W9-BMR-763

10 Things to Do When You Can't Get Started

1. Think of all the bad things that might happen if you don't do the task or complete it too late.

2. Remember how unpleasant it was the last time you put off something until the last minute.

3. Think of a time when you had a similar project that seemed overwhelming or difficult but that turned out to be not such a big deal once you started it.

4. Tell yourself you'll work on the task for just 10 minutes.

5. If #4 doesn't work, tell yourself to spend 10 minutes merely organizing the task or getting out the supplies for it.

6. Ask someone for advice, instructions, or hand-holding.

7. Listen for any negative self-talk going on in your head and turn it into positive statements.

8. Remind yourself why this task is a priority.

9. Daydream about a reward you'll give yourself or that you'll receive from others for completing the task. Or, if it won't be a distraction, treat yourself to that reward while working on the task.

10. Don't panic over your deadline. Focus on do dates, not due dates.

10 Things to Do When You've Started, but Can't Keep Going

1. Review what you've done so far and give yourself a pat on the back for getting at least something done, no matter how little.

2. Make sure you're comfortable; if not, get comfortable.

3. Don't worry about how you're going to be judged or how successful you'll be; *Just do it!*

4. Don't think about the next project or chores you're going to have to tackle when you finish this one; focus only on the task at hand.

5. Don't dwell on how little you've done or how much more you have to do on this project; focus on the present.

6. Remember the great sense of accomplishment you felt the last time you completed a project or task like this one.

7. Ask yourself if the reason you're not getting something done is that you don't know how to do it or don't know what steps to take next. If so, ask someone for help and/or review your original plan, schedule, or instructions.

8. If possible, clear your schedule of other commitments, at least temporarily, so you have more time and energy for this one.

9. Make sure you're using the chip-away technique, taking advantage of small windows of time to get things done and not waiting for the perfect block of time to finish.

10. Play beat the clock.

alpha
books

10 Good Reasons to Stop Procrastinating

1. Procrastination makes you feel lousy about yourself.

2. Procrastination makes other people have less respect for you or be angry with you.

3. Procrastination keeps your life in a constant or frequent state of turmoil. It makes you feel stressed and on the edge.

4. Other people who may be less talented, nice, or smart than you get ahead while you lag behind because of your procrastination.

5. Procrastinating costs money in fines, penalties, lost income, and price hikes for last-minute purchases and express mail, not to mention the cost of wasted time and lost opportunities.

6. Procrastination can be hazardous to your health.

7. You put your job and career in jeopardy when you procrastinate.

8. Your grades in school may suffer because of last-minute cramming.

9. You never get to relax fully because there's always something you should be doing.

10. You don't reach your goals or see your dreams come to life.

5 Ways to Remain an Ex-Procrastinator

1. Expect setbacks. You're not a robot; you're human.

2. Allow yourself to goof off occasionally and be sure to do it guilt-free. Keep your Wish-To-Do list in plain sight daily.

3. Keep clutter, both stuff and commitments, to a minimum in your life.

4. Rethink and revise your organizational systems from time to time so they work for you, not against you.

5. Remind yourself of your big-picture goals and priorities every day.

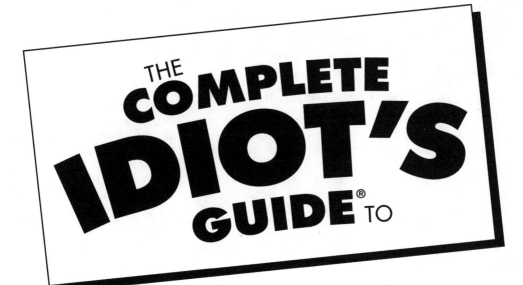

THE COMPLETE IDIOT'S GUIDE® TO

Overcoming Procrastination

by L. Michelle Tullier, Ph.D.

alpha books

Macmillan USA, Inc.
201 West 103rd Street
Indianapolis, IN 46290

A Pearson Education Company

For my grandmothers, Jessie Edwards and Jimmie Peterman, who ran businesses before the days of PCs and Palm Pilots, kept their households together without the help of professional organizers, and have never put off showing their love and support.

International Standard Book Number: 0028636376
Library of Congress Catalog Card Number: Available upon request.

01   00   99   8   7   6   5   4   3   2   1

Interpretation of the printing code: the rightmost number of the first series of numbers is the year of the book's printing; the rightmost number of the second series of numbers is the number of the book's printing. For example, a printing code of 99-1 shows that the first printing occurred in 1999.

Printed in the United States of America

ALPHA BOOKS

Publisher
Marie Butler Knight

Editorial Director
Gary M. Krebs

Product Manager
Phil Kitchel

Associate Managing Editor
Cari Shaw Fischer

Acquisitions Editors
Jessica Faust
Randy Ladenheim-Gil

PRODUCTION TEAM

Development Editor
Doris Cross

Production Editor
JoAnna Kremer

Copy Editor
Heather Stith

Cover Designer
Mike Freeland

Photo Editor
Richard H. Fox

Illustrator
Jody P. Schaeffer

Book Designers
Scott Cook and Amy Adams of DesignLab

Indexer
Nadia Ibrahim

Layout/Proofreading
Gloria Schurick
John Etchison

Contents at a Glance

Part 1: The Whats, Whys, and Woes of Procrastination   **1**

1 The Procrastinator's Wake-Up Call   3
Real-life stories about the negative consequences of delaying important tasks or not getting things done.

2 The Procrastination Epidemic   17
What procrastination is, why it's become such a common problem, and the love-hate relationship we have with it.

3 Blame It on the Environment   27
How procrastination results from the clutter, chaos, people, and atmosphere around you or sometimes from the nature of the task itself.

4 It's All in Your Head   41
How your thoughts, feelings, and self-talk cause you to put off tasks and goals.

5 It's About Time   55
The losing battle that procrastinators fight with this thing called time and how misconceptions about time lead to procrastination.

Part 2: Becoming an Ex-Procrastinator   **67**

6 Making Sure You'll Really Do It This Time   69
Why your past efforts to stop procrastinating haven't worked and what you need to know about the change process.

7 Rallying Support from the Pros   77
How to know whether you need help from mental health professionals, career counselors, personal coaches, and professional organizers, and where to find them.

8 Lightening Your Load   89
How to get rid of clutter so you can get more done at home or work.

9 Getting Your Act Together   105
Basic rules for living an organized life.

10 A Crash Course in Getting Organized   117
The role that schedules, filing systems, planners, and lists play in getting things done.

11 Decision-Making: The Root of All Action   133
      How poor decision-making leads to procrastination and
      what you can do about it. Plus, how to stop putting off
      important decisions.

12 The Secret Formula to Overcoming Procrastination   147
      Three simple ways to stop procrastination in its tracks
      and 10 strategies for starting and finishing absolutely
      anything.

Part 3: Tips and Tricks for Getting Things Done   161

13 Dirty Dishes and Other Household Chores   163
      How to keep up with chores on the home front, even when
      you hate to do them.

14 Family Matters   179
      Making tough decisions about getting married or starting a
      family, or keeping the family life you have sane, balanced,
      and functioning smoothly.

15 Get a Social Life—or Change the One You Have   191
      Steps to resolving relationship problems, improving your
      social life and interpersonal skills, entertaining, and
      having more fun.

16 New Year's Resolutions and Other
    Self-Improvement Promises   203
      Why it's so hard to stick to diet and fitness plans, seek
      medical treatment, find time for hobbies or lifelong
      learning, or set and meet any other personal goals.

17 Death, Taxes, and Other Important Stuff   217
      How to stop putting off writing or updating a will,
      preparing tax returns, and attending to other critical
      matters related to finances, insurance, and safety.

18 Put It in Writing   231
      Why you put off your social and personal business
      correspondence and how you can get past writer's block.

Part 4: Getting Things Done at Work and School   245

19 Get a Career—or Change the One You Have   247
      Strategies for making career decisions and transitions or
      for moving into self-employment.

20 Get a Job—and Keep It   257
      How to get moving on a job search and manage your job
      once you get it, including the challenges of working from
      home.

21 Cramming for Exams and Other
    Fine Academic Traditions   271
    Tips for getting your schoolwork done on time and
    jumping through other hoops of academic life.

Part 5: Living the Life of an Ex-Procrastinator   283

22 Your Procrastination Proclamation   285
    A simple plan for setting realistic goals and beginning to
    kick the procrastination habit.

23 Dealing with the Procrastinators Around You   299
    How to keep family, friends, co-workers, and bosses from
    slowing you down or driving you crazy—without nagging.

24 Keeping It Going   313
    Keys to making procrastination a closed chapter in your
    life and getting things done without sacrificing mind,
    body, or soul.

Appendixes

A Recommended Books   323

B Useful Organizations and Associations   333

C Online Resources   341

D The Procrastination Survey   345

   Index   353

Contents

**Part 1: The Whats, Whys, and Woes
of Procrastination**   **1**

1 The Procrastinator's Wake-Up Call   **3**

The Case of the Missing $12 Million
Lottery Ticket 3
The High Cost of Procrastination 5
Is Your Resumé Gathering Moss? 7
Darin, Can I See You in My Office—*Now?!* 9
Procrastination Can Be Hazardous to Your Health 9
Relationships on the Edge 11
Home, Sweet, Neglected Home 11
Procrastination Is a Security Threat 12
The Role of Fear in Overcoming Procrastination 12
    The Danger of Too Little Fear 12
    The Danger of Too Much Fear 13
Things We Procrastinate About 14
The Top 10 Things People Procrastinate About 15

2 The Procrastination Epidemic   **17**

You're Not Alone 17
Why We Love to Hate Procrastination 18
What It Is 18
    What It Feels Like 19
    All Talk, No Action 19
When It's a Good Thing 20
You're Not a Bad Person 20
    It's Not Laziness 21
    It's Not a Question of Discipline 21
    It's Not About Ambition 22
Why Procrastination Is Becoming an Epidemic 22
    Technology: Is It Really a Timesaver? 22
    The Pressure Cooker Workplace 23
    Nobody's Ruling the Roost 24

3 Blame It on the Environment   **27**

I Think, Therefore I Do—Or Do I? 27
Environmental Hazards 29
Peer Pressure Has No Peer 30
    The Culture of Procrastination 30
    Just Do It Already! 30
The Power of Discomfort 31
    Sitting in the Hot Seat 31
    Cubicle, Sweet Cubicle 31

Shine a Little Light on Me *32*
Straightjackets and Neckties..*32*
How a Cluttered Life Holds You Back.............................*33*
The Leaning Tower of Paper...*33*
The Collector's Curse *34*
Computer Clutter..*34*
Commitment Overload..*35*
Your 10 Life Roles *36*
Driven to Distraction...*38*
So Is It Really Not My Fault?..*39*

4 It's All in Your Head   41

The Psychology of Action *42*
You Think Too Much..*42*
You Just Didn't Think *43*
What's Causing Your Procrastination? *44*
Fears That Hold You Back *44*
Fear of Failure *45*
Fear of Being Judged *45*
Fear of Success...*46*
It Has to Be Perfect *47*
Letting It Get to You *48*
Feeling Overwhelmed *49*
This Is So Frustrating! *49*
The Adrenaline Rush *49*
I'm So Bored *50*
You Want Me to Do What?! *50*
I Have Plenty of Time *50*
Freudian Slips *50*
Attention Deficit Disorder *51*
Obsessive-Compulsive Disorder *51*
Anxiety Disorders *52*
Depression..*52*
Is There a Doctor in the House? *52*
Don't Worry; There Is Hope *53*

5 It's About Time   55

Why You Can't (and Shouldn't Want to)
Manage Time *55*
Your Relationship with Time *56*
Being Bullied by Time *56*
Who Controls Your Time? *57*
Making Peace with Time *58*
Don't Do More: Do Better...*58*
Handcuffed to Your Day Planner *59*
Balancing Acts..*60*

But I Just Can't Find the Time 60
   The Easy Way Out 61
   Doing What's in Your Face 61
Getting Your Priorities Straight 61
It's Not the Right Time to Do This 63
Creating the Illusion of More Time 63

Part 2: Becoming an Ex-Procrastinator   67

6 Making Sure You'll Really Do It This Time   69

Why Your Past Efforts Have Failed 70
Why Change Is So Darn Hard..73
Seven Stages of Change..73
How Likely Are You to Change? 75
Your Support Team 75

7 Rallying Support from the Pros   77

Do I Need Professional Help? 78
Mental Health Professionals 79
   What Do Psychotherapists Do? 80
   The Six Faces of Psychotherapy 80
Career Development Professionals 82
   Career Counselors 83
   Career Coaches and Consultants 84
Personal Coaches..84
Professional Organizers 85
Who You Gonna Call? 86
   Questions to Ask When Seeking Professional Help 86
   Finding Support Closer to Home................................87

8 Lightening Your Load   89

Assessing Your Clutter Crisis..90
Rationalizing Your Clutter Habit....................................93
Where Your Attachment to Stuff Comes From............94
   Guilt 94
   Value..95
   Sentimentality 96
   Time Capsule Syndrome..97
   Practicality 98
   Hopes and Dreams 98
   Identity 99
Getting Rid of Stuff 101

9 Getting Your Act Together   **105**

Organizational Rules to Keep from Coming Unglued 106
   A Place for Everything *106*
   Paper Shuffling 101 ....*107*
   Why To-Do Lists Don't Get Done *108*
   The Beauty of Routine *109*
   Expect the Unexpected on the Way to Appointments.......*109*
   Gluing the Pieces Back Together *110*
Balancing Acts 111
   Why It's Hard to Say No *111*
   How to Say No *113*
   Getting Out of Commitments You've Already Made *113*
The Organization-Procrastination Link 114

10 A Crash Course in Getting Organized   **117**

Three Ways to Get Organized 118
Find a Place for Everything and Keep It There...................118
   Chasing the Wild Goose: An Exercise............................*119*
   Why Things Don't Stay Where They Belong...................*120*
What to Do with All That Paper Jazz 120
   Ode to Stacking Trays *121*
   Let's Get Stacking! *122*
The Wonderful World of Filing.......................................122
   Pending Project Files...*124*
   Current Project Files..*125*
   Administrative Files...*125*
   Key People and Places Files *126*
   Topic Files *126*
Setting Up Mission Control 127
   Monthly Calendar *128*
   Daily Action Pages *128*
   To-Do Lists *129*
The Gentle Art of Scheduling 130

11 Decision-Making: The Root of All Action   **133**

I Just Can't Decide..134
Why Decisions Are So Hard to Make 134
   Too Many Choices and Too Much Information................*135*
   Not Enough Choices, Time, or Money............................*135*
   You Make Them Harder Than They Need to Be *136*
   Decisions Strike at the Core of Who We Are...................*137*
Major League Decisions..137
Little League Decisions 138
The Eight Decision-Making Styles....................................138
   Loner or Pollster?..*139*
   Forecaster or Bean-Counter?..*139*

Analyst or Feeler? 140
Hunter-Gatherer or Settler?...140
What's Your Decision-Making Style? 140
Ten Steps to Decision-Making Like a Pro 141
Step 1: Assess the importance of the decision.....................141
Step 2: Assess your readiness to make a decision. 141
Step 3: Define your priorities. 142
Step 4: Listen to your gut. 142
Step 5: Gather data....142
Step 6: Revisit your criteria. 142
Step 7: Analyze the data. 143
Step 8: Listen to your gut—again. 143
Step 9: Deal with any roadblocks standing in your way. 144
Step 10: Take the plunge....144
Don't Sweat It 144

**12 The Secret Formula to Overcoming
Procrastination   147**

Stop 147
Look 148
Listen 149
The Stop, Look, and Listen Formula in Action.....................150
Ten Sure-Fire Strategies for Getting Anything Done 151
Strategy #1: Get fired up. 152
Strategy #2: Get organized. 152
Strategy #3: Prioritize. 153
Strategy #4: Find freedom in routine. 153
Strategy #5: Get comfortable. 154
Strategy #6: Get connected to people and information. 154
Strategy #7: Use positive self-talk. 155
Strategy #8: Focus on do dates, not due dates. 156
Strategy #9: Use the chip-away technique. 157
Strategy #10: Play trick-or-treat........................................158
See? It's Not So Hard! 159

Part 3: Tips and Tricks for Getting Things Done   161

13 Dirty Dishes and Other Household Chores   163

Neatniks, Clean Freaks, and Slobs.....................................163
Why We Put Off Household Chores....................................164
Home Economics 101 165
Home Squalid Home 166
Tidying Up 167
Cleaning Up 169
Clearing Out 171

Laundry, Trash, and Other Dirty Words 172
  Laundry 172
  Dry Cleaning 173
  Trash 174
This Old House 175
Yard Work 176

14 Family Matters   179
Marriage American Style 179
  To Nest or Not to Nest 180
  Saying "I Do," Not "I'll Do It Later" 181
Putting Off the Pitter-Patter 182
  It's Not the Right Time 183
  How to Know When It Is the Right Time 183
Family Life 184
Making Home a Safe Haven 185
  Fire Safety 185
  Keeping Burglars at Bay 187
  Childproofing 188

15 Get a Social Life—or Change the One You Have   191
I Have to Get out More 192
  Finding the Time to Socialize 192
  The Importance of Follow-Through 193
Socializing Online 194
When Your Social Life Becomes a Chore 194
  Putting the Joy Back in Gift-Giving 195
  Taking the Rush out of Holidays 196
The Dating Game 198
  Getting Past the Dating Roadblocks 198
Dealing with Relationship Problems..199

**16 New Year's Resolutions and Other
     Self-Improvement Promises   203**
Why New Year's Resolutions Lose Their Resolve 204
Losing Weight and Lifting Weights 205
  The Day I Stopped Exercising 205
  A Losing Battle with Exercise 207
  Weight Lost and Fitness Found 207
Making Medical and Dental Appointments 210
Hobbies? What Are Those? 211
Getting Back on Your Hobby Horse 213
  Learning Something New 214
  Keeping a Diary or Journal 214
  Reading More 215

17 Death, Taxes, and Other Important Stuff 217

Why the Bottom Line Is Often Last in Line 218
Where Did I Put Those Canceled Checks? 218
Did I Even Need to Save Those Canceled Checks? 218
Your Love-Hate Relationship with Money 219
Paying Bills 219
Budgeting...221
Getting out of Debt 221
It's an Epidemic 222
The Symptoms of Debt Procrastination 222
Planning for a Secure Future 224
Saving and Investing 225
Insurance..226
The Annual Tax Procrastinator's Ball 226
The Reality of Mortality 228
Wills and Estate Planning 229

18 Put It in Writing 231

Dear Jane, Thank You for the 1992 Desk Calendar ... .232
RSVP—ASAP!! 234
We Want to Attend, but We Don't Know
How to Tell You 235
Writing Letters of Condolence 237
Sample Letters of Condolence 238
Postcards from the Edge of Procrastination 238
Keeping in Touch 239
Writing Letters of Complaint 240
Getting Your Outrage Down on Paper 241
Breaking Through Writer's Block 242

Part 4: Getting Things Done at Work and School 245

19 Get a Career—or Change the One You Have 247

A Career in Procrastination......................................247
Why Careers Stagnate 248
Finding Your Direction 248
Changing Your Career Field 250
Striking Out on Your Own: The Advantages of
Self-Employment 252
What's Stopping You? 253
Making It Happen 254

20 Get a Job—and Keep It **257**

Get a Job 258
  Too Comfortable to Leave, Too Miserable to Stay *258*
  Fishing with a Net..*259*
  No Target to Hit *259*
  Job Hunting Mind Games *262*
Keep Your Job 262
  The Bare Necessities *262*
  Write Like You Mean Business *264*
  The Human Component of a Job *265*
  When the Office Is at Home *267*
Make a Difference 268
Get Ahead 269

21 Cramming for Exams and Other Fine Academic Traditions **271**

A Procrastination Breeding Ground 271
Procrastination in High School..272
Procrastination in College..274
  Why College Students Procrastinate *274*
  What Can Be Done About It *275*
Procrastination in Graduate School 276
  One Foot in the Ivory Tower, One in Real Life *276*
  All But Dissertation, All Because of Procrastination *277*
  Getting from A.B.D. and A.B.P. to Ph.D. *278*
Returning to School Before the Twelfth of Never 279
Do Your Homework! 281

Part 5: Living the Life of an Ex-Procrastinator **283**

22 Your Procrastination Proclamation **285**

The Five Steps to Making a Procrastination
  Proclamation 286
1. Identify Your Life Roles Priorities 286
  Exercise: My Life Roles Rankings *286*
  Your Procrastination Proclamation: Part One *287*
2. Take a Procrastination Inventory 287
  The Procrastination Hot Spots Checklist.................................*288*
3. Choose Your Procrastination Priorities................................292
  Your Procrastination Proclamation: Part Two *292*
4. Make Your Priority B List 293
  Your Procrastination Proclamation: Part Three *294*
5. Build in Balance..294
  Wish-To-Do Lists *294*
  Your Procrastination Proclamation: Part Four *296*
The Procrastinator's Oath of Effectiveness 296

23 Dealing with the Procrastinators Around You   299

Convert Them? Or Turn the Other Cheek? 299
Do's and Don'ts for Dealing with Procrastinators 300
   Confronting the Procrastinator *300*
   Trying to Solve the Problem *301*
   The Recovery Process *303*
Procrastinators in the Workplace 304
   When You're Not the Boss *304*
   When You're in Charge, but Not in Control *305*
   When Your Coworkers Are Slackers *306*
When You Live with a Procrastinator 307
Spouses and Partners 308
   Roommates *309*
   Children *309*
   Friends *311*

24 Keeping It Going   313

Four Simple Things to Remember.................................314
Here We Go Again? No, Not This Time 314
Keeping Your Act Together 315
   Prevent Clutter from Piling Back Up *315*
   Put Things in Their Places *316*
   Avoid Overload *317*
Make Balance a Priority.................................317
Value Your Priorities and Prioritize Your Values 318
   Another Sort of Wake-Up Call *319*
   Being Hit Over the Head with Your Values *319*
   When "What Did You Do Today?" Takes on
    New Meaning *319*
   Sorting Out the Values and Priorities Confusion *320*
   Getting It Done *320*
It's Up to You.................................321

Appendixes

A Recommended Books   323

Careers: Choosing or Changing 323
Careers: Job Hunting.................................324
Careers: Managing and Advancing In.................................325
Change and Transitions 325
Decision-Making 326
Education and Study Skills 326
Financial Planning.................................326
Getting Organized 327
Health/Fitness/Diet/Nutrition.................................327
Inspiration and Motivation.................................328
Interpersonal Relationships and Social Skills 328

Mental Health	329
Personality and Behavior	329
Self-Employment	330
Time: Making the Most of It	330
Wills and Estates	331
Writing	331

B   Useful Organizations and Associations   333

Careers	334
Coaching	334
Education	334
Finance	335
Health/Fitness/Diet/Nutrition	335
Learning Disabilities and ADD	336
Mental Health	337
Organizers	338
Self-Employment/Business Development	338

C   Online Resources   341

Careers	341
Coaches	341
Education	342
Finance	342
Health/Fitness/Diet/Nutrition	342
Household Organizations	343
Learning Disabilities and ADD	343
Mental Health	343
Planners	343
Self-Employment/Business Development	344

D   The Procrastination Survey   345

Survey Method	345
Who the Participants Are	345
The Questionnaire and Instructions	347
Procrastination Survey	*347*
Survey Results	349

Index   353

Foreword

If you've color-coded all your files, answered all your e-mails, and gotten your holiday purchases wrapped by September 1, you can quit reading now. If, however, your mother called recently to see if you were still alive, the neighbors think your house is the recycling center, or the length of your to-do list qualifies for the *Guinness World Book of Records*, you've picked up the right book.

Just about everyone procrastinates. And for good reasons. Some of the things we never get around to doing are boring, difficult, overwhelming, and complicated. Any reasonable person would find "later" the best time frame to do them in. The sheer weight of the demands placed upon us can be paralyzing. If you think you have too much to do and not enough time to do it in, this is not your imagination. There really *is* too much to do. Some of us cope by putting off until tomorrow … what we won't have time to do then, either. Unfortunately, procrastination is a problem that not only doesn't solve problems, it creates them.

You are about to read the most comprehensive procrastination book on the market. It is full of nuts and bolts tips on how to stop procrastinating and take out that two-week-old trash, overcome your computer phobia, or make the career move that will change your life. Because people procrastinate for different reasons, this book provides a dual focus: It helps those of us who need to pay attention to the psychological roots of stalling, e.g., fears, perfectionism, and ambivalence, and it guides those of us whose main trouble stems from situational factors, e.g., overload, distractions, and disorganization. You will find nitty-gritty, specific, sure-fire ways to stop putting things off. The book's author clearly has her act together, and, lucky for us, has devoted her career to helping others do the same. But she also lets us know that she's no robot, and grapples with the same issues you and I face.

If I could retitle this book I would call it *The Secret Formula for Feeling Good.* As you read, you will swear Michelle Tullier looked inside your mind, heart, and soul and discovered, not only *why* you put things off, but precisely *what* will propel you off your procrastinating duff and into the life you want to live! What I love most about this book is that the underlying message isn't about making yourself exercise, paying bills on time, or keeping your closets clean. Michelle teaches us about the bigger issue of having some balance in your life. Getting *more* done is not helpful if you are not also doing what is important to you and to those you love. She reminds us that overcoming procrastination can help us connect with ourselves, our family and friends, our true mission in life, and our spirituality. And *that* is the secret formula for feeling good.

—Mary LoVerde

Life Balance expert, professional speaker, and author of *Stop Screaming at the Microwave! How to Connect Your Disconnected Life* (Simon and Schuster)

Introduction

How many things were you supposed to do yesterday that didn't get done? How likely are you to do them today? Tomorrow? Okay, how about if I give you until next week? Can you have them done by then?

Wait! Don't close the book yet! I know those are annoying questions, but I had to ask. Having fought a lifelong battle with procrastination myself, I know what the secret life of a procrastinator is like. You go through each day hoping no one will discover how far behind you are on projects at work, how much mold is growing on the leftovers in the back of your fridge, or how long it's been since you wrote to your Great- aunt Norma in Salinas.

This book is your chance to come clean, to admit to yourself and others that you've developed a habit of putting things off, not finishing what you start, and doing things at the last minute. Don't worry; you'll be in good company. As you'll see from the many real-life examples given in this book, just about everybody procrastinates, either occasionally or chronically. It's become something of an epidemic as life has become more complicated thanks to technological, workplace, and societal changes (which I describe in Chapter 2, "The Procrastination Epidemic").

Drawing from my knowledge base in psychology, my experience as a career and life planning counselor, and conversations with hundreds of procrastinators from all walks of life, I bring you practical, painless, easy-to-implement solutions to the problem. You'll learn why you procrastinate, how to break the habit, and how to keep it broken.

Most important, you'll learn that the key to being productive is not just to do more and more like some sort of time-management robot, but to focus instead on doing what's important to you and to the people you care about. In this book, I show you how to stop putting off things like cleaning out your closet, preparing your taxes before April 14, making a career change, and much more. But through it all, I urge you to have some fun, relax a little, and stop to smell the basil.

A Special Note to Readers with Disabilities

I make occasional references in this book to the role that learning disabilities, Attention Deficit Disorder, mental illness, and other such difficulties play in the problem of procrastination. If you suffer from any of those disorders, many of the usual behavioral techniques won't work for you. I hope you'll use the advice given here merely as a springboard for taking action and adapting it to fit your own needs, possibly with the help of a mental health professional or educational therapist.

If your disabilities are of a physical nature, then I apologize in advance for making statements such as, "Get up off that couch and wash those dishes," or "March over to that pen and paper and write out a list." In a book that's all about taking action, it's difficult to avoid using these sorts of physical analogies and expressions. I ask you to overlook the literal meaning of these statements and to focus instead on the message behind them.

How to Use This Book

Procrastinators are famous for wanting to skip around in books rather than methodically plod through them from page 1 to the end. Though I recommend that you try to read the chapters at least roughly in order, skipping around isn't such a bad thing if that's the quickest route to the answers you need. To that end, here's a brief overview of what's inside:

➤ **Part 1, "The Whats, Whys, and Woes of Procrastination,"** helps you get your bearings. It wakes you up to the dangers of procrastination so that you'll be motivated to break the habit. And it tells you what procrastination is and why it's so common. You'll also find chapters that help you pinpoint the reasons why you put off things and a chapter on how your relationship with time (being at war with it, for example) fuels the problem.

➤ **Part 2, "Becoming an Ex-Procrastinator,"** provides the foundation for getting over your problem. You'll learn what change is all about, why your past efforts to break the procrastination habit haven't worked, and how you're going to really do it this time. There's a special focus on getting rid of clutter, getting organized, simplifying your life, and learning to make decisions. Achieving these things plays an important role in overcoming procrastination. The final chapter of this part lets you in on the secret formula for overcoming procrastination.

➤ **Part 3, "Tips and Tricks for Getting Things Done,"** is the meat of the book. In these chapters, I roll up my sleeves and help you get those dishes washed, keep those New Year's resolutions, and stop putting off those home repair projects. You'll find nitty-gritty tips for taking care of chores and reaching goals related to your life at home, your family life, and your social life (or for getting a life if you feel you don't have one!). You'll also learn how to attend to your health, wealth, safety, and, most important, happiness.

➤ **Part 4, "Getting Things Done at Work and School,"** continues the theme of Part 3 in that it provides specific, practical tips for accomplishing tasks and reaching goals. The focus in this part is on your professional life rather than your personal life. You'll learn why you procrastinate on the job—or even about getting a job in the first place—as well as put off making decisions or taking action about your career in general. You'll also find tips for students on everything from avoiding the last-minute rush to write papers and cram for exams to completing degrees and dealing with academic red tape.

➤ **Part 5, "Living the Life of an Ex-Procrastinator,"** ensures that your efforts to break the procrastination habit aren't another failed attempt. You'll make a Procrastination Proclamation, a sort of contract with yourself to prioritize what you want to work on and lay out how and when you plan to do it. You'll also learn how to deal with people around you who procrastinate. (You know how irritating ex-smokers can be when they're around smokers; well, the same self-righteousness can afflict ex-procrastinators.) Finally, you'll learn how to keep it all going and keep it all in perspective by getting things accomplished without sacrificing your mind, body, and spirit.

Extras

To highlight special tips and resources, useful facts, pitfalls to watch out for, and insights from fellow procrastinators, there are boxes scattered throughout each chapter. You can spot them by their icons, which are as follows:

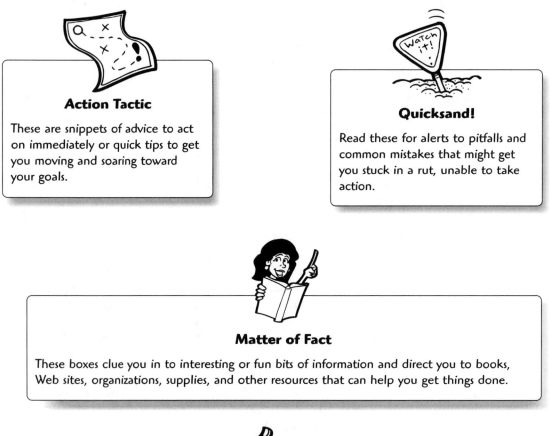

Action Tactic

These are snippets of advice to act on immediately or quick tips to get you moving and soaring toward your goals.

Quicksand!

Read these for alerts to pitfalls and common mistakes that might get you stuck in a rut, unable to take action.

Matter of Fact

These boxes clue you in to interesting or fun bits of information and direct you to books, Web sites, organizations, supplies, and other resources that can help you get things done.

You're Not Alone

These are quotes from real people talking about their procrastination problems, insights from experts, and words of wisdom from famous or historical figures.

Acknowledgments

Even the author of a book on overcoming procrastination needs help getting past writer's block, meeting deadlines, and maintaining some degree of sanity in her life. Many people had a hand in making those things happen.

My deepest gratitude goes to my husband Michael and my daughter. M.G., you not only provided everything from emotional to technical support as I wrote this book, you also have been incredibly patient with my book-writing addiction these last several years. I hope to make up for the sacrifices you've made! And, A.K., you're too young to understand this now, but you deserve a big thanks, too, for all the times you let me pay more attention to my computer than to you.

I also found support for writing through many helpful hands in my daily life who gave me peace of mind, a functioning household, and a sense of connection to the world. I thank Lubna, Kadijeh, and Olga for doing the hardest job in the world: keeping the little one safe, happy, and entertained. And I thank Alex, Shalini, and Leona for pitching in with that job, too, and for making me feel at home, but not alone. From a distance, I appreciated the support I received, as always, from my parents Scott Tullier and Patricia and Ronald Gann.

A great deal of appreciation goes to Amy Zavatto for initially bringing me into the Macmillan fold and to my friend and fellow author Marci Taub for generously sharing that lead and always being there to offer encouragement. I thank Jessica Faust for her enthusiasm when I proposed this topic and for her support and time along the way. Many thanks go as well to my development editor Doris Cross for being such a pleasure to work with and an excellent editor, and for indulging and sharing my obsession for details. Thanks go also to my research assistant Rebecca Rand, who skillfully collected many useful resources and was always willing to pitch in. And special thanks to my new friend Mary LoVerde for being willing to connect with me and with this project.

I am also grateful to Denis Gaynor, Judy Hernandez, Eileen O'Reilly, and their staff at Monster.com for being patient while I had to shift my priorities temporarily away from Monster and onto the writing of this book. And I haven't forgotten the early support Tish Chamberlain and Marion Flomenhaft of New York University gave me years ago when I first had the idea to write about procrastination.

And last, but by no means least, I thank the hundreds of people who contributed to this book with quotes, stories, and insights into the procrastination experience. This is a better book because so many of you took the time to respond to my survey, forward the survey on to others, share your stories, and provide valuable suggestions. To protect your anonymity, and because I don't have space to list the many names, I can offer only a collective thanks, but I hope to express my appreciation to each of you privately. I can, however, thank Stacey Prenner and Lauren Sperling by name for organizing and hosting the spring focus group that provided so much rich information for this book and re-motivated me during one of my dry spells.

Special Thanks to the Technical Reviewers

Also making this book a reality were the technical reviewers, John Hotard and Linda Rothschild, who so enthusiastically lent their wisdom and time despite their busy schedules. John Hotard is a psychologist and career counselor in private practice and director of the Career Center at Fordham Business School. Linda Rothschild is president of the National Association of Professional Organizers, and of Cross It Off Your List, a company in New York City that organizes everything from corporate filing systems to residential kitchens.

Part 1

The Whats, Whys, and Woes of Procrastination

Whew, you've gotten this far. You've bought, borrowed, or begged for this book. You've vowed to do something about your procrastination problem once and for all. And here you are about to start Chapter 1. Congratulations!

But are you already worrying about whether you're going to finish the book and make some real changes in your life? Well, worry no longer! These first five chapters will show you that procrastination is not some mysterious, insidious demon that you can't control. Rather, it is something that you can figure out, psych out, and snuff out.

In the first two chapters, you'll see how widespread a problem procrastination is and why it's a habit that needs to be broken. Then, you'll get right down to business in Chapters 3, 4, and 5 and learn why people procrastinate (because to get rid of a problem you have to dig it out at the roots) and why fighting time is a losing battle.

Chapter 1

The Procrastinator's Wake-Up Call

In This Chapter

➤ Waking up to the dangers of procrastination

➤ Real-world stories from chronic procrastinators

➤ What delaying does to your health, wealth, and happiness

"I'll do it later" seems like a harmless enough statement. The problem is that when later comes, that split-second decision you made to put off something can have lasting negative consequences. Occasional procrastination is usually fairly harmless. But procrastinating on a regular basis—ignoring important responsibilities and creating chaos for yourself and the people who depend on you—can be dangerous business.

At a minimum, procrastination inconveniences you and others. At its worst, procrastination takes a serious toll on your finances, career, mental and physical health, relationships, and personal safety. If you've brushed off your procrastination problem as a minor nuisance, a silly habit, or even a charming personality quirk, then this chapter is your wake-up call.

The Case of the Missing $12 Million Lottery Ticket

One of the most alarming procrastination stories I've ever heard is that of Ted, a chronic procrastinator who might have become 12 million dollars richer had he only gotten around to getting organized. For several years, Ted purchased a ticket in his

You're Not Alone

I typically don't do things until dire action requires it. I put off calling the plumber until the leak gets really bad, put off calling the exterminator until I see the mouse myself, procrastinate paying parking tickets until I've received my third urgent notice. Sometimes only the urgency of final deadlines or serious retribution motivates me to do things I don't like doing.

—Jill K., writer

Action Tactic

Think of one thing in your life that is disorganized and that would not take a lot of time and effort to straighten out. (Finding one convenient place to keep your keys or cleaning up your computer monitor's desktop are two examples.) Designate a specific time in the next three days to take care of it.

state's weekly lottery whenever the jackpot rose to more than 10 million dollars. His rationale was that the 10 million dollars rule limited how often he played and thus kept him from throwing away too much money on a game with such long odds of winning.

After buying his tickets, Ted would stick them in all sorts of places—clothes pockets, wallet, desk drawers, a catch-all bowl on the entrance hall table—a different spot practically every time. He often would say to his wife, or think to himself, "I really need to find one place to keep my lottery tickets so that I won't lose any." Despite those intentions, he never got around to setting up one simple organizational system for the tickets and continued to put them anywhere and everywhere.

Every couple of months, Ted would gather up any tickets he could find and sign on to the lottery's Web site to see whether any of his tickets matched winning numbers from previous weeks or months. They never did.

Then one day Ted was walking past the newsstand where he always purchased his tickets. Much to his surprise, he saw a sign indicating that a winning 12 million dollar ticket from a game a couple months back had been purchased at that very newsstand. Knowing that he had probably bought a ticket that day, he went home intent on finding the winning one. Of course, there was no guarantee that he had it, but the odds were certainly more in his favor this time. Now he was competing with only the people who had bought their tickets at that tiny, off-the-beaten-path news kiosk rather than the usual bazillions of entrants from across the state.

You can probably guess what happened next. Ted couldn't find a ticket with that date on it. According to his calendar, his routine had been normal that day, indicating that he most likely did buy a ticket for that jackpot. He found lots of other old tickets from around that time but not the one that would possibly make him a wealthy man. He and his wife searched for the ticket for several more months to no avail (lottery rules give winners a year to claim their prize).

Because he procrastinated over something as simple as finding an old shoebox or file folder in which to keep the tickets, he and his wife will never know if they were the winners. To make matters worse, no one else presented a winning ticket even after a year was up, so they really could have been the ones. Ted's wife told me that the *not* knowing felt almost as frustrating as she imagined it woul d be to know they had won but had lost the ticket.

The High Cost of Procrastination

Most procrastination doesn't make you 12 million dollars poorer, but it often does have some serious financial consequences. Take a look at the following ways that procrastination can hurt your bottom line. Put a check mark next to any that you're guilty of.

By paying bills late, I

_____ sometimes have to pay late payment penalties.

_____ pay interest on credit balances.

_____ have damaged or might damage my credit rating.

_____ have services such as phone or electricity cut off.

_____ inconvenience myself or others by having to pay bills in person or by phone at the last minute.

By not making advance reservations and plans, I

_____ pay higher fares for plane tickets or other travel rates.

_____ miss out on early-bird registration fees for events.

_____ let memberships and subscriptions expire and then pay a premium to renew.

By waiting until the last minute to buy things, I

_____ don't have time to comparison shop for bargains and quality.

_____ pay higher prices for purchases on holidays.

_____ miss out on sales and limited-time offers.

_____ waste money on express mail delivery services.

By not preparing and/or following a budget, I

_____ don't reach my financial goals.

_____ get into debt.

_____ rely too much on credit or borrowing.

_____ always feel that I don't have enough cash to spend.

By not getting around to saving money, I

_____ am concerned about my retirement.

_____ don't have money to cover emergencies.

_____ have to delay major purchases or expenditures.

By not filing taxes on time, I

_____ pay penalties for not filing or for filing late.

_____ pay interest on installment payments.

You're Not Alone

My worst procrastination problem is that I put off paying bills, even to the point of having services cut off. The stupid thing is that I always have the money in the bank; I just put off writing the check and mailing it out. It is embarrassing how poorly I manage this. I can't explain it. It's almost like I'm addicted to being a bum bill payer.

—Chad P., insurance broker

Then there are the many little ways procrastination costs you money. Maybe you pay fines for overdue library books or for not taking the time to rewind a rented videotape. Or you regularly park in metered spaces and put off getting back to the car in time to add another quarter. What should've been a dollar's worth of parking becomes an expensive parking ticket.

Even rushing to get places can cost you. When my husband and I put off leaving from our home just outside Manhattan for an event or appointment in the city, we have to make up driving time by taking the faster route, a tunnel instead of a bridge. Problem is, the tunnel has a four-dollar toll, but the bridge is free (not to mention the spectacular view of the Manhattan skyline we enjoy from the bridge versus the view of the back of 18-wheelers and the smell of exhaust fumes you get in the tunnel). A four-dollar toll is not exactly big bucks, but it's an unnecessary expenditure that can add up over time.

If you want to get a more precise idea of how procrastination has hurt you financially, estimate a dollar value per year for each item you put a checkmark next to in the preceding list, and then add it all up. How bad is the grand total? What else could you have done with that money?

We often don't realize what a significant financial toll procrastination is taking on our lives. If that's the case with you, don't dwell on the "lost" money; just use this realization as a wake-up call to get you motivated to take action against the problem. The strategies offered later in this book will show you what action to take.

Is Your Resumé Gathering Moss?

As a career counselor, I've witnessed countless examples of procrastination in people who put off getting their acts together professionally. When I was working face-to-face with hundreds of clients a year in my private practice, close to 50 percent of them told me in the first appointment that they had been meaning to do something about their job or career for at least six months but had put it off. Many of those people said that they had been unhappy with their jobs or nervous about their career futures for a couple, or even several, years.

Now that most of my career advising is done online for a Web site, I still see the same career-related procrastination epidemic. Many of the postings on my message board and questions in the chat room come from people who are down to the wire in choosing a career direction or finding a new job.

In fact, as I was writing this chapter in May 1999, I read a question on my board from someone who said he planned to make a career change "next June" and wanted to know how early he should start his job search. I was so floored that someone would start planning in May 1999 for a career change in June of the following year that I had to write back before answering his question to clarify that "next June" really did mean June 2000, not the next month, June 1999. He did indeed mean June 2000, so I congratulated him on his foresight and gave him an answer. (By the way, in case his situation is relevant to you, the answer was that he shouldn't start his job search until three to six months before the date he could start working, but he should use the time up until that point to research his new chosen field and network to build contacts in it.)

You're Not Alone

Perhaps the most difficult part of the career planning process for career changers is identifying a target career. Often, adults feel ashamed to admit that they are confused about their career options. They wonder how someone at age 30, 40, or older could still be unsure about what to pursue in terms of a career.

—From *Career Change*, by Dr. David Helfand

Quicksand!

If you're having trouble getting your work done on time or dealing with any aspect of your job, don't wait until you are seriously reprimanded or even fired. If your boss is understanding, talk to him or her. If not, ask your human resources department for a referral to a career management coach or to relevant seminars.

Some of the most common examples of career-related procrastination are the following:

➤ Students who are overwhelmed by the thought of trying to choose a career direction or find a job and who wait until they're close to graduating to start the entire career planning and job hunting process.

➤ Adults who are somewhat dissatisfied in their jobs and would probably be happier elsewhere but are too comfortable with their familiar routine and surroundings to get motivated to make a move.

➤ Adults who know that they might be laid off soon or that their employer is on shaky ground and could fold but who are in denial and don't make advance plans to find a new job.

➤ Job seekers who miss out on opportunities because they don't send their resumés or make the necessary phone calls in time to be considered for an opening.

➤ People who want to change not just their jobs but the career field or profession in which they work and are overwhelmed by the career options they have to choose from. Or they know what they want, but they don't know how to make the transition.

➤ Stay-at-home parents who want to get into the work world for the first time, or back into it after an absence for parenting, but let fear or lack of knowledge hold them back. (They might also be held back by the time-management challenge of getting out of the house to network or job-hunt while still taking care of the kids.)

➤ Budding entrepreneurs who never get around to making a business dream a reality.

➤ People who are not performing well on their job, have conflicts with co-workers or clients, or would like to ask for a raise or promotion but don't get around to taking action on these issues.

In Chapter 19, "Get a Career—or Change the One You Have," you'll find strategies for moving ahead in your professional life.

Darin, Can I See You in My Office—*Now?!*

There's more to success on the job than simply showing up on time and going through the motions of your basic job description. You have to manage your workplace relationships effectively, take charge of your job advancement, and make a real contribution toward the employer's goals. Always being behind the eight ball on the job may cause you to

➤ Be reprimanded or even fired.

➤ Miss out on promotions and raises.

➤ Be excluded from important projects or overlooked for plum assignments because you can't be counted on.

➤ Receive poor performance reviews or references.

➤ Anger and alienate your bosses and co-workers.

➤ Tarnish your professional reputation.

➤ Have less leisure or family time because work spills over into your personal life.

If you feel like you're walking a tightrope every day that you show up for work, the tips offered in Chapter 20, "Get a Job—and Keep It," may come in handy.

Matter of Fact

Lots of books on the market help with the nuts and bolts of job hunting or changing careers, but relatively few inspire you to think about your career in innovative ways. Two books I highly recommend for getting a new perspective on how to improve your career situation are *I Could Do Anything If Only I Knew What It Was* by Barbara Sher and *Zen and the Art of Making a Living* by Laurence Boldt. They won't tell you how to dot the I's and cross the T's in your resumé, but they will get you thinking out of the box.

Procrastination Can Be Hazardous to Your Health

Okay, so maybe federal law doesn't require your boss to give you a warning from the surgeon general on the health hazards of procrastination when handing you an assignment you're likely to put off doing. But it might not be a bad idea.

Some procrastination has an obvious impact on your physical health. If you put off stopping smoking, adopting a healthier diet, exercising, or making medical or dental

Quicksand!

Don't be fooled by the feeling of relief that often comes from putting off a task you've been dreading. Feelings of stress and anxiety are sure to follow.

appointments, your body will suffer. Some health consequences are not so obvious. The constant state of worry and turmoil procrastinators often live under, coupled with the disappointment from missed opportunities or unrealized dreams, can wreak havoc on your mental health as well. Procrastination can cause stress, anxiety, low self-esteem, and even depression.

Karen, a successful (and highly ethical) colleague of mine, told me a particularly poignant story about procrastination's effects on someone's stress level and sense of self-worth. When Karen was a freshman in college, she procrastinated so severely on writing a paper for a history class that she felt she had no choice but to lie to her professor. She told him that a family member was ill, and she would need extra time on the paper. The professor happened to be a Catholic priest, and Karen felt so guilty about her lie that she burst into tears while talking to him and ran out of the classroom. In describing the incident to me, she said, "I walked around for weeks feeling like I had jinxed myself, and that if someone in my family were to become ill, it would be all my fault."

Matter of Fact

Some people suffer from "hurry sickness," a term coined by Dr. Larry Dossey in *Meaning and Medicine*. Dossey conducted a study of stressed-out executives in which he asked them to sit quietly and guess when one minute had passed. The most stressed-out test subject of all stopped the clock after only nine seconds, assuming that a full minute had passed!

Procrastinators who continually race to meet deadlines or worry about unfulfilled obligations face not only emotional consequences but possibly physical ones as well. In *The Stress Management Sourcebook*, J. Barton Cunningham, Ph.D., defines stress as "any action or situation that upsets the body's normal equilibrium." He notes that stress has been found to be a contributing factor to such problems as asthma, chest and back pain, coronary heart disease, headaches and migraines, ulcers, and skin rashes.

Throughout this book (particularly in Chapter 16, "New Year's Resolutions and Other Self-Improvement Promises"), you'll find strategies for overcoming the types of procrastination that often lead to emotional and physical distress.

Relationships on the Edge

When you procrastinate, you run the risk of greatly annoying other people. Maybe you know this already. Your wife complains that you put off taking out the trash. Your husband is fed up with the fact that you keep saying you're going to stop working on the weekends but haven't gotten around to making any real changes yet. Your secretary has made it clear that your last-minute rushes disrupt the workflow of the whole department.

Or maybe you aren't yet aware that your procrastination inconveniences, disappoints, and angers the people around you. Be careful: Friends, family, and co-workers may be letting their feelings build up, and they will explode at you one day. That's usually not a very pleasant experience.

Your procrastination might also cause you to put off dealing with relationship problems that need to be worked out. Maybe you keep postponing ending a friendship or relationship you'd be better off without. Perhaps you do the opposite: You put off getting a relationship started or delay making a firm commitment to a good one that's already underway.

In Chapter 11, "Decision-Making—The Root of All Action," you'll learn techniques for making difficult life decisions, such as those related to relationships. In Chapter 15, "Get a Social Life—or Change the One You Have," you'll find tips on how to stop dragging your feet when it comes to dating, developing friendships, and dealing with other interpersonal situations.

Home, Sweet, Neglected Home

A household that is home to one or more procrastinators is likely to be in a constant state of disarray. Dirty dishes in the sink, piles of laundry to be washed, meals planned at the last minute, kids rushing out the door late for soccer practice, and all sorts of other chaos mean that the quality of life there is not what it could be. When one member of a family or group of roommates procrastinates, everyone else suffers.

People who live alone suffer, too. They get frustrated with themselves over not being able to find things among all the clutter, are embarrassed to have guests over, and leave home repair projects half-done. In households of one, there are no "enablers" to come along after the procrastinator and pick up the pieces. In Chapter 13, "Dirty Dishes and Other Household Chores," you'll find lots of tips and tricks for putting some order into a disorderly home life.

Procrastination Is a Security Threat

Some of the most frightening and devastating consequences of procrastination concern issues of your and your loved ones' personal safety and that of your property. It's amazing how many of us think nothing of putting off changing batteries in smoke alarms, equipping our kitchens with fire extinguishers, childproofing or burglarproofing our homes, or doing any other simple tasks that can protect us and our possessions.

You're Not Alone

Two of my smoke alarms have been chirping for seven months because the batteries need changing. You can hear it through the phone, so everyone I talk to knows it. More people have offered to buy me a battery and come over and change it for me than you can imagine. What did I do? I bought the batteries myself months ago and still haven't changed this thing!

—Lisa D., marketing consultant

We know it's just plain stupid not to do these things, but for some reason we don't do them. In Chapter 17, "Death, Taxes, and Other Important Stuff," you'll explore why you delay taking steps that can literally mean the difference between life and death and how to get yourself to take the necessary action.

The Role of Fear in Overcoming Procrastination

Edgar Watson Howe, an American editor and novelist from the early twentieth century, once said that "a good scare is worth more to a man than good advice." Recognizing that procrastination can have some pretty frightening consequences—or at least very inconvenient ones—is one of the first steps in breaking the procrastination habit. When faced with life-or-death matters or grave consequences like some of those I've described in this chapter, most people can manage to get themselves in gear and do what's needed to prevent such unwanted outcomes.

The Danger of Too Little Fear

But what about when the consequences aren't so serious? There's no fear, or at least much less fear, to motivate you to act. You might assume, for example, that no harm can come from taking a few months to return a jacket you had borrowed from a friend. But what if your friend decides that this is the last straw and that your repeated lack of consideration means the end of the friendship? Occasional bouts of procrastination over relatively trivial matters are harmless, but you can't always be sure that the matter really is no big deal.

The Danger of Too Much Fear

A healthy dose of fear—whether it's fear for your safety, happiness, health, career advancement, financial security, or anything else—is a good thing. Too much fear is not. If you let yourself get overly worried about what might happen if you don't get something done, you can build up so much anxiety that you procrastinate even more. The anxiety and fear make you feel frozen in a sense, unable to take even the smallest action.

I experienced this one time when I put off billing a client for career counseling services. He was a young college student who had come to me for help in finding a summer job. His father had made the initial contact to schedule the appointment and to tell me that he, not his son, would be paying for the counseling. The father was a single parent and a very busy, high-level professional who wanted his son to get extra attention from me. He asked that I check in with the son by phone between our face-to-face sessions to help keep him on track with his job search.

You're Not Alone

The only way to get myself moving on things I've been putting off is to logically think through the negative consequences that have resulted when I've procrastinated about something similar in the past. If the negative consequences were disproportionately large compared to actually doing the damn thing, then I can get myself to do it.

—Hal F., executive coach

The client happened to come to me at a time when my caseload was very heavy and my life in general was quite busy. I gave the young man my full attention during our face-to-face meetings, but I did not keep tabs on him by phone as often as I should have. After a couple of months of working with him, I let him drift away without calling to encourage him to come back in to meet with me.

I built up such guilt over what I saw as my negligence that when it came time to bill the father, I couldn't bring myself to do so. A part of me knew that I had provided more than adequate service to the client, but the part of me I listened more closely to was saying that I didn't deserve to be paid. A few months went by after my last meeting with the client, and, as summer arrived, I began to fear that I would get a phone call from the father, berating me for leaving his jobless son in the lurch. I knew that the responsible thing to do was to initiate a call myself, either to the father, the son, or both, apologize for having been out of touch, and see how I could be of further help. But fear kept me from doing so.

Then one day out of the blue, I did get a call from the father. Much to my surprise, he called to thank me and find out what he owed me. He said that his son had found my advice very useful and had found a summer job he was looking forward to starting in a few days. He said that he thought it must be about time that he received a bill and was worried that I might have already sent one that he'd overlooked. Talk about relief!

Matter of Fact

If you find that worry, fear, or a general sense of dread is something you experience often in your daily life, you might want to learn more about anxiety disorders. The Anxiety Disorders Association of America promotes the prevention and cure of anxiety disorders and works to improve the lives of people who have them. You can visit the organization's Web site at www.adaa.org or telephone them at 301-231-9350.

Despite the happy ending, I still felt that I could've done a better job and that the ending was due just as much to luck as to any effort on my part. I vowed that from that point on, I wouldn't let fear keep me from addressing my mistakes head on. I also vowed to remember that problems, tasks, or projects that seem so overwhelming usually turn out to be much less difficult or stressful than I've built them up to be. You can learn more about the role fear plays in procrastination in Chapter 4, "It's All in Your Head."

Things We Procrastinate About

Procrastination can rear its ugly head in any area of your life. Some people are efficient and productive at work but never get anything accomplished on the home front. Others vacuum, floss, and exercise regularly, but they procrastinate so often at work that they put their professional future in jeopardy.

For some people, it's not a question of whether the task is related to home or work but whether it's big or small, critical or unimportant. There are those who dust furniture regularly, complete routine paperwork at the office, promptly reply to invitations, and wash the car, but never get around to making major life decisions or reaching long-term goals. Others are out saving the world and accomplishing great things, but they put off picking up the dry cleaning.

The things we put off or don't finish usually fall into six main categories:

1. Home
2. Work
3. Relationships and social life
4. Self-improvement

5. School

6. Biggies like finances, insurance, estate planning, and safety

The chapters in Part 3, "Tips and Tricks for Getting Things Done," and Part 4, "Getting Things Done at Work and School," cover hundreds of specific tasks and activities within those six categories. You'll learn where your procrastination hot-spots are, and what you can do about them.

The Top 10 Things People Procrastinate About

I conducted a survey in which more than 300 respondents from across the country told me about their procrastination problems. They answered a questionnaire which listed 45 tasks, ranging from paying bills, to sending birthday cards, preparing a will, and getting together with old friends. The respondents checked off everything that they procrastinate about and made a special note of the three things that are their biggest procrastination problems, their personal Procrastination Hall of Fame.

With #1 as the task most often cited, those that made it into the Procrastination Hall of Fame were the following:

1. Exercising

2. Cleaning out closets, drawers, and other cluttered spaces

3. Losing weight

4. Household cleaning

5. Preparing a will or other estate planning

6. Keeping up with reading related to work

7. Writing letters (personal correspondence, not work-related)

8. Investing/saving for the future

9. Making home repairs or arranging for others to do them

10. Getting organized (in general)

Would any of those belong in your own Procrastination Hall of Fame? If you'd like to take the survey and find out, there's a copy of the original questionnaire, as well as more information on the survey and the results, in Appendix D, "The Procrastination Survey."

The Least You Need to Know

➤ Estimating how much money your procrastination habit costs you can be a useful way to get motivated to break the habit.

➤ Putting off dealing with problems on the job can cause major damage to your professional reputation and might even lead to job loss.

➤ Not doing anything about dissatisfaction with your career in general can cause you to have serious regrets later in life.

➤ Chronic procrastination can take a toll on your mental and physical health.

➤ Procrastination puts friendships and relationships in jeopardy and lowers the quality of your home life.

➤ A little fear about the potential negative consequences of procrastination can be good for getting you moving, but too much fear can overwhelm you.

Chapter 2

The Procrastination Epidemic

In This Chapter

➤ What it means to procrastinate

➤ Why it's sometimes a good thing

➤ Why procrastination is a growing problem

You know the feeling. It's that sense of dread or even panic that comes when you realize how many unfinished projects have piled up around the house or that you haven't started the report your boss is expecting tomorrow. Or maybe it's how cheated you feel shopping for exorbitantly priced red roses at 5:00 P.M. on February 14 or the embarrassment of not sending a thank-you note for a thoughtful gift received months ago.

Adding insult to injury is probably a backlog of e-mails and phone messages waiting for replies, boxes that haven't been unpacked from your last three moves, and the New Year's resolution to lose weight that succumbed to a hot fudge sundae on January 3. Face it: You're a procrastinator.

You're Not Alone

Procrastination is everywhere, and everybody does it, either chronically or occasionally. Yes, even the most seemingly organized, together people do it. With life on this planet getting more complicated every day, procrastination is becoming something of an epidemic. There's more for us to do and higher expectations for when we'll get it all done. When the going gets tough, procrastination often rears its ugly head.

Matter of Fact

For those who haven't yet bought into the idea that stopping procrastination is a good thing, there's the Procrastinators Club of America (PCA), founded in 1956. The club has 14,000 members and estimates that there are millions of would-be members who just haven't gotten around to joining. According to Acting President Les Waas, the club's most recent activity has been working on the Y1K problem. (By the way, Les has been Acting President since his first term ended in 1956 because the 1957 nominating committee still hasn't held elections for any years since.) You can reach PCA at 215-947-9020 or P.O. Box 712, Bryn Athyn, PA 19009. (PCA hasn't gotten around to developing a Web site yet.)

To overcome this problem, you first have to know exactly what procrastination is and why you do it. That's what we'll look at in this and the next few chapters.

Why We Love to Hate Procrastination

Most of us have a love-hate relationship with procrastination. We hate the way it wrecks our lives, jeopardizing our health, careers, relationships, and more. We hate the way it puts us in a state of constant worry. We stress over what we should be doing, what we haven't done, and what we've started but might not finish.

At the same time, though, we love the way procrastination relieves us of our responsibilities. It's our little escape from the real world. It gives us permission to go see a good movie instead of studying for a test. It lets us stay in bed an extra hour instead of going to the gym before work. Procrastination makes us human. We like the way it lets us enjoy life and keeps us from being automatons who get everything done but never stop to smell the roses. There's nothing wrong with that—at least not until it starts to take its toll in some of the ways described in Chapter 1, "The Procrastinator's Wake-Up Call."

What It Is

You might do it all the time or some of the time, but have you ever stopped to analyze just what procrastination is? Procrastination is the act of putting off something until later by either not starting it, starting at the last minute, or starting but not finishing. It comes from the Latin words *pro* and *cras,* which can be translated as "for tomorrow" or "belonging to tomorrow."

If you're a procrastinator, there are probably some things you never get around to doing. You make vague promises to yourself or others, saying, "I'll do it later." You don't have any idea when later might be; you just know it's not now.

Procrastination often happens with tasks that you expect are going to be difficult, such as quitting smoking. It also happens with projects that seem overwhelming or that you don't know how to begin, such as clearing out clutter that's been building up for years. Or you might put off doing something because it's boring, opting instead to spend your time on more fun or challenging pursuits.

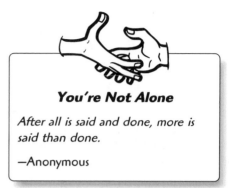

You're Not Alone

After all is said and done, more is said than done.

—Anonymous

On the other hand, you might be the type who is pretty good about getting things started but runs out of steam midway through and doesn't finish. This kind of procrastination happens frequently with projects that involve many steps and have to be carried out over a long period of time, such as writing reports or reaching self-improvement goals such as losing weight, getting fit, or learning something new. You start out with the best of intentions, but you give up or get distracted before reaching your goals.

What It Feels Like

Procrastination can feel like an addiction. You may have the sensation of being out of control and powerless to do anything about it. You feel as though some force within is controlling your actions. You can't figure out where that force comes from or how to curb it. Just as is sometimes the case with addictions to alcohol, drugs, gambling, or food, procrastinating behavior is often the result of giving in to impulses, having a negative self-concept, or being in an environment that enables the habit. Unlike some other addictions, however, procrastination is not a disease. It is simply a habit, a habit you can have power over.

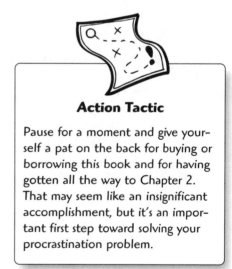

Action Tactic

Pause for a moment and give yourself a pat on the back for buying or borrowing this book and for having gotten all the way to Chapter 2. That may seem like an insignificant accomplishment, but it's an important first step toward solving your procrastination problem.

All Talk, No Action

Procrastinators usually know what they need to be doing. They talk about their obligations and commitments, either publicly or to themselves. They complain, vent, rant, rave, worry, and stew. They may even obsess over what they're supposed to be doing and think about a project or task constantly, but those thoughts don't get translated into action. In Chapter 4, "It's All in Your Head," you'll learn how your thoughts, feelings, and self-talk affect your action—or lack thereof.

When It's a Good Thing

If you've come to see procrastination as an evil demon that worms its way into your life to mess up things, then you may find it hard to believe that procrastination is sometimes a good thing. Deciding not to take action is often the best action you can take.

You might, for example, need to spread out commitments and tasks to keep your schedule manageable and to be most productive. That's what I did with this book. I proposed the topic to an editor several months before I would be able to start writing it. I wanted to get the book project on my schedule and on the publisher's calendar far in advance so that I wouldn't miss out on the chance to do it. But I needed to delay the writing of it until my schedule lightened up. That's the good kind of procrastination. It's based on conscious thought and rational decision-making.

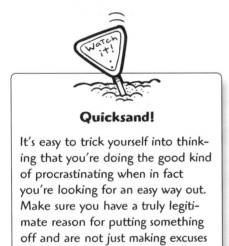

Quicksand!

It's easy to trick yourself into thinking that you're doing the good kind of procrastinating when in fact you're looking for an easy way out. Make sure you have a truly legitimate reason for putting something off and are not just making excuses or hoping the task will "go away."

You might also delay something because of an anticipated change in circumstances. You say to yourself, "I'm not going to begin this project yet because it's very likely that the new manager who starts next week is not going to want any of the old manager's projects to be carried out." As long as you would still have time to get it done if the new person did indeed want it, then you've made a wise decision. But if there's little chance that the project would get cancelled and you're just using the management transition as an excuse to procrastinate, then that's the bad kind of procrastination.

You're Not a Bad Person

If you're fed up with procrastinating, then you're probably fed up with yourself, too. You might feel lazy, undisciplined, irresponsible, and doomed to a life of missed opportunities. Although it certainly doesn't hurt to be a little tough on yourself to help get you moving, don't take the self-criticism too far, or you'll only make matters worse.

Procrastination is not a character flaw you were born with. It's a behavior problem you've developed, a habit you've learned. (One exception to this rule is when procrastinating results from something like Attention Deficit Disorder, Obsessive-Compulsive Disorder, a learning disability, clinical depression, or other difficulties you might have been born with or have developed. These problems are explained in Chapter 4.)

Matter of Fact

The external factors fueling your procrastination may go beyond distractions in your immed-iate home and work environment. Trends and developments in society-at-large have a trickle-down effect on our daily behavior. You can read about some of these in *The Future Ain't What It Used to Be: The 40 Cultural Trends Transforming Your Job, Your Life, Your World* by Vickie Abrahamson, Mary Meehan, and Larry Samuel.

It's Not Laziness

Think of the time and effort that goes into concocting excuses for why you're not going to do something. Think of the energy you expend doing the things you do to kill time. Think of the brainpower you use worrying about what you're supposed to be doing but aren't doing. Anybody who has that much energy isn't a lazy person.

You may have your lazy moments when you need nothing more than a kick in the seat of the pants to get moving and doing. But don't label yourself as lazy just be-cause you occasionally goof off. Procrastinators usually have the energy it takes to get things done and the ability to make an effort; they just use that energy and ability in misguided ways.

It's Not a Question of Discipline

Procrastinators sometimes wake up one day and declare that they're going to turn over a new leaf, buckle down, and get things done. They think it's a matter of being more disciplined. Unfortunately, what they don't realize is that trying to get more dis-ciplined only makes matters worse.

Think about times when you've tried to lead a very regimented life. Maybe you said you were going to go jogging every day of the week or would clean the kitchen immediately after finishing dinner each night. You probably felt so constricted and overwhelmed by the standards you'd set for your behavior that when you slipped up and didn't do something just one time, you labeled yourself undisciplined and gave up hope of ever getting your act together.

Discipline is not something you can dictate yourself to have. Trying to be disciplined is a form of all-or-nothing thinking that sets you up for failure. Instead, think about gradually adopting new habits and approaching everything with a sense of modera-tion, not an all-or-nothing attitude.

Action Tactic

If you're feeling down on yourself for procrastinating too much, take a few moments to think about times in the past when you accomplished something, or things you accomplish now. Even if you're feeling lousy about yourself, realizing how much you have done and do on a regular basis should provide some encouragement.

It's Not About Ambition

Just because you don't reach long-term goals or get day-to-day tasks accomplished doesn't mean you lack ambition. Procrastinators are often very motivated, ambitious people who have the best of intentions but can't seem to get things accomplished. They either have developed a procrastination habit that overpowers their ambition or don't make use of their time well enough to get things done and reach their goals.

Why Procrastination Is Becoming an Epidemic

Life is more complicated than it used to be. Technological advances, changes in the workplace, and the evolution of family life have made people feel overwhelmed, overextended, and resentful of all they are supposed to be doing or think they should be doing.

Technology: Is It Really a Timesaver?

Remember what life was like before rampant use of cellular phones, pagers, and e-mail? Are you even old enough to remember life before fax machines, voice mail, and overnight mail delivery? Then you probably recall a time when the pace of life was slower and you didn't feel so pressured.

Now think about what the expectations are for your performance these days. People demand immediate results because they know you can whip up a quick pie chart with up-to-the-minute budget figures with a few clicks of a mouse. Plus, they expect that chart to be visually appealing with fancy graphics and colors because everyone is an amateur desktop publisher these days. To make matters worse, they want it in an hour because you can send it by e-mail.

Quicksand!

If your goals aren't realistic and feasible, you'll never reach them. Goals that aren't doable are just fantasies.

Technology raises the expectations others have for the speed, content, and quality of your work to such an extent that you might get overwhelmed when facing what used to be the simplest task. You may let fears of how you're going to be judged keep you from doing it and may build the task up in your mind as something so complex you could never begin to tackle it. Or you may simply get fed up with others' unreasonable expectations and rebel by not doing something or by holding off until the last minute and then doing it grudgingly.

Although technology has certainly made our lives easier in many ways, it has also magnified many of the factors that lead to procrastination. Services and technology that enable you to do things at the last minute aren't foolproof. That Fed Ex office you thought was open until 8 P.M. might have started closing at 7. Or your Internet server could hit some snags and not be able to get your e-mail to its destination right away. Always work as if you had to mail things the old-fashioned way, leaving a cushion of a day or two to allow for unforeseen delays.

Action Tactic

Try designating one day a month or even one day a week, if possible, as a technology–free day. Don't use your cell phone, pager, computer, fax machine, or other electronic gadgets. Give yourself a break from the pressure of being constantly in touch with the world.

The Pressure Cooker Workplace

Unless you've been living under a rock for the past several years (which procrastinators sometimes feel like they're doing), you've no doubt heard that dramatic changes have taken place in the world of work. This has led to increased procrastination in several ways:

➤ **Overload.** Massive downsizing and lay-offs have meant that the people who remain in a company end up carrying a workload that was intended for two or three people, or even more in extreme cases. The result is employees who become less productive because they feel overwhelmed.

➤ **Change.** The name of the game in the workplace has been change: change of management, change of mission and philosophy, change of rules and procedures, change of location, and changes in health plans and benefits. So much change makes people confused and overwhelmed. It messes up routines and breaks down organizational systems, making it more difficult to know how to get things done or to find the resources needed to accomplish tasks.

➤ **Insecurity.** Employers can no longer promise a lifetime of secure employment, which can make employees feel less loyal. If you feel less committed to a person or organization, you'll have less incentive to get things done for that person or organization.

➤ **Self-employment.** More people than ever before are opting for the entrepreneurial route in their careers by starting businesses, freelancing, or consulting, and they are often doing it from home. Self-employment brings major time-management and organizational challenges. Plus, the success or failure of the business is riding on your shoulders. Such external and internal pressures are prime breeding ground for procrastination.

Matter of Fact

In the last several years, a whole new genre of career and business books has cropped up to explain what's going on in the workplace and how the changes are affecting individual workers. Some of the best of these books are *The Career Is Dead—Long Live the Career* by Douglas T. Hall; *The Organization of the Future* by Frances Hesselbein and Marshall Goldsmith; and *Managing Transitions: Making the Most of Change* by William Bridges.

Nobody's Ruling the Roost

Not many households these days have a June Cleaver at home full-time doing the cooking, cleaning, and organizing. What you're more likely to find is a dual-income couple trying to juggle the demands of jobs with household chores and possibly children. Or you find single people, either with or without children, working long hours and relying on take-out food and lots of luck in keeping their households functioning.

Action Tactic

For one week (don't try to do it for any longer), keep a log of the time you spend doing household chores versus working at a job. At the end of the week, compare the totals for each. How do they compare? How much time is left over in the week for sleeping and personal time?

What ends up happening is that no one's ruling the roost. Most adults in the household are too tired or distracted to plan the meals, cook, and clean. Plus, the old gender stereotypes of who should do which chores are gone in many households, so no one feels an innate sense of obligation to take out the trash, do the laundry, or put dinner on the table. Sometimes the children end up having more household responsibilities than the parents do, but kids don't necessarily have the ability or desire to do the same kind of job an adult would.

The result is a lot of people who feel resentful that they have to take care of so many chores on top of their work-related responsibilities and a lot of people who don't have the time or energy to do it all. Those are two sure-fire sparks for an outbreak of procrastination and an invasion of dust bunnies and cold pizza.

The Least You Need to Know

➤ Procrastination is the act of putting off something until a later time, either by not starting a task or not finishing one you've started.

➤ Procrastination is a habit that can be broken.

➤ People tend to procrastinate when they are overwhelmed by too much to do or high expectations others have for them or they have for themselves.

➤ Procrastination is becoming more and more common as technological, work-place, and societal changes make life more complex and challenging.

Chapter 3

Blame It on the Environment

In This Chapter

➤ Where procrastination comes from

➤ Obstacles that slow you down

➤ How clutter is a roadblock to action

➤ Common distractions to watch out for

You'll probably be relieved to hear that procrastination is not completely your fault. Although there's no denying that what goes on in your head has a lot to do with procrastination, the root of the problem may be in your environment. Most people don't need years on a shrink's couch to overcome procrastination. (The psychological side of procrastination is covered in Chapter 4, "It's All in Your Head.") All they may need is a comfortable, uncluttered, organized, and distraction-free environment that makes it easy to get things done.

I Think, Therefore I Do—Or Do I?

Getting started on tasks or completing projects you've begun relies on a critical thought-action link. You have the thought, "I need to do X now," and expect action to follow, but action doesn't always come, does it? Sometimes obstacles get in the way, breaking up the flow of that thought-action sequence.

You're Not Alone

"I think I was marked for life as a procrastinator when I saw Gone with the Wind *as a young man and heard Scarlett O'Hara say, "I'll think of it all tomorrow. After all, tomorrow is another day."*

—Scott T., dentist

Action Tactic

Next time you're sitting on the couch or lying in bed and don't want to get up to take care of some task, tell yourself to just stand up and stretch, with no expectation that you'll do anything more than that. You may be surprised to find that simple motion propels you into more movement and even into completing the dreaded task.

Here are some common examples of how your environment can be more to blame than your mind when you procrastinate:

➤ You may not have a major mental block against exercising; you just don't feel like wading through your messy closet to find clean workout clothes, so you never make it to the gym.

➤ You might not have a genetic predisposition to avoid housework (then again, you might!); you just don't feel like stooping down to fish around under the kitchen sink for all the cleaning supplies. You particularly don't want to reach for the sponge that always gets hidden behind the pipes where water leaks and where who knows what kind of creepy-crawlers reside. So you put off housework until a later time because there are just too many steps involved to get to the actual cleaning.

➤ The reason you're not finishing a project at work may not be that you have a fear of failure, fear of success, or any other fancy psychological hang-up. It could simply be that the disarray of papers and files that have accumulated on your desk makes it difficult to keep track of where you are in the project or the information you need to finish.

➤ You don't necessarily want to put off your income tax preparation until the last minute because of some deep-seated resentment toward the IRS (though that's a likely reason!). Instead, you might have to put it off because your life is overwhelmed with commitments and obligations that occupy every free minute of your waking hours until April 15.

When clutter, disorganization, an overload of commitments, or other distractions get in the way, the link between thought and action becomes weak. These obstacles break the momentum that's needed to get an object into motion. (That object is you, lying on the couch, staring blankly into space at your desk, or in some other state of inertia.) The obstacles give us a chance to pause or make excuses. We say things like, "But if I'm going to do C, I'll have to do A and B first, and that's a real hassle, so I'll do C another time."

Environmental Hazards

The obstacles that cause procrastination come in three easy-to-remember categories:

➤ People

➤ Places

➤ Things

The people are your partners in crime, the fellow procrastinators who convince you that there are about a million other things you'd rather be doing than the task you're supposed to be doing. They may also be people who are not procrastinators themselves but who drag you down by nagging or by not giving you the support and resources you need to get things done.

The places are your workspaces, the physical setup, lighting, temperature, and general comfort level of the areas in which you try to get things done, whether that's home, office, or elsewhere.

The things are objects like papers, files, household knick-knacks, junk, old clothes, and anything else that crowds your life and qualifies as clutter. Clutter can also come in the form of commitments and obligations that keep you overworked and overloaded.

Matter of Fact

If you can't see your desk for the papers and are afraid to open a closet or garage door, you might find the organizing tips in these books to be a lifesaver: *Clutter Control: Putting Your Home on a Diet* by Jeff Campbell; *Lighten Up!: Free Yourself from Clutter* by Michelle Passoff; and *Not for Packrats Only: How to Clean Up, Clear Out, and Live Clutter-Free Forever* by Don Aslett.

The remainder of this chapter focuses on how each of these factors can be a roadblock to action. As you read on, be thinking about your daily life, and see if any of these problems rings true for you. Then, in Part 2, "Becoming an Ex-Procrastinator" and Part 3, "Tips and Tricks for Getting Things Done in Life," you'll find practical solutions for dealing with these roadblocks.

Peer Pressure Has No Peer

My college roommate probably would've graduated Phi Beta Kappa and gone on to a top ten law school (those were her ambitions when we entered as freshmen) if I hadn't egged her on to procrastinate just about every time she needed to be studying or writing a paper. On countless occasions, for example, I persuaded her that it was much more important that we drive into Boston's Chinatown to the one restaurant that was open 24 hours a day than to stay in our rooms studying until the wee hours.

It wasn't that my powers of persuasion were so impressive but that I was, without realizing it, capitalizing on that weak thought-action link. I was presenting my roommate with a diversion, a thought that was more appealing than the one she had just had. The thought of moo shu pork and pot stickers made her mouth water in a way that her microeconomics textbook just couldn't compete with. So all hope of action—at least the kind that leads to straight As—was gone. You probably have similar examples from your school days, workplace, or home life.

Action Tactic

Make a list of all the people you come across in your daily life who may be contributing to your procrastination. Think of ways you could stand up to them and keep them from dragging you back into procrastination mode.

The Culture of Procrastination

Procrastination is like a contagious disease; if you're around someone who wants to put off things, you may feel more of an urge to do the same yourself. Like any social behavior, procrastination is fueled by the strength-in-numbers phenomenon. You feel less stigmatized by being a procrastinator and are more likely to give yourself permission to put off things when you see other people doing it. Plus, it's sometimes just plain fun to goof off with your friends, family, co-workers, or online pals, and most people find fun hard to resist.

Just Do It Already!

People who nag you to get things done or who belittle you for not doing something are just as guilty of fueling your procrastination as are the partners-in-crime described in the preceding section. In Chapter 23, "Dealing with the Procrastinators Around You," you'll read more about why nagging and chastising procrastinators won't get them to stop. For now, just keep in mind that if anyone around you is using those tactics to get you motivated and they're not working, it may not be your fault. The tactics are probably to blame.

The Power of Discomfort

Sometimes you aren't getting things done simply because you're uncomfortable. The chair you're sitting in, the temperature, the constricting clothing you're wearing—all of these things can make you less productive.

Sitting in the Hot Seat

Sometimes people don't get things done because of something as basic as the temperature. Changing the room temperature may be the easiest way to overcome procrastination! Get up and adjust the air conditioning or heat, open a window, step outside for some fresh air—do whatever you need to do to make your work environment more comfortable and to feel refreshed.

Cubicle, Sweet Cubicle

The design of most offices—if you can call them offices, given that they usually have no walls, doors, or windows—is not at all conducive to productivity. It's a wonder that anything gets accomplished in corporate America given some of the working conditions. Those lovely cubicle dividers covered in oatmeal colored carpet, the desk chair that's uncomfortable to sit in after about five minutes, the fluorescent lights that make you feel like a lab experiment—they all add up to one lousy setting for getting things done.

Fortunately, the rats-in-a-maze setup that you find in most office buildings is slowly, although too slowly, becoming a thing of the past. More and more employers are realizing that comfortable work environments breed creativity, productivity, and high morale. (They don't want you to be *too* comfortable, though, so don't try to wheel a recliner and big-screen television into your office Monday morning.)

Quicksand!

Don't abuse the discomfort excuse. If you find that you're often saying things like "I can't work until I find the perfect desk chair" or "It's too hot to do laundry," then you might need to stop making excuses, and just do it.

You're Not Alone

You're only as important as your furniture ... assuming you're not in senior management, you might be lucky to have a big ol' board that stretches the length of your cubicle and keeps the telephone from falling in your lap. Let's call it a 'desk' for the sake of argument. This desk-like arrangement is the perfect complement to the tiny chair that will be your home for 70 hours a week.

—Scott Adams, *The Dilbert Principle* (HarperBusiness, 1996)

They're also realizing that having workstations that are ergonomically correct (safe and comfortable for you physically) is good business because such workstations save them money on health claims and lawsuits. Not all employers are so progressive, however, so you may find yourself in a workspace that inhibits your productivity and encourages procrastination.

Matter of Fact

To find out how to make your workspace more comfortable and safer, check out the meta-site of Human Factors & Ergonomics at http://www.usernomics.com/hf/html. There you'll find links to many other sites that provide information, products, and services.

Of course, not everyone works in a corporate environment or even indoors in an office. The same principles apply, though, regardless of the setting. Your physical workspace affects your productivity no matter what type of job or household chore you're trying to do.

Shine a Little Light on Me

Just as the temperature can make you uncomfortable and unproductive, something as basic as poor lighting can make you procrastinate. You may be hard at work on a task and start running out of steam, not realizing that the energy drain is not coming from the project itself, but from eyestrain. If you are working in an area that is too dark, too bright, has too much glare, or is harshly lit, you might find that your eyes are telling your mind, "Enough of this. Let's quit for now and finish it another time."

Straightjackets and Neckties

If you have a job that requires you to wear formal business attire most of the time, do you find yourself more productive on casual Fridays or other occasions when you get to dress down? Folks who work from home know that there's sometimes nothing more satisfying than working in your bathrobe and scruffy slippers or favorite sweat-pants and bare feet.

If you work outside of the home, your employer or clients probably won't be too impressed if you show up in pajamas, but you should think of little ways to make your work attire more comfortable. You might be surprised at the difference in your attitude toward work when your feet aren't being pinched and your shoulders aren't constricted in a suit jacket.

How a Cluttered Life Holds You Back

If you look behind closed doors at the daily life of a procrastinator, you're likely to find too much stuff (papers, files, magazines, newspapers, knick-knacks, and the like) as well as too many obligations and commitments that eat up time. If that description fits you, you probably find that clutter slows you down and makes you feel less in control of life.

The Leaning Tower of Paper

Is there a phone call you need to return, but you can't find the phone number among all the scraps of paper on your desk, so you've decided to make the call later? Are you supposed to fill out forms this week to renew an insurance policy, submit a health care claim, or to take care of some equally important matter but don't know where you put the papers you need, so you miss the deadline? Are you late mailing a wedding present because you can't remember if the groom's last name is Perkle or Pickle and you can't find the invitation in the seven layers of memorabilia and dry cleaner's receipts on your bulletin board?

Having too much paper, or papers that are disorganized, is one of the major causes of procrastination. It's that thought-action link again. You have the desire, or at least the need, to do something, but you get bogged down in all the paper you have to muddle through before you can take action.

You've probably noticed by now that the paperless office or home that was promised to us by some trend analysts at the dawn of the personal computer era never materialized. Most of us have more paper than ever before because we can create and receive so many documents, bits of data, and graphics on the computer—much of which is pretty useless.

You might also keep papers because they're important for legal or reference purposes or because you're emotionally attached to them. Sometimes there are perfectly legitimate reasons for holding on to certain papers, even just for sentimental reasons, but the key is to keep only those which are truly important or special and to keep them well organized. In Chapter 8, "Lightening Your Load" and in Chapter 9, "Getting Your Act Together," you'll find lots of tips for getting yourself to throw things out and for finding a good place for the papers you do keep. (And I'm not talking about the proverbial safe place that eats paper like some homespun Bermuda Triangle.)

Quicksand!

Don't add to your paper clutter by printing out and saving e-mails you get with the joke of the day or some other words of wisdom or humor that are circulated to thousands of people. If it's so special that you must save it, print it on nice paper, frame it, and hang it on your wall.

You're Not Alone

It is preoccupation with possession, more than anything else, that prevents men from living freely and nobly.

—Bertrand Russell

The Collector's Curse

Not all clutter comes in the form of paper. Those 30-plus camel figurines scattered about my house that cause me to put off dusting until the last possible moment probably count as clutter. I love my camel collection, but I hate the way it makes a fairly easy chore (dusting) much more difficult than it ought to be.

What do you have around the house or office that makes your life more difficult? There's nothing wrong with collecting things you like or saving objects that have sentimental or monetary value. I'm not saying you have to live like a monk. But if you've been collecting things that don't have any great meaning for you or any current or future market value, is there any reason to keep them? If you've become a slave to your collections, then it might be time to part company with them. You'll read more about how to do this in Chapter 8.

Computer Clutter

It would take an awful lot of file cabinets to store the amount of information that can fit on a computer's hard drive and on diskettes. The storage capacity of personal computers is impressive, but it's also dangerous in that computers can easily become repositories for vast amounts of useless or irrelevant data.

Action Tactic

Get out your appointment book or calendar (yes, *now*) and schedule a block of time on a specific date (probably one to two hours are needed) when you'll go through your hard drive to discard files and programs you don't need and to reorganize your files and folders.

If I were to take a look at your hard drive right now, what would I find on it? Your 1994 holiday gift list? The letter you wrote to your next-door neighbor ten years ago complaining about noise? A fact sheet on the migration patterns of Tasmanian marsupials downloaded from the Discovery Channel's Web site? A folder of unimportant e-mails you saved during the first month you got online because you were so taken with this amazing new communication method that you just had to preserve them for posterity?

Computers in homes and offices are among the most overlooked clutter traps. They look innocent enough, sitting there on the desk with no telltale signs of the junk hidden within (unlike closets and drawers, which always seem to have something spilling out of them as a reminder of the chaos that lurks within). Like any type of clutter, an excess of computer files, folders, and programs slows you down when you're trying to get things done.

For example, I've used my computer and the Internet to find and store tidbits of information and ideas that relate to books I was writing or wanted to write. Although this convenient access to information is extremely helpful, I find that when it comes time to write a book, I'm overwhelmed by all the random bits of data I've accumulated. I often don't know where to begin to wade through it all or to organize it into a particular chapter, so I sometimes end up saying to myself, "This is too much trouble; I'll work on that chapter another day."

There's no denying that in many ways computers enable us to be more productive than we ever would be without them. But, if we let them become clutter traps, they can make us feel dazed and confused and unable to do what matters.

Commitment Overload

Clutter doesn't have to consist only of tangible objects. It also comes in the form of things you have to do. Your life may be crowded with so many commitments and responsibilities that you can't handle being pulled in that many different directions. When this happens, you may become overwhelmed, shut down, and not do anything.

Even ordinarily productive and efficient people procrastinate when there's too much to do. I, for example, am notorious for taking on too many responsibilities. During one period in my life, I was writing a 400-page book in 12 weeks, caring for my infant daughter with only part-time child care, launching and teaching a new online nine-week course for career counselors, and beginning a new part-time job (from home) as a career expert for a Web site. I managed to survive those few months of hell and get it all done, but not without frequent bouts of procrastination and huge amounts of stress.

Many people find that they are more productive when they're busy than when they have nothing to do and no structure to their lives. But when that busyness is taken too far and becomes an overload of responsibilities, the opposite happens. People become overwhelmed and unable to function. Every time they think of working on one project, their minds start spinning with all the other things they have to do. The energy they expend worrying about those other commitments drains the energy they need for the task at hand. In Chapter 9, you'll learn ways to turn down commitment requests as well as ways to get out of or minimize obligations you've already committed to.

Quicksand!

Having an extraordinary amount of responsibilities and obligations in your personal and professional life is nothing to brag about. Don't make the mistake of judging your or others' self-worth by how much you have to do. Truly accomplished people have balanced lives, not overextended ones.

If only you could be cloned! These are the 10 areas where you might have commitments and obligations at any given time.

Your 10 Life Roles

As you can see in the figure, commitments and responsibilities in life usually fall into these 10 basic categories:

Action Tactic

Think of one commitment you can get rid of within the next 30 days and vow to take whatever steps are necessary to remove it from your life during that time.

Family Member

Depending on the makeup of your family, you might have responsibilities related to being a child, grandchild, parent, grandparent, sibling, spouse or long-term companion, guardian, or other relative such as aunt, uncle, or cousin.

Homemaker

Whether you run a busy household like Carol Brady and Alice the housekeeper or live alone with nothing but a futon and lots of take-out menus, homemaking is a role everyone has to play for better or worse. Activities in this category can include: shopping for groceries and planning meals; preparing food and cooking; cleaning and organizing; making or overseeing home repairs, renovations, or decoration; making purchases related to the home; doing laundry or arranging for it or dry cleaning to be done; hiring and supervising domestic workers; relocating, including arranging for a move, packing, and unpacking; and managing and coordinating household schedules.

Income-Earner

You may be the sole breadwinner for yourself or your family through a job or business you run, or maybe you work part-time to supplement the income of the primary breadwinner. You might also have responsibilities related to earning money in other ways such as through investing, saving, or arranging for loans.

Careerist

Different from your role as an income-earner, your role as a careerist involves devoting time and energy to choosing, changing, or managing your career and to finding jobs or developing a business. Of course, your career probably brings in some income, but money is not the main focus here.

Leisurite

When you're in the leisurite role, you might be pursuing hobbies; playing sports or games; expressing yourself creatively or artistically; being entertained by movies, television, theater, or other media; taking vacations or short trips; or just getting rest and relaxation.

Social Being

Everyone is a socialite to some extent. You may not carry it as far as the beautiful people who grace the society pages in evening gowns and tuxedos, but you are a social being who has some degree of interaction with other human beings as a friend, date, romantic partner, or host.

Community Member

You may also connect with your fellow human beings or contribute to the betterment of society as a volunteer, philanthropist, public servant, concerned citizen, community leader, neighbor, or simply someone who brings a dish to the block party's pot-luck supper.

Learner

Whether you're a full-time student working toward a degree or merely someone who likes to read, you are a learner throughout your life. This category includes the roles of student, scholar, self-teacher, reader, explorer, researcher, thinker, and participant in intellectual life.

Quicksand!

Beware of playing roles in life that you think you *should* have; instead, take on only those responsibilities that mean something to you.

Physical Being

At various times in your life you might pay more or less attention to your physical self. You might exercise; focus on your diet or nutrition; attend to your health-care needs; work on recovering from illness, injury, or addiction; or make an effort to improve your appearance and attractiveness.

Spiritual Being

Though this role category is listed last, it is one of the most important, in that your spirit enables you to carry out and cope with the other roles; it guides your daily behavior. This category includes your ethics and morals; philosophy of life; attitude and moods; mental health and well-being; creativity; overall life balance; and religious affiliation, beliefs, worship, rituals, and traditions.

No one can devote significant energy, time, and attention to all 10 of these life role categories at once. Yet circumstances sometimes force you to have to try to. You might be laid-off and looking for a new job; caring for an elderly parent who has recently become incapacitated; having to run a household because you can't afford help; trying to date and develop a lasting romantic relation ship; keeping up your obligations to a community board; and getting some occasional rest. You didn't necessarily set out to become this overextended, but various twists of fate have thrown you into this predicament, a predicament that's prime breed ing ground for procrastination.

Driven to Distraction

We are constantly bombarded with distractions or potential distractions. There's the telephone in your office that brings calls from friends who want to chat or your mother who wants to know why you haven't called in a week. There's the lure of the television, kitchen, and who knows what else that home-based workers face. Television may be the biggest culprit of all, keeping many people from getting things done, whether on the work or home front.

You're Not Alone

The average American watches more than four hours of TV each day, equal to two months of nonstop TV watching per year and equal to more than 12 solid years of nonstop TV watching in the life of a person who lives to age 72.

—cited by Jeff Davidson in The Complete Idiot's Guide to Managing Your Time

Computers are also distracting. You get on an Internet people directory to look up one person you're trying to find and end up searching for your high school sweetheart, your third-grade teacher, your next-door neighbor's mother's beau from 1939, and everyone else you or your friends have ever known or met.

Then there are the games. Who can resist a quick hand of computer solitaire or slaying some dragons during that post-lunch slump at the office? The problem, of course, is that playing one hand of solitaire is about as easy as eating one potato chip, and there are always more dragons to slay.

There is something you can do about it. Computers these days usually come with complimentary games software built in. If you get a new computer, go ahead and erase the games from your hard drive during setup (or don't load them at all) so that you won't stumble upon them later in a vulnerable moment.

So Is It Really Not My Fault?

Now that you see how many obstacles in your life might be fueling procrastination, you might be tempted to close this book here at Chapter 3 and say, "I don't need to know any more. I now know that I procrastinate because my office is always too hot." I'm sorry to tell you that it's not that simple. Factors such as clutter, commitments, other people, and distractions may be the catalyst for your procrastination, but they don't tell the whole story. It's still up to you and all those thoughts and feelings in your head to determine how you react to your environment. You can choose to give in to the obstacles and procrastinate, or you can choose to get things done. The next chapter will look at how that process works.

The Least You Need to Know

➤ Procrastination often has less to do with psychological factors and more to do with people, places, and things.

➤ An excess of paper and possessions and an overload of commitments slows you down and leads to procrastination.

➤ Procrastination can result from working in a physically uncomfortable space.

➤ You might procrastinate because people around you encourage and enable the procrastination.

➤ Television and computers are the biggest enemies of action.

Chapter 4

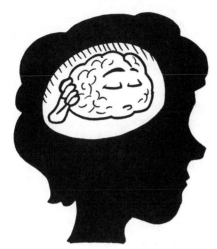

It's All in
Your Head

In This Chapter

➤ How thoughts and feelings lead to procrastination

➤ Where habits come from

➤ How to know whether fear is holding you back

➤ When being perfect gets in the way

➤ When procrastination signals a more serious problem

Procrastination may not be completely your fault, as Chapter 3, "Blame It on the Environment," explained. Plenty of people, places, and things can prevent you from starting or finishing a task or reaching goals. That's the good news because you can usually deal with those real, tangible obstacles.

The bad news is that no matter who or what is conspiring against you as you try to take action, it's still you and only you who is ultimately responsible for the action you take—or don't take. So if you thought you were off the hook, think again. To beat procrastination, you have to own up to the fact that what goes on in your head has something to do with the problem.

The Psychology of Action

All actions result from thoughts and feelings. If those thoughts and feelings are negative, irrational, or unrealistic, then the behavior they spark may turn out to be procrastinating behavior. If they're neutral or positive, then the behavior that results from them is more likely to be productive and appropriate.

You're Not Alone

When I try to make myself do something I don't want to do, it's as if I'm in that movie, Invasion of the Body Snatchers. *I know I have ultimate control over what I think and feel, but sometimes I feel like someone else is in my head telling me I don't have to do something. I feel like I'm my own worst enemy.*

—Adrienne G., homemaker and mother

Let's look at how thoughts and feelings can influence actions, first with a rational thought and positive emotion at the root of an action:

Thought: It's cold in this room, probably because the thermostat is set too low.

Emotional reaction: I feel uncomfortable, but I feel that I have control over the situation. I have the ability to go to the thermostat and see whether the setting is the problem.

Action: I go to the thermostat and turn up the heat.

Now, take a look at how an irrational thought and negative emotional reaction can lead to unproductive behavior in the same situation:

Thought: It's cold in this room, probably because that useless boiler is on the blink again.

Emotional reaction: I feel so angry and frustrated. Why is this hunk of metal wrecking my day? What did I do to deserve this?

Action: I spend the rest of the day complaining about the cold, unable to get any work done, but not taking rational steps to see what the problem is.

Adjusting the temperature in your home or office may not be something you procrastinate about or see as a major problem, but I chose this example because it illustrates the thought-feeling-behavior link that may be causing your procrastination in other situations.

You Think Too Much

Sometimes procrastinating behavior results from thinking too much. You worry about the outcome of an endeavor you're about to undertake or stew over how far behind you are on an assignment for school. Instead of following the advice of Nike to "just do it," you work yourself into a frenzy by thinking about what's wrong with your situation or what could go wrong. You end up making the task much more difficult or overwhelming than it needs to be and start feeling down on yourself for slacking off. Those feelings lead to a negative self-concept and low self-esteem, which in turn fuel further procrastination.

Matter of Fact

The thought–feeling–action link described here is based on the work of psychologist Albert Ellis, who pioneered a very practical and well-respected type of cognitive psychotherapy called Rational-Emotive Therapy (RET). What I cover in this chapter is just the tip of the iceberg, so if you want a more in-depth look at RET and cognitive psychology, read the work of Dr. Ellis in *The Albert Ellis Reader: A Guide to Well-Being Using Rational Emotive Behavior Therapy* by Albert Ellis and Shawn Blau, and *How to Stubbornly Refuse to Make Yourself Miserable about Anything—Yes, Anything!* by Albert Ellis.

You Just Didn't Think

You might also procrastinate because you don't think *enough*. You may act impulsively without thinking through what you are doing. Suppose that every night after dinner you say to yourself, "I ought to clean up the kitchen now rather than leaving everything sitting here until morning." Then, without thinking about the negative consequences of putting off that task (such as the fact that the pots and pans will have all sorts of crud stuck to them by morning), you go off to do something else and ignore the dishes and leftover food sitting out.

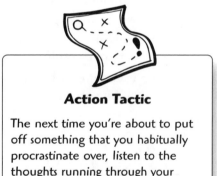

Action Tactic

The next time you're about to put off something that you habitually procrastinate over, listen to the thoughts running through your head. Do you hear any self-talk like "I'll do it later" or "I don't have to do this now"? If so, think about how much power those simple little statements have been having over your behavior.

Somewhere between that first thought and the action of leaving the kitchen was a fleeting thought that said, "I'll do it later." You block from your mind all thoughts of the messy kitchen and go on to more pleasant thoughts and activities.

If you don't stop and zero in on that "I'll do it later" thought, and if you don't consciously think through the consequences of your decision to put off the cleaning, then you'll stay in the same old pattern of acting on impulse. Habits develop in this way, and procrastination is one of the worst habits of all. In Chapter 12, "The Secret Formula to Overcoming Procrastination," you'll learn about the Stop, Look, and Listen formula, which helps you focus on the faulty thoughts and feelings that are causing you to act on impulse.

What's Causing Your Procrastination?

The thoughts and feelings swirling around in your head can lead to procrastination in several ways. Those ways fall into 10 main categories:

1. **Fear:** Fear of failure, success, or how you'll be judged

2. **Perfectionism:** Making things more difficult and critical than they need to be

3. **Being overwhelmed:** Finding a task so difficult or cumbersome that you don't know where or how to begin or end it

4. **Feeling frustrated:** Having a low tolerance for the ambiguity or delayed gratification that comes with some projects

5. **Adrenaline rush addiction:** Relying on the thrill that comes from getting something done at the last minute

6. **Negativity toward the task:** Disliking or being uninterested in the task itself

7. **Rebellion:** Having negative feelings toward the person who assigned a task or who will benefit from it and resenting that you have to do it

8. **Unrealistic view of time:** Having a faulty sense of time and how much you can get done within it

9. **Psychological issues:** Disorders such as depression or Attention Deficit Disorder, among others, make it difficult to get things done

10. **Physical problem:** Having a physical ailment that drains your energy and makes you less likely to get things done

You probably procrastinate for different reasons at different times, so more than one of these 10 causes is likely to ring a bell. To overcome your procrastination and implement the strategies suggested in Parts 2 and 3 of this book, you must first understand the source of your problem. As you read the rest of this chapter, try to relate each cause to your situation and focus on the ones that are relevant for you.

Quicksand!

If the idea of having to address the internal causes of your procrastination makes you want to quit before you start, don't do it. For the most part, internal causes are no more difficult to overcome than the external obstacles of people, places, and things.

Fears That Hold You Back

Fear is a handy defense mechanism. Being fearful keeps us from trying new things, taking risks, or accepting challenges. Fear defends and protects us because it keeps us from doing the things that we could fail at or be harshly judged because of. What this means for procrastinators is that fear keeps us from starting or finishing projects that could have possible negative outcomes or consequences.

The fears that relate to procrastination include the following:

➤ Fear of failure

➤ Fear of being judged

➤ Fear of success

The following sections describe how each of these fears could be holding you back.

Fear of Failure

If you don't enter the race, you can't lose. By not entering, you miss out on the satisfaction and rewards that might come from winning, but at least you won't have to face the disappointment of losing or lose face in front of others.

Action Tactic

To make fear of failure less of a problem, try to remember a time when you did fail at something but found that the people you care about were supportive and didn't think any less of you.

Failure is something most people want to avoid. It hurts emotionally by making you feel disappointed, sad, and rejected. It might embarrass or even humiliate you if the failure is at all public. It also can damage your self-esteem and self-confidence. From a practical standpoint, failure can have dire consequences. You might not earn an academic degree, get the job you want, or be rewarded with more money, a better parking space, or whatever it is that you want or need. If you are avoiding "entering the race" because you're afraid you won't win, fear of failure may be causing your procrastination.

Fear of Being Judged

The fear of being judged is related to the idea of fearing failure but has more to do with the quality of your work or your performance. You may have experienced fear of being judged during your years as a student. Whether your school days are in the distant past or part of your present, the fear of getting a bad grade is probably etched in your mind. If you received a lousy grade from time to time (or often), it was always easier to deal with the situation when you could say, "But I didn't study at all," or "I didn't start writing the paper until the night before." Telling others (and yourself) that you made no effort or didn't give it your all lets everyone know that the grade didn't reflect your ability, so you were off the hook.

You're Not Alone

Fear can be headier than whisky, once man has acquired a taste for it.

—Donald Downes

Not everything we do in life gets a grade from A to F, but most things we do are judged in some way. Whether it's a fussy guest giving your cleaning ability the white glove test or co-workers and bosses judging your presentation skills at a staff meeting, someone is always scrutinizing the things you do. If you are particularly sensitive to or concerned about how you're going to be judged on a certain task, then you may be more likely to delay starting it or finishing it.

Fear of Success

I first heard the term *fear of success* in the late 1970s when there was lots of talk about superwomen, women who were finding success in their careers while meeting the demands of family life. Fear of success was sometimes given as an excuse for why some women were not reaching even higher levels in the professional world.

My first reaction was, "How bogus! Why would anyone be afraid of success, especially someone who has made a point of positioning herself or himself on the road to success? Who wouldn't want fame, fortune, and glory?" About 50 psychology classes and a little life experience later, I came to realize that the term does make sense. It's not that some people don't want to succeed. They are just afraid of how their lives may change if they do achieve success. Fear of success happens because we have thoughts such as the following:

> **Fearful thought:** If I accomplish this task or reach this goal, people's expectations of me will increase greatly and then I'll have to do even better the next time, or at least keep up the same standards.
>
> **Example:** If the boss praises my sales figures this month, I'll have to perform just as well, if not even better, in all the months that follow.
>
> **The procrastinator's escape route:** Put off making the phone call that's necessary to close a deal until it's too late and the sale has already gone to a competitor.

> **Fearful thought:** If I accomplish this task or reach this goal, I'll then have to go on to the next set of goals or tasks, and I'm not sure I have the stamina, ability, or desire to keep going.
>
> **Example:** If I am successful at cleaning out the garage, then I'll have to move on to the attic, the kitchen cabinets, the closets, and who knows what else.
>
> **The procrastinator's escape route:** Don't clean out the garage and instead say that you'll do it next spring when it will be "the right time" to do all the cleaning and organizing chores.

Fearful thought: If I accomplish this task or reach this goal, my life will change in ways that I can't handle or might not want to handle.

Example: If I am successful at getting onto television talk shows to promote the unique small business I've just started, I might have to travel more than I want to, or I might not have lost 10 pounds by then and will look fat on television.

The procrastinator's escape route: Don't get around to writing the press release necessary for publicizing your business and keep putting off making a call to the TV producer a friend referred you to.

Fearful thought: If I accomplish this task or reach this goal, I will become a different person.

Example: If I am elected to city council, my friends and family might not treat me like the old me anymore. They may be threatened or jealous and think of me as a different person. I might not even recognize myself anymore. I'm just not the successful type. That wouldn't be me.

The procrastinator's escape route: Don't run for office so there's no chance of winning, even though friends and family are telling you that you should enter the race and that you have a good chance of winning.

As you can see, having a fear of success doesn't mean that you wouldn't want to be successful. It just means that you aren't comfortable with what would be expected of you or how your identity might change if you did achieve success. To avoid that discomfort, you might engage in self-defeating behaviors such as those described in the preceding examples.

It Has to Be Perfect

Striving for excellence is a good thing. Striving to be perfect is not. What's the difference? Perfectionists are extreme and obsessive in their thinking. They become preoccupied with being perfect and are often controlling in their efforts to reach perfection. There's nothing wrong with wanting to give 100 percent effort to a project or having high standards for how you carry it out. There *is* something wrong with thinking that everything you do must be done flawlessly.

People who are not perfectionists and who merely have high standards for their behavior and their work are more realistic and flexible. They want to do well, but they understand that perfectionism is an impossible goal and that being slightly less than perfect is still acceptable.

You're Not Alone

Every time I find that I'm getting in my own way, the advice of my first boss (Ronald Mansbridge, former Director of Cambridge University Press) rings in my ears. He told me, "Don't let the perfect stand in the way of the good."

—Sally Dougan, executive vice president, Bert Davis Publishing Placement Consultants

Quicksand!

If you're a perfectionist trying not to be one, don't make the mistake of thinking you have to lower your standards of performance. You can still aim to do good work; just don't obsess over making it perfect.

Perfectionism is one of the most common causes of procrastination. If you are determined to have everything you do turn out flawlessly, then you probably make every task more difficult than it needs to be. To a perfectionist, even the smallest task becomes a major ordeal, and the truly big projects seem insurmountable. As perfectionists embark on new projects, they remember how much effort went into a similar one in the past and feel tired and overwhelmed before even beginning the task at hand. Perfectionists try to maintain such impossibly high standards that they end up burning themselves out.

For example, I am a perfectionist who is struggling not to be one. As I was writing this section on perfectionism, I was thinking, "I have to write the most intelligent, original, innovative, and clinically accurate description of perfectionism that's ever been written. A lot of people have written about perfectionism, and I want my account of it to be different and better."

So what did I do after having that thought and writing the first three sentences of the section? I went to the kitchen and poured another glass of water. I walked outside to talk to my neighbor. I checked my answering machine to see if I'd missed any calls. I called my husband at his office for no particular reason. I went online to look up the name of a book title that I needed for a Matter of Fact sidebar. In other words, I procrastinated.

What got me back to writing? Besides the pressure of looming deadlines in my contract (nothing like a legal document to get a person motivated!), I got back to writing by telling myself, "it doesn't have to be perfect, it just has to be very good, and, most important, it has to get done."

Letting It Get to You

The same faulty thoughts and feelings that lead to perfectionism can also cause you to procrastinate for other reasons. You might give in to feelings of being overwhelmed, frustrated, or bored by a task and not attempt to do it or give up before completing it. You might also react by rebelling against the people or institutions that expect you to get something done. Or you might misjudge how long it will take to complete a task or project and wait until the last minute to start it.

All of this cognitive and emotional turmoil means that you're letting your responsibilities and commitments get the best of you. You're being controlled by your to-do list instead of taking control of your thoughts, feelings, and actions and behaving responsibly.

Feeling Overwhelmed

Some people let themselves get overwhelmed by the size, scope, or nature of a project. If you find a task you're facing to be difficult or overly challenging, you might not even attempt it or may give up too quickly rather than seeking the information and support that would help you complete it. Feeling overwhelmed also happens when a project involves many steps. You get in the middle of the project and lose sight of what to do next, particularly if your surroundings are cluttered and disorganized.

Action Tactic

If you don't know how to begin a project because you weren't given adequate instructions, ask for more guidance. You'll look less stupid asking for clarification at the beginning than you will down the road when you haven't finished it or have made mistakes.

This Is So Frustrating!

Feeling frustrated is a lot like feeling overwhelmed. Frustration is often a problem when a project is underway and is either not going well or seems never-ending. Some projects require that you stay patient and wait for delayed gratification. If you're the sort of person who needs to see immediate results, then you might end up giving up and saying you'll try again another time. This outcome is especially common with long-term endeavors such as weight loss. If you've tried to lose weight, how many times have you given up because you weren't losing quickly enough to keep yourself motivated to stick with the plan?

The Adrenaline Rush

Some procrastinators are addicted to the rush of adrenaline that comes from completing a task at the last minute. They get a sort of natural high from the thrill of pulling out all the stops and beating incredible odds to meet a deadline. (Of course, that high might also be from the huge amounts of caffeine procrastinators usually consume in order to stay awake and alert to get things finished!)

If you're the type who is always racing against the clock, think about why that might be. Some people who love the last-minute adrenaline rush simply crave some excitement in their lives. They put off things until the last minute because their work or their lives are so dull that they need to introduce a little excitement. Others do so because they believe they do their best work that way. (I used to be one of those.) Maybe they do good work, but might their results be even better if they gave themselves a little more time?

Others addicted to adrenaline need it to boost their self-esteem. If they create a crisis by waiting until the last minute to do something, and then solve the crisis by getting that thing done, they end up looking like heroes who have saved the day in their own minds and to others who witness their accomplishment.

I'm So Bored

You might put off doing something because it doesn't interest you. How you feel about a task is directly linked to how likely you are to get it started or finished. You may know the feeling of starting on a project with a gung-ho attitude only to find that you get so bored with it midway through that you abandon it and never finish. That may be why there are so many unfinished home do-it-yourself projects and incomplete filing systems around the world.

Quicksand!

You might enjoy the adrenaline rush that comes from doing things at the last minute and see no harm in it as long as you ultimately get your work done; but think how your procrastination affects the people around you. It may be unfair to force friends, family, or co-workers to live on the edge with you.

You Want Me to Do What?!

Procrastination is a powerful tool for rebellion. If you hate your boss, it can feel awfully good to show how insignificant her little pet project is by not getting around to doing it. If your husband nags you to wash your car more often and you don't understand why the matter should concern him, you show your power by driving around in a car that always looks like you just came back from off-roading.

When other people try to control the way we do our work or carry out our lives, we often rebel by not doing what they want us to do. By putting off or never getting around to completing chores or projects that they think are important, we exert some control over our lives and keep others from taking over. A little rebellion is necessary for our sanity and independence, but when carried too far, it can put our jobs, businesses, and relationships in jeopardy.

I Have Plenty of Time

Some people have unrealistic views of time. They underestimate how much time they need to accomplish something or even overestimate the time and end up getting lost in an unnecessarily long, drawn-out process. The issue of how you view time and how your perspective on it may be causing your procrastination is dealt with in detail in Chapter 5, "It's About Time."

Freudian Slips

For most people, procrastination is a bad habit they've picked up and can't seem to shake because of the powerful psychological hold that habits can have. But sometimes procrastination signals a more serious mental health issue. The following disorders are often associated with procrastination:

➤ Attention Deficit Disorder (ADD)

➤ Obsessive-Compulsive Disorder (OCD)

➤ Anxiety

➤ Depression

I'm not saying that procrastination and psychological disorders always go hand in hand, but if you find that your procrastination is chronic and extreme and is having a seriously negative impact on your life, then one of these issues could possibly be the culprit. Diagnosing any of these disorders is beyond the scope of this or any other book; you'd have to meet with a psychologist, psychiatrist, or learning disability specialist and describe your feelings and situation in order to get a complete, accurate diagnosis.

As a first step, you might want to learn more about these disorders by browsing the Web sites listed in the "Learning Disabilities and ADD" and "Mental Health" sections of Appendix C and contacting the organizations listed in those sections of Appendix B. You can also read more about them in the "Mental Health" section of Appendix A.

In the meantime, to give you an idea of what these disorders can feel like, I've taken the formal diagnostic criteria that psychiatrists and psychologists use (that is, the definitions and checklists they use when trying to figure out whether someone has one of these problems) and have summarized them in layperson's terms for you in the following sections. Once again, don't take this information as the last word on ADD, OCD, anxiety, and depression. These summaries just scratch the surface of the complete, clinical definitions of those disorders. You can't tell whether you have one of them just from reading these descriptions; for that, you need to turn to the resources and professionals I previously recommended.

Attention Deficit Disorder

People with ADD (or the related problem of Attention Deficit Hyperactivity Disorder, known as ADHD) tend to have great difficulty getting and staying organized. They may have trouble focusing on one task long enough or intensely enough to complete it. They may be easily distracted, forgetful, and prone to losing things.

Obsessive-Compulsive Disorder

OCD, on the other hand, brings about procrastination from a different direction; people with OCD are obsessed with organization. They are often perfectionists who attend to minute details, such as alphabetizing the spice rack, but they never get around to the more important task that those details are a

Quicksand!

Only a qualified, licensed mental health professional can accurately diagnose a psychological disorder. Don't try to diagnose or treat yourself, and don't be afraid or embarrassed to seek help.

51

part of, such as cooking with those spices. They may make endless lists and schedules, but they get so caught up in the planning that they never get around to doing the things they've listed or scheduled, or they wait until the last minute to do them. Some OCD sufferers become so obsessed with organization, so worried about finding just the right place to put an object, or so concerned about how to prioritize their time that they are unable to take any action and often become very unorganized and unproductive.

Anxiety Disorders

Anxiety disorders relate to the fears (already talked about in this chapter) that can keep people from accomplishing things. People who are diagnosed with an anxiety disorder are plagued with intense and/or chronic anxiety that goes beyond normal levels of worry. They may find themselves worrying so much that they feel they don't have any control over the worrying. They can't stop it, and it affects their sleep patterns, moods, ability to concentrate, or other aspects of daily life to the point that they can't function normally at work, in social situations, or at home.

Depression

Depression, as well, can keep people from reaching goals or taking care of routine responsibilities because of the overall lethargy and apathy that may come with it. Most everyone feels down or blue from time to time. But true clinical depression is more than that. As with anxiety disorders, clinical depression usually doesn't let up quickly. It is intense and prolonged. It may cause its sufferers to sleep too much or not be able to sleep at all, to eat too much or too little, or to experience other changes in daily behavior. At its more serious levels, depression can lead people to harm themselves or others. But even if it doesn't reach that point, clinical depression is nothing to brush off as a temporary or minor problem. If you can't seem to shake the blues, then it may be time to seek professional help.

Is There a Doctor in the House?

The physical symptoms you have when procrastinating may feel a lot like the ones you get with the flu or jet lag. You lack energy, feel sluggish, and walk around (or lie around) in a kind of daze. Sometimes, the similarity is more than a coincidence. Your behavior (delaying starting something or running out of steam after starting) may be rooted in a physical problem rather than a psychological one.

Although you should, of course, see a physician for regular checkups, you may particularly want to pay attention to your physical health if you're experiencing serious problems with procrastination. That way, you'll know if you can rule out something like a fatigue syndrome or other illness and can get on with tackling the environmental or psychological causes of your procrastination.

Matter of Fact

If you suspect that your lack of energy could be related to what you've been eating, consider consulting with a nutritionist for advice on ways to boost your energy. You can get a referral to one in your area from the American Dietetic Association at www.eatright.org or 1-800-366-1655. Don't forget about the role that exercise plays in upping your energy level. The Web site of the American Council on Exercise (www.acefitness.org) might motivate you to start moving.

Don't Worry; There Is Hope

The point of this chapter was to introduce you to some of the causes of procrastination that might result from thoughts and feelings you have when facing a task. If you think that any of these issues are responsible for some or all of your own procrastination, and if they seem like insurmountable problems, don't despair. Parts 2 and 3 of this book are devoted to showing how you can cross these hurdles with a minimum of pain and suffering. In particular, Chapter 7, "Rallying Support from the Pros," helps you navigate the confusing world of mental health counseling and other professional advice.

The Least You Need to Know

➤ Procrastination often results from irrational or illogical thoughts and feelings you have that lead you to unproductive behavior.

➤ Some people procrastinate because they fear how they'll be judged or fear success or failure.

➤ Problems like perfectionism or feeling overwhelmed or frustrated can keep you from starting or completing tasks.

➤ Some procrastinators are addicted to the adrenaline rush that comes from doing things at the last minute.

➤ Procrastination can be a way of rebelling against something you don't want to do or someone you feel hostility toward.

➤ It's sometimes a good idea to consult a mental health professional or physician to make sure your procrastination is not related to a mental or physical condition.

Chapter 5

It's About Time

In This Chapter

➤ Fighting with time

➤ Controlling your time

➤ Maintaining balance in life

➤ Unlocking the day planner handcuffs

➤ Finding time to get things done

Time exists. Period. Contrary to popular belief, it doesn't fly, drag, or accomplish any of the other feats we ascribe to it. You get 24 hours a day and 7 days a week whether you're Martha Stewart or Homer Simpson. If you live to be 90 years old, you'll get 47,304,000 minutes of time. It's your choice how you spend them. (With that many minutes, you can probably afford to waste a few now and then!)

Why You Can't (and Shouldn't Want to) Manage Time

It's presumptuous of us to think we can manage time. Can anyone alter the speed at which the earth spins on its axis or revolves around the sun? Maybe George Lucas or Bill Gates could have a go at it, but most of us mere mortals are powerless over forces of nature. We can't control time; all we can control is our behavior. We can conduct ourselves in a way that makes the most of the time we're given.

You're Not Alone

Time is man's most precious asset. All men neglect it; all regret the loss of it; nothing can be done without it.

—Voltaire

Action Tactic

It's a morbid thought, but imagine you found out you were going to die in 48 hours. What would you regret about how you've spent your time up until now, and what would you do with the remaining time? Think about it and see if clues to your true priorities emerge.

The fact that you can't manage or control time shouldn't come as a major disappointment, because if you think about it, you probably wouldn't want to manage time anyway. How you spend your time is your life. Do you want to think of your life as having to be "managed"? Life is to be lived, not managed.

Your Relationship with Time

Whether you're the type who's naturally inclined to want to manage and control time or is usually fairly go-with-the-flow and oblivious to where the time goes, you have your own unique relationship with it. Just as in your dealings with other human beings, your relationship with time probably has its ups and downs.

Being Bullied by Time

Some people are in a perpetual fight with time. They believe that it's not on their side or that it passes too quickly. Think about the colorful and sometimes even violent expressions some people use when describing how time pressures make them feel:

➤ Pulled in too many different directions

➤ Spread too thin

➤ Burning the candle at both ends

➤ Treading water

➤ Swamped

➤ Pressed

➤ Pushed to the breaking point

If you feel that time is out to get you, then it's probably more than a coincidence that you also happen to be a procrastinator. As long as you keep fighting with time and trying to control it, you're perpetuating your procrastination. The fight with time is a losing battle that distracts you from doing the things you need to do to deal with your problem.

Who Controls Your Time?

Do you sometimes feel you don't do the things you need to do or want to do because other people are controlling how you spend your time? Look at the following list of people and put a check next to any who control your time:

Husband/wife/life partner _____
Boyfriend/girlfriend _____
Roommate(s) _____
Children _____
Parents _____
Other family members _____
Friends _____
Boss(es) _____
Co-workers _____
Clients/customers _____
Teachers/professors _____
Neighbors _____
Pastor, rabbi, or other religious official _____
Therapist/personal coach _____
Physician or other medical professional _____
Attorney _____
Accountant _____
The government _____
Politicians _____
People on television or radio _____
Aliens from outer space _____
Other: _____

How many did you check off? You should've checked none. That's right, none. All these people can make demands on your time, but they can't control it. (With the possible exception of space aliens, who can probably do whatever they want to do with you.) Only you control your time.

Even bosses, no matter how demanding and unreasonable they might be, can't control your time because you have free will to determine what you do and when and how you do it. Sure, your job might be on the line if you don't meet all their demands, and changing jobs and getting a new boss may not be such a great alternative, but you do have options.

Matter of Fact

The idea for the checklist of who controls your time came from *The Complete Idiot's Guide to Managing Your Time* (Alpha Books, 1998) in which author Jeff Davidson makes the provocative point that we don't have to be helpless punching bags when it comes to how we spend our time. In his book, you'll find lots more about this concept, as well as more interesting insights into the issue of time and practical tips on making the best use of it.

Quicksand!

Don't run out of time when you could've prepared for a foreseeable crunch: Returning from vacation or a business trip means extra laundry and dry cleaning, plus unpacking. Coming off a busy weekend means you'll have household chores to catch up on. Meeting an important deadline means that other areas of your life have been neglected and will need your attention.

Making Peace with Time

An important step to becoming an ex-procrastinator is to make peace with time. Stop obsessing over how little you have or how quickly it passes. Own up to the fact that time simply exists. It's not out to get you, and it's up to you to make the most of it.

Also, don't get caught up in blaming others for controlling your time. Other people may serve as distractions or roadblocks to getting things done, but they can't control you.

Don't Do More: Do Better

In *Stop Screaming at the Microwave: How to Connect Your Disconnected Life*, Mary LoVerde gives us a wake-up call with this statement:

> In mathematics, when you add and add and add without stopping it's called infinity. In life, when you add and add and add without stopping it's called insanity. Something's gotta go.

Even though the *Complete Idiot's Guide to Overcoming Procrastination* is all about getting things done, I don't want you to think for a minute that it's only about getting *more* done. Your aim should be to do the important things, not just more things. The issue I'm addressing is quality of life, not quantity of tasks.

Handcuffed to Your Day Planner

Being a slave to your appointment book and obsessing over to-do lists is no way to live. As the general pace of life has picked up in recent years due to the technological, workplace, and societal changes discussed in Chapter 2, "The Procrastination Epidemic," many people feel the need to schedule their time more tightly than ever. They crowd their calendars and appointment books with more tasks and engagements than any human being can reasonably handle.

Think of all the visual reminders you might have of things you should be doing or could be doing:

➤ Appointment book or planner (for example, Day Runner or Filofax)

➤ A time management system in your computer

➤ The calendar on your desk or office wall

➤ The calendar hanging in your kitchen

➤ A calendar of classes from your health club

➤ Calendar of events for a social club or community group

➤ Your children's school calendar

➤ Project flow charts in your office or department

➤ Newsletters with calendars of events for various groups you belong to

➤ Church or other religious institution's calendar

➤ Electronic organizer

➤ To-do lists

➤ Grocery list

➤ Alarm clocks

➤ Watches or pagers that beep to remind you to do something or be somewhere

That list should give you some idea of the ways we visually assault ourselves with reminders of what we could, want to, or ought to be doing with our time. Relying on more and more calendars, lists, and electronic gadgets as reminders of how you should spend your time isn't the answer. Making the most of time is not a matter of piling on the obligations or rigidly scheduling your days.

You're Not Alone

Burnout is not about working too hard but about not being able to control when you work or spending the day doing things you don't want to do.

—Louise Lague, midlife counselor and trend analyst for The Wisdom Group in Greenwich, Connecticut

A life that is nothing more than appointments written into a day planner or items on a to-do list fuels procrastination. It does so by making you feel that you're in a rut, that your life is overly regimented, and that life is nothing more than a collection of obligations to meet. You wake up, go to appointments, check things off a list, go to sleep, and start it all over again the next day.

This routine can bring about feelings of resentment, stress, and burnout, and these emotions fuel procrastination. You start to dread each day because you wake up to a litany of things to do at precisely scheduled times, things that don't necessarily bring enjoyment or bring you closer to your professional and personal goals. Rather than getting more things done, you put off more things as a way to rebel against the drudgery.

Balancing Acts

The beauty of overcoming procrastination is that you'll enjoy life more. By getting routine chores taken care of, major responsibilities met, and backburner projects out of the way, you free up time to pursue activities that you find rewarding, fun, or relaxing. You can spend more time making meaningful connections with people, places, and things rather than merely going through the motions of life. If you're wondering how this change is ever going to happen, don't worry. When you get to the chapters in Part 2, "Becoming an Ex-Procrastinator" (yes, you will get there!), you'll find strategies for being productive without sacrificing your personal life and values.

Quicksand!

Multitasking (taking care of two or more obligations or chores simultaneously) can be a good way to make the most of your time, but watch out for hidden dangers in this strategy. You might not do as good a job with the individual tasks because you're dividing your attention, and you may start to feel burned out if you're always tackling too much at once.

But I Just Can't Find the Time

You know that I'm not trying to turn you into a workhorse who never has any fun, and you understand that you determine how you spend your time. But you can't quite buy into the concept that not only will you be able to get your big responsibilities and routine tasks taken care of, you'll also have time left over to kick back and contemplate your navel or whatever else you'd choose to do with some free time. (I would sleep, read novels, and have a conversation with my husband about something other than whose turn it is to change our daughter's diaper.)

You can barely find the time to get yourself and the kids (or yourself and the houseplants) fed and watered each day. How will you ever find the time to catch up on all the things that have piled up while you've been procrastinating? You can't get things done because you just can't find the time.

Isn't it interesting that you can almost always find the time to do things that are easy or enjoyable? You can while away two hours on a Saturday afternoon watching a classic movie on television, but you can't find 30 minutes to weed the garden. You find time to chat on the phone with friends throughout the workday, but you can't find time to get that expense report filled out.

The Easy Way Out

It seems to be human nature that most people, especially procrastinators, do the things that are fun or easy first. Remember that thought-action link that's so vulnerable to distractions? (If you don't remember what that's all about, go back to Chapter 3, "Blame It on the Environment," and Chapter 4, "It's All in Your Head.") When you develop the habit of procrastinating, you act on impulse rather than thinking through your actions. Your impulses often point you to the quickest, most pleasant activity rather than the more difficult or complex ones.

You're Not Alone

Like an Egyptian mummy, I am pressed for time.

—Jean Garten

Doing What's in Your Face

People often neglect their long-range plans and ambitions or current priorities be-cause they spend too much time responding to what's urgent or pressing. Suppose that your two top priorities in life right now are to get physically fit and to spend more quality time with your family or friends. But no matter how important those goals are to you, your daily actions don't reflect them.

You have high hopes of exercising at least a few days a week after work, but you keep getting waylaid by last-minute crises that pop up on the job. You want to go on an outing every weekend with the kids (or friends) for a healthy dose of fun and maybe even some culture or education, but you don't plan enough ahead to make it happen. Or you become sidetracked by household chores that have to be done by Monday.

Getting Your Priorities Straight

Unless you plan in advance and put some organizational and procedural systems in place at home and work, you'll spend all your time responding to the pressing needs of the moment and will never get around to doing the things that relate to your true priorities and long-term goals.

You may say that developing that sideline business is a priority, but you never seem to have time to work on it in the evenings. You may say that searching on the Internet for old friends you've lost touch with is a priority, but every time you get online, you only have time to do your business for the day, not to search for them.

Stephen Covey, author of several books, including *The Seven Habits of Highly Effective People,* has contributed some of the best common sense ideas regarding the issue of time and losing sight of what's important. He sees the activities we engage in on a daily basis as falling into four categories:

1. **Urgent and important.** Most of us spend too much of our time dealing with pressing matters and crises that are important enough to have to be dealt with right away but that don't get us any closer to our major life priorities. Our time gets tied up with putting out fires and racing to meet deadlines rather than working toward our personal and professional goals.

2. **Not urgent but important.** This area is where we need to spend most of our time. These activities help us achieve balance in our lives and reach our goals. They include long-range planning, putting systems in place that will prevent crises from happening in the first place, and building relationships. Unfortunately, most of us neglect these activities because, even though we know they are important, they're not urgent, so they can easily be relegated to the back-burner.

3. **Urgent but not important.** These activities demand immediate attention, but they aren't necessarily critical matters: a co-worker standing at the door of your office needing a few minutes of your time, a ringing phone that's hard to ignore, a screen full of e-mail messages. These sorts of things may be eating up too much of your time because they're right there in front of you and hard to put off. They often aren't all that important, though, and can usu-ally wait until after you've taken care of more significant, priority-based matters.

4. **Not urgent and not important.** Procrastinators love this category. It includes the games we play or other fun time-wasters we distract ourselves with. It also includes busywork we engage in to make us look and feel like we're getting things done, when we're just avoiding more important responsbilities.

Action Tactic

Close your eyes and picture time. What do you see? Do you see a clock, a calendar, or a long, straight line? Do you see people and places? Do you picture the future or the past? There's no one correct mental image of time or one best way to interpret what you see. It's just an interesting exercise that might clue you in to your relation-ship with time.

Once again, you might agree with this idea of focusing on the big picture of what you want out of life and not getting bogged down in distractions and crises, but you may be wondering how you'll ever get yourself out of categories 1, 3, and 4, and into #2, where you can deal with what's important but not urgent. In Part 2 of this book, you'll learn ways to put systems in place at work and home that will keep you from having to deal with so many last-minute crises. In Part 3, "Tips and Tricks for Getting Things Done," you'll find lots of practical strategies that will help you make better use of your time.

It's Not the Right Time to Do This

For some procrastinators, the problem is not so much that they don't have the time but that the time isn't right. They're waiting for a day when the boss is in a good mood, the temperature is 72 degrees, the kids are with a sitter, they feel motivated and energetic, the swallows return to Capistrano, and the heavens part. They also wouldn't mind if hell froze over and the Libertarian Party controlled Congress.

You're Not Alone

Dost thou love life? Then do not waste time, for that is the stuff life is made of.

—Benjamin Franklin

Procrastinators who wait for the right time to do something are often waiting for the perfect time—a time that doesn't exist. As I said in Chapter 2, there is such a thing as good procrastination, consciously putting off something because it makes legitimate sense to do so. But many procrastinators abuse that principle and turn it into a contingency excuse, the excuse that they can't do one thing until some other chain of events occurs. Taking action becomes contingent upon other things happening and conditions being just right. When this excuse is used, productive action rarely takes place, because even if conditions do become just about right, another contingency always seems to come along.

Creating the Illusion of More Time

Whether you don't have enough time or can't find the right time, you probably wish there were 25 hours (or more) in each day. That's not going to happen, of course, but you can feel like you have more time by trying these tricks:

➤ **Focus on the moment.** Time doesn't seem to go by so quickly when you fully live in the present moment, instead of going through the motions of life not focusing on what you're doing.

➤ **Simplify.** The less clutter and commitments you have in your life, the less you'll feel pulled in so many different directions. When you simplify your life, you free up time.

➤ **Delegate.** Short of cloning yourself (which someone is probably working on right now), delegating is the best way to get twice as much done in a limited period of time. Turning projects and chores over to others saves you time and energy.

➤ **Develop systems.** If you feel like you waste a lot of time putting out fires, which are those crises and urgent matters that arise at home or work, you need to put organizational, management, and procedural systems in place so that those fires eventually stop igniting.

Quicksand!

If you think it's cool to brag about how little sleep you get each night to prove how much you work, then you're out of touch with the times. These days, the movers and shakers of the corporate and entrepreneurial worlds sleep a solid eight hours every night and don't mind saying so.

➤ **Slow down.** The more you bite off, the longer you have to chew. If you keep adding things to our to-do list and taking on more responsibilities in your life roles, you're going to feel as though the days are shorter and time is running out.

➤ **Change your sleep pattern.** As a big fan of sleeping long hours, I'm the last person to suggest that you deprive yourself of sleep. Nevertheless, you should take a look at how much time you're sleeping and see whether you can shave off an hour or even a half-hour at bedtime or in the morning. You'll find that you have more time to get things done.

➤ **Keep the big picture in mind.** Try to spend time doing things that reflect what is important to you and that will help you reach your goals. You'll feel like you're wasting less time every day because you'll be doing more things that have meaning for you and fewer tasks that you don't consider important.

➤ **Enjoy quiet.** Build into your day some quiet times that serve as mini-escapes from the world. These are times when you turn down the volume (literally and figuratively), go off by yourself, and relax. You might shut your eyes, take off your shoes and wiggle your toes, and take some deep breaths. Do whatever you need to do to relax and rejuvenate, even if only for a couple of minutes.

➤ **Pause and reflect.** Take some time throughout each day to step back from what you're doing and reflect on what you've done up to that point. Doing so will force you to look at how you spend your time and will make you less likely to feel as if time is just passing by.

➤ **Don't worry about what's next.** If you are continually thinking about what you have to do next or how much work is left on a particular project, you'll create the sensation of time speeding up. You'll forget about the time you do have left and will start worrying that you're running out of time.

You'll find more details about these and other tricks for "creating" time in the chapters in Part 2.

The Least You Need to Know

➤ Time can't be controlled or managed. You can only control how you use it.

➤ Other people can make demands on your time, but they can't control it. You have free will to use your time in whichever way you choose.

➤ Overcoming procrastination is not about packing more commitments into your schedule or chores onto your to-do list.

➤ Taking care of responsibilities and routine tasks frees you up to do things that bring you enjoyment and satisfaction.

➤ Saying you can't find the time to do something is not a valid excuse. You have to prioritize in order to make the best use of time.

➤ Saying that it's not the right time to do something is often not a legitimate excuse. If you keep waiting for the perfect time to do something, you probably won't do it.

➤ You can't add another hour to the day, but you can create the illusion of more time by using some simple time-saving techniques.

Part 2

Becoming an Ex-Procrastinator

*You've made it to Part 2, and you haven't given up yet. See, you don't put off every-
thing. Your momentum should build even more as you read these next chapters
because now you're getting to the good stuff. This part is where I tell you exactly how
you're going to stop procrastinating.*

*We'll look at why you might have had trouble overcoming procrastination in the past
and what you're going to do differently this time. You'll get rid of clutter, simplify
your life, and become organized so that no more obstacles stand in the way of your
getting things done. You'll also learn how to become a whiz at decision-making—
whether the decision's about what to have for dinner or what to do with your life. In
the final chapter of this part, you'll learn the secret formula for stopping procrastination before it starts, as well as a simple, 10-step plan for getting things started and
finishing what you start.*

Chapter 6

Making Sure You'll Really Do It This Time

In This Chapter

➤ What kept you from getting your act together

➤ Why change is such a chore

➤ How to calculate your chances of success

➤ Why having a support team is key

You should now have a handle on what procrastination is, why it happens, and why you owe it to yourself and the people you care about to get over it. This can mean only one thing: The time to take action is near. Soon, you'll have to venture into those bulging closets and drawers, return to that half-written novel, face up to a career or relationship that's going nowhere, or do whatever it is you need to do to get your life on track.

Now that you're faced with having to do something about your procrastination and not just read about it, you might be tempted to close the book and put it aside, making vague promises to come back to it at some future date. You and I know that that future date doesn't exist.

If you are getting cold feet at this point, it might be because you're remembering all the times in the past when you tried to turn over a new leaf and nothing happened. Maybe the new you lasted only a day, a week, or even a month, before you were back to your old ways. A backlog of projects piled up, your home or office became cluttered again, and life started to feel out of control once more. It doesn't have to be that way

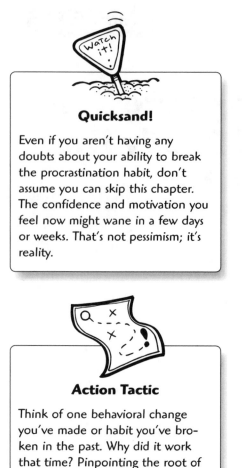

Quicksand!

Even if you aren't having any doubts about your ability to break the procrastination habit, don't assume you can skip this chapter. The confidence and motivation you feel now might wane in a few days or weeks. That's not pessimism; it's reality.

Action Tactic

Think of one behavioral change you've made or habit you've broken in the past. Why did it work that time? Pinpointing the root of your success helps you repeat the success.

again. In this chapter, you'll learn why your past efforts to overcome procrastination have failed and what you're going to do to make it work this time.

Why Your Past Efforts Have Failed

If you've struck out a few times when you've tried to stop procrastinating and make positive behavioral changes in your life, your failure was probably caused by one or more of the following factors:

➤ **You lacked commitment.** You may have thought that you wanted to stop procrastinating, but the reality was that you hadn't fully committed to the idea. Perhaps you were merely trying to do what others wanted you to do, but you didn't care all that much about making changes in your life. Or maybe you truly did want to change but weren't willing to make the sacrifices and put in the effort it would take to do so.

➤ **You tried to do too much, too soon.** Maybe you tried to solve everything at once. You took stock of all the current crises, looming deadlines, and backburner projects you'd been putting off and decided to tackle them simultaneously. That's a recipe for disaster. This time you'll be more successful because you'll take on only what's manageable.

➤ **You didn't get instant gratification.** If you expected to see dramatic changes in your behavior and your life simply because you said the magic words, "I'm not going to procrastinate anymore," you might have been disappointed when instant gratification didn't come. Old habits die hard, and change takes time. You can't expect immediate results.

➤ **You didn't prioritize.** Perhaps you dove right in and started trying to finish things without first determining what was most important to you and to the significant people around you. If you try to force yourself to become more efficient and productive in areas that mean nothing to you, that attempt is destined to fail. You have to believe in what you're doing in order to get it done.

➤ **You weren't angry enough.** Sometimes you have to get to the point of saying, "I'm mad as hell and I'm not going to take it anymore," before you can get yourself moving. At first, the anger is often directed at someone else, such as the person who gets ahead of you in life while you're busy procrastinating or maybe the person who monopolizes your time and keeps you from getting things done. But, eventually, you have to realize that the blame lies primarily with yourself and become so exasperated that you finally decide to do something about the problem.

Quicksand!

Some people think they're committed to kicking the procrastination habit for good, but in reality they just want a quick fix. In the back of their minds, they expect to go back to their old ways as soon as some immediate problems or urgent matters are dealt with. If you don't make a serious commitment, it'll be just a matter of time before you backslide.

➤ **You weren't scared enough.** As with anger, fear plays a big part in attempts to become an ex-procrastinator. You may have to realize how damaging the potential consequences of procrastination are before you can fully commit to changing.

➤ **You lacked support.** It's difficult to go it alone when trying to make major, or even minor, changes in life. If you tried to turn over a new leaf in the past and didn't have a team of key people helping you (friends, family, co-workers, or experts of some sort), you probably didn't manage to keep that leaf turned over for very long. Later in this chapter in the section called "Your Support Team" as well as in Chapter 7, "Rallying Support from the Pros," you'll find out who should be in your inner circle and how to bring them there.

➤ **You lacked information.** To accomplish something, you have to know how to do it. Depending on the nature of the task or project, you may need information, knowledge, instructions, direction, guidance, skills, and resources. If a lack of know-how or access to resources has held you back in the past, think about why that is. Were you afraid to ask for help? Did you not know where to turn for guidance? In the "Get Connected" section of Chapter 12, you'll find out how to get past the barriers to asking for help and finding the information you need.

➤ **Your timing was off.** Even though it's not a good idea to wait for the proverbial perfect time to do something, there is such a thing as choosing the wrong time to get over your procrastination. If your past efforts to stop procrastinating came at a time when you had too much going on in your life, then you probably weren't very successful with the antiprocrastination efforts. Never try to make behavioral changes when your life is overloaded with commitments and pressing deadlines or when major life-changing events are taking place (such as the death of a loved one, marriage, separation, moving, the birth of a child, and the like).

Matter of Fact

The best way to get an in-depth look at the change process and how to make it work is to read what psychologists have to say about it. My two favorite books on change are *Getting Unstuck: Breaking Through Your Barriers to Change* by Dr. Sidney B. Simon and *Change Your Life Now: Powerful Techniques for Positive Change* by Dr. William J. Knaus. Both books are grounded in solid psychological principles, but they are very practical and user-friendly.

➤ **You were too critical of yourself.** If your standards for your behavior were unreasonably high the last time you tried to stop procrastinating, then you were setting yourself up for failure. This time, be more realistic about what you can achieve and how quickly you can do it.

➤ **You weren't balanced.** If your life doesn't have a healthy balance of work and play, or action and relaxation, you'll burn out. Just what that balance should be is different for each person, but whatever it is, you have to pay attention to it. You have to nurture the part of you that wants to goof off as much as you nudge the part of you that has to be and wants to be productive. If you become single-minded and focus only on your calendar and to-do lists at the expense of leisure time, your brain and your spirit will shut down, and you won't get anything done.

➤ **You had an identity crisis.** Identity crises don't just happen at key age-related stages in life, such as adolescence, midlife, or retirement. They can pop up any time you try to change your behavior. Habits, both good and bad, become such second nature to you that they become a big part of your identity. When you try to change those habits, you also have to change the way you see yourself and the way you want others to see you. This process can be unsettling and may cause you to abandon your efforts to change.

➤ **You took the easy way out.** No matter what the obstacles are that stand in your way and no matter how difficult change is, there comes a time when you have to be tough on yourself and stop making excuses, whining, and looking for the perfect time or magic shortcut. If you've tried to stop procrastinating in the past and couldn't sustain any degree of change in your behavior, then you might have been letting yourself give up too easily. This time you're not going to do that. You may have a bumpier road to travel than the path of least resistance, but the results will be worth the trip.

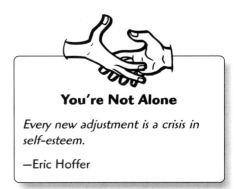

You're Not Alone

Every new adjustment is a crisis in self-esteem.

—Eric Hoffer

These reasons for abandoning your effort to break the procrastination habit are normal, human reactions to the challenges that the change process brings. Any way you cut it, making behavioral changes is difficult.

Why Change Is So Darn Hard

If it were easy to break bad habits and change problem behavior, the world would be a very different place. You'd see lots of slim, physically fit people walking around, the tobacco industry would crumble, companies wouldn't have to fire anybody, and relationship counselors would be hurting for patients. But the world doesn't look like that, because bad habits, especially procrastination, are as hard to get rid of as telemarketers at dinnertime. Change is difficult for the following reasons:

➤ It takes time

➤ It takes effort

➤ It's hard to do alone

➤ It leads you into unfamiliar territory

One of the best ways to bring about change in your life is to understand the process of change itself. If you realize that changes take time and effort to make, and you anticipate that they'll be a little unsettling and isolating, then you have realistic expectations. Realistic expectations will make you much more likely to succeed at any efforts to overcome procrastination.

Action Tactic

Make a list of at least 10 positive changes you've made in your life in the past. They might be changes in your appearance, health, financial status, career, social life, home, or anything at all. It doesn't matter whether the changes lasted. The important thing is that you made them. Seeing the list can get you motivated to make changes again.

Seven Stages of Change

When you're trying to overcome procrastination, you'll probably find yourself going through seven typical stages of the change process:

1. Acknowledge the need to change your behavior. Wake up to the fact that procrastination is not a cute personality quirk; it's a dangerous habit that threatens your health, wealth, and happiness, as well as that of people around you.

2. Declare to yourself and to others that you're ready to change. Make it official. Some people refrain from telling anyone that they're going to try to break a habit for fear of embarrassment if they don't succeed. But telling other people about your plans makes you accountable for your behavior and reinforces your commitment to change.

3. Mentally prepare yourself to commit to making a change. While you work on breaking the habit, think through how your life will be different when you change it and what you'll think and feel. Brace yourself for at least a little inconvenience and emotional pain.

4. Figure out how to change. Don't expect yourself to have an innate sense of how to make a behavioral change. Change is an acquired skill, not something you necessarily have an intuitive knack for. Rely on any of the many books written to help people with the nuts and bolts of the change process (such as those listed in Appendix A). Or seek professional help from the sorts of experts described in Chapter 7.

5. Implement your change strategy. Follow the step-by-step process that you outlined previously.

6. Get frustrated and accept setbacks. If the change process were plotted on a graph, it would look like those jagged lines and peaks and valleys we see on graphs of things such as interest rates or the level of unemployment in America. For every two forward steps you take, there's inevitably going to be a backward step. If you are aware of this from the outset, you'll be less likely to give up when you become frustrated. Instead, you'll accept occasional setbacks as a normal part of the process.

7. Work through the frustration and past the setbacks until a new behavior gradually replaces the old habits. As you keep plugging away through the change process, you will wake up one day and realize that your new behavior has started to feel like a habit. Instead of spending the day putting off things and worrying about what you should be doing, you'll get things done without having to put a great deal of thought and effort into your actions. You will have replaced the do-it-later habit with the do-it-now habit.

After you've made your way through these stages, you'll need to cycle back through them periodically to maintain your new way of doing things. This maintenance process is addressed in Chapter 24, "Keeping It Going."

How Likely Are You to Change?

So now that you know what change is like, what are the chances that you're going to be able to overcome procrastination? Take the following quiz to find out. Circle True (T), False (F), or Not Sure (NS) to indicate how you feel about each statement. Be honest!

T	F	NS	I am completely fed up with my procrastination.
T	F	NS	I fear that severe negative consequences are just around the corner (or already here) if I keep putting things off.
T	F	NS	I can be patient with the change process and comfortable with the fact that it might take a long time to break my bad habits.
T	F	NS	I am okay with the idea that I might have to give up some leisure and fun time for a while in order to get more critical things done.
T	F	NS	I have the courage to admit to other key people in my life that procrastination is a big problem for me.
T	F	NS	I am willing to put myself on more of a daily schedule and routine.
T	F	NS	I am willing to ask others for help and to delegate some responsibilities.
T	F	NS	I am aware that much of the paper and possessions in my home and/or office will have to be thrown out or given away, and I am okay with that.
T	F	NS	I can learn to say no to commitments and obligations.
T	F	NS	I can honestly say that I know I deserve to be happy and successful, in whichever way I choose to define those concepts.

The scoring for this quiz is simple: You either pass or fail; there's no middle ground. If you answered False or Not Sure to even one of these statements, you need to rethink your commitment to overcoming procrastination. It's normal and natural to be unsure about or unable to agree with a few of these statements. But if you do, be aware that your likelihood of success goes down a notch or two. In order to make significant changes in your behavior, you need to get to the point where you can agree with all 10 statements.

Your Support Team

Of all the tactics you'll use to overcome procrastination, having a support team is one of the most important. It's so critical that I've devoted all of Chapter 7 to describing who might make up your support team and how to find these people. For now, I just want to introduce you to the concept.

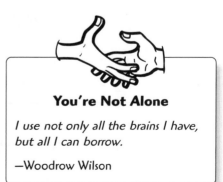

You're Not Alone

I use not only all the brains I have, but all I can borrow.

—Woodrow Wilson

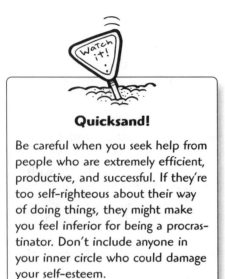

Quicksand!

Be careful when you seek help from people who are extremely efficient, productive, and successful. If they're too self-righteous about their way of doing things, they might make you feel inferior for being a procrastinator. Don't include anyone in your inner circle who could damage your self-esteem.

A support team isn't a team in the literal sense. You don't need to type up a roster and print up T-shirts with team members' names on the back and some sort of Procrastination Busters logo on the front. (Although, if it makes you happy to do so, by all means, knock yourself out.) A support team is an inner circle of people to turn to for advice, strategy, re-sources, encouragement, and emotional support.

The people you turn to for emotional support when the going gets tough or for advice and strategies when you run out of ideas may include the following:

➤ Family members

➤ Friends

➤ Co-workers or other work-related colleagues

➤ Teachers or professors if you're a student

➤ Experts such as mental health counselors, career coaches, professional organizers, and more (these and other experts are described in Chapter 7)

Out of these categories, exactly who you need on your team depends on the nature of the things you procrastinate about and the type of support you respond to best. Some people, for example, are more comfortable talking to friends about their problems than they are talking to their families. Others may not want to share their problems even with close friends and family and prefer to seek the confidential support that comes from a professional such as a psychotherapist. If you do prefer to turn to an objective source of support far removed from your family and friends, you can read about some of the people who can help in Chapter 7.

The Least You Need to Know

➤ If you feel like you're not going to be able to stop procrastinating, it's probably because your past attempts failed.

➤ Understanding why your behavioral changes haven't worked in the past makes you less likely to repeat your mistakes.

➤ Change is difficult because it takes time and effort, it is hard to do alone, and it leads you into unfamiliar territory.

➤ You're much more likely to succeed at overcoming procrastination if you have the support of friends, family, and professional counselors or organizers.

Chapter 7

Rallying Support from the Pros

In This Chapter

➤ Your choices for expert advice

➤ The many faces of psychotherapy

➤ Choosing a career counselor

➤ Coaches for the game of life

➤ Professional organizers to the rescue

Sometimes, friends, family, and co-workers are well-meaning but aren't up to the task of helping you get over a problem with procrastination. If your situation calls for expert, not amateur, advice on how to change your behavior, make decisions, or get organized, your choices for an objective ear fall into four basic categories:

➤ Mental health professionals

➤ Career development professionals

➤ Personal coaches

➤ Professional organizers

This chapter examines each of these categories in detail so you'll know who these professionals are and how to find them.

Do I Need Professional Help?

Before you start searching for professional help, you need to know whether expert advice is something you need or whether you can get by with just a little help from your friends. Take the following quiz and see where you stand. Read through the following statements and circle True (T) if a statement sounds like something you might think, feel, or say. Circle False (F) if the statement doesn't sound like you.

A

T	F	My procrastination habit makes me feel down about myself.
T	F	I sometimes feel so depressed or lacking in energy that I just don't feel like doing anything.
T	F	I wish I could talk about my procrastination problems to someone who is understanding and not judgmental.
T	F	I've tried to stop procrastinating, but I just don't feel like I have any control over it.
T	F	I think that much of my procrastination is due to psychological issues rather than environmental ones.

B

T	F	I'd like to choose a more satisfying career, but I have no idea what it is; or I have some ideas, but I'm having difficulty choosing among them.
T	F	Whenever I want to do something about my career, I find that bigger life issues stand in the way, such as decisions about where to live, who to be with, what my values are, and the like.
T	F	I think that fears, self-doubts, or a lack of confidence might be holding me back in my career.
T	F	I've been floating from career field to career field or job to job, and even though I want to settle down in one area, I don't know how to stop my drifting.
T	F	I'm the type who likes to take tests to figure out who I am and what I should be doing.

C

T	F	I know what steps I should be taking to plan my career or get a new job, but I just can't seem to take action.
T	F	I have problems being productive and efficient on the job, but I can't talk to my boss about it (or I've tried to, but my boss wasn't any help).
T	F	Whenever I start to make a career transition or look for a new job, I give up too soon if success doesn't come quickly.
T	F	I feel like I need to get my act together in general (personally or professionally), but my problems aren't serious enough to warrant seeing a shrink.
T	F	I have some ideas of personal or career goals I'd like to reach, but I'm not sure I can reach them on my own.

D

T	F	I'm drowning in a sea of clutter at home or work.
T	F	I feel like I've organized my closets, drawers, files, and garage (or any other space) a thousand times, but they always get messy and crowded again.
T	F	I have trouble setting priorities and making the best use of my time (at home or work).
T	F	I wonder if all those electronic organizational gadgets and software could help me get my act together.
T	F	I know how to get rid of clutter and organize my stuff, but I won't do it unless someone is watching over me.

To score the quiz, count the number of times you circled True in each of the four parts (the A, B, C, and D sections) of this quiz. Write the numbers in the following spaces to find out whose couch you should be lying on.

A: ___   B: ___

C: ___   D: ___

If you answered True to two or more of the **A** statements, you should consider meeting with a mental health professional to deal with the psychological side of procrastination. Two or more True replies in the **B** category means that you could benefit from working with a career development professional, specifically a career counselor who can help with the more complex issues related to career decisions and transitions. If you circled two or more Trues in the C category, then a career consultant or personal coach may be able to solve your procrastination problems. Two or more Trues in the D category means that you are probably organizationally challenged and should hire a professional organizer to help you with your problem.

Mental Health Professionals

If you are suffering from chronic or severe procrastination that is causing distress to you or the people around you, then it might be time to consult with a qualified mental health professional for some psychotherapy to work through the issues that are holding you back. Unfortunately, finding a therapist or counselor to work with can be an extremely confusing process. People who

You're Not Alone

Many people say 'I don't need a shrink. I'm not crazy!' We think we're not that upset or that out of control to warrant seeing one. We feel unhappy but not in an extreme enough situation to seek outside help. But why live like that?

—Dale Masi, D.S.W., social work professor and co-author with Robin Masi Kuettel of *Shrink to Fit: Answers to Your Questions About Therapy*

need professional help for a procrastination problem often put off getting that help because they don't know how to find the right person.

The key to sorting out the choices is to have a basic understanding of what psychotherapy or mental health counseling involves and what the various educational degrees, licenses, and titles mean.

What Do Psychotherapists Do?

Psychotherapy, or mental health counseling (the two terms are used interchangeably here), involves talking about your problems and concerns in a one-to-one or group setting. Some psychotherapy is short-term with a goal of seeing behavioral changes in a matter of weeks or months; other approaches to psychotherapy require a commitment of a year or more to work out issues fully. The way that psychotherapy is conducted depends on the philosophy of the person delivering it as well as on that person's education, training, and licensing or certification.

Anyone can hang out a shingle and call himself or herself a psychotherapist, but not everyone has the experience and training to do it effectively and ethically. Legitimate psychotherapy is a service provided by various types of licensed and degreed mental health professionals, such as psychologists, clinical social workers, and others with specialized training.

Matter of Fact

Working one-on-one with a mental health professional, career counselor, coach, or organizer in private practice is not the only way to get expert advice. You might save time and money in a group counseling or seminar setting. Plus, the camaraderie and networking opportunities of a group environment can be an asset when you're going through the often lonely and isolating process of trying to change your behavior. To find support groups or seminars, contact: universities (especially the adult education or continuing education division); professional associations for the field or industry in which you work; places of worship such as churches and synagogues; hospitals, clinics, and HMOs; and social service agencies or community centers.

The Six Faces of Psychotherapy

Choosing among all the different types of mental health professionals is like falling into a bowl of alphabet soup. Do you go to a Ph.D., Psy.D., M.D., M.S.W., C.S.W., M.A., M.S., M.Ed., or B.A., or do you just decide it's all a bunch of B.S. and give up?

To help you with your search, here are brief descriptions of the six types of mental health professionals you're most likely to come across when seeking psychotherapy:

➤ **Psychologists:** Psychologists who perform psychotherapy have a doctoral degree, either a Ph.D. or a Psy.D., in psychology (usually either clinical or counseling psychology) and a license issued by the state in which they practice. Through extensive education and training, they learn to diagnose and treat mental disorders, and some may have special expertise in learning disabilities or Attention Deficit Disorder. They also know how to counsel people who don't have serious psychological problems but who need help coping with problems of daily living (such as procrastination). Some may administer tests to help you understand yourself better, and a small percentage are qualified to prescribe medication.

> **Quicksand!**
>
> If your image of psychotherapy comes from Woody Allen movies, think again. He and his cronies may spend decades on the analyst's couch, but that's not the norm. Many psychotherapists provide short-term, practical counseling that helps you see results in weeks or months.

➤ **Licensed professional counselors:** These counselors have a master's degree in counseling and have completed the required length of clinical training to receive a state license. Although they are trained to recognize mental illness or serious psychological problems, they work primarily with people experiencing less serious difficulties and usually refer clients with severe problems to psychologists or psychiatrists. Some professional counselors specialize in certain issues such as relationships, substance abuse, careers, or other areas in which they have received special training and certification.

➤ **Social workers:** Social workers who offer psychotherapy usually have the M.S.W. degree (Master of Social Work) with an emphasis on clinical work (that is, counseling and therapy) or a C.S.W. (Clinical Social Work) degree. Some may go beyond master's level to earn a doctoral degree in social work, but a doctorate is not a necessary qualification for performing psychotherapy. As with professional counselors, clinical social workers tend to work primarily with people who have basic problems with daily life rather than serious mental disorders.

➤ **Certified mental health nurses:** These nurses receive training and certification in mental health in addition to general medical education and training. They are often qualified to offer some of the same psychotherapeutic services as other counselors or psychologists and are most likely to work in clinics, hospitals, or social service agencies rather than in private practice.

> ➤ **Certified pastoral counselors:** These professionals are members of the clergy who have received special training in counseling or are laypersons who have had in-depth religious or theological training.

> ➤ **Psychiatrists:** Psychiatrists are medical doctors, meaning they have earned an M.D. degree. They have the same general medical education as other physicians, plus specialized training in mental illness and mental disorders. Psychiatrists are qualified to prescribe medication to help alter your moods or behavior as well as to perform psychotherapy.

> A common stereotype of psychiatrists is that they are more likely to hand you a jar of pills than to talk you through your problems. This image of psychiatrists results from the fact that their training tends to focus on working with patients with serious mental disturbances and on a medical treatment model for dealing with those problems. So even for patients with less serious problems, psychiatrists might tend to reach for the prescription pad too readily. There are plenty of exceptions to this stereotype, however, and some psychiatrists are well qualified to talk to you, not just medicate you.

Career Development Professionals

If your tooth aches, you go to a dentist. If your eyesight needs to be checked, you see an optometrist or opthamologist. Rarely would you try to fix these problems yourself. So why suffer through job or career problems without the help of a professional trained in those matters?

Matter of Fact

If you're stuck in a career or job that's going nowhere or feels like the wrong fit, the Career Planning and Adult Development Network can help you find a career counselor or job search coach in private practice. This international organization has members who serve as Network Contacts in most U.S. states and several other countries. The Network Contact will either see you as a client in his or her own office or can refer you to another Network member in that geographic area. To find your local contact-person, e-mail the Network at info@careertrainer.com or call its main office in the San Francisco Bay area at 408-441-9100.

People with expertise in career development and job hunting can help you choose a career direction, make a career change, find a job, get a promotion or raise, or improve your on-the-job performance and satisfaction. If you've been putting off doing something about your career, then a visit to a career development professional may be what you need to get moving.

As with psychotherapy, career advice is dispensed by a dizzying array of professionals and so-called professionals. Here are some of the titles you're likely to come across:

➤ Career counselor

➤ Career consultant

➤ Career management consultant

➤ Career coach

➤ Career strategist

➤ Career advisor

➤ Job search coach

➤ Employment consultant

➤ Executive coach

Although a person's title gives you some clue as to what his or her expertise and training might be, it's up to you to ask the right questions to be sure that person can give you the kind of help you need. (See "Questions to Ask When Seeking Professional Help" later in this chapter for ideas.)

Career Counselors

Those who call themselves *career counselors* must have a master's degree or higher in psychology, counseling, or social work. Beyond that, their credentials and experience will vary widely, because career counseling is a largely unregulated field. Some states require licenses, and some career counselors have obtained an optional national credential making them National Certified Career Counselors.

A career counselor is a good choice if you need help getting focused on a career direction, because the process of choosing a career often has a psychological component. You may benefit from the listening skills, analytical abilities, knowledge of human behavior, and expertise in personality testing that a counselor can offer.

Action Tactic

Go online to get advice about your career or job hunt. Many of the Web sites recommended in the "Careers" section of Appendix D have much more than job listings. Their advice columns, chat rooms, and message boards are great sources of quick, free, expert advice.

However, just because career counselors (as opposed to career coaches or consultants) are especially adept at the more psychological aspects of career planning, don't assume they can't help you with the practical side of career transitions and job hunting. Many career counselors are just as skilled at helping you with resumés, interviewing, networking, and job hunting strategies as with exploring your psyche and administering tests.

Career Coaches and Consultants

Career development professionals who do not have a counseling or psychology background or degree often have backgrounds in business and call themselves career consultants or coaches. They usually tend to focus more on helping clients with strategies for the career change or job hunting processes than with the more psychological issues that come up when making career choices and wanting testing. Still others focus on helping you manage your job rather than helping you look for a new one. They usually go by the name *executive coach* or *career management coach*.

Career consultants and coaches are a good choice when you know what you want to do but you just don't know how to get there. If you are already in the right career field and job but need advice and support as you try to advance in the field or deal with day-to-day issues in your current job, then an executive coach or career management coach is also a good option.

Personal Coaches

The term *coach* used to refer exclusively to the man or woman on the sidelines of your school's basketball court or neighborhood Little League diamond wearing a whistle and a nervous expression. Or the term conjured up images of Bill Parcells or Phil Jackson. Now, the term *coach* doesn't necessarily have anything to do with sports. It can mean a personal coach: someone who helps you reach your personal and/or professional goals.

Personal coaches are a little bit like psychotherapists, career counselors, executive coaches, and professional organizers; but at the same time, they are like none of them. They don't deal with the major emotional or psychological issues that psychotherapists handle, but they do provide a nonjudgmental forum for expressing your hopes, dreams, fears, and concerns. They don't always have the in-depth knowledge of career development that a career counselor has, but they can help you set and reach your professional goals. They don't usually roll up their sleeves and tear apart your closet or filing cabinets like professional organizers would, but they do help you get your act together and keep it together in a more general sense.

Coaches act as partners who help you take action. You typically meet with a coach on a weekly basis (often by phone, if not in person) to structure a plan for reaching your goals and getting support along the way. They often take a no-holds-barred, no-nonsense approach that keeps you focused on your target.

Although some coaches are certified by a credentialing organization (see the ones listed in Appendix B), the personal coaching field is even more unregulated than the other counseling and coaching professions. Be sure to ask questions about your prospective coach's training, experience, and approach so you can make an informed decision about the coach you choose to work with.

Matter of Fact

If you've been putting off anything related to education, whether it's signing up your newborn for private nursery school, finding a summer program for your special needs teenager, or going back to college later in life, an independent educational consultant can help you and your family make the right choices. For information on how an educational consultant could help, or for referral to one near you, contact the Independent Educational Consultants Association (IECA) at 703-591-4850 or IECAassoc@aol.com. Or visit its Web site at www.educationalconsulting.org.

Professional Organizers

Do you look at the piles of paper on your desk and feel like you'd rather throw them out the window than try to sort through and organize them yourself? Have you cleaned out your closets more times than you care to remember but find that they just get messy again soon after? It may be time to call in someone who de-clutters, files, and organizes for a living. Yes, such a person does exist and may be just what you need to get your life on track.

According to the Web site of the National Association of Professional Organizers (www.napo.net), "a Professional Organizer has the skills and experience to provide information, ideas, structure, solutions, and systems which increase productivity, reduce stress, and lead to more control over time, space, actions, and resources." Professional organizer services usually fall into five main categories:

Action Tactic

The best way to find any sort of expert to help with your procrastination problem is to ask for suggestions from friends whose opinions you respect. A word-of-mouth referral is much more likely to be on target than sticking a pin in the Yellow Pages or asking someone who doesn't know you well.

➤ Space planning

➤ Paper and information management

➤ Time management

➤ Storage design

➤ Clutter control

Professional organizers can work wonders and are important allies in the battle against procrastination.

Who You Gonna Call?

Everybody needs a team of ghostbusters to help exorcise the procrastination demons. Who can you turn to for support and advice as you try to overcome procrastination? Put a check mark next to each type of professional you might like to work with:

_____ Mental health counselor

_____ Psychologist

_____ Psychiatrist

_____ Career counselor

_____ Career consultant

_____ Executive coach or career management coach

_____ Personal coach

_____ Professional organizer

_____ Other:

_____

_____

_____

_____

_____

_____

Questions to Ask When Seeking Professional Help

The following questions can help you zero in on the best psychotherapist, career counselor, coach, or professional organizer for your needs:

What is the approach or philosophy behind your work?

What can I expect to have happen when we first meet?

Do you work on a session-by-session basis, or do I have to sign up for a package of sessions?

Do you work on a one-on-one basis, in groups, or both?

What is the average length of time someone would work with you to reach his or her goals?

What is your professional background (education, work experience, and so on)?

Do you have any licenses, certifications, or credentials? Are these required in your field and state, or are they optional?

How long have you been in private practice or in your own consulting business?

Have you dealt with people with my problems/situation before?

Do you have a particular specialty or area of expertise?

What do you charge for your services, and which forms of payment do you accept?

Finding Support Closer to Home

Which of your friends, family, or co-workers are most likely to be supportive of your efforts to stop procrastinating? Make note of their names here:

_____

_____

_____

_____

_____

No matter who ends up on your support team, the important thing is to have one. Don't forget about household helpers (cleaners, baby sitters, lawn care workers, and others) as valuable members of your support team. Getting and staying connected with people who can offer support, encouragement, advice, and resources is a critical element in your efforts to banish procrastination from your life.

The Least You Need to Know

➤ Friends and family can provide support while you try to stop procrastinating, but you may need to turn to professionals for expert advice and strategy.

➤ Psychotherapy is delivered by many different types of counseling and medical professionals and can be useful when you feel that your procrastination problem has psychological roots.

➤ Career development professionals can help you stop putting off making changes and decisions in your job or career.

➤ Personal coaches are a new breed of helping professional who take a practical, cut-to-the-chase approach to guiding you in setting and reaching personal and professional goals.

➤ A professional organizer can help you take control of your paper, clutter, and time at home or at work.

Chapter 8

Lightening Your Load

In This Chapter

➤ Taking stock of your clutter crisis

➤ Deciding what to keep and what to throw out

➤ Experiencing the freedom that comes from de-junking

Imagine you walk down two blocks of a city street, both of which are littered with trash and debris. The trash cans on the first block are almost empty, but the cans on the second one are overflowing with garbage. If someone asked you to pick up one piece of trash from one of the blocks and throw it into a garbage can, which block would you be more likely to choose? Most people would choose the first block where the trash receptacles have plenty of room for whatever they want to toss into them.

How this scenario relates to procrastination is that clean, uncluttered spaces encourage action. If your closet weren't so crowded, you probably wouldn't put off hanging up your clothes. If your file cabinets weren't so stuffed with useless papers, you'd be more likely to get back to those great business ideas buried within them. The fewer obstacles standing in your way, the more likely you are to be productive. This concept was introduced in Chapter 3, "Blame It on the Environment." In this chapter, you'll tackle your clutter problem.

Assessing Your Clutter Crisis

The first step in getting rid of clutter (the physical kind: papers, objects, and miscellaneous stuff) is to take stock of where it is. You probably already have some idea of where the trouble spots are. You know which closet you'd hate a guest to open accidentally, because your insurance may not cover the head injury that unfortunate guest could receive from flying objects. You know which kitchen drawer always gets jammed by all the useless utensils you've been collecting for decades.

To find out where all your clutter hotspots are, the obvious and not so obvious ones, rate each of the following areas of your home or office by circling a number from 1 to 4, with 1 being the least cluttered and 4 being the most cluttered. (If the area doesn't apply to you—for example, if you don't have children—then mark it N/A for Not Applicable.) You can think of each number on the scale as follows:

Rating	Meaning
4	It should be declared a Federal Disaster Area.
3	A visit from the Red Cross wouldn't hurt.
2	It could use some clearing out, but it is not a total embarrassment.
1	This area would pass the mother-in-law/nosy neighbor/fussy roommate test.

Clutter Crisis Quiz

Kitchen cabinets and cupboards	4	3	2	1	N/A
Kitchen drawers	4	3	2	1	N/A
Kitchen counters	4	3	2	1	N/A
Refrigerator and/or freezer	4	3	2	1	N/A
Cleaning supplies	4	3	2	1	N/A
Canned and dry foods	4	3	2	1	N/A
Pots and pans	4	3	2	1	N/A
Glasses and cups	4	3	2	1	N/A
Plates, bowls, and other china	4	3	2	1	N/A

Plastic containers and old jars	4	3	2	1	N/A
Silverware	4	3	2	1	N/A
Other utensils	4	3	2	1	N/A
Spices and herbs	4	3	2	1	N/A
Plastic wrap, foil, and so on	4	3	2	1	N/A
Cookbooks	4	3	2	1	N/A
Recipes	4	3	2	1	N/A
Coupons	4	3	2	1	N/A
Take-out and delivery menus	4	3	2	1	N/A
Pantry	4	3	2	1	N/A
Breakfast room table	4	3	2	1	N/A
Dining room table	4	3	2	1	N/A
Bathroom medicine cabinet(s)	4	3	2	1	N/A
Bathroom closet(s)	4	3	2	1	N/A
Bathroom drawer(s)	4	3	2	1	N/A
Under the bathroom sink	4	3	2	1	N/A
Bathroom shelves/vanity	4	3	2	1	N/A
Surface of the toilet tank lid	4	3	2	1	N/A
Tub or shower stuff	4	3	2	1	N/A
Linen closet	4	3	2	1	N/A
Bedroom(s) (general)	4	3	2	1	N/A
Under bed(s)	4	3	2	1	N/A
Bedside tables	4	3	2	1	N/A
Bedroom closet	4	3	2	1	N/A
Clothes in drawers	4	3	2	1	N/A
Surfaces of dressers or chests	4	3	2	1	N/A
Children's toy areas	4	3	2	1	N/A
Children's closets	4	3	2	1	N/A
Children's clothes in drawers	4	3	2	1	N/A
Supplies/equipment for hobbies	4	3	2	1	N/A
Stereo area	4	3	2	1	N/A
TV or entertainment center area	4	3	2	1	N/A
Laundry room	4	3	2	1	N/A
Utility closets	4	3	2	1	N/A
Coat closet	4	3	2	1	N/A
Coat and hat racks or hooks	4	3	2	1	N/A
Entry hall area/mudroom	4	3	2	1	N/A

continues

Clutter Crisis Quiz (continued)

Windowsills	4	3	2	1	N/A
Bookcases	4	3	2	1	N/A
Coffee tables	4	3	2	1	N/A
Basement	4	3	2	1	N/A
Attic	4	3	2	1	N/A
Garage	4	3	2	1	N/A
Inside of your car(s)	4	3	2	1	N/A
Your car(s)' trunk(s)	4	3	2	1	N/A
Gift wrap and empty boxes	4	3	2	1	N/A
Artwork	4	3	2	1	N/A
Memorabilia/souvenirs	4	3	2	1	N/A
Knick-knacks	4	3	2	1	N/A
Photographs	4	3	2	1	N/A
Home movies/videos	4	3	2	1	N/A
Household files and papers	4	3	2	1	N/A
Catalogs	4	3	2	1	N/A
Magazines	4	3	2	1	N/A
Newspapers	4	3	2	1	N/A
Bulletin boards	4	3	2	1	N/A
Stationery and other paper	4	3	2	1	N/A
Office supplies	4	3	2	1	N/A
Computer floppy disks	4	3	2	1	N/A
CD-ROMs	4	3	2	1	N/A
Computer hard drive	4	3	2	1	N/A
Computer desktop	4	3	2	1	N/A
Desk drawers	4	3	2	1	N/A
Surface of desk	4	3	2	1	N/A
Work/business files and papers	4	3	2	1	N/A
Other home or office areas (fill these in):					
_____	4	3	2	1	N/A
_____	4	3	2	1	N/A
_____	4	3	2	1	N/A
_____	4	3	2	1	N/A
_____	4	3	2	1	N/A
_____	4	3	2	1	N/A

To score your quiz, count the number of times you answered with a 4, 3, 2, or 1 and write the total in the following blanks. Then do the multiplication to fill in the subtotals at right:

I circled 4 __ times.   4 × _____ = _____

I circled 3 __ times.   3 × _____ = _____

I circled 2 __ times.   2 × _____ = _____

I circled 1 __ times.   1 × _____ = _____

Now add up the four subtotals to get your grand total: _____

If your total is over 250, you have a major clutter crisis on your hands. Call in the National Guard or at least a professional organizer or lots of willing friends and relatives armed with trash bags to help you dig yourself out of the mess.

If your score is between 200 and 250, you have a minor crisis on your hands. Plan on having to devote a lot of time and effort to de-junking before you can deal with your procrastination problem.

If you scored between 150 and 200, you have some work to do, but your home or office is probably no more cluttered than the average one down the street or down the hall. A score under 100 means you're probably living a fairly simple, uncluttered life and deserve congratulations. Just watch out for any hot spots you rated as 3s or 4s.

Rationalizing Your Clutter Habit

Think of all the excuses you come up with for letting clutter accumulate:

➤ I'm just a packrat. It's how I am.

➤ I might need this some time.

➤ I'll be able to fit into this again someday.

➤ It will come back in style.

➤ I have special memories connected to this.

➤ I paid too much for this to just throw it out or give it away.

➤ They don't make them like this anymore.

➤ I might be able to fix this and make it like new.

➤ This was a gift, so it would be wrong of me to get rid of it.

Occasionally, these statements are valid. Maybe you can repair something and get some use out of it again. Maybe you just have to keep some gifts no matter how much you dislike them or how little need you have for them. Perhaps your diet and exercise program really is melting off the pounds weekly.

In most cases, though, these statements are nothing more than excuses for keeping your life in disarray. If you want to become more productive, stop using excuses like these. Keeping yourself surrounded by too much stuff in every nook and cranny of your home or office is like wrapping yourself in a warm, cozy blanket. The clutter protects you. It provides an excuse for not having to get on with life.

For example, if a room of your house is full of boxes and stacks of old magazines and newspapers, you have an excuse not to tidy up or clean that room. As long as all that clutter is in the way, there's no point in trying to make the room look attractive and clean. If your office is a disaster area, no one expects you to be able to get any work done, so you're off the hook.

Where Your Attachment to Stuff Comes From

In order to stop making excuses for a clutter habit, you have to know why you make these excuses in the first place. I can't just tell you to stop saying something like "This is too valuable to throw out." You'll come up with 10 more arguments to make sure you don't have to get rid of that allegedly valuable item. The only way you're going to stop making these excuses is to understand the psychology behind them or the circumstances that have led to them. Your reasons for keeping things probably fall into one of seven basic categories:

1. Guilt
2. Value
3. Sentimentality
4. Time capsule syndrome
5. Practicality
6. Hopes and dreams
7. Identity

The following sections detail some examples of each of these reasons along with solutions for dealing with your rationalizations.

You're Not Alone

It's the little things that drive you crazy—the broken heel, the stain, the drip. If you take care of the little things, the big things become manageable.

—Heloise, as quoted in *Simply Organized* by Connie Cox and Cris Evatt

Guilt

So you paid $300 for that fancy kitchen mixer, but the closest you've come to baking a cake from scratch is defrosting one of Sara Lee's finest. Even so, you can't bring yourself to give it away despite the fact that you curse it every time you see how much counter space it takes up in your kitchen. Or maybe it's tools, clothes, exercise equipment, or something else you paid an arm and a leg for but haven't gotten more than a week's use out of. You feel guilty for spending money on things you aren't using, so you keep them around to trick yourself into believing that they were worthwhile purchases.

It's not just the big-ticket items that cause the guilt, either. Maybe you tend to make impulse purchases while waiting in the check-out line of stores. If you threw out all the useless little trinkets and gadgets you've accumulated that way, you'd be admitting that they were foolish purchases.

Guilt also plays a role when you've received gifts that you don't like or need. It seems ungrateful to get rid of something that was a gift, so you keep it out of guilt.

Finally, you might be keeping things because you feel guilty about having what others don't have. Maybe you're unwilling to throw out that can of fruit cocktail that's been sitting in your cupboard for eight years because you feel bad for the starv-ing kids in some country halfway around the world. Never mind that you and no one you know likes canned fruit cocktail and you don't know how you ended up with it in the first place.

Solution: Stop buying things you don't need. If you have a problem with impulse buying, make yourself put more thought into each purchase. If your shopping in general is out of control, admit it and seek professional help. Also, tell people who regularly give you or your family gifts to stop doing so. Realize that letting a gift sit around un-used and unappreciated is just as bad as giving it away or throwing it out, so you may as well get rid of it. If you're worried about people less fortu-nate than you, then pack up your food, clothes, or whatever and send it to them, or drop your donation off at a local soup kitchen or shelter.

Value

"I'm keeping this because it might be worth a lot of money one day." How many times have you made (or heard) that excuse? Do you really think that pile of old magazines gathering dust in the corner is likely to turn into a treasure trove of rare journalism and let you retire a millionaire? Or maybe you're counting on rubber bands becoming obsolete someday so that rubber band ball you've grown to the size of a prize watermelon will bring in some fast cash.

Action Tactic

If you tend to hoard stuff and have limited space, then follow this rule: Every time you bring something new into your home (anything from a magazine, to an item of clothing, a piece of furniture, or whatever), discard or give away something comparable that's already there.

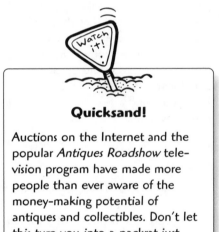

Quicksand!

Auctions on the Internet and the popular *Antiques Roadshow* tele-vision program have made more people than ever aware of the money-making potential of antiques and collectibles. Don't let this turn you into a packrat just because you think your junk might be a treasure some day. Save only what has at least a remote chance of becoming valuable.

Holding on to items you don't use, enjoy, or gain any current value from is a common mistake of packrats.

Solution: If you're keeping things because they might be worth some money in the future, verify that assumption. Do the necessary research to find out how likely it is that your junk will turn to gold. If experts tell you it's a long shot, you probably don't have much to lose by discarding it.

Action Tactic

If you find yourself reluctant to throw things out, think about people who lose everything in a major fire or tornado. No matter how devastating their loss of material possessions, most people say that they're just thankful that they and their loved ones are alive. Think about how much stuff you have and how trivial its loss would be compared with the loss of a loved one. I bet you'll find a few things you can throw out or give away!

Sentimentality

Keeping things for sentimental reasons is hard to argue with. I'm notorious for wanting to save every wedding invitation, birth announcement, and postcard I receive, as well as ticket stubs from special events, knick-knacks collected on trips, and just about anything else that is fun, significant, or touching. Then there are the shoes I bought in Florence, Italy in 1987; I held onto them long after they became worn beyond repair because they were the most fabulous pair of shoes I'd ever owned.

I'm sure you have your own items you can't seem to part with. Old photographs, correspondence, souvenirs, and other keepsakes are important reminders of special people, places, and things in our lives. I'm the last person to tell you to chuck it all and live a totally unsentimental life. But there comes a point when you have to remind yourself what the word *keepsake* means. You have to ask yourself what the sake, or purpose, is for keeping something. If it is near and dear to your heart, then by all means keep it. If not, it might be time to part company.

Solution: There are lots of ways to preserve the memory of events, people, or places without having to use up valuable space storing every physical reminder of them. You can take a photo of yourself holding or wearing something you're going to throw out or give away. You can keep a journal in which you write about special events so that you don't have to save the ticket stub, the program, and the parking lot receipt. If the silly paper hat you wore during Mardi Gras in 1977 is so special to you, frame it and hang it on the wall.

As for those things you want to save but that don't fit or belong in scrapbooks, keep them manageable by limiting the amount of memorabilia you allow yourself to save each year. Designate no more than one box per year as a memorabilia box that you can put things in throughout the year, then store away in your attic, garage, or a closet.

I do still save wedding and birth announcements and postcards in special files in my home office, which I empty into my memorabilia box at the end of the year. I've thrown out most of the ticket stubs, programs, magazines, and other papers that I don't need. And I finally threw out the spectacular Italian shoes, but I treasure the photo taken of me wearing them the day I bought them.

Time Capsule Syndrome

Related to the sentimentality excuse for keeping things is what I call the time capsule syndrome. Not only might you save things because they have emotional value for you, you are also determined to save them for that proverbial posterity, for some sort of historical value. According to *Webster's New World Dictionary*, posterity means "all of a person's descendants" or "all future generations."

As with sentimentality, there's nothing wrong with saving some things that will capture a moment in time for your grandkids or for future generations not even related to you. As our society's communication and creative expression become more and more electronic, and therefore not often saved in any real, physical form, it is important that we all do our part to keep some record of our times for future generations to learn from or just have a laugh over. The problem comes when you start saving anything and everything and the items become clutter rather than carefully chosen time-markers.

Matter of Fact

Is there a household in this country that doesn't have at least a few, if not several decades worth, of old National Geographic magazines taking up space? Now, you can buy 109 years of National Geographic on CD-ROM, available through its Web site at http://www.nationalgeographic.com/cdrom/complete/. This option won't thrill purists who prefer the smell and feel of rotting paper, but it will clear out lots of garages and attics around America.

Solution: If something is worth saving for posterity, then it shouldn't be stuck in a box somewhere. It should be on display to be enjoyed or at least be labeled and easily accessible. To make your own time capsules, consider these space-saving options:

➤ Scan documents, artwork, and other paper keepsakes onto computer disks.

➤ Make sure that someone isn't already saving the things you're saving. For example, most magazine and newspaper publishers now keep past issues online.

➤ Ask local schools and libraries if they are putting together time capsules which you could donate items to.

➤ If your items are of true historical or cultural significance, donate them to museums or archives.

➤ If you already have children or grandchildren you plan to leave your mementos to, go ahead and give them your mementos now rather than hanging onto them yourself.

You're Not Alone

I hate the idea of waste—of throwing something away that I may need again someday. The irony is that I keep so much junk that I don't even know what I have, so half the time I end up going out and buying something new instead of using what I've carefully stored away.

—Karen K., career consultant

Practicality

Some people are practical to the point of impracticality. They save every spare part, scrap of food, bit of cloth, torn sock, and anything else that could come in handy some day. This behavior is often typical of people who lived through the Depression or other hard times or who immigrated from a country where resources were scarce.

There's nothing wrong with not wanting to be wasteful, but keeping so many odds and ends on hand slows you down. You end up fishing through drawers filled with bits and pieces of what is essentially junk to the point where you can't find what's not junk.

Solution: Every time you're about to save something in the name of practicality, pause and ask yourself what the chances are that you will fix, use, or need that item. Also, think through the consequences of not saving it. Could you replace it easily? Do you already have a duplicate? Being practical is a good habit, but like all good habits, it can be taken to the extreme.

Hopes and Dreams

You thought you were going to start a home-based business, but the idea fizzled out. Now you're left with all sorts of papers and books from the research you did and maybe even some inventory if you had progressed that far. Or perhaps you took some graduate school courses but gave up hope of completing a degree and now can't seem to part with the textbooks and notes that take up valuable bookshelf space. Or maybe you had planned to lose weight and get fit, but your wardrobe of smaller clothes and unused exercise equipment just gathers dust and takes up space.

Some hopes and dreams may not be major life-changing goals like those just described but are small projects you thought you'd get to someday: the sweater you planned to knit, the chair seat you thought you'd re-cane all by yourself, the videos you were going to watch, or the cheerful holiday cards you planned to turn into a collage. Projects like these start out with the best of intentions but usually fall victim to the realities and demands of daily life. What you end up with is lots of stuff around you that could have been put to good use but instead becomes clutter.

Solution: Prevent the problem before it starts. Before you accumulate paraphernalia, think carefully about the likelihood that you will carry out the project or work toward that goal. As for the things you've already collected, be realistic about how likely you are to use them.

A few years ago I decided I wanted to do something with my hands, so I took up decoupage. One week and one little decoupage box later, all the supplies ended up hidden on a high shelf in the hinterlands of my closet. When I unearthed them two years later to prepare for a move, I had a hard time parting with them, thinking I'd get back to them some day. Then I realized that even if I did have more leisure time on my hands in the future, I might not want to do that particular craft again. If I did, the supplies would probably be all dried up and icky by then, and the cost of replacing them would be less than the housing cost of the one or two square feet it would take to store them for a few more years. So I got rid of them.

If your clutter relates to more significant unfinished projects, such as abandoned business ideas or personal goals, parting with the remnants of those lost dreams can be more difficult psychologically. The best way to let go of that type of clutter is to realize that everyone has unfulfilled goals. There's nothing wrong with that. You're only making matters worse by keeping the painful reminders around. By throwing them out, you free yourself to move on to new pursuits. (If you do end up revisiting an old idea, chances are you'd have to do all new research and collect new resources or equipment; just save a few notes or documents that won't get outdated so you don't have to start completely from scratch.)

You're Not Alone

I added to my clutter problem by buying a sewing machine that has sat unopened in its original box through two house moves, gathering dust and taking up space. I don't know what made me think I'd run up some curtains or make costumes for my son when I don't really even know how to sew, don't particularly enjoy it, and surely don't have time for it on top of a full-time job and chasing after a two-year old.

—Joanna H., pension fund manager

Identity

Some of us keep certain objects around because we draw our identity from them. The possessions we choose to surround ourselves with tell other people, as well as ourselves, who we are or who we'd like to be (or even who we used to be). We don't necessarily use these things or even get much enjoyment from them, but we feel tied to them, so we keep them.

I'm as guilty of this as the next person. I was reminded of this problem one day when I needed a map of New York City shortly after moving to a new neighborhood.

Quicksand!

Don't buy something simply because it's on sale or because you have a coupon for it. Put thought into every purchase; otherwise, you're just accumulating clutter.

I knew I had one somewhere, but all I could find in my huge supply of maps were ones to places as far-flung as downtown Cairo; Bergen County, New Jersey; and the entire Eastern Seaboard of the United States. (That last one would've come in handy if I'd wanted to take I-95 instead of the subway from Greenwich Village to Queens.) I also came across a driver's guide to Tunisia; an illustrated walking tour of Portland, Maine; and a street guide to Mississauga, Canada. I had to get out the atlas to figure out where Mississauga, Canada is, and I still don't know what I was doing there if, in fact, I had ever been there at all.

In my frustration to find the one map I needed, the thought crossed my mind that maybe I should get rid of some of these maps. Even if I were to visit the exotic, or not so exotic, locales of the places I had maps for, chances are good that streets and highways would have changed by the time I returned there. Driving through the Sahara Desert with an out-of-date map would not be a wise move.

Why was I keeping them? When I forced myself to give an honest answer to that question, I realized it was because I wanted part of my identity to be "world traveler," someone who can navigate an Arabian souk as comfortably as the New Jersey Turnpike. Never mind that my biggest travel decisions these days are more like whether to go to the farther away grocery store with the better buy on baby wipes or to save gas and time and buy the more expensive ones at the corner market.

Think about the things you might be keeping around because you like what they say about you. Then think about the inconvenience, if any, that they're causing. Do they take up space you could use for something else? Do you have to dust around them? Do you waste time sorting through them to get to what you need? Are they necessary to have on hand?

Solution: You are not your stuff. Your identity comes from what you do, not what you have on your bookshelves or on the walls of your office. There's no harm in keeping a few things around that tell the world "This is what I like and what's important to me." If we didn't, we'd be boring people living and working in boring surroundings. But when you could use the space for other purposes, it might be time to weed out your collections.

I didn't part with all my maps, but I got rid of many that seemed superfluous. Now instead of having nearly an entire file cabinet drawer stuffed with maps, I keep one small file box designated for maps on my home office bookcase. In it are eight hanging file folders representing various regions of the United States and the world with the appropriate maps in each. One of the hanging files is just for New York tri-state area maps, so I can quickly access the ones I need most often.

Getting Rid of Stuff

You know what you've been accumulating too much of and why you've done it. Now you have to get rid of it. Yes, you really have to. Throughout later chapters of this book, you'll find specific tips for de-cluttering chores you might have been putting off. You'll learn techniques for cleaning out and organizing closets, drawers, and other crowded spaces and for sorting through your papers.

Action Tactic

To make yourself more likely to throw out or give away things you don't need to keep, have someone (not a packrat!) watch over you while you attempt to de-clutter.

For now, start an anti-clutter notebook to keep on hand while you clean out various spaces. Use it to make note of items you need to return to someone, things that need to be repaired, and supplies you need to buy or find to organize an area or make necessary repairs. Also, schedule times to take action on the tasks you've written in your anti-clutter notebook. For example, get out your appointment book and write down that next Saturday you will go buy storage bins to organize the remaining sweaters in your closet.

To start ridding yourself of clutter, choose just one small area or one set of like items to clear out at any given time. One area might mean a single drawer, one pile of papers, the top shelf of a closet, or the tool wall of your garage. Don't try to tackle too much at once. Clearing out one small space will give you the incentive to go on and do the rest. Also, set aside a realistic amount of time to start and complete the project. Schedule it for a firm date and time as if it were an important engagement.

When it comes time to clean up the area you selected, set up and label sorting containers (boxes or trash bags) that you will put stuff in. You should have one container for each of the following categories:

➤ To Keep: Easy (for things that have a place and will be easy to put away)

➤ To Keep: Difficult (for things that you will need to find a place for)

➤ To Take Action (for things you need to deal with)

➤ To Return (for borrowed items)

➤ To Trash (for things you can throw away)

➤ To Recycle (for glass, aluminum, paper, and other recyclables)

➤ To Give Away (for things you'll donate to charity or give to other people)

➤ Not Sure (for items that aren't easy to categorize right away)

Go through one item at a time and put it in the appropriate box. To build some momentum, start by doing the easiest sorting first, such as throwing out things that you can get rid of without a second thought. Don't stop to read, reminisce over, try

You're Not Alone

When I was a kid, my parents used to send me out to the garage to bundle up old newspapers for recycling. Eight hours later, I'd still be there reading the papers instead of preparing them for recycling!

—John H., psychologist

Action Tactic

As an incentive to de-clutter your surroundings, calculate the cost of your home or office per square foot and estimate the square footage devoted to items you don't use, wear, or enjoy. How much is it costing you to store your clutter? What else could you be doing with that space if it were emptied out or less crowded?

on, or otherwise be distracted by items you're sorting through. If you need more time to look something over before deciding whether to keep or discard it, put it in the Not Sure box. Just don't let everything end up in that box!

In *The Complete Idiot's Guide to Getting Organized*, author Georgene Lockwood recommends asking the following questions when you're tempted to hang on to something you might not need to keep:

➤ When was the last time I used this?

➤ How often do I use it?

➤ If I don't use it very often, could I borrow, rent, or improvise the few times I might need it?

➤ Is it a duplicate?

➤ Is it out-of-date?

➤ If I didn't have this anymore, what impact would it have on my life?

➤ Do I value this item?

➤ Am I keeping this because I'd feel guilty if I tossed it?

After sorting everything into the boxes, deal with each of the boxes. Start with the easiest first: Bag up the trash and recyclables and take them out of your house; put the box of things to return or donate near your door or in your car so you'll remember to take them where they belong; put away or file the To Keep: Easy items. Give yourself a finite period of time to go through the more difficult stuff. That period might be one week or one month, for example, depending on the amount of items you have to sort through. Each day, go through the Not Sure box little by little. And, each day find a place for one or two items in the To Keep: Difficult box and deal with one or two items in the To Take Action box. Tell yourself that if these boxes are not empty by the end of the time period you've chosen, you'll have to throw out the contents.

When you rid your life of possessions that bring little or no joy or satisfaction, you lift an enormous weight off your shoulders. If you're a packrat now, you may find it hard to imagine life without all your stuff, but I guarantee that de-cluttering your surroundings will be a liberating experience.

The Least You Need to Know

➤ Before you can get organized and stop procrastinating, you have to simplify your life by getting rid of unnecessary possessions.

➤ Watch out for lame excuses you use to hang on to stuff.

➤ When clearing out clutter, focus on one area at a time and don't let yourself get distracted.

➤ Keep yourself inspired with the idea that lightening your load is a liberating experience.

Chapter 9

Getting Your Act Together

In This Chapter

➤ Five simple rules for getting organized

➤ How to keep from coming unglued

➤ Learning to say no

➤ How being organized helps you stop procrastinating

Do you ever have days when it seems like you just can't get your act together? Perhaps your whole life feels that way! I had one of those days recently, a day that revolved around a simple 1:30 doctor's appointment.

Earlier that same day, I dropped my daughter off at the baby sitter's, did the weekly grocery shopping, went to the gym, came back to my home office to take care of e-mails and phone calls, stood in the kitchen wolfing down some leftover Greek salad (a little soggy after a night in the fridge with dressing), and jumped in the shower at 1:00. Between 1:10 and 1:30, I had to dress, dry my hair, and get to the doctor's office about a mile from my house. Definitely doable. After all, I thought, I'm an organizational whiz kid, aren't I? Well, there were a few snags that day …

Organizational Rules to Keep from Coming Unglued

In those hectic 20 minutes, I discovered that over the previous few weeks I had managed to break five key organizational rules and was now paying the price for my sloppiness. Those rules are as follows:

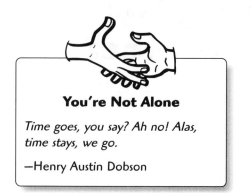

You're Not Alone

Time goes, you say? Ah no! Alas, time stays, we go.

—Henry Austin Dobson

1. Have a place for everything and keep it there.

2. Sort paper into action launching pads to make it easier to deal with, but deal with important papers immediately.

3. Don't just make to-do lists; schedule times to do the things on them.

4. Have a daily routine to bring order to your life, but be flexible and vary it when the need arises.

5. Always allow twice as much time as you think you need to prepare for, and get to, appointments.

Let's look at how I broke these rules and what you can do to avoid making the same mistakes I made.

A Place for Everything

The problems started when I realized I didn't have the address of the doctor's office. (I'd never been there before.) I had not written it in my appointment book when I scheduled the visit, so now I had to waste time looking it up in my health plan's directory. Only problem was, I hadn't yet designated a place to keep the directory, so I didn't know where to look for it. I ended up spending several precious minutes hunting down the book until I found it buried in a stack of magazines on the living room coffee table. (I couldn't have just called information to save time because the doctor had an unusual last name that I wasn't sure I was spelling correctly.)

The moral of this story: Whenever you get something new (a book, catalog, document, household item, or anything), take a couple of minutes to select a logical, accessible, easy to remember place for it. Then make an effort to keep it in that place. If you take catalogs to read in bed, put them back in their place the next morning. If you bury an important document in a pile of papers on your desk, unearth it at the end of the day and put it where it belongs. If you take the scissors out of the kitchen drawer to use them in the den, put them back in the drawer as soon as possible.

Matter of Fact

The first full week of October every year is Get Organized Week, sponsored by the National Association of Professional Organizers (NAPO). Local chapters of NAPO across the country hold special events for the general public, such as seminars on getting organized or expos and trade shows of organizing products. Individual members of NAPO may also give talks at bookstores or other public venues. Make a note in your calendar for August (not October, when it will be too late) to check their Web site at www.napo.net for announcements of any activities in your area or on the Web site.

Paper Shuffling 101

Now that I knew where to go, I needed to find my health insurance card because I knew the receptionist would ask to see it. It wasn't in my wallet. The clock was ticking, and panic was setting in. "Why didn't I look for it before now?" I asked myself in disgust. Because I had a new health plan, I had never used the card before and didn't even know what it looked like, much less where it was.

Then, I vaguely remembered getting an envelope in the mail in recent weeks that might have had the card in it. I sorted through my To Do: Non-urgent stacking tray, the place where I put mail and other papers that need to be dealt with but that can wait. (Stacking trays and sorting mail are described in more detail in Chapter 10, "A Crash Course in Getting Organized.") Sure enough, there was a packet from the insurance company with my card in it. I remembered I had stuck it there because I had said to myself, "I'm too busy writing a book to deal with this now, and I won't need it any time soon."

The moral of this story: You're never too busy to do something important. Taking a little time to deal with an important matter will save you a lot of time down the road. The minute you get an important paper in your hands, deal with it. Read it, respond to it, pass it on to the appropriate person, file it in a place where you can find it later, or do whatever action the paper calls for.

Papers that don't require immediate action get sorted into stacking trays, plastic trays that serve as action launching pads. You have a tray for things to read, one for bills to pay, another for things to file, and so forth. By sorting paper into these trays, you put it in a place where it won't get lost, and you make it easy to find and take action on these papers a few days or weeks later. More details on how to set up and use stacking trays are provided in the "Ode to Stacking Trays" section of Chapter 10.

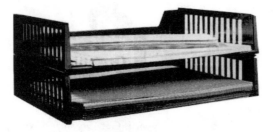

Stacking trays help you organize papers and act as action launching pads by making it easy to see what kind of action needs to be taken with each paper.

Why To-Do Lists Don't Get Done

I keep a personal to-do list, which is separate from my work-related lists. Every time I write something on my work-related lists, I schedule a day to do the task by writing it on one of my day-at-glance appointment book pages. The method works, and I get things done. When I'm in a crunch to meet work deadlines, my personal to-do list tends to get neglected. I write things on the personal list so that I won't forget to do them eventually, but I am not very diligent about scheduling specific days or times for getting them done. My rationale is that during the heavy workload periods, such as when I'm writing a book, my personal tasks have to go on the back burner for a while.

Action Tactic

Put trash cans around your house where you don't typically think of having them, such as the living room, dining room, or hallways. (Buy or make attractive ones if you're worried about wrecking the decor.) Having a trash can handy at all times makes you more likely to throw out papers and stuff you don't need, making it easier to take action on the things you do keep.

That practice came back to haunt me 15 minutes before my doctor's appointment. Weeks before that day, I had put on my list "Figure out new health plan." What I meant by that was that I needed to: review the coverage; locate important phone numbers and put them in my Rolodex and wallet; find the card and put it in my wallet; and put the directory of service providers in a safe place. Had I done any of that? No, and now I was paying the price.

The moral of this story: To-do lists are useless if you don't do two things:

1. Look at them frequently. That may sound like the most obvious advice in the world, but many people take the time to make elaborate lists and then never give them a second glance. If you're guilty of that, you probably tend to forget about things that need to be dealt with.

2. Designate times when you'll do the things on the list. To-do lists are merely inventories. By glancing at a list, you see what you need to do; you check inventory. Lists do not, however, spark action. To get things done, take each item on the list and mark it in your appointment book or calendar as part of a daily action plan. (List-making, scheduling, and calendars are described in more detail in Chapter 10.)

The Beauty of Routine

A routine is a wonderful thing. By knowing that the second Tuesday of every month is the day you pay bills, you don't have to spend all the other days of the month worrying and saying things like, "I should probably be paying some bills." A routine tells you what to do and when to do it. Although that may sound constricting, it's actually liberating. A routine frees you up to enjoy life or at least not to stress out over things. If you know that you regularly do certain tasks on certain days of the week or month, maybe even at specific times, you don't have to think about those things at other times.

On the day of that doctor's appointment, however, my routine complicated the day rather than making it easier. I tried to squeeze too many commitments into too few hours, making myself stressed, nervous, tired, and angry.

Quicksand!

Don't crowd your to-do list with tasks that you have no intention of doing in the remotely near future. Being overly ambitious and filling your list with nonessential tasks will only make you feel guilty and unproductive (when you don't do them), which might keep you from doing the important things. Keep a separate list of backburner projects and long-range goals.

The moral of this story: I should've varied my routine. Just as many people balk at the idea of a routine, thinking it seems too dull and rigid, some people get too dependent on a routine. I'm one of those. The doctor's appointment happened to be scheduled for the day of the week that is my busiest day. It's the day I try to do some household and personal chores along with work.

It was a mistake to schedule the medical appointment in the middle of that day. I should have realized that my household wouldn't crumble if I did the grocery shopping another day and that I could've skipped a day at the gym without any serious health consequences. (It wasn't an option to do those things after the doctor's appointment because I had to host my weekly online chat session later that afternoon and then pick up my child at the babysitter's and take her to a toddlers' gymnastics class that evening.) Deviating from my routine would have made the day much less hectic and allowed more time to prepare for the appointment, have a decent lunch, and stay relaxed.

Expect the Unexpected on the Way to Appointments

If you tell my grandmother you'll pick her up at noon to go out to lunch, I guarantee you'll find her sitting in the lobby of her building no later than 11:10 A.M., with matching shoes and handbag, all ready to go. My mother and I always have a laugh over this, but there's a serious lesson to be learned from her timing. Not everyone has the luxury of being ready nearly an hour early for appointments, but most of us do have enough control over our schedules to allow at least a little extra time cushion.

Action Tactic

Always tell yourself that an appointment or event is half an hour before it is. Even though you'll know the real time, if you keep that real time pushed far enough to the back of your mind, you'll forget about it and will start to think that the fake, earlier time is the actual one.

Giving myself only 20 minutes to dress and drive to a doctor's appointment a mile away was not exactly a wise move, but it wasn't totally unrealistic. If no snags had come up during that 20 minutes, I could've made it. But snags did get in the way. Not only did I have the problems already mentioned, I also realized I had only a few dollars on hand, not enough cash to cover the co-payment I would probably owe (and, of course, I didn't know what that amount would be because I hadn't reviewed my health coverage earlier).

Plus, I realized that parking spaces were just about impossible to find in the area of the doctor's office, so I would need to walk. I'm a fast walker who could probably have gotten there on foot in less time than it would have taken to drive there and park, but there was one problem: The temperature was 90 degrees with about 100 percent humidity. I didn't want to show up at the doctor's office all sweaty, but leaving at 1:30 for a 1:30 appointment, I didn't have much choice but to race-walk.

The moral of this story: Unforeseen delays just about always come up, so the key to getting places on time is to start preparing much earlier than you think you need to. I could've organized my health insurance information days before the appointment. I could have written the doctor's address and phone number in my appointment book on the daily action page for that day. I could have rearranged my schedule to allow more time to get dressed and walk at a leisurely pace to the appointment. Even if delays don't come up, and you end up being ready a little early, what's the harm in that? Maybe you'll sit around all dressed up with no place to go or will arrive somewhere and have to wait a few minutes. But isn't that better than fighting a battle with time?

Gluing the Pieces Back Together

To salvage some sense of order in that chaotic day, I called the doctor's office to say I'd be late, which enabled me to relax a little bit. I also asked about the co-payment amount I would owe and the forms of payment accepted. I then made sure to put my checkbook in my purse so I wouldn't have to take time to stop at a cash machine. I also made the decision to save time by leaving home with wet hair. After all, I wasn't going to be in a beauty pageant, and it would probably dry in the heat by the time I got there anyway. I then walked there swiftly but not at breakneck speed, arriving only 12 minutes late and not too sweaty.

You can always find a few shortcuts and ways to minimize the inconvenience to others when you don't have your act together, but of course, the best policy is to be organized in the first place to avoid getting into last-minute jams.

Matter of Fact

If you're having trouble keeping things around your home or office organized, check out some of the handy organizational tools available from the Container Store. Whether you need closet shelving, a CD organizer for your car visor, kitchen storage jars, laundry bags and bins, or desk organizer, this company probably has it. It has retail stores nationwide, or you can contact it at 800-733-3532 (catalog sales) or www.containerstore.com.

Balancing Acts

As you may have learned in Chapter 3, "Blame It on the Environment," not all clutter is the kind that grows in your closet or filing cabinet. You can also get slowed down by a glut of obligations in any of the 10 life roles described in that chapter.

Suppose you're rolling along with your daily routine, managing to get everything done, when something comes along and upsets the apple cart. Perhaps you have to care for an elderly relative or a family member who suddenly becomes sick or injured. This happens at the same time that you're nearing critical deadlines at work, remodeling your kitchen, trying to stick with an exercise plan, and devoting energy to a new romantic relationship in your life. Just when you thought you had your act together, a case of commitment overload kicks in.

Some commitments, such as those related to unexpected illness, are difficult, if not impossible, to control. Others, however, like pointless meetings you're asked to attend, committees you're volunteered for, household projects you ambitiously take on, are within your control. You can say no!

Why It's Hard to Say No

If you find yourself too often saying yes to obligations that end up eating up your time and making you feel stressed, then you need to figure out why it's so difficult to say no. Check off the following reasons that ring true for you, and then start using the strategies suggested after the ones you checked:

❑ Your sense of duty compels you to take on any obligation that comes your way.

Strategy: You can be of more service to people if you carefully pick and choose your commitments so that you have enough time and energy to devote to each one. Remember that you also have a duty to treat yourself well—not just other people!

❏ You want to be liked.

Strategy: Are people going to dislike you if you decline their invitations or requests? In most cases, people take a no much more easily than you expect them to. But people won't be too thrilled if you take on something you don't want to do or that you can't commit to fully.

❏ You like to feel needed.

Strategy: It's nice to feel that others rely on you, but commitment is a quality issue, not a quantity one. You don't have to overextend yourself to feel needed. Instead, focus on the satisfaction you get from devoting your time and energy to a select group of people and organizations, and don't let yourself get spread too thin.

❏ You want to avoid confrontation.

Strategy: It's very unlikely that anyone is going to yell and scream and stomp their feet when you say no to a request for your time. Telling someone no isn't necessarily the most pleasant exchange you'll ever have, but it's not likely to trigger World War III.

❏ You feel flattered to be asked.

Strategy: Flattery doesn't bring 25 or 35 hours to your day. Not far behind that warm and fuzzy feeling you get from the flattery is the resentment you'll feel over the time and effort you have to put into a particular project. If it's flattery you need, tell your loved ones to say nice things to you more often.

❏ You're afraid to miss out on something.

Strategy: If honoring the request is practically guaranteed to propel you closer to your personal or career goals, then do it. If not, realize that, if this opportunity came along, there will probably be more like it down the road.

❏ You're losing sight of reality.

Strategy: Some demands for your time are presented as quick and easy little blips on the calendar. If you tend to fall for vague promises that a particular project won't disrupt your life or take up much of your time, then you need to be more careful when the request is made. Think through the day-to-day reality of what this obligation would entail and what it would do to your life.

Once you understand why the word yes rolls off your tongue far too often, you'll be ready to start replacing yes with no.

How to Say No

To say no painlessly and politely, follow these rules:

➤ Keep your priorities in mind at all times. If a request for your time doesn't fit in with your values and goals, you should probably say no.

➤ If you know right away that you don't have the desire or time to do something, turn down the request as soon as possible. The longer you wait, the more likely you are to back down and change your mind, and the more difficult it will be for the other person to find someone else to do it.

➤ When you're asked to take on a particular commitment, if your first reaction is uncertainty, don't decide immediately. Never let anyone rush you. Take the time you need to think through all the possible consequences of doing the project.

➤ Ask other people for input on your decision. If you decide to decline the offer, you'll feel more confident in saying so because you didn't make the decision alone.

➤ Say no in a succinct but polite way. Giving too much detail about your situation opens the door for the other person to try to find ways to fit the obligation into your schedule. Simply say you'd like to do it, or that you're flattered by the offer, but your schedule does not allow it.

Remember that no matter how difficult it may be to say no, it's much easier to do so before you've committed to something than to bow out after the fact.

Getting Out of Commitments You've Already Made

Never bail out on an important project at a critical time when other people are counting on you. But if you are not totally indispensable, then don't be afraid to bow out if you feel you must. Here are some of the ways to do it:

➤ Find a replacement to take over your responsibilities.

➤ Regardless of whether you handpick the replacement, offer to update that person on where you left things.

➤ Give an adequate explanation for why you have to bow out so that it will be clear that you have valid reasons and are not just abandoning responsibility.

➤ Point out to the others involved that you can no longer devote an adequate amount of time and energy to the commitment and

Quicksand!

Before you back out on a commitment you've already made, make certain that you are in no way legally bound to carry out that obligation.

Action Tactic

If there's no way to get out of a project you've already committed to and you no longer can find the time to do it, try to delegate as many tasks as possible to an intern or assistant of some sort to ease your burden.

that they'd be better off having someone else take over. They'll appreciate the candor and might even prefer that you leave!

➤ If you aren't too deep into the project, point out that it's better to leave now while someone else can still fairly easily take over than to leave them in the lurch farther down the line.

Needing to leave a project you've started on or to relinquish responsibility when people are counting on you is usually an extremely uncomfortable situation. It can be done, though, especially if you keep in mind that you're not only doing yourself a disservice by hanging on against your wishes, you're also letting down others who need a genuine commitment from you.

The Organization-Procrastination Link

Getting your act together relates to procrastination in two ways:

1. **You put off getting organized.** Getting organized may be something you've been putting off doing. In other words, your procrastination habit may be keeping you from getting your act together. You keep saying you'll get around to cleaning out the garage, the attic, a closet, your files, or whatever, but you put it off and put it off. You keep meaning to set up some organizational systems for your household routine or business operations, but you never get around to it.

2. **Putting off getting organized is what causes you to put off other things.** A lack of organization may lead to procrastination in other areas of your life. It sets the stage for putting off other tasks. Maybe you delay writing thank-you notes because you can't find the addresses you need or decent stationery to write on. Perhaps you run a small business and put off billing clients because you've never set up an organizational system for keeping track of services rendered, dates, price quotes, and other key data that goes into the bills.

The five basic rules of organization described in this chapter are the building blocks for getting your act together, whether disorganization is the problem or the cause of other problems. In Chapter 10, you'll find details on how to follow these rules. Then, in the chapters in Part 3, "Tips and Tricks for Getting Things Done" and Part 4, "Getting Things Done at Work and School," there are lots of examples of how these rules of organizing can be applied in specific ways in your personal and professional life.

The Least You Need to Know

➤ Having logical, easily accessible spots for objects and paper is an important foundation for being organized.

➤ The reason that to-do lists so often don't work is that people forget to check them and don't schedule times to do the things on them.

➤ Having a daily or weekly routine brings order to your life and frees you from worrying about all your commitments and obligations.

➤ Always allow twice as much time as you think you need to prepare for, and get to, appointments.

➤ Being organized is not only a worthy goal in and of itself, it also sets the stage for getting things done in all areas of your life.

➤ Saying no to requests for your time is easier than you might think.

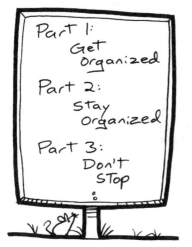

Part 1:
Get
Organized

Part 2:
Stay
Organized

Part 3:
Don't
STop

Chapter 10

A Crash Course in Getting Organized

In This Chapter

➤ Finding the proverbial safe place for things

➤ Filing for function, if not fun

➤ Low–tech and hi–tech organizing options

➤ Where to put all that paper

Getting organized is not only an art and a science, it's also a booming industry. Everyone from Oprah, to supermodels, to major corporations and housewives have enlisted the services of professional organizers. Not only are there people who make a living wading through and sorting out other people's stuff and helping them get their acts together, there are also plenty of books with tips on how to clear off your desk or clean out your closets and any number of seminars that motivate you to make the most of your time.

Any time there are that many consultants, authors, and seminar leaders working in the same field, you're going to have a wide range of opinion about the specifics of how to get organized. Whether it's how to set up a filing system that works, or whether you should keep your appointments in an old-fashioned appointment book or in a fancy, hi-tech electronic organizer, the advice on getting organized presents a confusing array of choices. The important thing to remember is that there is no right or wrong way to organize. Sure, some techniques and systems are typically more effective than others, but organizing is a personal thing. You have to take all the expert advice and use the parts of it that work for you.

I don't claim to be a professional organizer, but I've spent more than a decade reading all the latest books on organizing and attending many seminars on the topic. (It's kind of a hobby of mine.) I've even led my own seminars on it and have seen what works for the many clients I've helped get their acts together. Most important, I've tested out various methods, systems, and techniques in my own busy personal and professional life.

The Complete Idiot's Guide to Overcoming Procrastination is not a book on organizing per se (there's *The Complete Idiot's Guide to Organizing Your Life* for that). What I offer you in this chapter, and throughout the chapters in Parts 3 and 4, is a simple system that works for me and can work for you (or can be adapted slightly to fit your particular needs).

Three Ways to Get Organized

Just as Chapter 8, "Lightening Your Load," provided general guidelines for minimizing clutter, this chapter outlines the basic techniques for getting organized. In Part 3, you'll find more specific ideas for organizing various aspects of your life. This section deals with the three keys to organization:

➤ Putting things, and keeping them, where they belong

➤ Dealing with and filing paper

➤ Making lists, scheduling, and working with calendars and planners

Becoming and staying organized in these three basic areas will bring you one step closer to being an ex-procrastinator.

Matter of Fact

The first step in getting organized is to get rid of clutter and simplify your life. If you skip those steps, you'll never succeed in keeping paper, stuff, and schedules organized.

Find a Place for Everything and Keep It There

Let's play a game: Look at a watch or clock with a second hand, or use a stopwatch, and start timing yourself when I say, "Go." You're going to tell me where certain items are located at this very moment around your home. Ready, set, go!

Where's your *Yellow Pages* phone directory? Your checkbook? The TV remote control? Your passport? Your birth certificate? A new light bulb? The warranty or instruction manual for your microwave? A first class stamp? A roll of masking tape? A thick, black felt-tip marker? A spare key to your car or house? A bottle opener? A flashlight? Your doctor's phone number?

Getting annoyed yet? How long did it take you to think of where those things are? Too long? Maybe it wasn't merely a question of needing time to remember; you may have had no idea at all of where some of them could be.

That list represents just a sampling of the sorts of items you need to be able to find without a moment's hesitation. Some are more important than others. You could live without the remote control for a few hours (though I'm sure some of you would disagree with me), whereas a missing flashlight or emergency phone number might be critical.

Quicksand!

Make sure that all other members of your household know where various items belong. In an emergency, it does no good for you to be the only one who knows that the flashlight is kept in the drawer to the left of the dishwasher.

Chasing the Wild Goose: An Exercise

If you find yourself on wild goose chases on a daily, or at least frequent, basis, then it's time to find a place for everything and keep it there. To do that, take these three simple steps:

1. Walk around your house with a pad of paper and a pen and write down everything you see that's a "floater," something that never seems to stay in one place.

2. Take a look at your list and think of convenient, logical places for the frequently used items and less accessible (but still logical) places for the items that can be stored away for less frequent use.

3. Put those things in their places. Then every time you remove something from its home, put it back where it belongs as soon as possible. There's nothing particularly original or profound about this advice, but it's a simple step that so many people don't take, so it's important to pay attention to it.

If you follow these steps but still find that certain items disappear or take too much time to track down, re-think the places you've chosen to keep them. What may seem like a so-called logical spot when you first do the exercise can turn out to be not so logical or convenient after you've lived with the floaters' new homes for a while.

Why Things Don't Stay Where They Belong

Remember that spaces get messy for any or all of four reasons:

1. They're too crowded; something needs to be thrown out or moved.

2. The items aren't arranged well, so it's difficult to keep them organized.

3. Items don't have a place they belong, so they never get put away and instead sit out as floaters.

4. Items do have a place they belong, but they don't get put back there.

The next time you look at your office, home, or even your car and complain about how messy it is, don't act as though you can't do anything about it. Keep the preceding four reasons in mind and see whether you're guilty of any of them. If so, do something about it!

> **Action Tactic**
>
> Bedside tables are notorious clutter traps. To keep them clear of all but the most essential items, get into the habit of picking up at least a couple of things from your nightstand each morning when you first get out of bed. As you make your way to your morning coffee or the bathroom, drop the items off in the rooms they belong in.

What to Do with All That Paper Jazz

Whether it's paper in the form of letters, bills, invitations, catalogs, magazines, pamphlets and brochures, product warranties, or any other kind of document, correspondence, or publication, there are seven basic things you can do with paper:

1. **Take immediate action on it.** Respond with a letter, phone call, or e-mail; reply to an invitation; register for an event; pass the paper on to someone else; or take some other action. Immediate usually means within about 24 to 48 hours.

2. **Take action on it in the near future.** Handle it in the same ways as the immediate action category, but within a longer time frame, such as weeks or months.

3. **File it.** Put it in a file folder already set up for papers in that category, or establish a folder and a location for it. (Tips on filing are given later in this chapter in "The Wonderful World of Filing.")

4. **Pay it.** Bills, subscription renewals, membership fees, and any other demands for your hard-earned dollars go into the Pay It category. This category can also include lists, order forms, or pictures of things you want to buy.

5. **Throw it out.** Decide it doesn't need to be saved and immediately toss it into a trash can or recycling bin.

6. **Read it.** By keeping things to read in a separate place from your other action files, you can easily grab something to read when you anticipate having some time to do so, such as when waiting in line, sitting on a bus or train, or waiting for an appointment to start. With a Read It file, you can easily reach for a professional journal, a funny article a friend sent, or anything else that will keep you entertained or productive during periods of down time.

7. **Keep it for reference.** Some things, such as documents or notes you've made, don't require immediate action because they're related to pending projects, not current ones. But you might need to refer to or use them in the near future, so they shouldn't be buried in a file somewhere.

Quicksand!

If you get a decent filing system set up for the first time in your life (and use it and keep it in good order for the first time ever), beware of getting carried away with your newfound organization. You might be tempted to save every piece of paper you come across just because you now have a place to put it. Resist the temptation. Only file things that need to be kept.

Now that you know the seven things to do with paper (not including making paper airplanes and origami), you need to know how this system works on a day-to-day basis. First, you need to set up stacking trays so that you can sort papers according to these seven action categories. Then you need an easy-to-use filing system to store documents and a good calendar/appointment book system to keep track of the action you need to take on some of the items in the stacking trays.

Ode to Stacking Trays

If I were stranded on a desert island, I would want to have with me some strong sunscreen, Revlon's Apricot Fantasy lipstick, and a set of stacking trays. I might not get any mail to put in those trays, but I could use them to sort palm leaves and seashells. Maybe I'm a little weird, but stacking trays are quite handy items; in fact, I'm not sure I could live without them.

Stacking trays are those plastic, three-sided, rectangular boxes that hold 8.5" × 11" documents. (You can also find fancier ones that are made of wood or wicker.) Some people know them as in-baskets, but they're much more than that. If you have just one or two trays in which you dump everything that's going in or out of your office (or household work area), you won't be very motivated to do the stuff that's in them.

Instead, you need to set up a whole series of stacking trays in which to sort papers. This way, instead of having one or two giant piles of papers accumulating on your desk or kitchen table every couple of days, you have your papers neatly tucked away in slots that are clearly labeled with the action you need to take to deal with them. I think of the trays as action launching pads. They're the answer to a procrastinator's prayers.

Matter of Fact

To help you better understand the uses for a Reference stacking tray for paper, I'll give you a glimpse into my own Reference tray. It currently contains: a store credit for an item I returned; an acknowledgement from a mail-order catalog that a baby gift I ordered was mailed to the recipient; directions to the home of some friends my husband and I will be visiting next weekend; and the confirmation number for a change-in-service order I requested from the phone company.

Let's Get Stacking!

When you have your trays, the next thing to do is label them. Most stacking trays don't come with labels, so you'll probably have to make your own. I use the clear plastic tabs with little paper inserts that are designed to go on top of hanging file folders. I write the name of the tray on the insert, slide it into the plastic tab, and tape it to the front center of each tray. Typical labels, based on the seven things to do with paper, are: To Do: ASAP, To Do: Non-urgent, To File, To Pay, To Read, and Reference. (Of course, papers to be thrown out don't need a stacking tray.)

Finally, you have to use the trays. Don't just look at them and admire your organizational prowess. Put things in them. But make sure you put things in the right place rather than randomly sticking papers wherever they fit. And be sure you only put what belongs there. The trays are not storage spaces for any odds and ends you need to stick somewhere. Then, of course, you have to go through the trays from time to time before they start overflowing. How to do that is covered later under "The Gentle Art of Scheduling."

The Wonderful World of Filing

Prepare yourself for a whirlwind tour of filing. Okay, so it doesn't exactly sound like a romp in the park or a stroll through the Louvre, but what you'll discover will be infinitely useful—I promise! Call me crazy, but I happen to enjoy filing. I know I'm in the minority here, so I'll make this tour quick and painless for those of you who don't enjoy filing in your spare time.

Because I do get a kick out of setting up filing systems and using them, I've had lots of practice doing it and have managed to come up with a simple system that works. You may need to vary my method slightly depending on what you need to file and how you need to use it, but you can use my system as a starting point for getting yourself organized.

Even the smartest people can feel like complete idiots when it comes to setting up a filing system that is complex enough to keep your papers in order but is at least a notch down in complexity from rocket science. Having struggled with this problem myself, I've come up with a simple system.

First, you need two types of file folders: regular manila file folders (or colored ones if you want to spice things up a bit or color-code your files) and hanging file folders. The regular ones should be "one-third cut," which means they have a raised tab at one of three locations across the top: left, center, or right. Most office supply stores sell them in boxes of 100 for just a few dollars. The hanging folders (Pendaflex and Globe-Weis are two popular brand names) come in a drab olive green or assorted colors. I recommend the assortment of colors, so you can group like files by color. These folders have metal arms that let the file hang from file cabinets with metal frames or from portable plastic file boxes.

After you have your file folders, you need three pieces of equipment to hold your file folders: file cabinet(s), portable file boxes, and standing file racks. A file cabinet is that big hunk of metal that eats paper. I happen not to like file cabinets because they act like a sort of paper graveyard. The files way in the back can seem dead, buried, and forgotten, unless you keep them alphabetized or color-coded so that you know what's in the back of the drawer. They are useful, however, for files that don't need to be referred to or added to often. If you have the space for them, lateral file cabinets are great because all the files are in plain view when you open a drawer. (Lateral cabinets are usually about 30 inches wide and hold letter-size files sideways, as opposed to regular vertical file cabinets that are about 15 or so inches wide and hold files front to back.)

Lateral file cabinets make it easy to find frequently referenced files and have a nice, wide surface that can double as a credenza. Vertical file cabinets are good for narrow spaces and files that aren't used often.

Quicksand!

Reusing file folders is a great way to recycle. But watch out: File cabinets or boxes full of extremely old, tattered file folders can deter you from filing. You'll feel more organized and be more likely to maintain your filing system in good working order if you periodically replace the worn-out folders with crisp, new ones.

File boxes, which are my preferred storage unit, are usually plastic, but they may be wooden or cardboard and can fit on a bookcase shelf as long as it's about 12 inches deep. File boxes hold hanging file folders and have handles or cut-outs on each end so that you can pick them up and put them on your desk or other work surface while you're using them.

Standing file racks are simple, inexpensive, wire or solid metal stands that hold regular (not hanging) file folders, usually about 10 to 20 at a time, depending upon how much paper you have in each folder. File stands are useful for current projects and active files that you need to have out on your desk or close at hand. They can also be used as a substitute for stacking trays to sort paper if you don't plan to put a lot of paper into them (trays hold more than file folders can).

Using the folders and equipment you have acquired, set up five categories and locations of files. Don't become overwhelmed when you start setting up files. Rather than trying to deal with every piece of paper in your office or home office, start with current papers and go forward. In other words, set up files (or reorganize existing files) for papers and projects you're dealing with today or will be in the near future, and don't worry about the old stuff. Then after you've gotten adjusted to the new filing system and are feeling caught up, go back to clearing out the old piles, boxes, or bags of paper and setting up files for the ones you need to keep. The following sections describe the five categories.

Pending Project Files

Most people don't set up files for projects until that project is officially underway. The problem with that approach is that lots of paper and information is likely to come trickling in (if not pouring in) between the time you first find out about the project and the time it starts. What ends up happening is that important papers and bits of information are scattered all over the place. Then when it's time to get to work, you can't find the information you need. You're likely to procrastinate at that point because you don't have what you need to get started and finding all the information seems like too much of a chore.

The answer to this chaos is to start a file for a project the minute you find out about it. Then whenever you come across information related to that topic, you can drop it in the file. When you have phone conversations or exchange e-mails about the project, you can file your notes in one place to have a complete record of the communication.

That's all there is to pending project files. Just set up one folder and use it as the one and only place you keep information related to that project. (You might also start a file or folder on your computer, too, if you want to save e-mail, typed notes, or downloaded information more easily.) Keep pending project files in a file stand or a file box that you keep in a convenient enough spot to make it likely that you'll put things in it, but not right in front of you; you don't want to stress out over projects that haven't yet started.

Action Tactic

If you tend to stuff your manila or hanging file folders pretty full, consider using pocket or jacket folders. These folders have enclosed sides to keep papers from falling out and accordion-pleated bottoms to expand as needed. Some even have a special little pocket to keep a computer disk in.

Current Project Files

Current project files are essentially the same as the pending files except that the project is already underway, so the big differences here are location and size of files. You should keep current project files within easy reach of your desk chair or wherever you'll be working. I'm a big fan of file stands for this purpose because the files stay visible and very accessible. When you jot down an important phone number on a sticky note and need to keep it on hand for a current project, you're more likely to put it in that project's file if the file folder is in sight than if it's buried in a drawer.

As for size of the files, you might find that a project has enough stuff related to it to warrant setting up a file box with multiple hanging folders in it. That, too, should be kept nearby, perhaps on a bookshelf near your desk or on your desk if space allows.

Administrative Files

Some files need to be fairly accessible, but not necessarily in your face. A file cabinet is fine for administrative files that you need to refer to occasionally, maybe about once a week or even less often. Your household administrative files might include

- ❑ Bills you've paid; use one hanging file folder for each account, such as credit card companies, utilities, phone companies, and the like

- ❑ Medical records and health insurance information

- ❑ Financial documents (recent ones only—old tax records and cancelled checks get relegated to archival files)

- ❑ Household papers such as mortgage or rental documents, construction projects, personnel files for household equipment warranties, receipts, and instructions

❑ Miscellaneous documents and records (examples from my files are frequent flyer mileage statements, car maintenance records, and a Christmas file in which I keep records of gifts I've given in past years and a card recipient list)

Some administrative files don't even need to be in an easily accessible file cabinet. If you're keeping certain documents merely for the record and are unlikely to need to refer to them frequently, if at all, those documents become archival files. Archival files can be stored away in cardboard boxes in a closet, the attic, an office storage room, or any other appropriate space.

Matter of Fact

Using different colored hanging folders for various categories of your administrative files keeps your files from being one big blur and makes it easy to spot the one you need. For example, in one locked file cabinet drawer, I have about 20 red folders for paid bills and other important documents related to our car, home, and insurance; several blue folders for medical and dental records and health insurance information; and several green files for investment account statements, general financial information such as budgets, and the past two years' tax files.

Key People and Places Files

You probably have people you correspond with on a regular or occasional basis or that you like to keep tabs on in some way. At work, these might be clients, customers, professional colleagues, networking contacts, and the like. In your personal files, these might be friends, family, babysitters, or classmates. The places are associations, companies, schools, and other organizations you belong to, do business with, conduct research on, or otherwise collect information about. Places might also be geographic locales that you have papers related to. Unless you need to refer to your people and places files on a regular basis, these files can usually go in a filing cabinet.

Topic Files

Topic files hold articles and other papers related to topics of interest to you. For example, my personal topic files include information on art, photography, horses, camels, cartoons, and jokes, among others. My work topic files are more extensive and include such topics as procrastination (obviously), job hunting, career management, and self-employment issues. If you're the type of person who lets old magazines, newspapers, or professional journals pile up because they contain articles you might want to save, then you probably need to set up a good topic files system. That way, you can go through the publications, read and tear out the articles of interest, and file them in folders designated for those topics. As with key people and places files, topic files usually belong in file cabinets.

Action Tactic

If your brain just doesn't seem to be wired for organizing, you might find that the book *Organizing for the Creative Person* by Dorothy Lehmkuhl and Dolores Cotter Lamping speaks to you.

Setting Up Mission Control

This entire book is about getting things done, but a particularly important element in being productive is to start with the basics: appointment books (planners), calendars, lists, and scheduling techniques. The first thing you need is a mission control where you keep a calendar, appointment schedule, to-do lists, and daily action lists, as well as additional optional data such as addresses and phone numbers and ex-pense records.

Your mission control can be a ready-made organizational system that you buy in an office supply store or get through an organizational seminar. These planners have brand names like Filofax, Day Runner, Day-Timer, or Franklin Quest, to name just a few. If you need to carry your planner around with you during the day or in a briefcase or bag between office and home, these are good options because they are portable and come in a variety of sizes. They also come with a choice of attractive cover materials and colors, if that matters for your professional image.

If you prefer electronic gizmos, there's software that you load onto your hard drive and that usually contains, at minimum, a calendar, appointment book, to-do lists, contact section (like an electronic Rolodex), and a notepad. There are also hand-held options, like the chic Palm Pilot, which is better for people who are frequently on the go. The electronic organizing options work only if you are comfortable using them and if they are convenient for you.

Then there's the low-tech, primitive approach that I greatly prefer. Take a regular three-ring binder that's about 2 inches thick. (That's the old-fashioned loose-leaf notebook you probably carried to school as a kid.) Get a set of divider pages with tabs that you can write on to label different sections. Then, and this is where this method is not entirely low-tech, print up 12 monthly calendar pages and one daily action page. I did mine on Microsoft Office, which has a section of predesigned calendar templates you can customize for your own needs. If you're not handy on the computer, find a friend who is.

Open the rings of the notebook and put the monthly calendar pages in the front. Then put a divider after the December page (or whichever month you end with) and insert the daily action pages. Then, put in dividers for each sphere of commitment

that you will have to-do lists for. Put a few pieces of notebook paper in each section to write your to-do lists on. That's all there is to it. You have a customized, simple mission control.

Once you have the place for your mission control, you need to use it. The following sections provide a brief rundown on the three basic parts of mission control: monthly calendar, daily action pages, and to-do lists.

Monthly Calendar

When I see people who use those little pocket-sized appointment books that show only a couple of days or a week at a time on two facing pages, I don't know how they function. To have a clear sense of the balance in your life, or lack thereof, and to schedule well, you have to have a month-at-a-glance section where you see an entire month on one page (or spread across two facing pages).

That way, when someone says, "Can you volunteer at the church two Saturdays this month instead of your usual one Saturday?" you know how to respond. Rather than just looking at the two weeks in which those Saturdays fall and saying yes because you see your calendar is clear those days, you look at the whole month and get a big picture view of how your life will be affected by volunteering two weekends. If you see that the other two weekends (and maybe many of the weekday evenings, too) are jam-packed with commitments, then you know that filling in two more Saturdays is going to put you on overload that month. You'll end up getting behind on household chores and any work that you might've needed to do in the evenings or weekends, not to mention quality time with friends and family and rest.

Daily Action Pages

A monthly calendar is important for managing your overall schedule and maintaining balance, but it doesn't help you get things done on a daily basis. Just because your calendar says that June 10 is your mother-in-law's birthday doesn't mean you'll remember to mail a card on June 5. Just because the calendar says that a major report is due in two weeks doesn't mean you'll take the right steps each day until then to get it done on time. You need daily action pages to do that.

With some planner systems, you can buy sets of pages that have two pages per day of the year. The page on the left looks like a traditional appointment book page, with times of days down the left side and spaces along the right for you to mark scheduled appointments for that day. The page that faces it on the right has blanks for writing your daily to-do list.

On my homemade daily action page, I have separate sections for To Do: Work, To Do: Household, To Do: Out, To Call, and To E-mail. That way, instead of having one confusing list of things to do each day, I can tackle one category at a time. When I'm online, I can send all the e-mails at once. When I'm in the mood to make phone calls, I have a quick list to scan to see who I need to call. When I'm on my way out to do one errand, I see what other errands I can take care of to make the best use of my time.

If you've heard it once, you've probably heard it a thousand times, "Break big projects down into manageable steps to get them done." That's the idea behind your calendars and daily action plan. By focusing on "do dates" instead of due dates, you get things done.

Action Tactic

You'll have an easier time keeping track of events and appointments in your personal and work lives (hey, it's all one life!) if you have only one monthly calendar. The recommended maximum is two: one in the planner you use throughout the day and one on the refrigerator for family or roommates to keep track of major events, occasions, and appointments.

To-Do Lists

So how do you know what to do each day? There are three simple steps. First, take stock of the different spheres of commitment in your life. What I mean by that is, think of the different projects, life roles, or areas in which you have things to do. For each of those spheres, you need a to-do list.

Because I am self-employed, I usually have two or three main freelance or consulting projects going on at any given time, plus some occasional smaller, short-term projects. I have a section in my mission control book for each of those main projects, plus a section labeled "Miscellaneous Work." Then, I have a section labeled "Personal." In each section is one to-do list where I write down everything I need to do the minute I think of it or as soon as it is assigned to me. Over the past few months, my personal to-do list has included the following tasks:

➤ Buy baby gift for Nancy H.'s new son

➤ Make copies of the photo M.R. wants

➤ Get photo inspection of car for new insurance company

➤ Send housewarming card to Stevie

➤ Make invitations for daughter's birthday party

➤ Schedule day to visit the Bermans

➤ Catch up on baby's scrapbook

➤ Arrange for shower to be re-grouted

➤ Buy new exercise tights

➤ Figure out new health insurance

Quicksand!

Don't be a slave to your schedule. If you follow it too rigidly, you'll start to resent it and may abandon it altogether.

You get the picture. The personal list contains all those things that you usually never get around to doing or do late. But now that they're on one clear list and, more important, now that you're going to schedule them on daily action pages, you'll start doing them. Use the same approach with your work-related to-do lists. By the way, I did everything on this list except the last item (and in Chapter 9, you saw what kind of trouble that got me into!).

If you find it confusing to have multiple to-do lists, start by making one giant list of everything you have to do in all areas of your life. Then, after you have become comfortable with the system of using a list and scheduling to-do items on your daily action pages, you can graduate to the more advanced systems of separating out your lists.

The Gentle Art of Scheduling

I call scheduling a gentle art, because one of the most common mistakes of scheduling is to be unrealistic about how much you can get done in a certain period of time. To avoid that mistake, follow these guidelines:

➤ Have a routine schedule for the weekly chores and appointments you regularly have. Type it up on one horizontal piece of paper with the days of the week along the top and times down the left side. Put it in a visible place over your desk or in your planner.

➤ Whenever you schedule a nonroutine appointment, think through every step that it would involve: advance preparation, getting ready on the day of the appointment, travel time, and so on. Then schedule it on a day and time when you know you can get through all the steps with a minimum amount of hassle.

➤ Consult other key people, such as co-workers, friends, or family, before scheduling. It does you no good to arrange a meeting or social engagement only to find that the time is no good for others who need to be involved.

➤ Keep your overall priorities and goals in mind when scheduling your day-to-day action. For example, writing a thank-you note might be a priority, but is it a bigger priority to get past a particular work deadline first? Maybe the thank-you note can wait a few days. As long as you write it down on a daily action page, even if you send it a few days later than the ideal time, it won't be forgotten and will get done.

➤ Maintain balance in your life. Don't schedule every minute of the day. Allow some time to be spontaneous and do nothing (or to do something fun on the spur of the moment). If your life is extremely busy, you might have to build balance into your schedule. I know that sounds kind of crazy, but scheduled spontaneity is better than none at all.

➤ Work with your natural rhythms. Don't schedule a fitness workout at 6 A.M. if you're not a morning person. Don't plan to make cold calls after lunch if that's the time of day you feel most sluggish. Use your common sense and schedule routine tasks or occasional appointments at times that make sense for your energy level.

Just as your schedule should fit your mind's and body's natural rhythms, so should all your organizational systems. The examples you've seen in this chapter of filing methods, calendars, and other ways to get your act together will only work for you if you adapt them to fit your preferred style of living and working.

The Least You Need to Know

➤ When you don't have a place for everything and keep it in that place, not only do your surroundings become messy, you also get slowed down when you're trying to get things done.

➤ To deal with all the paper that comes your way, use stacking trays to sort it into such categories as To Do: ASAP, To Do: Non-urgent, To File, To Pay, To Read, and Reference.

➤ To design a filing system that works, set up files in locations that make sense for the frequency with which you'll use them and group related files together.

➤ To get things done, keep a to-do list for each project or sphere of commitments rather than one giant list. Also, schedule a time or day to do each item.

Chapter 11

Decision-Making: The Root of All Action

In This Chapter

➤ Decision-making: Innate talent or learned skill?

➤ Why we make decisions harder than they need to be

➤ Identifying your decision-making style

➤ Deciding like a pro

Ann is a conscientious mother who wanted to find a good preschool for her son. She kept putting off enrolling him somewhere because she was waiting for the perfect option. She extended her search so long that she missed all the deadlines and had to send him to a school that was near the bottom of her list.

Donny is a magazine editor living in New York City where it costs an arm, a leg, and a kidney to rent an apartment. Thirteen years ago, Donny had the opportunity to get on a waiting list for a nice building known for its extremely reasonable rents and spacious apartments, a waiting list you could wait on for several years before you got to the top. At that time, he put off adding his name to the list because he was in the process of deciding whether he wanted to settle down in Manhattan permanently or move somewhere else. It took him so long to decide to stay that, as he now realizes, if he'd been more decisive, he could have been living in a nice, large apartment by now instead of in an overpriced one-room studio that doesn't even have a closet!

I Just Can't Decide

When you put off making a decision, you put your life on hold. You miss out on opportunities, have to settle for second-best, and disappoint yourself, as well as the people you care about or work with.

As with getting organized, decision-making is related to procrastination in two ways:

1. Decision-making may be the thing you procrastinate about. You delay making decisions that are difficult, take time, or have a lot riding on them. You might not put off cleaning the oven, making your annual dental checkup, or going to the gym, but when it comes to making a decision, you're a major procrastinator. You wait until the very last minute to commit yourself to one direction or another.

2. Delayed decision-making may lead to procrastination in other areas of your life. Decision-making is at the root of all action, so the things you put off doing might get put off because you can't decide when, how, or where to do them.

Quicksand!

If you dwell on the poor choices, you'll never develop the confidence you need to make good choices. Just because decisions you made in the past didn't work out so well, don't assume you're doomed to keep making the same mistakes.

Whether the decision is a major life choice or merely a choice of what to do in the course of your workday or what to have for dinner, decision-making is often one of the biggest sources of frustration and confusion for procrastinators.

Why Decisions Are So Hard to Make

Decisions are sometimes difficult to make because we've never learned how to make them. We rely on hit-or-miss methods that work if we're lucky or lead us down the wrong paths if we're not so fortunate. We don't realize that decision-making is a skill that can be learned. Instead, many of us think we ought to have some innate talent for making perfect decisions. We become frustrated and disappointed in ourselves when we don't come by decision-making naturally.

In "The Eight Decision-Making Styles" later in this chapter, you'll learn how your own approach to decision-making might be at the root of the problem. Then in "Ten Steps to Decision-Making Like a Pro," you'll learn a simple decision-making method that I bet no one has ever taught you. For now, though, let's look at four other reasons why you may be stymied by your choices:

1. You have too many choices and too much information.

2. You have too few good choices or too little time or money.

3. You make the decision harder than it needs to be.

4. You're grappling with the identity issues that decision-making raises.

As with most instances of procrastination, putting off making decisions usually results from a combination of psychological and circumstantial factors. In other words, the options you have to choose from (the circumstances) and how you deal with those options (the psychology of decision-making) can create one whopper of an indecision cocktail.

Too Many Choices and Too Much Information

Think about any purchase you might need to make: a car, a telephone, a piece of furniture, or anything at all. No matter what the item is, you probably have more products to choose from and more consumer information at your fingertips than at any time in history. You can go onto the Internet and most likely call up hundreds of thousands of references to the product in question. There are Web sites that want to sell you the product, sites that warn you about the brands not to buy, sites with objective consumer information about several of your choices, and bulletin boards or chat rooms where people are ranting and raving about the product at this very moment.

It can all be more than a little overwhelming, particularly if you're the type of person who finds that even just one issue of *Consumer Reports* contains more information than you can handle. The fact that you can get not only every back issue of that magazine online but millions of other resources as well is no doubt mind-boggling.

This abundance is also overwhelming for those other people who believe that you can't have too much information before making a decision and who enjoy the research process a little too much. They might wander off into research never-never land and not come back to make the decision they set out to make.

Not Enough Choices, Time, or Money

Sometimes tough decision-making is not a matter of too much, but too little. You might, for example, experience decisions that are difficult because you don't have enough good options to choose from. Take the case of someone who wants to go back to school, but must do so close to home due to family or work obligations. What happens if the only colleges close by aren't particularly strong in the field that person wants to study? The decision becomes one of opting for

Action Tactic

Think of at least one good decision you've made in the past. Why did it turn out so well? What can you do to repeat the same success with a decision you currently need to make?

what's second-best or third-best, rather than what's ideal. When the choices are no great shakes, the decision is not an easy one to make.

Making matters worse is the fact that so many decisions come with a deadline. If you don't choose X, Y, or Z by such-and-such a date and time, you'll miss out on the chance of a lifetime: a great bargain, your ticket to success, or some other life-changing opportunity. Sometimes, the time deadlines are just come-ons by salespeople or are self-imposed and therefore controllable. Often, however, they are all too real and put such pressure on us that we can't imagine how we'll ever wade through all the choices to get to the right one in time.

Money is an additional factor that can have an impact on decisions. If your financial resources are limited when a purchase or investment is required, then the pressure to make the best decision becomes exacerbated.

You Make Them Harder Than They Need to Be

We can't blame all of our decision-making difficulties on external factors, though. Many of us make decisions more difficult than they need to be because of the way we approach them in our minds. We agonize, analyze, deliberate, and debate until what should have been a fairly simple process becomes a torturous ordeal.

Often, perfectionism is the culprit. We feel we can't settle on one option until it is proven to be the perfect choice. Of course, rarely is there one option that's clearly head and shoulders above the others. Waiting for that ideal choice is like searching for sunken treasure. You aren't quite sure if the ideal choice is really out there somewhere, but you hope that it is, and you're willing to go out on a limb to find it. Unfortunately, going out on that limb may keep you from just making a decision with the choices you do have and getting on with your life.

Some people not only expect the perfect choice to emerge, they also think it's going to do so in some sort of dramatic way; they'll wake up one day and "see the light," as in some sort of religious experience. Or, they'll walk into the department store for the tenth time to try to buy a sofa, and finally, the blue sofa will "speak to them." They've found the buried treasure and they snatch it up quickly. Unfortunately, the decision-making process is usually much more mundane than that. You assess what you want in, let's say, a sofa. You browse around to compare prices, styles, and quality. You sit down on several to see how they feel. Then you make a logical choice based on the data you've collected. No bells, no whistles, no flashes of

You're Not Alone

Procrastinating about consumer purchases is my downfall. I'll shop till I drop before actually buying something as simple as a toaster. I'm as indecisive about clothes. And furniture? Forget it. I've been searching for the perfect sofa-bed for over a year. I know my research obsession is a perfectionist mind game I play with myself, but I just can't seem to break this pattern.

—Jeanne K., publicist

light—just a sound decision based partly on objective data and partly on gut feeling. (Or in the case of buying a sofa, how it feels to another part of your body.)

Decisions Strike at the Core of Who We Are

Action Tactic

Think of any big decisions you are currently trying to make. Ask yourself what's holding you back.

Some decisions raise difficult issues about who we are or who we'd like to be. Take the example of relocating to another city or town. Any Web site or book you might turn to on relocation will ask you to rate how important various criteria are to you so that it can tell you which locations match what you're looking for. You have to know, for example, if it's more important for you to be near good hospitals or big universities. Would you rather have cultural attractions and sophisticated nightlife or solid community centers and nice parks? The choices force you to look at what kind of life you lead or would like to lead. No wonder so many people put off finding a place to live. The process requires that you not only look outward at your geographic choices but inward as well.

The same happens with choosing a career, choosing a spouse or life partner, buying a house, or making any other major decision. You have to have a solid handle on who you are as a person before you can know whom you want to be with, what you want to do, or where you want to live.

Major League Decisions

What are the decisions that cause you trouble? Some of them belong in the major leagues; they're the ones that can have a serious impact on your life or the lives of people who depend on you. These decisions generally fall into seven categories:

➤ **Relationships/marriage:** Who to be with; whether to make the commitment; if and when to end it

➤ **Family decisions:** Decisions related to the care, education, and upbringing of children; care of aging parents or other relatives; and even care of your pets

➤ **Relocation/home:** Where to live; whether to rent or buy; how much to spend on a rental or purchase; if, when, and how to remodel, renovate, or decorate

➤ **Career decisions:** Choosing your first career direction or changing an existing one; deciding which types of jobs to seek and evaluating job offers; deciding if and when to start your own business; other issues related to developing or managing your career

➤ **Business decisions:** Any decisions that have to be made in the course of the day on the job or in your own business

Quicksand!

Don't waste your time agonizing over too many minor decisions on a day-to-day basis. As often as possible, let someone else (especially when they care more) decide which restaurant to go to, where to hang the new painting for the office lobby, or whether to buy the package with six rolls of toilet paper or eight. Keep your mind clear for the bigger, more critical decisions.

➤ **Financial decisions:** Decisions related to budgeting, spending, and saving; how much, when, and where to invest

➤ **Personal decisions:** Any decisions related to yourself, including: health choices such as which doctors to see or whether to have certain medical procedures; whether to make changes in your appearance; choices related to your spirituality such as where to worship or whether to change your religious affiliation

These major league decisions are the ones that keep us up at night when we're trying to make them and come back to haunt us if we never get around to making them at all.

Little League Decisions

Our daily lives are filled with micro-decisions, the little decisions we don't even notice we're making but that we usually have to make in order to get anything done. Should you give your child bananas or peaches for breakfast this morning? Will you wear the red tie or the yellow one? At the office, do you answer e-mails or make phone calls first? Most of these are not life-or-death decisions, but they can seem that way for people who find decision-making in general difficult.

Although these decisions may not be as significant as the major league ones, letting yourself get stressed out over too many little decisions day after day adds up to one big problem. Not only does doing so drain your mental energy (energy you need for more important matters), it also keeps your life in a constant state of disarray. By wasting too much time fretting over the small stuff, you're likely to become disorganized and fall behind on more critical tasks in the process.

The Eight Decision-Making Styles

Each of our brains is wired differently when it comes to decision-making. In order to start making better decisions or to stop putting off making them at all, you need to understand your natural decision-making style.

The styles described in this section are based loosely on personality dimensions identified by the famous Swiss psychiatrist, C.G. Jung, and popularized by the Myers-Briggs Type Indicator, a personality test administered by career and mental health counselors. As you read through the eight decision-making styles that follow (described in four pairings of opposite styles), be thinking about how each does or does not describe you.

Matter of Fact

The decision-making styles described in this chapter are based on a personality test, the Myers–Briggs Type Indicator (MBTI), administered by career and mental health counselors. If you're interested in taking the MBTI to assess your personality type, contact the Association for Psychological Type at www.aptcentral.org or call its Kansas City, Missouri headquarters at 816-444-3500. This association can tell you more about the MBTI and can refer you to a professional in your area qualified to administer and interpret it.

Loner or Pollster?

If you're a loner type, you probably try to make most decisions on your own. It's not your natural inclination to involve others, even if the ultimate decision will affect people around you, such as a spouse or co-worker. You trust your own judgment or feel that the dilemma is not something you should bother people with. If it's a business decision, you don't call a meeting to get input from colleagues. If it's a personal decision, you don't call a family meeting or e-mail all your friends. You go it alone.

Taken to an extreme, the loner position is a handicap, because the input of others is an important element of sound decision-making. On the other hand, a little bit of loner attitude is a practical approach to decision-making; after all is said and done, it's up to you and you alone to decide how you cast your vote.

If you're a pollster type, you do the opposite. You survey anybody and everybody to find out what they know about the options you're choosing among, or you ask them what they would do in your situation. Taken too far, the pollster style can mean that you secretly hope someone else will make the decision for you and will tell you what to do. Used responsibly, though, the pollster method is a good way to make an informed decision. It can also be useful for building consensus when a decision you make will affect the lives or work of others.

Forecaster or Bean-Counter?

Forecasters are, as you might have guessed, future-oriented. They tend to focus on the implications of decisions they're making. They think through where various forks in the road would lead. This visionary approach ensures that a decision you make today won't mess up your life tomorrow, because you've thought through its long-range consequences. A common pitfall of this approach, however, is that you might see the forest but lose sight of the trees; in other words, you consider the big picture but overlook critical details.

That's where the bean-counter approach becomes important. Bean-counters focus on the details and the bottom line. They gather the nitty-gritty data that's needed to make a fully informed decision. The key here is to strike a balance between the long-range view of the forecaster and the attention to detail of the bean-counter.

Analyst or Feeler?

I once saw a client in my career counseling private practice who was a 55-year-old engineering professor who had just been admitted to medical school. He was having an extremely difficult time deciding whether to embark on such a long, arduous route at that point in his life. This man was a perfect example of the analyst style of decision-making. He would come into my office with elaborate flowcharts, spreadsheets, and graphs that laid out his options and analyzed the pros and cons of each. Unfortunately, all that fancy data analysis wasn't getting him any closer to a decision. What was missing was the perspective of the feeler.

Good decisions are based on the right balance of head and heart, on analyzing objective data but also listening to what your gut instincts tell you. Feelers listen to what their values tell them is the right thing to do, and they listen to their intuition. Those aren't things that can be plotted on a chart or graph, but they are often just as valid as the analyst's data.

Hunter-Gatherer or Settler?

Do you tend to leave no stone unturned when hunting for information to help you make a decision? Do you gather so much information you can't begin to sort through it all? Or do you lose patience with the research process and become so uncomfortable about not having made a decision that you just settle on an option, even if you're not 100 percent sure it's the right one?

Action Tactic

If you've made bad choices in the past, try to identify where you took the wrong turn in your decision-making process. If you can zero in on what led you to make the wrong choice, you'll be less likely to repeat the same mistake.

As with all of these pairs of decision-making styles, striking the right balance between hunter-gatherer and settler is essential. You have to collect enough information to make an informed decision but not use the research process as an excuse to keep delaying it. You have to call an end to the debating, deliberating, and weighing of options at some point. But you shouldn't make too hasty a decision just for the sake of having one made.

What's Your Decision-Making Style?

You probably see at least a little bit of yourself in each of the eight styles I just described. You may also tend to use one approach with certain types of decisions and the opposite approach with others. For example, you might tend to go with gut feelings when it comes to personal decisions, but you've learned to be an analyzer when it comes to business decisions. Nevertheless, most everyone has a natural inclination toward one direction or the other, regardless of the type of decision or the setting in which you're making it.

Think about decisions you've made in the past or currently have to make on a regular basis. In the space next to each pairing in the following table, make a note for yourself of which style you seem to gravitate toward. If you feel completely divided between two styles, then write both in the space that follows that pair.

Loner or Pollster?	
Forecaster or Bean-Counter?	
Analyst or Feeler?	
Hunter-Gatherer or Settler?	

Keep your decision-making styles in mind as you read through the following 10 steps to decision-making. You'll need to pay more or less attention to the various steps depending on your natural tendencies.

Ten Steps to Decision-Making Like a Pro

An easy way to master the art of decision-making is to follow the simple, 10-step process described in the following sections each time you have a difficult choice to make.

Step 1: Assess the importance of the decision.

Is this a major or minor league decision you're facing? If it's minor, ask yourself how much of your time and mental energy it deserves. If the matter is fairly trivial, then you should probably just do something and not worry too much about exactly what it is you're doing. Or maybe you can delegate the decision-making to someone else. If it is important, then you need to pay close attention to the steps that follow.

Step 2: Assess your readiness to make a decision.

Sometimes, decisions are difficult to make because it's not the right time to be making them. If you have too much going on in your life in the way of major projects, commitments, and stressors, then you might not have the time and energy to devote to making a good decision. Or if you're in the midst of some sort of transition, or if people and places around you are in transition (as often happens with employers you work for, for example), then you may need to wait until things settle down before you can make any major decisions.

Quicksand!

All the best decision-making strategies in the world are useless if you don't set aside enough time to make the strategies work. You have to schedule times to conduct research and times to sit back and think about your choices, just as you would schedule an appointment or meeting.

Step 3: Define your priorities.

As with the relocation example given earlier in this chapter, most major decisions require that you define some criteria on which to base the decision. Let's say someone is trying to decide between two communities that offer nearly equal features in terms of quality of life and cost of living, but one gets more snow, and the other has better professional sports teams. That person has to know whether climate is more important to him or her than being a sports fan before making a choice between the two locations.

If you run a small business and need to decide whether to take on a partner, then you need to have your long-term business and personal goals in mind before you can decide if partnership is a good idea. All sorts of decisions require that we know where we want to end up in the long run before we can feel comfortable deciding what to do today.

Step 4: Listen to your gut.

Before assessing your options in a logical, methodical way, it helps to start by listening to what your gut instincts tell you. (Or listen to your heart, your spirit, or whatever you personally choose to have guide you.) Sometimes, people embark on a long, involved research process to make a decision only to find that their first instinct had already given them the answer they were looking for. It's usually unwise to base a decision entirely on something as subjective and intangible as a gut feeling, but that's a good place to get your first read on the direction you may be headed toward.

Step 5: Gather data.

Most good decisions are based on information. You need to talk to people, read about your choices, or do whatever kind of research makes sense for the type of decision you're trying to make. Collect enough data to know what each option entails and how each would affect you and your loved ones personally and professionally.

Step 6: Revisit your criteria.

After gathering some information on your options, you might find that your priorities shift a bit. Something you thought was extremely important to you may seem less important now that you know more about the realities of your choices. At this point, it's helpful to go back to Step 3 and reevaluate how critical each of your priorities actually is.

Step 7: Analyze the data.

Most people get out the old pad of paper and a pen to make a list of the pros and cons for each option they're considering. And most people end up still unable to make a choice. The problem is that they're often comparing apples and oranges. The best few options out of the bunch usually end up having about the same balance of pros and cons. If they didn't, then you probably wouldn't be faced with a tough choice in the first place; one option would clearly emerge as the best.

Action Tactic

No matter what kind of decision you're trying to make, ranking your decision-making criteria in order of importance is the key to making the tough choices.

The way to get around the apples and oranges dilemma is to go back to the priorities you identified in Step 3 and that you revisited in Step 6. If you know what's most important to you in the area of your life that a particular decision will affect, then you should be able to define some criteria on which to base your decision.

If you're trying to decide between two computers to buy, for example, your top two criteria might be expandability and lowest price for best quality. Out of all your choices, you narrow the options to two computers. One has a very low price and good reputation, but it might not have the capability to grow with your business or other computing needs. The other one can be expanded, but it will hit you harder in the wallet. Do you go with the one that will save you money now but may cost more in the long run because you'll outgrow it? Or do you shell out the bigger bucks now and save money in the long run? The only way to make the choice is to know what your priority is. Is your priority to make an investment in your future or is it to get the best equipment you can find now on a limited budget?

Step 8: Listen to your gut—again.

Enough with being rational, logical, and methodical; now you need to put aside all that objective data for a moment and listen to what your heart and your gut are telling you to do. Are they still saying the same thing they said before you collected information in Step 5? Or has your instinct changed its tune now that you're better informed about your options?

I'm not saying that you should completely forget about the research you've done and make an impulsive, emotional decision. A good decision is based on both objective and subjective information. At this point in the process, you need to take the tentative decision you've made based on the data analysis in Step 7 and see how that decision sits with you. What looks like the right choice on paper and makes sense in your head may not feel right in your heart.

Step 9: Deal with any roadblocks standing in your way.

If you've tried to balance the objective analysis with the subjective approach and are still stuck, try to figure out what's holding you back. When you find yourself unable to make a decision, ask the following questions:

➤ Could I benefit from more outside input?

➤ Have I done enough research?

➤ Do I need to force myself to stop researching and start deciding?

➤ Am I trusting my instincts and judgment enough?

➤ Am I keeping my priorities and goals in mind?

➤ Is fear of making the wrong decision holding me back? Is that fear justified?

➤ Am I delaying this decision because I'm concerned about what I'll have to do after I make it?

If you demand honest answers from yourself to all of these questions, you'll zero in on the root of your paralysis, and you'll be able to get past the roadblocks. If you still can't get around the roadblocks on your own, consider working with a coach, career counselor, or psychotherapist for an objective and supportive perspective on the situation.

Step 10: Take the plunge.

At some point, you have to do one simple thing: Decide already! Keep in mind what I said earlier about how most decisions come without bells, whistles, and light bulbs over the head. You might find this tenth step to be somewhat anticlimactic. Don't let that deter you. If you've carefully progressed through the previous nine steps, then you're in a good position to make a sound decision. Go ahead and do it!

Don't Sweat It

Very few decisions in life are totally irreversible. It might be inconvenient, expensive, and even a little embarrassing to admit that you made the wrong choice and need to go back to square one or plan B, but doing so is almost always an option. If you find yourself putting too much pressure on any decision you make, keep in mind that having freedom of choice is supposed to be a good thing; it should not be something that causes undue stress.

The Least You Need to Know

➤ When you delay making decisions, you put your life on hold and miss out on opportunities that might not come around again.

➤ Decision-making is a skill that can be learned.

➤ We often make decisions more difficult than they need to be because we expect the perfect choice to materialize before us.

➤ Avoid spending too much time on minor decisions that someone else could handle for you or that don't warrant much of your mental energy.

➤ Good decisions are based on a combination of rational analysis of the choices and listening to your gut instincts.

➤ When you're faced with difficult decisions, follow the simple 10-step method described in this chapter.

Chapter 12

The Secret Formula to Overcoming Procrastination

In This Chapter

➤ Three simple steps that stop procrastination in its tracks

➤ The Stop, Look, and Listen formula

➤ Ten techniques for getting anything done

When you were a child, your parents or teachers might have taught you to cross the street safely by warning you to do three things: Stop, look, and listen. That same advice works when you feel a bout of procrastination coming on. In this chapter, we'll look at why you're going to stop, as well as what you need to look and listen for. After you've pushed the impulse to procrastinate aside with the Stop, Look, and Listen formula, you'll need to take action. The second half of this chapter describes 10 sure-fire techniques to get you moving on any kind of task or goal, whether it's washing your car or finally making a career change.

If you read only one chapter of this book (though I hope you'll read more), this is the one to read. This chapter is where I give the secret formula that turns delayers into doers. So strike up the band, send in the clowns, and let's get to it.

Stop

It's a lazy Saturday afternoon, and you've gone into the kitchen to make a sandwich. After you finish, you leave the open bag of bread, a messy mustard knife, and lots of crumbs on the counter and head back to the television or wherever it is that you're

Action Tactic

Imagine you're watching a video-tape of yourself and you push the pause button. Picture yourself on the screen, frozen in time. That's what I want you to do in real life. Every time you're walking away from your desk to avoid doing work, slinking out of a room that needs cleaning, or avoiding any other task, push an imaginary pause button and freeze your movement.

going to enjoy your sandwich and not think about the mess you've just made. Somewhere in that process, the fleeting thought "I'll clean it up later" probably runs through your mind.

Leaving a few crumbs and a knife that will get crusty is probably not going to wreck your life, but it may be just one example of many instances of procrastination that do start to take their toll on your quality of life and that of the people around you. To break the pattern of putting things off until some vague future time, the first thing to do is to pause. Stop to think about what you're doing and try to figure out why you're doing it.

When you say, "Stop!" you do several important things:

➤ You are no longer acting on impulse, but you instead become conscious of your behavior.

➤ You gain power over procrastination instead of letting it be some insidious force that sneaks up on you.

➤ You give yourself the chance to think about the consequences of delaying the task you're about to put off.

➤ You give yourself the chance to get angry or fed up over your procrastination habit, and these emotions may inspire you to do something about it.

If you end up still deciding to put off the task, it's okay as long as that decision is based on pausing to think about what you're doing. You might decide, for example, that Saturday afternoons are meant for relaxing and that there's nothing wrong with waiting until later to clean up the kitchen. That's fine, just so long as you've stopped to think about what you're doing and aren't merely acting on impulse.

Look

When you've called a halt to that first impulse to procrastinate, the next step is to look around for the reasons you're tempted to put something off. You're basically looking for five types of problems, much like those described in Chapter 3, "Blame It on the Environment":

➤ Is clutter getting in your way?

➤ Is something distracting you?

➤ Is someone distracting you?

➤ Are you uncomfortable?

➤ Do you not have enough information to get the task done?

After you've pushed the pause button on that imaginary video of yourself, imagine you're examining what you see on the screen as though you were looking for a movie prop that was out of place or something else you couldn't catch when the video was playing. Do the same in real life. Literally look around for distractions or missing information that's keeping you from taking action.

When you've identified what's getting in your way, think about what you can do to remove the roadblocks. Take some time to clear out and organize the clutter, remove the distractions, get comfortable, or find the information and guidance you need.

You're Not Alone

My sister and I once won a free pair of snow skis. We couldn't decide which length would be better for us in terms of our level of experience and the amount we ski. It's now been two years, and my sister still hasn't called to claim the skis. I imagine it's now too late to get them.

—Rebecca R., graduate student

Listen

The next step is to listen to what's going on in your head. As you may have read in Chapter 4, "It's All In Your Head," your thoughts, feelings, and internal messages (self-talk) drive your actions. Those games your mind plays that give you the excuse to put off something is the psychology of procrastination. To put an end to those games, ask yourself these three questions and listen closely to the answers.

1. **What am I feeling?** Am I giving in to fear or feelings of inadequacy about the task that lies before me? Am I feeling overwhelmed when it's not necessary to feel that way? Am I feeling pressured to get this done by a certain time or in a certain way? Am I bored or tired?

2. **What am I thinking?** Are my thoughts irrational, unreasonable, inaccurate, or self-sabotaging? Am I assuming this task is going to be more difficult or unpleasant than it is likely to be? Am I believing that I don't have enough time to do this? Is that true? Am I convincing myself that X has to happen before I can do Y? Am I justified in waiting for X?

3. **What am I saying to myself (or out loud to others)?** Are negative or unproductive statements running through my mind? Am I giving myself permission to put this off or making excuses? Am I saying things that I haven't even been conscious of and that are powerful barriers to action? For example, am I saying things such as: I don't have to do this now; I'll do that later; I'm just not the sort of person who does that?

Matter of Fact

It's not realistic to expect yourself to remember, much less use, the strategies and formulas discussed here long after you've finished reading this book and put it aside. To make it easier to put them into practice, be sure to tear out the Complete Idiot's Reference Card from the front of this book and keep it over your desk, in your briefcase or appointment book, or wherever you can easily refer to it. The tips listed on it are based on the ones described in this chapter.

By asking these questions, you break down your internal barriers to action. You stop functioning on autopilot and start becoming conscious of the thoughts, feelings, and self-talk behind your acts of procrastination. Later in this chapter, in "Strategy #7: Use Positive Self-Talk," you'll learn techniques for replacing these paralyzing thoughts, feelings, and statements with more positive ones.

The Stop, Look, and Listen Formula in Action

To make sure that the Stop, Look, and Listen formula works, I've been field-testing it in my own life for a few years now. I'm happy to report that it works like a charm. It's what gets me through writer's block, keeps me from putting off household chores (well, most of them), and enables me to make it to the gym a few times a week. But of all the things I've accomplished thanks to this formula, it's not the six published books, the organized house, or the major weight loss I recently achieved that I'm most proud of. It's the fact that I no longer procrastinate about refilling the water jug and putting it back in the refrigerator.

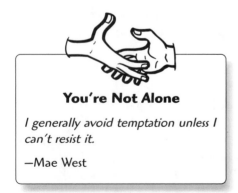

You're Not Alone

I generally avoid temptation unless I can't resist it.

—Mae West

Yes, that simple task used to be my most irritating procrastination habit, to me and to others. It's been a problem since childhood. My parents used to complain that I would drain our water pitcher of its last drop, then leave it on the kitchen counter for someone else to deal with. My father still uses that same old blue plastic water pitcher, and when I visit him, I sometimes catch myself wanting to do the same thing.

In my own home, we keep water in a clear plastic jug with a screw-on cap that flips open for pouring. It's not exactly a complex piece of equipment to operate, so my husband always found it mind-boggling that I seemed incapable of refilling that jug. I'd even clean the entire kitchen but leave the empty water jug sitting out on the counter. I had no good explanation for why I did that. I just did it. Making matters worse was the fact that I've always consumed vast amounts of water, so I was usually the one who emptied the jug.

One day, I was about to walk out of the kitchen, leaving the empty water jug sitting on the counter, when I decided to tackle the problem. I stopped, walked back over to the counter, and stared down the empty jug as if I were in some sort of stand-off in the Old West. Then I looked around for barriers that might be in my way, but I couldn't find any. The cap screws off easily. The jug fits well under the faucet. We have running water in the kitchen sink. I am able to lift a gallon of liquid. There's no padlock on the refrigerator door. No excuses there.

Then I listened to what I was saying to myself during those split seconds when I would choose to put off the task. I discovered that I was saying things like: I really hate doing this. It's such a hassle. I don't have to do this now. I'll do it later. I just don't do that sort of thing. Ah ha! I found the source of the problem. Irrational, irresponsible, meaningless self-talk had led me to develop this habit.

What I did to break the cycle was to think about the benefits of filling the jug with water and refrigerating it. I thought about how nice it is when I want a glass of water and find a full, cold jug of it in the fridge and how annoying it is to find an empty one. I thought about how healthy it is to drink water and about the fact that on days when I don't refill the jug, I don't drink as much because I don't want to drink tepid tap water. I also thought about how silly it is to procrastinate over something as easy, quick, and minor as refilling a container of water and opening the refrigerator door.

It worked. Now when I pour the last drop of water, I refill the container immediately and put it in the fridge. My husband's happier, I'm happier, and we're both maybe even a little healthier.

Ten Sure-Fire Strategies for Getting Anything Done

The Stop, Look, and Listen formula squashes the impulse to procrastinate and forces you to deal head-on with the reasons why you're about to put off something. What it doesn't do, however, is get the thing done. That's where the 10 strategies that follow come in. Think of them as a bag of tricks you can pull from when you find yourself about to put off starting something or not finishing what you've started.

The 10 strategies don't have to be used in the order in which they're listed here. This is not a

Quicksand!

The 10 strategies are described here only briefly. To get a more complete picture of how you can use them in various, specific situations, be sure to read the chapters in Part 3, "Tips and Tricks for Getting Things Done" and in Part 4, "Getting Things Done at Work and School."

10-step process in which you have to do Strategy #1, then #2, and so on. Instead, use whichever one works for the situation you find yourself in. If you're facing a tough procrastination situation, you might have to try several strategies before you get to the one that motivates you to take action. The idea is to pick and choose until you get to the one that works for you.

Strategy #1: Get fired up.

This strategy involves doing a reality check. Depending on the situation, that might mean getting real fed up with yourself, real embarrassed by your behavior, or real angry that other people are leaving you in their dust while you procrastinate. Getting fired up means reaching the end of your rope, hitting bottom, or getting your competitive juices stirring.

Procrastinators often float through life in a state of denial, believing that there's not much harm in what they're doing (or not doing). Or even worse, they don't think about their behavior at all, much less whether it's doing any harm. The idea behind this strategy is that it's not just a reality check: It's a wake-up call. By getting fired up, you think through the potential negative consequences that can result from putting off something or that have resulted in the past when you procrastinated about something comparable. The emotions that result when you get fired up can spark some powerful action.

Action Tactic

Designate one day a week, one day a month, or whatever works for your schedule as a Stop-the-World-I-Wanna-Get-Off day. On this day, you don't have to take care of any of your usual chores or responsibilities. You use the entire day to catch up on busy work or a time-consuming project, get reorganized, or in some other way regroup and reconnect.

Strategy #2: Get organized.

As you already know from Chapter 8, "Lightening Your Load," Chapter 9, "Getting Your Act Together," and Chapter 10, "A Crash Course in Getting Organized," getting rid of clutter and unnecessary obligations and becoming organized are important foundations to productivity. They were presented as ways of cleaning out your life to clear the way for taking action, sort of prerequisites for becoming an ex-procrastinator. Now you can use those same strategies when you're right on the brink of procrastinating.

If you're in the middle of a project and find yourself losing steam, look around to see if clutter has accumulated since you first began. If so, is it making you feel unmotivated to do any more or making your job harder than it ought to be? If you haven't even started on something yet, the same principle applies. If you're faced with clutter and chaos or a life that's on overload, you're going to be reluctant to tackle the task that lies within the mess. Taking a little time to get organized clears the way for being productive.

Strategy #3: Prioritize.

You can't get things done unless you make it a priority to do them. I realize that sounds so obvious that it hardly seems worth mentioning, but most people don't prioritize effectively, so it needs to be said. It's so easy to go through your daily life in your usual routine saying, "I wish I could get X done because it's a priority to me, but I just can't seem to find the time for it." Or even worse, you might say, "I wish I could get X done, but it just isn't happening." Things don't just happen by themselves, and if you read Chapter 5, "It's About Time," you know that a few extra hours per day aren't going to miraculously appear. You have to rearrange the way you're choosing to spend the 24 hours a day that you are given.

If there are some major things you'd like to accomplish in your life, such as making a career change, improving a relationship, losing weight or getting physically fit, starting a business, or anything else that takes time and commitment, then you have to declare that it is a priority for you. That may mean you'll have to make some tough trade-offs in how you spend your time, and it may mean that you have to put some other so-called priorities on the back burner for a while. But doing so will be worth it in the long run.

Quicksand!

Be careful about how you prioritize. Merely saying that something is important to you is not enough. It doesn't become a priority until you rearrange your schedule, reevaluate all your commitments, rally support, and do any other preparation necessary to devote time, energy, and resources to it. Thoughts don't make something a priority; actions do.

Strategy #4: Find freedom in routine.

As I discussed in Chapters 9 and 10, a routine, which is a schedule that determines the days and/or times when you'll do recurring tasks and chores, is anything but constricting. First of all, you can vary your routine as the need arises or when you don't feel like doing something at its designated time. You control your routine; it doesn't control you.

Second, a routine is liberating in that it keeps you from worrying about what you should be,

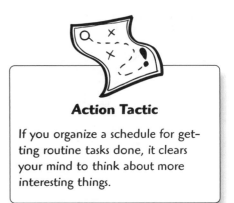

Action Tactic

If you organize a schedule for getting routine tasks done, it clears your mind to think about more interesting things.

ought to be, or could be doing. Some people shun the idea of a routine because they think it will make their life dull and not give them the freedom to be spontaneous or creative. The irony is that the things you need to schedule into a weekly routine are usually pretty dull in the first place, so you're not missing out on anything by working them into a routine. When you designate days and/or times to do these mundane tasks, you don't have to worry about them the rest of the time.

Strategy #5: Get comfortable.

One of the simplest ways to get motivated to do something is to get more comfortable. When I'm in the middle of writing a chapter or an article and find myself stuck, unable to write any more, the technique that often works is to print out what I've written so far, get out of my not-so-comfortable desk chair, and curl up on the sofa in another room with my printout, a pen, and a pad of paper. I find that getting my hands off the keyboard, changing my position, and getting a fresh perspective on my writing from the hard copy rather than the screen does wonders for getting past writer's block. (Yes, it is possible to move to the couch without falling asleep.)

Strategy #6: Get connected to people and information.

Isolation is the kiss of death to action. You have to reach out to people and to sources of information to find the guidance, new ideas, support, and companionship that enable you to stop stalling and get moving. I don't mean that you're going to do your best work on a crowded city bus or in the middle of an amusement park. Working alone or in a quiet environment is a great way to get things done. What I do mean is that there's a difference between working independently and being isolated.

The danger in isolation is that you become disconnected from people and from information that could help you do your work better, faster, or more easily. You can easily become a hermit if you do your job from home, do housework alone, or try to tackle any personal, self-improvement issues on your own. Even if you work in a large company, it's easy to close that office door (or hole up in your cubicle) and disconnect yourself from the people around you.

Quicksand!

Beware of losing touch with people and ideas when you're trying to get things done. Isolation only encourages procrastination.

Letting yourself become isolated and disconnected encourages procrastination. But when you reach out and connect with people, you can prevent procrastination in several ways:

➤ Delegate the task to someone else so that you don't have to do it at all.

➤ Delegate part of a task or project to someone else. In other words, follow the old saying, "Many hands make light work."

➤ Admit to someone that you're having a problem getting something done. Not only might that person have some helpful advice for how you can get it done, the mere confession that you're struggling also can work wonders.

➤ Have someone talk you through the steps involved in what it is you need to do. Or have someone listen while you talk yourself through them. This technique is especially helpful if you're in the middle of a complex project or working slowly toward a major goal and lose sight of what you want to, or need to, be doing next.

➤ Consult and confer with people in a position to advise you or offer solid strategy. They might be some of the professionals described in Chapter 7, "Rallying Support from the Pros," or anyone else who knows something about what it is you're trying to do.

➤ Ask for handholding. You might benefit from simply having another warm body keep you company and cheer you on while you clean out your closet, go through your files, or do whatever it is that you find to be a lonely or boring task.

As you can see from those examples, getting connected can mean anything from emotional support as you trudge through a chore to having someone else do the task. It might also mean connecting with people who can serve primarily as sources of information and advice. Use whichever method of connection works for you and the task you're facing.

Strategy #7: Use positive self-talk.

As I've discussed in previous chapters, the messages that play in your head have a great deal of power over your behavior. When you give in to negative emotions, irrational thoughts, and destructive self-talk, you open the floodgates to procrastination. An important strategy that works for just about every procrastination situation is to play more positive messages in your head.

You start by substituting positive thoughts for negative ones, then you learn to speak a new internal language to make your self-talk more likely to lead to action. I like to think of it as having my self-talk play on compact disc instead of cassette tape. CDs are clearer, sharper, and easier to use than cassettes.

Self-talk on cassette tapes	*Self-talk on CDs*
I don't think I can do that.	I know it seems difficult now, but I can get it done.
I can't get that done on time.	If I make this a priority, I can get it done on time.
I'm not the kind of person who does X.	I used to be a procrastinator, but now I'm the type of person who gets X done.
I'm afraid I won't do this well enough.	It doesn't have to be perfect; it just has to get done.

I should do that.	Do I really have to do that? If not, I don't need to feel guilty for not doing it.
I can't see myself doing that.	I can visualize myself starting and finishing it as if I were watching myself on videotape.
I would do that, but …	I will do that because …

Those are several of the most common examples of negative self-talk. If yours have a slightly different ring to them, you can still convert them into more positive sounds, like those in the Self-talk on CDs column. The key is to eliminate the negative language, words such as *not, afraid,* and *but,* and also to be creative in thinking about the flip side of the negative thought behind that language.

Strategy #8: Focus on do dates, not due dates.

In a way, deadlines are meaningless. The date that something is due is simply the date that you turn it in, hand it over, mail it, or stop working on it. Whether it's a deadline at work, a deadline to apply for something, or a deadline you've set for yourself, that deadline or due date has almost nothing to do with action.

A major reason why people put off things and end up racing to meet a deadline is that they focus too much on the due date and not enough on do dates. Do dates are the specific days or times when you schedule and plan to complete certain tasks. Do dates are where the action is.

Matter of Fact

According to *Why Do We Say That?* by Graham Donaldson and Sue Setterfield, the word *deadline* originated during the Civil War in a crowded prisoner-of-war camp in Andersonville, Georgia. There was a line drawn in the dirt around a wire fence that surrounded the camp. If a prisoner crossed the line, he was shot dead on the spot with no warning. Thus, we have the term *deadline*, which still causes as much anxiety today as it did then, even when the circumstances aren't life-or-death!

Many experts in productivity and project management suggest setting mini-deadlines that come before the final deadline. The mini-deadlines give you something more manageable and less remote to work toward. This system is still not enough for a true procrastinator, though. You just end up with more deadlines to race toward or miss. Although there's no harm in using the mini-deadline system, it won't work unless you also schedule do dates that will lead you to those deadlines.

Scheduling the things that you put on your to-do lists was dealt with in Chapter 10. That's what this strategy is all about. Take an inventory of the things you need to do or the deadlines you're facing and schedule specific times or days when you'll do them. That way, the emphasis is on do dates, not due dates.

Strategy #9: Use the chip-away technique.

The chip-away strategy involves tackling big projects or working toward major goals by chipping away at them with little bits of action here and there. If your goal is to get in better physical shape, you might find five minutes to do some exercises at your desk when you can't drag yourself out for an hour at the gym. If you're trying to write a term paper for school but can't seem to get started, you could take two minutes to skim through a relevant article while you're waiting for class to start. Some ideas in that article might inspire you to get cracking on the paper. If you've been putting off weeding the garden and find yourself standing in the driveway waiting for your spouse or the kids to come out to the car, you could use that time to pull up just a few weeds from the front path.

Even though it is extremely important to schedule times when you'll do routine tasks or take steps in major projects, it's just as important that you be on the lookout for unexpected windows of opportunity. Using this hidden time, time when you aren't necessarily scheduled to work on a particular task, is a great way to chip away at that task. Doing so helps you get things done little by little without even realizing that you're working on them. It's quick and painless.

The chip-away technique doesn't require major advance planning. All you need to do is spot a small window of opportunity and ask yourself if there's one little thing you could be doing during that time. This strategy is what enables me to keep my house tidy most of the time. (Although I'm certain that the day Publisher's

Action Tactic

For more ideas on how to chip away at your goals and projects, refer to *Stop Screaming at the Microwave: How to Connect Your Disconnected Life*, in which Mary LoVerde describes a concept similar to the chip-away technique, which she calls "microactions."

Clearinghouse shows up at my door with cameras rolling to award me my million-dollar prize, the house will be a mess, and I'll be in a ratty bathrobe.) Every time I walk from one room to another, I pick up one item that doesn't belong in that room and take it where it belongs (or at least one room closer to where it belongs). By the end of the day, there's not a huge task of tidying up waiting for me because I've chipped away at it throughout the day. You can read more about this and other examples of the chip-away technique in the chapters in Part 3.

Strategy #10: Play trick-or-treat.

Just as the procrastination habit can sneak up on you, you can sneak up on it with tricks and treats that motivate you to take action:

➤ **Distract yourself.** You might feel that in order to get things done, you have to turn off the television, radio, or phone, shut down the video games, stay away from the shopping mall, keep your chatty friends and co-workers at bay, or avoid any other so-called time waster or distraction that limits your productivity. The fact is, though, when you deprive yourself of something you enjoy or put yourself in an artificially sterile environment, you are often less productive.

I'm not saying you should try to write your Great American Novel while engrossed in an action-suspense thriller on television, but putting a small television in the kitchen might make you more likely to scrub those pots and pans or even to cook. The idea is to look for ways to combine doing what you enjoy with doing what you don't necessarily like to do but need to do.

➤ **Dangle a carrot.** There's nothing like the promise of a reward for a job well-done to get you motivated. Delayed gratification doesn't work for everybody, but looking forward to a treat you've promised yourself is a handy technique to try. Plus, it helps ensure that you're keeping some balance of work and fun in your life.

➤ **Beat the clock.** Pretend that you have a limited period of time in which to get something done and see how fast you can do it. Suppose you're trying to clean out the garage. You estimate that you have about three hours of work left to do, but you don't feel like working for three more minutes, much less three more hours. Pretend that you have only one hour left before someone will be coming over to see the finished product. Play a game of seeing how much you can finish in that hour. You might be surprised to find that you get three hours' worth of work done in an hour because of the imaginary time limit. But even if you don't, you've at least done more than if you had given up altogether.

➤ **Pretend you're about to go on vacation.** You may know the feeling of going on vacation from a full-time job or a business you run. In the last few days, or even the last few hours, before that vacation, you probably get more work done than in a typical week or month on the job. The necessity of getting projects wrapped up or loose ends taken care of provides an adrenaline rush that propels your action into warp speed. (Plus, it helps to know that there's a light at the end of the tunnel in the form of white, sandy beaches or wherever it is that you're headed.)

You may not be able to go on an actual vacation, but you can play a trick on yourself based on that pre-vacation productivity boost. Imagine you're about to leave on a long trip and have to get certain things done by then. The game may encourage you to take stock of what you've fallen behind on and get it done or to move forward with something you've been putting off starting.

➤ **Just do something.** I'm no physicist, but I believe physicists when they say that an object at rest will remain at rest until some force propels it into motion. It's a handy principle to keep in mind when trying to get yourself to do something. Sometimes nothing works better than to take one little baby step toward a particular task. You'll more than likely find that the first step propels you into motion and leads to more steps. If you wash one dish, you'll probably end up washing the whole sinkful. If you write one thank-you note, you'll probably go ahead and thank everyone on your list. Even if you don't, you'll be one step closer than where you were.

The act of procrastinating involves all sorts of mind games we play on ourselves. By playing trick-or-treat, we can turn those mind games to our advantage.

Matter of Fact

The "just do something" strategy and the chip-away technique may sound like the same thing, but they're not. The chip-away technique is based on making use of down time or hidden time to do anything at all related to a bigger task, even if what you do is not necessarily the first step. The "just do something" strategy is all about taking the first step toward a task in the hope that that step will immediately lead you into the next step. It's a subtle difference, but a difference nevertheless.

See? It's Not So Hard!

If you feel an invasion of the procrastination body-snatchers headed toward you, you now know what to do. First, you stop, look, and listen to break the pattern of acting on impulse and to figure out what's keeping you from taking action. Then, you choose from the 10 strategies for getting things done until you find the one that works for you and for the situation you're stuck in.

The Least You Need to Know

➤ When you feel yourself starting to put off something, use the secret formula for halting procrastination in its tracks: Stop, Look, and Listen.

➤ Procrastination is a habit based on impulsive action, so stopping, or pausing, to think about what you're doing and the consequences of delaying is the first step toward breaking the habit.

➤ When you're tempted to put off something, look around you to see what's tripping you up, such as distractions or clutter in your environment or something that's making you uncomfortable.

➤ Listening to your thoughts, feelings, and self-talk is critical for understanding why you're about to start procrastinating.

➤ When you just can't seem to get yourself to take action, refer to the list of 10 strategies to get moving and pick the ones that work for you and for the type of task you're putting off.

Part 3

Tips and Tricks for Getting Things Done

In Part 2, you laid the foundation for becoming an ex-procrastinator and learned basic principles for getting things done in most any situation. In Part 3, I focus on more nitty-gritty techniques for specific chores, tasks, and projects you need to tackle, whether it's washing that sinkful of dishes or making an overdue doctor's appointment.

You'll find tips for managing your household, your career and job, and your health or other self-improvement issues. You'll explore ways to make some changes in your family or social life, improve or solidify relationships, keep in touch with people, and make the holidays fun, rather than a chore. You'll also find out how to get past writer's block and any other blocks you might have and move forward with the big stuff in life: your finances, safety, and the fact of your mortality.

Chapter 13

Kitchen

Dirty Dishes and Other Household Chores

In This Chapter

➤ Why you hate housework

➤ Effortless tidying and cleaning—well, almost

➤ Laundry, trash, and other drudgery

➤ Tool time

➤ Yucky yard work

Have you ever come across those people who enjoy household chores? The ones who find it relaxing to iron clothes or invigorating to vacuum and who consider weeding the garden a Zen-like experience? If you're reading this chapter, you're probably not part of that rare breed. Don't worry; I'm not going to try to sell you on the joys of housework. (I haven't bought into that concept myself.) I merely want to help you understand why you put off projects around the house and offer you tips for getting them taken care of relatively painlessly. Because let's face it: They have to get done somehow by somebody, and lots of times the only somebody is you.

Neatniks, Clean Freaks, and Slobs

Do you align the edges of magazines on the coffee table while ignoring the tumble-weeds of dust under the table? Do you neatly put away dishes and clear off counter-tops in the kitchen every night but never mop the floor until your feet stick to it like

You're Not Alone

You know things are bad when you've got five minutes before company arrives and have to make decisions like, "Do I put on my makeup and get dressed, or do I vacuum?" Makeup and clothes always win hands-down, and the dust gets swept under the couch.

—Barbara W., business manager

mice to glue traps? If so, you're like me: a neatnik who can go a year without vacuuming (I'm satisfied just to pick up the big pieces of debris by hand), but who can't stand to see sofa cushions that need fluffing and throw pillows that are out of kilter.

Or maybe you're like my husband. I tell him that company is coming over in 20 minutes and ask him to help me tidy up the house. He says, "Don't you worry about it. I'll take care of it." Nineteen minutes later, I find that he's taken apart the toaster to render it impeccably crumb-free, scrubbed the bathtub (which our guests won't even see, much less be using), and vacuumed every nook and cranny of the carpets and floorboards. If he'd had an hour before guests were to arrive, he would also have rewired a lamp or two and repotted some houseplants.

What he doesn't do during those critical minutes is pick up and put away the toys, clothes, papers, magazines, books, and other assorted items strewn across every surface of the house. I end up spending a frantic final minute clearing a path from the front door to the couch for our guests. He means well, but his efforts are misguided because there's only enough time for some superficial straightening and maybe a little dusting. But he can't help it; he's a clean freak, through and through.

Then, of course, there are those poor souls who don't care much for either tidying up or cleaning up. Those of us who fall in one of the other two categories think of them as slobs. Chances are they aren't slobs by nature, and they don't enjoy living in squalor; they just can't seem to find the time or energy to maintain their households. They procrastinate.

Whichever label rings a bell: neatnik, clean freak, or slob, or a little of each, this chapter has something for you. You'll learn why you procrastinate doing household chores (including ones outside the home, such as keeping your car, yard, and garage clean or well-maintained). You'll also find tips for getting past the mental and physical barriers keeping you from doing household chores.

Why We Put Off Household Chores

The roots of procrastination on the home front are pretty obvious. Household chores are boring, messy, and sometimes strenuous. Often, we avoid doing them simply because we have no interest in them. Or we feel too tired after work, school, or parenting to get down on our hands and knees and scrub the bathtub or lug heavy bags of trash out the door. However, three additional factors that are involved in putting off household chores may not be so obvious:

1. You don't have the right cleaning supplies or equipment; you have too many cleaning supplies, or the ones you have are not easily accessible.

2. There are too many other demands on your time, so housework gets relegated to the bottom of your priority list.

3. Your family, friends, or roommates have unrealistic standards for how you should maintain your home. Or you feel pressured by the standards of society-at-large for housekeeping (made worse by the glistening kitchen floors and toilet bowls in cleaning product advertisements). You feel like you can't live up to everyone's demands, so you waste your time worrying instead of doing.

Action Tactic

If your excuse for not cleaning or making home repairs is that you don't know how, or don't have the time, visit the very helpful Web site Tipz Time (www.tipztime.com). It has hundreds of tips for more efficient and effective cleaning and household maintenance.

Recognizing the role that these factors play in household procrastination can get you three steps closer to getting your chores done. You may not ever come to love doing housework (or yard work or washing the car), but you can use some simple techniques to solve these supply and demand problems and stop putting off tasks at home.

A 1999 survey by *Better Homes and Gardens* magazine asked readers to rank their dream amenities from a choice of 27 household problem-solving devices. Most of these gadgets exist only in our imaginations (or in the SkyPad Apartments where the Jetsons reside); others, such as no-stain countertops and self-vacuuming baseboards, are already heaven on earth in some well-equipped homes. The top ten choices, in order, were self-cleaning windows; never-paint house trim; a built-in, automatic bug zapper for yard and windows; self-cleaning fixtures; self-clearing driveways and sidewalks; no-stain countertops; cordless lamps; tile that feels warm in winter, cool in summer; a remote control module for all household lighting, electronics, locks, thermostat, and alarms; and fireplaces with self-cleaning glass doors. Until such dream amenities as self-cleaning windows and self-clearing driveways materialize, you'll have to face up to the fact that you have to take rag, rake, or shovel in hand and do it yourself.

Home Economics 101

If you think you're doomed to a life of grungy stovetops, crunchy carpets, messy closets, and uncut grass, don't despair. No matter what the chore is, there are easy steps you can take to get it done. The remainder of this chapter looks at specific techniques

Quicksand!

Don't assume that these techniques work only for cleaning and straightening. You can also use them to get past your blocks against doing yard work, making home repairs, and completing other home-related chores.

you can use to complete chores you've been putting off. Six of the 10 techniques from Chapter 12, "The Secret Formula to Overcoming Procrastination," are especially useful for just about any kind of household chore, so they're repeated here:

➤ **Organize.** Cleaning, tidying up, and maintenance are easier when the spaces you're working on, or working in, are uncluttered and have a place for everything and when the supplies or tools you need are organized and within easy reach.

➤ **Have a routine.** Putting regular and seasonal chores on your monthly calendars and daily planners will help you get things done without having to live in a constant state of worry. Having a routine for when you do household chores is the key to getting past the "I don't feel like it" excuses.

➤ **Connect with people and information.** Delegate chores to family members or roommates, hire someone to do them, or even just have someone keep you company while you do the chores. Connect with the information you need on how to get things done so that you can't use lack of knowledge as an excuse. Books, Web sites, and TV shows are filled with household tips.

➤ **Chip away.** Because much of household procrastination is based on simply not enjoying a particular task, the chip-away technique is especially useful because it's a way of getting things done little by little so that you almost don't even realize you're doing it. You'll read examples of how this works throughout this chapter.

➤ **Play trick-or-treat.** As with the chip-away technique, playing tricks such as "beat the clock" and rewarding yourself for getting the job done are particularly useful when the job is one that you just don't like doing.

Don't forget that before you can put these techniques to work, you have to stop, look, and listen so that you squash the impulse to procrastinate and start taking action.

Home Squalid Home

The holy trinity of household chores has to be tidying up, cleaning up, and cleaning out. By tidying up, I mean collecting all the random items that end up scattered around the house while you're busy living in it and putting them in their places.

Cleaning up is that thing some people do to keep germs, dust, mildew, mold, bugs, and even rodents at bay. Cleaning out is, essentially, de-cluttering. It means clearing junk, as well as useful stuff, out of closets, drawers, cabinets, garages, attics, basements, automobile trunks, storage boxes, and other spaces that tend to be clutter traps. The following sections look at ways to stop putting off any aspect of these three categories of chores.

Tidying Up

Even if it doesn't bother you that your home isn't neat as a pin, keeping it reasonably neat makes the rest of your life easier in a number of ways. You don't have to panic or be embarrassed when guests drop by on short notice. You can find things when you need them without having to turn the house upside down. You'll be more likely to clean (or make it easier for others to clean) because you can get to the surfaces and spaces that need cleaning. Perhaps most important, keeping your surroundings tidy can give you a sense of tranquility and of having your life under control.

Action Tactic

If you tend to sit around a messy house watching television, use the chip-away technique to get things done during commercials. Get up off your duff and pick up a couple of things, load the dishwasher, or wash a few dishes. After a couple of hours of watching television, you might be pleasantly surprised to find that you've made a big dent in your household chores.

To keep your home neat and tidy, follow these six rules:

1. **De-clutter.** It is infinitely easier to straighten up when you have fewer things and fewer obstacles to climb over to get to them so you can put them away.

2. **Have places to put stuff.** If you have a hook to hang your house keys on (or a bowl to drop them in) every time you step in your door, then you know how simple it is to put them away and find them the next time you're headed out. Your goal should be to have that sort of system for everything in your home. Many people put off tidying up because there's no place to put things.

3. **Use collection bins.** You can chip away at tidying up throughout the day when you keep a basket, box, or other portable container in each room. Suppose that over the weekend, your entrance hall tends to accumulate items of clothing, shoes, papers, sports equipment, books, and anything else that gets dropped there as people come and go. Putting all that back in the various rooms where it belongs can seem like a daunting task. If you have some sort of collection bin that everything can be dropped into and that you can easily carry around to other rooms, you'll be more likely to put everything away. If you have to gather up only what you can carry in your hands and make several trips to collect it all and put it back where it belongs, you'll procrastinate.

Quicksand!

If you live in a household with roommates or family members, don't let their sloppy habits counteract your efforts. They might come along and mess up the house as fast as you clean it up. Not only do you need to get over your own procrastination problems, you also have to learn the techniques suggested in Chapter 23, "Dealing with the Procrastinators Around You."

4. **Never walk through your house empty-handed.** Get into the habit of taking something with you every time you go from one room to another. For example, at night I sometimes read things in bed that belong in my home office. It's easy for those items to accumulate in the bedroom unless I make a point of carrying at least one or two of them out with me the next morning. I often take them only as far as the kitchen rather than all the way to my office, but at least that way they're one room closer to where they belong. I can move them to the correct room when I leave the kitchen.

5. **Play beat the clock.** Most of us are familiar with having to race against the clock to tidy up when guests are coming over. What we usually don't do, however, is play beat the clock when no one is expected. If you have a competitive streak, you might find that you get motivated to tidy up if you time yourself and see how quickly you can get one room, or even several rooms, picked up. The race will also help you stay focused on the task at hand instead of getting distracted by reading or fiddling with the items you're picking up.

6. **Focus on one room at a time.** One of the biggest mistakes people make when tidying up is to try to work on more than one room at a time. For example, a father of small children uses his collection bin in the den to carry toys to the kids' room. When he gets to that room, he puts all the toys away where they belong and then decides to start straightening up that room or finds some distraction that keeps him there for a while. He ends up forgetting about the tidying up he was doing in the den and may never get back to it. What he should've done instead was drop the toys in the kids' room and quickly get back to the den to finish his job there. By concentrating on one room at a time, you just about guarantee that you'll get at least one area of your home in good shape. Your sense of accomplishment when you see one room looking nice can also encourage you to move on to other rooms.

If you start with an uncluttered house or apartment and then tidy up as you go along, you should be able to get your home looking neat as new in just a matter of minutes at the end of each day or weekend.

Cleaning Up

People who know me well know that I'm about the last person on earth to be qualified to offer cleaning tips. Beyond knowing that club soda can slurp up a red wine stain from the rug and that vinegar isn't just for salad dressings but can actually clean things, I'm no Heloise. I do, however, know a lot about the psychology of cleaning, and when it comes to procrastinating about cleaning, that's what we're dealing with.

Action Tactic

If your home is in bad shape, plan a party so that you'll have to straighten up and clean. Just make sure the party date is far enough in the future to allow you time to whip the house into shape!

One way to motivate yourself to clean is to eliminate the number of steps involved (such as having to drag the vacuum cleaner out of a crowded closet and up the stairs to vacuum the second floor of a house). When you minimize the number of steps you have to take to find cleaning supplies or equipment (by forking over the bucks to buy a second vacuum cleaner to keep on the second floor, for example), you give yourself fewer chances to say, "This is too much trouble; I'll do it later." You also have to minimize the thought that goes into cleaning by having a routine for it so that it becomes a habit instead of something you worry about but don't take action on.

Try these additional tips and tricks to move yourself from thinking that you ought to be cleaning to actually cleaning:

➤ Get someone else to do it! If you hate to clean, or have other ways you need to be spending your time, then this is the obvious answer. If you think you can't afford to hire someone to clean your house, make sure that's really the case. Maybe you can't squeeze a full-time or even once-a-week housekeeper into your budget, but think of some alternatives. Maybe you could have someone come once every two weeks or have a cleaning service come in once a month to do the heavy-duty chores. Perhaps a neighborhood kid would like to earn a few bucks by coming in to do nothing but vacuum or mop the kitchen and bathroom floors or do any other single chore that you dread doing. Be resourceful.

➤ Have a daily, weekly, and periodic cleaning routine. Whether you're doing it yourself or have brought in a cleaning whiz, having a routine takes the worry out of cleaning. Start by making a list of everything that needs to be done, and then assign days and times to do it all.

➤ Get your supplies in order. Weed out the ones that don't work well, are too complicated to use, or have expired. Keep just a few basic, multipurpose cleansers on hand (such as ones that clean both glass and surfaces, or both kitchen and bathroom) so that you don't have to fish through lots of clutter to get to them.

➤ Use supplies that do most of the work. As you select those few basic cleansers to have on hand, look for ones that let you be a little lazy. For example, you can spritz certain cleansers on the tile after showering, and grime and mildew magically disappear without scrubbing.

➤ Chip away. If you wait for a big block of time to clean, you'll start to dread all the chores that face you and will be more likely to put it off. Instead, try to clean little by little. If you're cooking, for example, and find that you're waiting for water to boil before you can do anything else, why not grab a hand-vacuum and suck up the crumbs that have accumulated around the toaster or bread box? Or you could wipe off a shelf in the refrigerator.

➤ Combine cleaning with something fun. Put on some favorite music or let yourself watch something totally useless but amusing on television. Do anything that will make cleaning less of a chore.

Matter of Fact

When did you last dust the tops of tall bookcases, clean out the gutters, and disinfect your trash cans? Don't remember? Then you probably need to make lists of cleaning chores you should be doing on a daily, weekly, monthly, and seasonal basis, and schedule those chores into your planner and calendar. The lists can also help you see which chores should be part of your regular routine and which could be delegated to a cleaning service you bring in periodically. *The Complete Idiot's Guide to Organizing Your Life* has a great set of lists, as do books by cleaning guru Don Aslett, including *The Cleaning Encyclopedia*.

No matter which tricks and techniques work for you, one of the most important strategies is not to stress out over keeping your home perfectly clean. Do what is necessary to make it a comfortable, safe environment (germs are no laughing matter, so I'm not saying don't clean at all), but don't set impossibly high standards that make your life miserable.

Finally, don't let cleaning get in the way of your relationships at home. A 1999 national study by the Soap and Detergent Association (www.sdahq.org) and Opinion Research Corporation looked at ways household cleaning causes friction among married and living-as-married couples. Here's what they found:

➤ Of all couples who make a home together, 46 percent argue about cleaning.

➤ Women claim to do 79 percent of the cleaning in their households. Men admit to doing only 35 percent of the cleaning.

➤ Of couples with children in the household, 55 percent argue over cleaning; only 38 percent of households with no children fight about it.

➤ Of couples 55 and older, 34 percent argue about cleaning; 59 percent of couples aged 18 to 24 years old argue about it.

The study also asked about men's and women's common cleaning complaints:

Complaint	Men say about women	Women say about men
Doesn't clean enough	41%	56%
Doesn't clean the bathroom enough	16%	50%
Doesn't clean up after using the kitchen	24%	47%
Vacuums or dusts around items instead of moving them	41%	41%

If some of these complaints sound familiar, see what steps you can take to minimize the conflict. One important first step may be to be more tolerant of your partner's cleaning style. Unless your home is on the verge of being condemned, cut the other person a little slack and give him or her credit for at least making an effort. If, however, the division of labor in your household is very unfair, put your heads together and try working out a schedule for who does what and when it gets done. That way, cleaning chores won't have to be a constant topic of discussion. You'll only have to nag if the other person doesn't hold up his or her end of the bargain.

Clearing Out

Second only to exercising, clearing out cluttered spaces is the biggest procrastination problem experienced by the more than 300 people who participated in the procrastination survey. (The procrastination survey, detailed in Appendix D, asked respondents to indicate what they tend to put off out of a list of 53 personal and work-related tasks and which of those procrastination problems causes them the most distress.) It's no wonder that it's the household chore most likely to be put off. No matter what needs to be cleared out and organized—a closet, cupboard, drawer, garage, attic, basement, car, or just a pile of boxes and old newspapers taking over a room—doing it is a big job. It takes time and energy, and it raises all sorts of psychological issues. As we sort through all the stuff, we're forced to confront the

Quicksand!

All-or-nothing thinking can keep you from doing anything at all. Just because you wipe off the bathroom mirror doesn't mean you have to scrub the toilet and tub. Sure, those other chores have to get done eventually, but if you always think in terms of whole rooms, instead of chipping away at mini-tasks, cleaning will seem too overwhelming, and you won't do any of it.

You're Not Alone

Believe it or not, I've been carrying 200 unopened boxes with me from apartment to apartment for the past five years. I've had to move three times during my four years in my current city. Unpacking only to pack again seems like a fruitless endeavor, so I just let the boxes sit and wait.

—Dianne D., communications coordinator

ups and downs of our weight loss, spending habits, incomplete projects, and unfulfilled dreams.

Also, clearing out is a project we put off because it's not a part of our daily routine. We can let clutter and chaos accumulate day after day because we don't see it as pressing compared with something like washing dishes or having clean clothes to wear.

To get cluttered spaces cleared out, you have to do three things:

➤ Make it a priority by recognizing the negative impact clutter is having on your life.

➤ Make an appointment with yourself to do the initial big job of clearing out and reorganizing the contents of the cluttered space.

➤ Make clearing out a part of your routine by scheduling days and times on a monthly or seasonal basis to look for clutter that has re-accumulated.

As for the nitty-gritty of what to do next, review the 10 steps outlined in the "Getting Rid of Stuff" section of Chapter 8, "Lightening Your Load."

Laundry, Trash, and Other Dirty Words

Do you know why it's so easy to let trash and dirty clothes pile up? It's because they can be tucked away out of sight. Unlike the layers of dust that are so visible on furniture and the coats of grime that make bathrooms disgusting, garbage is hidden away in cans or bags, and laundry is in a hamper or closet. Yes, I know that the trash can often get pretty darn visible when it overflows and becomes smelly, and dirty clothes might spill out of the closet or hamper and start to fill the bedroom floor. But they are still easier to put out of sight and, therefore, out of mind. Let's look at why you might put off doing laundry, having dry cleaning done, or taking out the trash, and what you can do about it.

Laundry

Do you buy new underwear more often than you do laundry? If so, you're a laundry procrastinator. I used to be one, too. When I moved to New York City after graduate school, one of my first apartments was a fifth-floor walk-up in an old brownstone. It was charming with its exposed brick wall and working fireplace, but charm didn't get the clothes washed. To do that, I had to load up the laundry bag, drag it down five flights of stairs (10 flights, really, because each floor cruelly had two flights), and schlep it down the street three blocks to a laundromat. Then, of course, there was the fun of sitting there for hours watching the dryer spin around, because I didn't dare leave my precious cargo unattended.

After a couple of months, I'd had enough of that and decided to splurge on having my laundry done for me. For about the cost of a movie ticket, I was able to drop off my laundry on the way to work in the morning and pick it up all fresh and neatly folded on my way home. Sure, I still had to get it there, but I made that a no-brainer by taking it on the same day every week so that it became a habit. Knowing that I wouldn't have to wash and dry the clothes myself gave me lots more incentive to drag it down those steps.

Whether you have to haul your dirty duds to a laundromat or just down the basement stairs to your own washer and dryer, think of strategies that will work for your own laundry procrastination. Maybe it's delegating the task to a roommate or family member with the promise that you'll take over one of their chores. Don't think you're the only person in the household capable of doing laundry; teach someone how to do it. It's not rocket science.

If delegating or sending it out isn't an option, look for other ways to get it done. Have a routine for it so that you don't have to worry about it all the time. Make sure your laundry area is clean and uncluttered. If space allows, use those nifty laundry bags or hampers that are divided into two or three sections so that you can sort your dirty clothes by color as you toss them in, rather than having to do it just before you wash them. As added incentive, think about how much nicer it is to have clean underwear and towels.

Dry Cleaning

Twenty-five percent of the people who took the procrastination survey said that dropping off or picking up dry cleaning is something they procrastinate about, but only 15 percent put off doing laundry. At first glance, those results seem surprising because laundry is typically a bigger, more time-consuming job than tossing a few shirts on the dry cleaner's counter and picking them up all pressed and starched a couple of days later.

You're Not Alone

I never do laundry in any week with a Monday.

—Barbara Walters on *The View*, March 26, 1999

But when you think about it, dry cleaning is a multistep process that offers lots of opportunity for procrastination. First, you have to get the clothes out the door, because they can't walk to the cleaner's on their own. To make that happen, keep a shopping bag or tote bag hanging on your bedroom or closet drawer to drop your dry cleaning into so that it's always ready to grab at a moment's notice.

Then, unless your dry cleaner picks up and delivers, make sure you take the clothes to a cleaner's that's convenient (on your way to work, your kids' school, or your usual errands). Some cleaners even have drive-through windows to make the process easier.

Next, you have to keep track of the receipt. Find one place in your wallet, purse, car, or wherever and always put receipts there. Just make sure that you'll always have them with you when you need to pick up the clothes. To get the clothes picked up, try to have a standard day(s) of the week (or month, if you have dry cleaning less frequently) that you drop them off and pick them up. As with any other task, having a routine makes it a habit instead of a chore.

Trash

Hearing family members and roommates nag each other about not taking out the trash (and recyclables) often enough or promptly enough is part of the fabric of American culture and probably many other countries' cultures as well. Why is it such a big deal? Like many household chores, it's a dirty, sometimes heavy, job that nobody likes to do. Some of the excuses that otherwise hygienic, conscientious people give for letting their trash pile up include the following:

"The trash can (or trash chute, if in a building) is out of my way."

Excuse buster: If it's not on your way, make it on your way. Work it into your daily routine so that you don't have to make a big deal out of doing it. If you don't already pass the trash cans or chute on your way to work, vary your route every other day (or however often you need to take out the trash) so that you do pass them. Don't give in to laziness! The trash cans or chute can't be that far away.

"I don't have time to go out of my way. I'll be late for work/school/whatever."

Excuse buster: Stop the problem before it happens by not letting yourself get so pressed for time. When you're calculating how much time you need between waking up and walking out the door, you factor in things like brushing your teeth, getting dressed, making coffee, wolfing down some breakfast, and scanning the paper. Added to that time should be a couple of minutes for bagging up the trash and walking down the hall, out back, down the driveway, or wherever to dump it.

"I have too many other things to carry when I leave the house."

Excuse buster: First of all, do you have to carry so much stuff? Sometimes, people are not only packrats at home but also when they go places. Try to take less stuff or consolidate what you must take into fewer bags. If you collect your trash in large bags, try switching to smaller bags, such as plastic grocery bags with handles. They'll be easier to carry when you don't have a free hand, just a couple of free fingers.

"The bags always break by the time I get to the trash receptacle, so I dread doing it."

Excuse buster: Buy stronger bags and don't cram so much trash into them. This excuse is really lame (but one that I've used myself, so I know how tempting it is!).

Most of these excuses are just plain old habit. When you stop to think about them (using the Stop, Look, and Listen formula described in Chapter 12, "The Secret Formula to Overcoming Procrastination"), you'll realize that they aren't particularly valid excuses at all.

Matter of Fact

Some people put off household repairs or home improvement projects because they get lost shopping in those gargantuan stores that seem to sell everything and the kitchen sink. You might find it easier to shop by catalog. The *Renovator's* catalog (800-659-2211) has every-thing from patio furniture to bathroom vanities, weathervanes, and light switch wall plates. Equally handy is the *Improvements* catalog (www.improvementscatalog.com), which contains hundreds of quick and clever problem-solvers such as caulking tools, gutter pumps, and a 13-foot window washer brush for second-story windows. (There goes one excuse for not washing the windows.)

This Old House

In the procrastination survey, making home repairs or arranging for others to do them was one of the tasks respondents most often cited as being a problem for them. Much of the reason for this may be that having something break, leak, squeak, or otherwise get out of whack is not at all part of one's daily routine. We drop off dry cleaning on Monday mornings and pick it up on Thursdays. We vacuum on Saturdays and cut the grass on Sunday afternoon. What we don't have as part of our routine is fixing a closet door that suddenly doesn't close right or finding a plumber to repair a leaky faucet and rearranging our schedules to be home while the work is being done. To keep the roof over your head not only standing, but functioning well, try these tricks:

➤ Keep a running list of non-urgent repairs to be done and schedule times to do them, just as you would schedule any other appointments or chores. In addition

Action Tactic

If you put off buying tools, kitchen equipment, and other household items, consider shopping online. A good place to start is www.buyitnow.com

to doing them at scheduled times, you can also do them whenever you have some down time. Having the list helps you get a quick glimpse at what needs to be done, so when you have a few minutes free and are feeling motivated to do something, you won't have to try to remember what needs fixing. You'll see it on the list.

➤ Also keep a running list of supplies or tools needed to make the necessary repairs or improvements, and schedule times to buy the supplies.

➤ Designate one weekend per month as home improvement weekend. (Obviously, you can do it more or less often depending on your needs.)

➤ If you never feel like making home repairs or renovations on the weekend, try doing them at a different time. It's kind of silly that millions of people ruin their weekends worrying about the projects they should be doing but aren't doing. Nothing says that a loose doorknob or leaky pipe can't be fixed on a weekday evening or any other time.

➤ Keep the phone numbers and business cards of repair people in one visible spot so that you'll be less likely to put off calling someone to do the work.

➤ If you put off having repairs or renovations done because it's hard to schedule time away from work or other commitments so you can be at home, contact the National Association of Professional Organizers (contact info is available in Appendix B). Ask them if any members in your area offer concierge services. What that means is that the professional organizer or someone on his or her staff can come sit at your house to wait for a repairperson, oversee the work, and handle any other details involved. Another good resource is the National Concierge Association (NCA). Some NCA members provide services to individuals who need help getting things done; not all concierges work in hotels and building lobbies anymore! (NCA is also listed in Appendix B.)

Yard Work

Let me begin this section by making an important distinction: Yard work is not gardening. Yard work is all that mundane, repetitive maintenance you have to do, such as cutting the grass, trimming hedges, watering plants, raking leaves, and weeding. Yard work is what you do to keep your neighbors from mistaking your family for the Munsters. Gardening, on the other hand, is fun (at least it is to a lot of people). You get to plant pretty flowers, be creative with landscaping designs, and nurture little seedlings into sturdy trees and bushes. Many people find the time to plant some petunias, but then can't seem to find the time or desire to water them.

The reasons for procrastinating about yard work are much the same as for other household chores. It doesn't seem as urgent as some indoor tasks; it's often messy and strenuous; you may not have the right supplies or equipment, or the ones you have are hard to get to in a crowded garage or tool shed. Plus, it usually seems to be hot and sticky when yard work begs to be done.

Action Tactic

To get motivated to do yard work and to get ideas for the fun parts (gardening), check out all the neat information, tips, and timesavers at www.gardenweb.com.

Solutions for getting it done are also similar to those for other chores: Delegate it whenever possible, schedule it into your routine so that it becomes a habit, and keep your supplies in good working order and easily accessible. To minimize the problem in the first place, keep your lawn as low-maintenance as possible so that there's less to do or to put off doing.

The Least You Need to Know

➤ You may never grow to love housework, but you can make it easier with a few simple techniques.

➤ Getting rid of clutter, organizing supplies, and using the chip-away technique makes it easier to do any chore.

➤ Getting laundry and dry cleaning done and taking out the trash is a matter of finding more convenient ways to do them.

➤ Chores like home repairs and yard work are easier to get done when you delegate them or schedule times to do them.

Family Matters

> **In This Chapter**
>
> ➤ Saying I do or I don't
>
> ➤ Making the baby decision
>
> ➤ Managing family life
>
> ➤ Keeping your family safe

The noted anthropologist Margaret Mead was once quoted as saying, "No matter how many communes anybody invents, the family always creeps back." There does seem to be some truth in that statement. Maybe having people connected to us by blood or bound by a legal document is a deep-seated survival strategy. Perhaps it's a biological need to procreate. Whatever it is, something draws many people to marriage and children. Despite the attraction, however, good old procrastination often gets in the way.

This chapter looks at why people put off making the commitment to marriage (or to a living-as-married partnership) and to having children. This chapter also examines how procrastination affects daily life for those who already have families.

Marriage American Style

Year after year, U.S. Census Bureau statistics reveal that married adults are the majority in this country. In 1998, approximately 56 percent of all adults (111 million people) were married and living with their spouses. The numbers are even higher when marriage rates are examined for certain age groups:

Marriage Rates by Age and Sex

Age Group	Percentage of Women Married	Percentage of Men Married
18–24	21%	11%
25–34	62%	54%
35–64	71%	74%

If marriage is that common, why do we hear about so many people dragging their feet on the road to matrimony? Their procrastination may be due to the simple fact that they can put off marriage. Societal changes over the past several decades have made it more acceptable and popular for men and women to get married at a later age and to live together before, or instead of, marrying.

Estimated median age at first marriage for Americans since 1890. (U.S. Census Bureau)

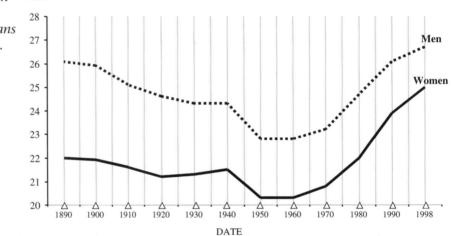

Women in particular have more choices than in the era of *Ozzie and Harriet*, when being a wife and mother was the most sought-after career. Now many women are more likely to see how they can fit marriage and kids into a booming career than to see work as a way to bide their time until the right man comes along.

To Nest or Not to Nest

Some instances of marriage-related procrastination can be attributed to societal conditions that fuel it, but the rest of it is undoubtedly due to what's going on in the minds of these bachelors and bachelorettes. As with any other sort of procrastination, fears, anxiety, and misconceptions can cause people to delay making the commitment to a lifetime together. If you're experiencing cold feet when it comes to marriage, or think you feel a chilly draft on the way, see whether any of these common causes apply to you:

➤ Having concerns about long-range compatibility with your partner

➤ Not being ready to give up the freedom of single life

➤ Looking for perfection in your partner or in the relationship

➤ Not knowing what you want out of life

➤ Having lousy decision-making skills

➤ Making the commitment aspect of marriage more overwhelming than it needs to be

➤ Being frightened by the statistic that half of all marriages end in divorce

➤ Being too comfortable with the status quo in your relationship to feel the impetus to take the next step

➤ Not feeling settled or secure enough in your career or finances to merge your life with someone else's

Quicksand!

If it's your partner, not you, who is procrastinating making the marriage (or the living-as-married) commitment, be careful how you use your powers of persuasion. Nagging, badgering, and being demanding or manipulative won't get you anywhere. Follow the advice in Chapter 23, "Dealing with the Procrastinators Around You," if you're not sure what to do.

Because marriage is one of the biggest commitments you'll ever make, it's a good thing to have these concerns. You obviously need to give a great deal of thought to the decision. On the other hand, if your tendency is to procrastinate when it comes to any difficult decisions in life, then you need to distinguish between being careful and being indecisive.

Saying "I Do," Not "I'll Do It Later"

You can make the marriage decision easier by asking yourself three questions:

1. **Do I have doubts about my long-range compatibility with my partner?** If the problem lies with the nature of the relationship itself and with the doubt that you can love, honor, and cherish this particular person from here to eternity, then you need to address that problem head-on. Rather than floating along indefinitely in a dating relationship and pushing your concerns to the back of your mind, deal with them. Talk to your partner about your doubts. If the attachment is meant to be, it can withstand what might be a very difficult discussion. If the problems are too big for the two of you to sort out on your own, consider talking them through with a counselor who specializes in relationships before you write off the relationship as doomed. (Information on how to choose and find a counselor is provided in Chapter 7, "Rallying Support from the Pros.")

Matter of Fact

If you're thinking of delaying marriage until you're older, you might want to factor in the odds of finding your soulmate at that later age, especially if you're a woman. According to the U.S. Census Bureau's 1998 statistics (the most recent ones available), there are 114 unmarried men ages 18 to 44 (divorced, widowed, or never married) for every 100 unmarried women of those ages. At older ages, however, the ratio reverses to 146 unmarried women for every 100 unmarried men among 45- to 64-year-olds and 315 unmarried women for every 100 unmarried men among the 65 and older crowd.

2. **Do I know what I want out of life and out of a life partner?** Before you can make a life with someone, you have to know what kind of life you want. You need to have a handle on what's important to you, how you want to spend your time each day, and what your long-range goals are before you can venture into marriage with confidence.

3. **Is this yet another example of my difficulty with making decisions?** You might be in a wonderful, solid relationship, adore your partner, and value the institution of marriage, but your lack of decision-making skill is keeping you from taking the next step. If that's the case, then try to zero in on how and why you might be making the decision harder than it needs to be and use the techniques suggested in Chapter 11, "Decision-Making: The Root of All Action."

Action Tactic

If having the inside scoop on pregnancy and parenthood would help you get moving on the baby decision, read the *Unofficial Guide to Having a Baby* by Ann Douglas and John Sussman or any of the irreverent *Girlfriend's Guides* by Vicki Iovine (for example, *The Girlfriend's Guide to Pregnancy* and *The Girlfriend's Guide to the Toddler Years*).

Putting Off the Pitter-Patter

It is easy to get so caught up in living your life and doing your job that you can realize quite suddenly that the window of opportunity for starting a family is closing. Whether it's a woman's biological clock or either partner's desire to raise kids while still young enough to chase after them, time and age are factors when making the baby decision.

It's Not the Right Time

Because time is of the essence, you'd think people wouldn't put off making the decision, but, of course, procrastinators always find a way. This is usually where the classic excuse, "It's not the right time" pops up. Here are some typical reasons why healthy women and men might feel it's not the right time to have a baby:

You're Not Alone

Who of us is mature enough for off-spring before the offspring them-selves arrive? The value of marriage is not that adults produce children but that children produce adults.

—Peter de Vries

➤ Being too busy in a career or not yet having reached certain professional goals

➤ Not being financially secure enough

➤ Not having ample health insurance coverage

➤ Not having a home that's spacious enough or set up right for kids, or not feeling settled in one geographic location

➤ Not being ready to give up the freedom of a childless life

➤ Not being ready or willing to give up habits like smoking and drinking (in the case of the prospective mother, although this can apply to the father as well)

➤ Not being in good enough physical shape (again, this applies mostly to the mother, but it can be an issue for the daddy-to-be also)

➤ Doubting your parenting capabilities or even doubting how much you like kids in the first place

What's interesting about this list is that these reasons are all much more valid than the usual excuses for procrastinating. After all, deciding to have a child is just as great a commitment as deciding to marry. Having doubts is a good thing. If you look at all the cons, not just the pros, before you decide, you'll have a better idea of what you're getting into and whether bringing a child into your world is the right thing to do.

Action Tactic

If you're concerned about being financially ready for a family, take a look at some of the parenting Web sites, particularly www.babycenter.com, which have nifty tools to help you calculate the cost of raising a child.

How to Know When It Is the Right Time

So how do you decide? First, recognize that only you and your partner (or you alone, if you plan to be a single parent) can make that decision. To make it a little easier, and to help yourself make the right decision, don't just look inward, but look for input from outside as well. Reading books on parenting, spending time with other people's kids (the brats and the angels), getting some hard data on the cost of raising a child, having a pre-pregnancy checkup with a physician or Certified Nurse Midwife, meeting with a nutritionist—all these efforts can help you take an objective look at what's involved and whether it's the right move for you. Beyond that, you have to listen to what your heart is telling you to do.

Matter of Fact

If you're a single father trying to run a household, there are probably times when you feel like the only one around, but that's not the case at all, according to the U.S. Census Bureau. Although the number of single mothers (9.8 million) has remained the same over the past three years, the number of single fathers has grown 25 percent, from 1.7 million in 1995 to 2.1 million in 1998. Consequently, men comprised 1 in 6 of the nation's 11.9 million single parents in 1998, up from 1 in 7 in 1995 and 1 in 10 in 1980.

Family Life

If you do have a family of more than one, you've probably reaped not only the joys and rewards of family life, but also a whole host of new things to procrastinate about. The parents who participated in the procrastination survey (that survey is described in detail in Appendix D and highlights of the results are given at the end of Chapter 1) and others I've talked to mention putting off such tasks as the following:

➤ Planning, shopping for, and preparing meals

➤ Getting kids packed up and out the door for school, appointments, and activities

➤ Taking care of evening rituals such as bath time during toddlers' (and parents') meltdown time of day

➤ Picking up toys

➤ Doing the extra laundry

➤ Signing up kids for classes, activities, and summer programs

➤ Shopping for clothes and shoes (keeping up with kids' rapid growth)

➤ Getting organized in general

➤ Planning family outings and vacations

➤ Finding time to slow down and relax with the family

Almost all of these procrastination problems are organizational problems, which can be solved by following the suggestions in Chapters 8, 9, and 10, as well as in the books and Web sites on organizing that are listed in Appendixes A and C. Particularly important is having a routine, having places to keep things, and not overloading your schedule or your kids' unnecessarily.

Making Home a Safe Haven

Isn't it odd how responsible and safety-conscious we are in the middle of the night when we hear a strange noise in the house or think we smell something burning? Not only do we usually jump up right away to go investigate, we also vow to take some action first thing in the morning to make our home and family safer. We promise to put fresh batteries in the smoke alarms, install stronger locks, call the burglar alarm company, or take whatever other steps are necessary to feel safe and secure.

Action Tactic

Instead of wasting time writing out a new grocery list every time you need to go to the store, keep one permanent list of the items you typically buy. Arrange the list in the order that you'll find the items in your supermarket's aisles. Post it on the fridge, and as you discover things you need throughout the week, mark them on the list.

So what happens when the light of day hits? As with so many other situations in the life of a procrastinator, the incentive to take action dies down when the imminent presence of danger is no longer felt. We say we'll deal with it later. What we forget is how serious the consequences can be when we make that fateful decision to put off safety issues until later.

Fire Safety

According to the United States Fire Administration, fire kills more Americans every year than all natural disasters combined. It's the third leading cause of accidental death in the home, with up to 80 percent of all fire deaths taking place in residences. The majority of home fires begin while cooking, usually as a result of human error rather than the mechanical failure of stoves and ovens. Heating systems are the second leading cause of residential fires, especially in single-family homes, where the heating systems are often not professionally maintained as they are in apartment buildings.

Fortunately, there's one simple thing you can do to increase your chances of stopping a fire before it gets out of hand or of escaping one that has already gotten going: If you don't already have them, install smoke alarms in your house or apartment and keep them functioning by keeping them clean and changing the batteries when needed. Fire experts say that smoke alarms are the single most important means of preventing residential fire fatalities; they reduce the risk of dying by nearly 50 percent. It's estimated that over 40 percent of residential fires and three-fifths of household fire deaths occur in homes with no smoke alarms.

Matter of Fact

Information on preventing and surviving household fires is so easy to come by that there's no excuse for putting off getting it. Three good places to start are the following:

FireHouse.com (www.firehouse.com) has fire safety tips in the site's InfoZone.

Look for the United States Fire Administration's *Fire FactSheets* at www.usfa.fema.gov or write to the administration at 16825 South Seton Avenue, Emmitsburg, Maryland 21727.

The American Red Cross's *Are You Ready?* brochures on disaster preparedness are available through your local Red Cross office or online at www.redcross.org/disaster/safety.

I don't have any fancy statistics on why so many people don't get around to installing or properly maintaining smoke alarms (even where they're required by law) or taking other fire safety steps. I think it's safe to say, however, that procrastination probably plays a major role.

Action Tactic

Unless you have the newer smoke alarms with 10-year batteries, you'll need to change the batteries at least once a year. Pick an easy date such as your birthday or a holiday to replace your batteries every year. You should also dust and test the alarms once a month, so pick a date like the first of the month or payday to make that an easy-to-remember, routine chore.

Smoke alarms are inexpensive and very easy to install. Maintaining them is no more complicated than changing the batteries in your Walkman and dusting off your favorite knick-knacks. So why don't you do it? The usual suspects are at work here. You probably don't think about fire safety during the course of a normal day, so the task gets put on the back burner, unattended. (Pardon the pun.)

1. Open up your daily planner or calendar and schedule a time to log onto a fire-related Web site or call your local fire department or American Red Cross office to get fire safety tips. Better yet, do it right this minute. (This is one time when I don't mind if you put this book aside and get back to it later.) Educating yourself about fire prevention and safety will help you assess where your home stands and what you need to do to get up to speed.

2. Also schedule a time to buy the supplies you need based on what you learned in Step 1. Smoke alarms are easy to find at hardware, home supply, and general merchandise stores, as are fire escape ladders, fire extinguishers, flashlights, and other items you might need. Of course, if all you need is fresh batteries, you can find those almost anywhere.

3. Within the next 24 hours, install the smoke alarms, change the batteries, devise your family's escape plan, or take any other necessary measures as identified in Step 1.

Do these things now. I mean it! I don't care who or what is clamoring for your time. Make fire safety a priority, schedule do dates (because this is one due date you don't want to reach unprepared), and take care of it.

Keeping Burglars at Bay

You hear those things that go bump in the night and say to yourself, "I ought to do something about that loose window lock or that broken porch light." But the next morning, just as with a fire scare, you get caught up in the daily grind, and it's easy to forget about fire fatalities and crime statistics.

According to the very informative Web site of "The Crime Doctor," Chris E. McGoey (www.crimedoctor.com), more than 30 percent of all home burglars gain access through an open door or window using ordinary household tools such as screwdrivers, pliers, pry bars, and small hammers. If it's easy for the bad guys to get in, it ought to be easy for you to keep them out. But, of course, just because something's easy doesn't mean a procrastinator is going to get around to doing it. Unless you make burglar-proofing a priority and schedule times to educate yourself about it and make some changes in your home, it won't get done.

You might also put off protecting your home and family from intruders because you figure there's not too much you can do about it. Maybe you know of someone who was robbed even though he had an expensive alarm system. Or perhaps you've heard too many stories of burglars jimmying heavy-duty locks that your neighbors took great pains and spent big money to install. You just assume that if it's going to happen, it's going to happen, and there's not too much you can do except hope that you're not home when it happens.

Although home burglaries might seem random, experts find that burglaries involve a simple selection process. Burglars tend to choose homes that appear unoccupied and have the easiest access, the greatest amount of cover, and the

You're Not Alone

The best way to keep children home is to make the home atmosphere pleasant—and to let the air out of the tires.

—Dorothy Parker

Quicksand!

If your home isn't safe because of domestic abuse or violence, don't make the all too common mistake of putting off dealing with it and never assume there's no place to turn. Whether the violence is directed at you or someone else in your home, you can contact the National Domestic Violence Hotline 24 hours a day at 800-799-SAFE or at the number for the hearing impaired 800-787-3224.

quickest escape routes. If you know that, there are some common-sense things you can do to make your house or apartment less of a target and harder to get into. They include simple steps such as keeping windows and doors locked securely, leaving lights on inside and outside the house, and considering installing an alarm system.

For more detailed suggestions and expert advice, schedule a time to contact your local police department or to research home safety on the Internet and make a promise to yourself and your family to act on that advice. It's one of the most important promises you'll ever keep.

Childproofing

According to the National SAFE KIDS Campaign, more children die each year from preventable injuries than from all childhood diseases combined. Nearly 6,700 children ages 14 and under are killed from unintentional injuries, and over 60,000 are permanently disabled.

Matter of Fact

Having a checklist of ways to make your home safe for babies or children is a simple first step you can take to get motivated about child safety. The National SAFE KIDS Campaign is a good place to begin. Look it up at www.safekids.org or contact it at 1301 Pennsylvania Avenue NW, Suite 1000, Washington, DC 20004; telephone: 202-662-0600. You'll also find lots of tips at these sites:

Childproofer's USA, Inc.: www.childproofing.com

Children's Safety Zone: www.sosnet.com/safety

The Paranoid Sisters: www.paranoidsisters.com

The BabyNet.com: www.thebabynet.com

National Safety Council: www.nsc.org

Those statistics are frightening enough, but they're more so when you realize that even children of the most attentive, caring parents can, unfortunately, become victims of preventable accidents. Part of the problem is that kids grow so fast that you never know from one day to the next what they'll be getting into.

I'll never forget the day that I left the kitchen for about 30 seconds while my 15-month-old was standing at the refrigerator door playing with some child-safe magnets. When I came back, I found her standing in her high chair trying to reach the ceiling light. How was I to know that she'd discovered that she could drag the metal trash can several feet across the kitchen floor and use it to climb up into her chair? Luckily, her brush with danger was just a brush that day, but it made me realize that I had to stop putting off all sorts of childproofing measures that I'd assumed weren't yet necessary.

Child safety experts have identified the following areas as some of the major causes of concern: falls, burns, cuts, choking, poisoning, drowning, and electrical shock. If there are infants, toddlers, or young children in your household, where do you stand on safety precautions to prevent these and other accidents?

Procrastinators rarely plan ahead; they tend to work on what needed to be done yesterday or what absolutely has to be done today. Rarely do they get around to doing what might need to be done tomorrow. With kids, you never know what tomorrow will bring, so take steps today to make tomorrow a safe one.

The Least You Need to Know

➤ Putting off marriage results from practical concerns, such as money matters, as well as fears and doubts.

➤ Putting off the decision to start a family is an example of good procrastination, because such a major commitment requires careful thought.

➤ Procrastination in daily family life usually results from a lack of organization.

➤ Making your home safe has to be a top priority.

Chapter 15

Get a Social Life—or Change the One You Have

In This Chapter

➤ Getting out more often

➤ Putting the fun back into holidays and special occasions

➤ Mustering the courage to date

➤ Leaving loser relationships

So you want to make a change in your social life. Maybe you've recently ended a relationship or marriage and want to meet someone new or haven't been in a relationship at all in quite a while. Perhaps your spouse or partner passed away some time ago, and you now feel ready to date again. Whatever the situation, you might say that you'd like to date more and meet someone special, but the procrastinator in you comes up with all sorts of excuses for why you don't have the time, why it's not the right time, or why you shouldn't do it.

Or maybe socializing for you is less about meeting Mr. or Ms. Right and more about just having fun and a change of pace. You might even be married or seriously involved with someone already but have a social life that consists of nothing more than cozying up to a rented video and take-out food every Friday night. There's nothing wrong with relaxing that way, whether you're single or attached, but when those quiet evenings at home start to feel like a rut, it's time to make some changes. You might say that you'd like to get out more, do new things, and meet new people, but your procrastination habit causes you to let work or family demands keep you stuck in that unsocial rut.

Maybe you are socializing enough, but the way you're going about it is not quite working. Instead of having plain old fun when getting together with friends, hosting parties, and celebrating holidays and other special occasions, you find that your social life has become a chore. It brings all sorts of tasks to procrastinate over, such as shopping for gifts, sending greeting cards, and preparing for parties.

This chapter looks at how procrastination can have an adverse affect on your social life and what you can do to stop delaying the fun and games.

I Have to Get out More

You know you're in trouble when you're starting to remember the puzzles on *Wheel of Fortune* reruns or when your closest friend is the guy who delivers take-out food to your office while you burn the midnight oil night after night. Whether your problem is having no life or having only a work life, it's easy to find yourself doing the same old thing day after day. You end up falling out of touch with old friends and not making new ones, and have more dates with the television and a bag of potato chips than with live human beings.

Finding the Time to Socialize

If you're not getting out to have a social life, the issue may be time. You don't seem to have enough of it to get all your responsibilities out of the way and still have some time left over for fun. This is particularly true for people with demanding careers and/or busy family lives. In addition to using the insights about time and how to deal with it offered in Chapter 5, "It's About Time," try to spur yourself into action with the following strategies:

Action Tactic

To motivate yourself to get out of a rut and into having more fun, read *Beyond Love and Work: Why Adults Need to Play* by Lenore Terr, M.D. This fascinating book takes a scholarly, yet practical, look at how important it is to lose ourselves and find freedom in the act of play, just as we did when we were kids.

➤ **Make it a priority.** If you don't make a conscious effort on a daily basis to be on the lookout for opportunities to socialize and to make the necessary plans, then week after week will pass by with no change in your social life.

➤ **Make advance plans.** If you schedule get-togethers with friends, reply early to party invitations, and make advance reservations for meals or events, you'll be more likely to stick with those plans. Without a clear plan, you can give in to excuses like, "I just don't feel up to going out tonight," or "I'll see them next week." Even better, buy nonrefundable tickets to events far in advance so that you'll have more incentive to honor your commitment to go.

➤ **Combine socializing with another activity.** If finding spare time is a major problem, look for activities that have double rewards. If you'd like to get more exercise, consider group sports where you can get in shape and meet people at the same time. If there's something you'd like to learn or a skill you want to brush up on, take a course; it's a chance to make some new friends and socialize after class.

You're Not Alone

If my wife and I don't book a baby sitter in advance, we end up not going out. It's not that the sitters' schedules are the problem. It's that we use baby sitting as an excuse to be lazy. If we wait to the last minute, we say, "Oh we probably can't get a sitter, so let's stay in." But if one is on the calendar, we go.

—Mohammad M., banker

Many people put off improving their social lives because they believe they're lousy at meeting people or making conversation. Although some social butterflies do seem to have a natural gift of gab and an innate ability to maneuver any social situation, that doesn't mean social relations skills can't be learned. Adult learning centers and some universities' night schools offer courses in such fine academic pursuits as the art of flirting, how to talk to anybody anywhere, and how to attract the opposite sex.

The Importance of Follow-Through

How many times have you met a nice person, exchanged phone numbers, said you'd call each other next week to get together, and then never laid eyes on each other again? Whether you're looking to date more or merely make new friends and infuse some excitement into a stale social life, it's easy to put off the follow-through that's necessary for making those things happen. There are three basic causes for this type of procrastination:

1. **Lack of organization.** You simply lose the person's business card or the slip of paper where you had scribbled down a name and number. To avoid this problem, write the name and address in your daily planner if you have it with you at the time. If not, then take the card or paper out of your pocket or wallet as soon as you get home and make a note in your planner for the day you plan to call the prospective new friend.

2. **Lack of prioritizing.** You might be complaining to a friend or your spouse that you'd like to meet new people, but you don't translate that wish into reality. When you do meet someone new, you don't make it a priority to follow through. You have to change your mindset to one that has "Make new friends" in its forefront.

Action Tactic

When you meet someone new, try to get an e-mail address in addition to, or instead of, a phone number. Then, if you're hesitant to pick up the phone and call the person for fear that the person might not want to hear from you, you can use the less direct (and therefore less intimidating) method of e-mailing first.

3. **Lack of confidence.** Under most circumstances, you might be a fairly confident person who considers yourself someone who can be a good friend to others and is pleasant to be with. But you get home and stare at that name and phone number of the person you met briefly last weekend and hesitate to pick up the phone. Even if getting together with that person would have nothing to do with romance, you might have all the same concerns that someone has before calling for a date.

You might say, "Oh, he didn't really mean it when he said let's get together." Or, "I'm sure she was just being polite. She doesn't really want me to call. She's too busy." Or you worry that you'll look like a loser, someone desperate for a friend. What a shame to let those sorts of self-defeating—and usually unfounded and irrational—thoughts hold you back. Pick up the phone and call. What's the worst that could happen?

Socializing Online

Americans send 2.2 billion e-mail messages a day, compared with 293 million pieces of first-class snail mail. At least a third of the country sends e-mail. Without a doubt, the Internet has not only revolutionized how people do business, it's dramatically changed social life as well.

Socializing online is a godsend for procrastinators. Meeting people in chat rooms or staying in touch with old friends by e-mail removes all of the inconvenience factors of face-to-face socializing. It also removes some of the anxiety associated with a social life in that it is relatively anonymous, and unless photos are exchanged electronically, it doesn't matter what you look like.

Of course, it does have its down side. Not only can it make you a hermit, it can also be dangerous if that charming screen name on the other side of cyberspace ends up being a psychopath. Safety on the Internet is no joking matter, so if you opt for socializing online, tread carefully.

When Your Social Life Becomes a Chore

You have a social life, but does it bring challenges and extra commitments that can sometimes be overwhelming? We tend to think of procrastination as being a problem with tasks that are drudgery, a hassle, or difficult. Yet most of us have the same problem when it comes to the fun things that go with an active social life: shopping for the right cards and gifts for birthdays and other occasions, planning celebrations, and preparing for major holidays. Does it have to be that way? Not if you have a strategy.

Putting the Joy Back in Gift-Giving

If you'd like to meet some fellow procrastinators, just visit any shopping mall on December 24 or any florist at about 5:00 P.M. on February 14. Like last-minute income tax filers who get a kick out of the carnival atmosphere at post offices on April 15, last-minute shoppers often take a sort of warped pride in their procrastination. They love the adrenaline rush that comes from doing all their Christmas shopping on Christmas Eve or from finding just the right gift five minutes before they're due at a birthday party or bar mitzvah.

If you're one of those last-minute shoppers but would gladly get your thrills in other ways, then you have to do just one simple thing: Focus on do dates, not due dates. Of all the techniques described in Chapter 12, "The Secret Formula to Overcoming Procrastination," that's the most important one when it comes to shopping for holidays and special occasions.

Here's how the do date, not due date, method works for gift-selection and shopping. (I use Christmas as an example, but if that's a holiday you don't celebrate, just substitute any other one.)

Old think: I have to get my Christmas shopping done by December 25.

New think: I can pick up Christmas gifts throughout the year.

Quicksand!

If you don't have a strategy, you'll find yourself in the Belated Birthday section of your card store most of the time or phoning in your greetings at the last minute. Instead, try buying a supply of cards in advance. Take your birthday list and shop for a full year's worth of cards. Pick up some blank ones and spares, too, for other occasions you're likely to encounter. If you do wait until the last minute and your birthday person is plugged in, send an online greeting card!

Action Tactic

Eliminate the decision-making aspect of gift-giving by coming up with your one signature gift for each type of occasion. For example, every time you get a birth announcement, turn to your favorite catalog or Web site and order a monogrammed baby blanket. You can vary the gift slightly to personalize it for each recipient, but having a basic idea makes you less likely to procrastinate.

Old think: These gifts I'm buying on this vacation or business trip are souvenirs I'll give my friends and family as soon as I get home.

New think: Trips out of town are a great time to look for Christmas gifts, no matter how far away December 25 is. So I'll save some of these souvenirs until then.

Old think: There's no way to know in July what I'll want to give someone in December, so I can't shop early.

New think: My friends' and relatives' tastes and interests aren't likely to change that much in six months, so I can shop ahead. Even if I do end up wanting to give them something else, I can probably think of someone else to give the original gift to.

Old think: If I shop ahead, I'll just lose the gifts or lose track of who each one is for.

New think: I can find one box or designate one shelf of a closet for gifts and label them clearly. I can also keep a running list of gifts and gift recipients in a Christmas file.

Matter of Fact

Just about any kind of present you'd like to give can be ordered on the Internet. Here are several of the best sites for two of the most common gift-giving occasions: marriage and birth.

For engagements, bridal showers, and weddings, go to www.WeddingNetwork.com, www.Ross-Simons.com, or www.TheKnot@iqvc.com.

For baby showers and new baby gifts, go to www.Thebabynet.com, www.Etoys.com, or www.Babycenter.com.

Gift-giving is supposed to be pleasurable. You should enjoy selecting items that your friends and family (or business colleagues) would like. It's not supposed to be a major hassle, but that's what it becomes when you wait until the last minute. So start early. And if clawing your way through stores and fighting for parking spaces is not your idea of fun, use time-saving conveniences like shopping online or from catalogs or employ a personal shopper (many stores have in-house personal shoppers who can cost less than independent ones).

Taking the Rush out of Holidays

Holidays, whether religious or secular, conjure up all sorts of images and feelings. Some people find them a happy time of reunions, good food, comforting traditions, and perhaps spiritual renewal. For many, however, they simply mean more things to add to an already stuffed to-do list.

Christmas and Hanukkah bring gifts to buy, cards to send out, travel plans to make, meals to prepare, and decorations to set up. Independence Day might bring a picnic and family outing to coordinate and cook for. Halloween brings costumes to make or buy and candy corn to stockpile. Just about any holiday has its traditions, which, when taken to extremes or tackled at the last minute, are more of a burden than a blessing.

I promised early on in this book that my focus wasn't going to be about doing more just for the sake of doing more, but about doing what you enjoy and what's truly important to you. My advice to you concerning holidays is perhaps the best example of that philosophy. Instead of giving tips on how to be more efficient with holiday preparations, I'm suggesting that you think about the holidays differently by doing the following:

➤ Remember why you like and celebrate a particular holiday. If you don't particularly enjoy it, and if your friends and family don't care much for it either, then don't make a big deal out of that holiday, even if the greeting card and retail industries do.

➤ Eliminate the aspects that are a hassle. Holidays can be some of the few times a year, besides maybe a summer vacation, when we get to stop working and relax. If you spend all of that time off doing things you don't enjoy just because you've always done them or think you should do them, that's a classic waste of time.

➤ Simplify your celebrations. Give gifts to fewer people, and give fewer gifts to each person. Most won't mind at all, assuming they even notice the difference. (Even kids can be taught from an early age to be less materialistic.) Cut back on decorations, unless you love making them and setting them up and have all the time in the world. Simplify in any way that will make each holiday less of a complex project and more of a manageable, fun occasion.

Action Tactic

If Christmas is a holiday you observe, but you find that it's become more of a chore than a celebration, read *Simplify Your Christmas: 100 Ways to Reduce the Stress and Recapture the Joy of the Holidays* by Elaine St. James.

The key to holiday-related procrastination is to stop focusing so much on becoming super-efficient and re-think how many tasks you should put on your to-do list to begin with. If you scale down your holiday commitments, you'll find it easier to find time and energy for the preparations, planning, and socializing that you do enjoy.

The Dating Game

Dating is a whole branch of socializing unto itself. Many people socialize in the hope of finding that special someone, a soulmate, or whatever they choose to call the person they can spend holidays with, buy those cards and gifts for, and just have fun with.

According to the U.S. Census Bureau, there are nearly 80 million single people in this country (40 percent of the population). Walk into a crowded singles bar on any Saturday night, and it can feel like all of those 80 million pairs of eyes are checking you out—or even worse, not checking you out!

Quicksand!

Don't put off dating because you assume that the singles scene isn't for you. If you assume that the only way to start dating is to hang out at bars or flirt with strangers in the produce section of supermarkets on a Saturday night, you're leaving out a lot of other ways to meet people. The so-called singles scene is whatever you choose to make it.

When it comes to dating, the intimidation factor is one major cause of procrastination. You may say you'd like to meet that proverbial special someone, but there seem to be all sorts of roadblocks keeping you from going to the places and events where you might meet some potential dates. Or you may already have a few phone numbers tucked into your wallet, numbers of friends-of-friends or people you happened to meet and thought you might like to see again. But something keeps you from picking up the phone and asking for a date. Your dating procrastination might result from these feelings:

➤ Feeling out of practice if it's been a while since you dated

➤ Not knowing, or being confused by, current dating rules

➤ Fear of rejection

➤ Lack of confidence

➤ Hesitation because you got burned in your last relationship

➤ Complications caused by being a single parent

➤ Guilt over meeting someone new, even if your last relationship or marriage is definitely over

Dating is supposed to be fun, but it's a complex process that calls up all the usual suspects of psychological and situational obstacles found in any sort of procrastination.

Getting Past the Dating Roadblocks

To stop saying, "I'll deal with it later," and start doing it now, consider these painless ways to ease into dating:

➤ Don't put pressure on yourself to look or act perfect.

➤ Make it your main aim to have fun, not to connect with your life's soulmate.

➤ When you meet a potential date or go out on a first date, make the focal point an activity that can deflect attention away from the awkwardness of a first meeting, such as going to a sports event, the theater, or anything else you enjoy. You might feel less pressure than you would on the traditional drinks or dinner date.

➤ Keep your expectations realistic.

➤ Consider using a reputable dating service. The old stereotype of their being just for losers is not at all the case.

➤ Don't let yourself feel stigmatized by being single. Having a chip on your shoulder won't attract people to you.

You're Not Alone

Despite the numerous single role models today working in entertainment, sports, politics, business, and other high-profile fields, people still feel tremendous internal pressure to marry. We are not talking here about the natural desire to mate or to fall in love. We are referring to an outdated cultural mandate to marry.

—From *Being Single in a Couple's World* by Xavier Amador, Ph.D., and Judith Keirsky, Ph.D.

Most important of all, date because you want to, not because you think you're supposed to. Don't let yourself get caught up in feeling stigmatized by your single status. Plenty of people choose not to marry or get involved in serious relationships. They enjoy going out with friends and maybe having an occasional date, but they don't stress out over looking for a life partner just because that's what society expects them to do (or because their relatives nag them about when they're going to settle down).

Dealing with Relationship Problems

Just about everyone (except maybe those who marry their college sweetheart and live happily ever after) has had the experience of staying in a relationship far too long. You may know the feeling; something's just not quite right, and the attachment doesn't seem to have any future, but you put off doing anything about it. It often seems easier to stick with the status quo than to make the tough decisions and have the difficult discussions necessary to make the relationship better or leave it confidently.

This dilemma is expressed well in the book *Too Good to Leave, Too Bad to Stay: A Step-by-Step Guide to Help You Decide Whether to Stay In or Get Out of Your Relationship*, by Mira Kirshenbaum. Procrastinating taking a firm stand on where a relationship stands is the result of what she calls "relationship ambivalence."

When in this ambivalent state, you do all the wrong things to try to make decisions about whether to cut loose or stay and try to make the relationship work. This list is a synopsis of those wrong things, described in more detail in Kirshenbaum's book:

➤ You go through long stretches of bad times and ill will in the relationship, but then the atmosphere changes, the outlook is rosy again, and you sweep the problems under the rug until the next time they pop up.

➤ You complain about the relationship or the other person but contradict yourself by saying you don't want to leave.

➤ You talk to everyone about the problem, hoping someone will tell you what to do.

➤ You obsess over the problem, thinking and worrying about it constantly, but you don't take any action.

➤ You assume that the matter is just about your own fear of commitment, not a problem with the relationship itself.

➤ You wait for some sort of sign, that light bulb over the head, that tells you what to do.

➤ You take an overly rational, objective approach, listing the pros and cons, assigning each a number, and hoping that with enough number-crunching you'll come up with the answer.

➤ You keep leaving, hoping that breaking up will stir things up, but it doesn't, and you always come back to give the other person yet another second chance.

In *Too Good to Leave, Too Bad to Stay* the author also goes on to advise that, instead of relying on those ineffective or hit-or-miss approaches, you diagnose the problem step-by-step as a physician would diagnose a physical ailment. You have to try to remove yourself from the situation (mentally, that is) enough to cast an objective eye on it and to take all factors into account while still letting your gut feelings have a say in the matter.

Turn to Kirshenbaum's book, as well as the many other books available on relationships (such as those recommended in the "Interpersonal Relationships and Social Skills" section of Appendix A), for advice on how to obtain that objective vantage point. For even more personalized assistance, consider seeking help from a mental health counselor who specializes in relationships. These sorts of decisions are often difficult to make on your own or with your partner alone, so to stop procrastinating; connect with the information and people who can help you through the process.

The Least You Need to Know

➤ Getting stuck in a social life rut is often caused by not making it a priority and by anxieties about putting yourself out there.

➤ To stop procrastinating choosing and buying gifts, focus on do dates, not due dates.

➤ Holidays are not about doing more but about simplifying so you can celebrate them in the way you want.

➤ Deciding whether to stay in or end a relationship is made easier when you seek expert advice.

Chapter 16

New Year's Resolutions and Other Self-Improvement Promises

> ## In This Chapter
>
> ➤ Understanding why New Year's resolutions don't resolve anything
>
> ➤ Waiting for weight loss
>
> ➤ Exercising your right to put off exercise
>
> ➤ Getting and staying healthy
>
> ➤ Finding the time for hobbies

Quick: Name one New Year's resolution you've ever kept. Still thinking? Nothing coming to mind? Not one? That's what I figured. And that's why I wrote this chapter. Not keeping New Year's resolutions, or a resolution made at any time of year for that matter, is in large part a procrastination problem. You say you're going to turn over a new leaf on January 2, but when that day arrives, you don't quite feel ready. You decide it would be better to wait and turn over that new leaf after the Super Bowl, or when the winter doldrums pass and spring kicks in, or when work slows down, or when, well, you get the picture. Before you know it, it's pretty clear that you're not going to quit smoking, stop biting your nails, lose weight, learn to speak Urdu, or whatever it is you want to do, until hell freezes over. With global warming and all, you figure that's a very long time away.

You're Not Alone

I think I procrastinate in my personal life because I'm so overwhelmingly busy with a full-time career and a part-time business that when it comes to doing things for myself, I put them off. In my work, I can't miss deadlines, so when I have a moment free, I hate to burden myself with something else to do.

—Fran K., communications manager

Why New Year's Resolutions Lose Their Resolve

It's a miracle that any New Year's resolutions are ever kept. When you make one, you expect dramatic changes to take place in your behavior overnight. Think about how silly it is that you could be one person on January 1 (and all the days that came before) and a totally different person on January 2. As you found out in Chapter 6, "Making Sure You'll Really Do It This Time," change happens gradually and requires a shift in both mindset and daily routine. There are three main flaws in most people's New Year's resolutions (or resolutions made at any other point in the year):

1. **The resolution is too broad.** If you say, "I want to lose weight this year," or even if you're more specific with a resolution like, "I want to lose 20 pounds by April," the statement is too broad.

Those statements are goals or end results. They're not resolutions. A resolution is the act of resolving to do something. You resolve to eat fast food only once a week instead four or five times a week. You resolve to join a weight-loss group on Monday morning. Resolutions will work only if you make them concrete, specific, and doable. Start with a simple baby step you can achieve on January 2. Then with the confidence and momentum built from that accomplishment, set the next step for a week later, or whatever time frame makes sense. Keep going with weekly or monthly resolutions until you reach the ultimate goal.

2. **The resolution doesn't get worked into daily life.** You might have so much determination to keep your resolution that it's practically spilling out of you. But no matter how much you are psychologically ready to work toward your goals, you won't reach them unless your daily routine incorporates the steps necessary for reaching those goals. As you learned in Chapter 5, "It's About Time," extra time doesn't just appear out of nowhere. If you resolve, for example, to spend less time working and more time with your kids, that resolution won't happen unless you take some pretty drastic measures to reorganize your work and home lives and rethink how you schedule your days.

3. **Resolutions are based on an all-or-nothing attitude.** When we're trying to make changes in our behavior, even the strongest of us develop very fragile egos. We set out toward our goals with the highest of hopes yet with nagging doubts about our ability to reach them. Then when we hit the first snag, our egos are shattered. Instead of rolling with the punches and realizing that all

change comes with setbacks and relapses, we let the setback get to us. We say, "It's hopeless. I'll never keep a New Year's resolution, so I'm not even going to try anymore."

The key here is to think not so much in terms of the timing of the resolution. Sure, it's a new year, a fresh start, old acquaintances can be forgot, yadda, yadda, yadda. The reality, though, is that New Year's Day is just another day in your life. And whether it's January 1, June 1, or October 1, you're not going to make changes in that life unless you understand the change process, as touched on in the preceding list of three problems and in more detail in Chapter 6.

Quicksand!

Waiting for the brink of a new year to make changes in your life or your behavior is a form of rationalized procrastination. Instead of making positive changes in the summer, fall, or any other time, you say, "I'll wait until January and make it a New Year's resolution." That's still procrastination any way you cut it. Don't fall for it.

Losing Weight and Lifting Weights

The American Dietetic Association has found that at any given time, 45 percent of women and 25 percent of men are on a diet to lose weight. Recent government surveys show that almost 51 percent of women and 59 percent of men are overweight, according to the government's updated ideal weight charts and figures. The weight-control industry makes $30 to $50 billion a year from diets, drugs, and other products and programs. Even my little procrastination survey of 309 people (see Appendix D, "The Procrastination Survey") found that losing weight and exercising are two of the three biggest procrastination problems. All the numbers add up to the fact that a lot of people are seeing higher numbers on the scales than they'd like.

As for exercising, it, of course, is not always done for weight loss. Weight loss is a major reason people exercise, but some people exercise to feel good, be healthier, or look better. A recent *Newsweek* poll for a special issue on women's health found that 66 percent of women exercise to look better and feel healthier, while only 18 percent do so because they enjoy it. (Ten percent said they never exercise, and 5 percent had other reasons not stated.) I wouldn't be surprised if the statistics for men are similar. Considering that we're a society that places such importance on looking good, those who don't exercise often end up feeling inferior somehow. I know the feeling!

The Day I Stopped Exercising

I can pinpoint the day that I became an exercise procrastinator. I was in my mid-20s and in my first year of graduate school in Los Angeles. Up until that point, I had been an extremely active and athletic child and teenager. In college, I still considered myself a basically athletic person even though I didn't do much in the way of exercise. It wasn't an issue of procrastination; I simply found too many other fun things to do during the undergrad years (including eating way too much pizza, which led to putting on the proverbial "Freshman 10"—okay, maybe 15).

Matter of Fact

For many people, struggles with weight are caused by, and made worse by, a poor self-image and low self-esteem. Working with a psychotherapist or other mental health professional can therefore be a valuable complement to any weight-loss effort. You can think of it as working on your appearance from the inside out. To work on your self-esteem from the outside in, consider meeting with an image consultant, who can help you feel better about yourself by looking better—no matter what your weight is. You can find one through the Association of Image Consultants International at 800-383-8831 or www.aici.org.

In graduate school, I thought that I would get back into exercising and sports, but for some reason, I did so only sporadically. I now know why. It all started one day when I attended a psychology conference. At the suggestion of a fellow student (and against my better judgment), I sat in on a speech given by a motivational speaker/psychobabbling guru popular in the 1970s and 1980s. I'm not saying that all motivational speakers are bad; hey, I've even bordered on being one myself at various times in my counseling and consulting career. I've certainly been guilty of spouting some psychobabble. But from what I knew of this guy, there was much more superficial, feel-good pabulum than substance in his best-selling books.

My worst fears were realized when he began his talk by boasting that he had not missed a day of jogging, except for one day when bedridden with the flu, for something like 10 years. I think he wanted us to see that he walks the talk of his *Just do it* message for people trying to reach personal goals. My first thought was, "Nobody gets the flu for only one day, which means he went running while sick, which is just plain stupid." My second thought was a much less confident one. It was, "I'll never be one of those people who exercises, really exercises, consistently."

I know I can't blame all the struggles I've had with exercise since then on that man and that one annoying statement. But it is amazing to me how etched in my mind that moment is. I can hardly remember what I wrote my dissertation on, but I can picture that speaker on stage as if it were this morning. Since that day, I can hardly remember a time when I didn't have negative, self-defeating thoughts about my relationship with exercise. In retrospect, I now see that that was the day I developed a "me versus them" attitude toward exercising (and, indirectly, toward weight loss as well). I decided that there are people who have self-discipline and people who do not and that I was in the "not" category.

A Losing Battle with Exercise

From that point on, I joined more health clubs than I care to count, always starting out with the best of intentions only to end up playing hooky for weeks and then months at a stretch. It would get to the point where I was too embarrassed to slink back in the place. I also dabbled in some of my favorite sports from time to time, playing tennis a few months here and there, riding horses on and off for a few years, swimming when I had access to a pool, and other activities that were convenient at any given time. I didn't see these brief stints of exercise as a normal range

You're Not Alone

It's unfortunate how many people put off exercising because of misperceptions about what's necessary to reach reasonable fitness goals. They assume they'll have to work out for hours, seven days a week, to get in shape, when in fact, if they exercised efficiently, a few hours a week would probably suffice.

—Tim Haft, A.C.E., certified personal trainer, New York City

of physical activities in an average life span. (We go from sport to sport, or gym to gym, as our interests, schedules, and geographic locales change.) Instead, I saw my exercise stints as evidence of a major failure—my inability to stick with one program.

I was letting perfectionism and all-or-nothing thinking get in the way. I felt that if I didn't go to the gym three days a week, every week, for the rest of my life (or at least for more than a few months straight), then I had failed. I also believed that if I played tennis fairly regularly for one summer, then I was a failure if I didn't keep it up through the fall.

Weight Lost and Fitness Found

Then, something changed. I decided to examine my procrastination problem and apply the same principles that I espouse in this book. Guess what? They worked. I don't claim to have everyone's magic answer to losing weight and keeping it off and getting fit and staying that way. If someone had that magic answer, that person would be even richer than the people who *don't* have the perfect answer but who make a lot of money by leading us to believe that they do. This book is on procrastination, not on diet and exercise, so for expert advice from nutritionists, fitness trainers, exercise physiologists, physicians, and more, turn to the books, Web sites, and organizations on health and fitness listed in the appendixes.

What I *can* help you with is exercising and weight loss from the perspective of psychology and organization, which are the two elements of any effort to overcome procrastination and the two elements that worked for me. Here's how you can use the techniques for fighting procrastination to help you exercise and eat right:

Matter of Fact

You've heard of whistling while you work; well now you can exercise while you work, and all without leaving your desk. Before a stiff neck and cramped hands set in, pop in some exercise software and watch fitness experts on your computer screen lead you through a routine. Some even spy on you by keeping count of the number of keystrokes or mouse movements you make, and signaling when it's time to take a break and stretch. Choices for working out at work include:

CyberStretch by Jazzercise (888) 797-8738; www.cyberstretch.com

The ErgAerobics System (800) 689-9199; www.ergaerobics.com

StretchWare (800) 307-0131; www.stretchware.com

➤ **Banish all-or-nothing thinking.** Realize that a little progress is better than no progress at all, that eating a sensible diet is better than trendy crash diets, and that being a moderate exerciser is just as worthy as being an exercise fanatic.

➤ **Make it a priority.** Believe me, I *know* that is easier said than done. There are two things you can do to help yourself make weight loss or exercising a priority. One is to think through the consequences and benefits. It's the "get real" technique from Chapter 12. Every time you start to put off losing weight or getting fit, give yourself a reality check. Think of the health hazards that can result and think of the benefits you'll gain by doing it. Federal government health statistics show that we're all living longer than humans used to. Don't you want to look and feel better during those extra years? Use realities like that data to get you fired up to make your health a priority.

➤ **Make it a habit.** I may have knocked that guy who boasted about jogging every day for umpteen years, but there is something to be said for the regularity of his exercise routine. By doing something on such a regular basis, he made it a habit. No doubt he factored time for running into his daily schedule when making other commitments and appointments. I don't advocate aiming for doing something every single day of your life because it entails all-or-nothing thinking. But the more you can schedule any weight loss or fitness efforts into your daily routine, the less you'll have to think about them, and the less likely you'll be to think of excuses not to do them.

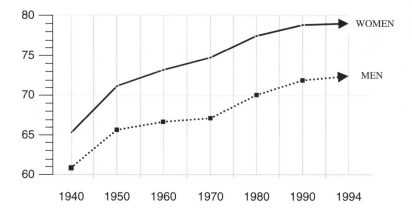

Life expectancy for Americans has increased steadily since 1940. (Centers for Disease Control)

➤ **Do what you enjoy, or at least do what you don't hate.** I used to think that I wasn't trying hard enough to lose weight or get fit because I wasn't going to aerobics classes. Then I remembered that I wasn't going to aerobics classes because I hate them. I hate the loud, obnoxious music. I hate the grunting and counting chants from the instructor. I hate feeling like a klutz because I can't follow choreography so complicated it would impress Debbie Allen. So I don't do them. I go to the gym and do nothing but weight training because I kind of enjoy it. I try to walk to the gym and back (it's about a mile) and to take long walks on the alternate days, so I do get some cardiovascular workout. You might love aerobics classes and hate weightlifting. That's fine. The point is to do what you enjoy—or at least what you don't hate—rather than what you think you're supposed to be doing.

➤ **Play tricks.** Playing little tricks on yourself can be a powerful way to help you stay motivated while losing weight or getting fit. Over a year after having a baby, when I was going to the gym to get back in shape (yes, I put it off that long!), I used to play a silly game that worked wonders. At each visit, I would use a locker whose number corresponded to my weight that day. As I lost weight, I'd move to a locker with a lower number. It seemed like a meaningless little game, but I found that I looked forward to going to the gym to see that visible symbol of my weight loss. Plus, it helped that the lockers with lower numbers were in more desirable locations in the locker room!

As I said before, what worked for me won't necessarily work for you. But adapting these methods to fit your needs, your psyche, and your life can work. In my case, by banishing all-or-nothing thinking, writing exercise into my schedule, rewarding myself for reaching goals, and letting myself skip the gym from time to time or gorge on cookies occasionally, I've managed to lose weight and keep it off and to maintain a moderate exercise routine. I know you've heard people say this before, but it's true: If I can do it, I know you can.

Making Medical and Dental Appointments

Losing weight and getting fit are health procrastination issues just as much as they are issues of appearance and self-esteem. Another health procrastination issue is putting off medical and dental appointments.

You know that doctors, dentists, and other health professionals can make the hurt go away or can keep it from coming in the first place through preventive care. You know you're supposed to have regular checkups. You know you should be screened or immunized at certain ages for various conditions (for example, having mammograms, rectal exams, cholesterol checks, and other pokes and prods most women and men would gladly put off). You know how important medical and dental care is, but you don't always get around to getting it, do you?

Here are some of the classic excuses, along with a reality check for each one:

"I feel fine. The doctor will only find something wrong."

Reality: If you're fine, that's what the doctor will find. If you're not fine, you should know about it before the problem goes undetected and worsens.

"There's no history of serious disease or illness in my family, so I don't have to worry."

Reality: It's a major myth that genetics account for most major health problems. You can get breast cancer, colon cancer, and many other terrible diseases with no family history.

"The pain will go away."

Reality: And just how do you think that's going to happen? Maybe you can cover it up for a while, and maybe it will even disappear for a while, but like a bad debt and bad ex-lovers, pain usually comes back to haunt you.

"It won't make a difference. If I'm going to get cancer, I'm going to get it."

Reality: Of course it will make a difference. Early detection does wonders in improving your chances of surviving most treatable diseases. If you'd rather not undergo debilitating treatments for a terminal condition, no one can force you to.

"It hurts."

Reality: The things that doctors, dentists, physical therapists, and other health care providers have to do to you sometimes don't exactly feel like lying in a bed of rose petals. But 9 times out of 10, the pain that comes with preventive care or treatment for a problem is much milder than what you'd experience if problems went undetected and untreated.

"I don't have time."

Reality: You do have the time for something this important.

"I don't like my doctor."

Reality: Get a new one. Even with HMOs, you usually have a choice of at least a few doctors.

"I don't know who to go to."

Reality: I know this is often a valid reason for delay. For a variety of reasons, my family's health insurance has changed several times in the last few years. Sometimes, doctors we've seen are in the new plan, but often we find ourselves having to choose new general practitioners or specialists. I know that frustrating feeling of randomly choosing a doctor out of a directory based on nothing more than the office location or how you like the sound of his or her name. You can make the process less haphazard by asking for referrals from friends and neighbors, and then seeing which ones are part of your plan. Some health plans can provide patient ratings of member doctors.

Action Tactic

If you've been putting off quitting smoking, look for some motivation in the success stories, advice, and resources available in the iVillage Kickbutt Community at www.betterhealth.com/kickbutt.

"My health plan/health insurance doesn't cover it."

Reality: Most plans cover basic checkups and many tests. If you have a dollar limit you can't go over in a given year, however, and an expensive test would require out-of-pocket expenses, or if the visit isn't covered at all, look for alternatives. Contact hospitals in your area, as well as your state's Department of Health, for suggestions of any free or low-cost services you might use.

"I can't afford to go to the doctor."

Reality: Sadly, this is the reality for far too many people who don't have health insurance. Follow the same advice given for those who do have insurance but just aren't covered for certain procedures.

Hobbies? What Are Those?

Most resolutions are about things that are good for us or that we need to do but don't necessarily want to do. Sometimes, though, we see the New Year, or any other time we envision a fresh start, as a chance to inject some new life into our daily routines. That often means revisiting a long-forgotten hobby or taking up a new one.

Matter of Fact

Hobbies are usually thought of as solitary activities. In fact, it's that quiet time alone that draws many people to arts and crafts, collecting, and other leisure activities. But if you'd like to connect with other people who share your interests, go to www.forhobbies.com. This comprehensive site has links to all sorts of hobby groups, from the British Origami Association to the Federation of Historical Bottle Collectors. The site also links you to sources of supplies, equipment, and how-to information on pursuits as varied as making Scottish bagpipes to collecting PEZ dispensers.

It seems almost passé to talk about hobbies in an age of fast-paced lives where work, hectic family lives, and more work take up most of our time. We think of hobbies as being the domain of retirees and the idle rich. I recently attended a conference for career counselors, where a woman presenting a session on how to help clients identify their skills asked the audience for examples of some hobbies they had. She wanted to show us how the things people do in their leisure time usually involve skills that they enjoy using and might want to incorporate into their paid work. A surprisingly small number of hands went up, particularly considering that the group had been very talkative and not shy about participating up to that point. Among the audience members within earshot of my seat, I heard whispered comments like, "If only I had time for a hobby!" and "I used to have hobbies," or "Hobby? What's that?"

Finally, someone spoke up and told the group that she does Ukrainian egg painting. "How neat!," I thought. The workshop leader then took us through an analysis of the skills that person uses to pursue her hobby. As expected, we found that some skills were related to her profession, such as researching (she has to know the history of Ukrainian art and culture), attention to detail, and working independently. Other skills, however, were completely different from those she utilizes on her job: creative and artistic expression, working with her hands, and so forth.

The point here is that hobbies serve as an important escape for us. They let us flex our mental, and maybe even physical, muscles in a way that our jobs don't allow. A full-time mother, for example, might find solace in pursuing her hobby of collectibles by logging onto Internet auction sites after the kids are tucked in bed, the dinner dishes are put away, and the house is quiet. A salesman who spends all day talking to people and dealing with business matters may find comfort in writing poetry and short stories in his free time. Whether you call it a hobby, a leisure pursuit, recreation, or just that thing you do in your spare time, it's essential for keeping balance in life.

Getting Back on Your Hobby Horse

If you're a procrastinator who has trouble getting the important things in life taken care of, how will you ever get around to doing something as non-urgent, and seemingly insignificant, as a hobby? Whether you're trying to take up a new hobby or pick back up one you used to have, try this six-step process:

1. If it's a former hobby you're trying to revisit, ask yourself if you really want to pursue it again. Sometimes people feel obligated to pick a hobby back up because friends or family say things like, "What a shame it is that you don't paint anymore. You had such talent." Or, "Are you going to let all those expensive supplies go to waste?" Don't let yourself be coerced into doing something you don't particularly enjoy or no longer have an interest in. Find a new hobby or take a break from hobbies altogether for a while. If, however, you would like to get back to it, but just can't seem to rally yourself to do anything about it, then read on to the next steps. (The same goes for taking up a new hobby: Make sure you choose something you'd really like to do; otherwise, you're just wasting your time.)

2. Schedule a date in your calendar to assemble any supplies or equipment you might need. If you already have what you need, but it's buried in a closet or the garage, plan a time to unearth it. If you'll need to purchase some new things, write that task on your to-do list and schedule a time to do it.

3. If you have enough room in your home to do so, set up a hobby workspace. Most people do this for hobbies that require a great deal of space and equipment, such as woodworking, but they don't always think of setting up a workspace for "smaller" hobbies. Even if all your hobby paraphernalia can fit in a shoebox, make sure that that shoebox has its designated place.

4. If you don't have enough room to set aside a separate workspace, then at least keep your supplies in a place that makes them visible and easily accessible. If you have to go to a great deal of trouble to unpack and set up your supplies and equipment every time, you might get slowed down by the set-up step and never get to the hobby.

5. Find a regular time to pursue the hobby. Schedule it into your weekly or monthly routine just as you would any other important appointment or household task. Let your friends, family, and roommates know that that particular time or day is hobby time so that they won't try to get you to do something else.

6. If your hobby is one that can be done in a group, try to find other people who do the same thing, and do it with them. Or whether your hobby is a solitary or group-oriented one, consider taking a class in it. You'll not only brush up on your skills and learn something new, you'll also be making more of a commitment to it.

Action Tactic

To find out where you can go to learn something new, check out the Seminar Finder at www.seminarfinder.com. This Web site lists seminars offered around the country in a wide variety of fields.

Finding the time and energy for a hobby is much like any other task. It's a matter of making it a priority in your life and then working it into your routine so that it becomes a habit.

Learning Something New

It's easy to say you'd like to get up-to-speed on computers, learn to speak another language, figure out how your car's engine works, or improve your public speaking skills. It's much harder to rally yourself into doing it. When learning something new is not absolutely essential for your job, it's easy to put off. Besides the obvious problem of not seeing it as a priority, there are three main reasons why that happens:

1. **You don't know where to go.** The choices of schools, universities, seminar centers, and other venues for taking a course or two (as opposed to going back to school for a degree, which is discussed in Chapter 21, "Cramming for Exams and Other Fine Academic Traditions") can be confusing. Use the educational Web sites listed in Appendix C as a guide for making sense of the choices.

2. **You don't have enough time.** Remember those 10 life roles described in Chapter 3, "Blame It on the Environment"? Being a lifelong learner is an important piece of that puzzle. That doesn't mean that if your other life roles are on overload, you should add more responsibilities to your plate by going back to school. Learning something new does take effort and energy, so you need to make sure your other roles aren't too crowded. But don't use lack of time as an excuse if you can find the time through some minor reworking of your schedule and priorities.

3. **You can't afford it.** Some courses taken on an individual basis through university continuing education divisions or private institutions are expensive. There are, however, other options. Public libraries, community centers, religious institutions, senior citizens' centers, and other nonprofit agencies might offer what you're looking for at a low cost or possibly even for free.

You're always going to put off learning something new until you recognize that, even though your job might not depend on it, learning new things is important for being a well-rounded, content person.

Keeping a Diary or Journal

Writing for self-expression or to record events in your life is a most worthwhile pursuit. I procrastinated writing about this topic, however, because I myself have never been able to keep a diary or journal for more than a few days or weeks at a time intermittently throughout my life. I thought, "What could I say to my readers if I can't practice what I preach?" Then, while writing this book, I attended a conference and received just the inspiration I needed to write this section.

The inspiration came while I was dining alone in the hotel restaurant one night before the conference began. I was seated at a table just a few inches away from where two women who appeared to be in their 70s were having dinner. I didn't mean to eavesdrop, but until I had placed my order and become engrossed in the book I'd brought, I couldn't help but listen to what they were saying. My ears perked up when I heard one of them mention coming across a journal she'd kept 40 years earlier, during the first year she knew her future husband. She said to her friend, "I haven't been able to get myself to keep a journal since then, but I'm grateful that I did for just that one year." That's when I realized that I had been applying all-or-nothing, perfectionist thinking to the task of keeping a diary or journal. It doesn't matter if you write in it religiously or just jot down some thoughts from time to time. You'll enjoy looking back on it someday.

Reading More

I was surprised by how high "Keeping up with things I want to read" rated on the procrastination survey. In the rankings of questionnaire items based on how often they were cited as procrastination problems, reading for pleasure was fourth. It showed that what I've been saying about people not having time for much besides work and household demands is true. If you have a stack of books waiting to be devoured or can't even find the time to buy or borrow any books, try these tips:

➤ Consider listening to books on tape as a way to fit reading into a busy schedule, particularly if you drive a lot or listen to a personal stereo while commuting or exercising.

➤ Pay a weekly visit to an online bookstore as a convenient, quick way to get up to speed on what everybody's reading and to order your books (usually at a discount) from the comfort of your home or office.

➤ Schedule a visit to the library into your weekly, or even just monthly, routine. Make it a habit to stop by and pick up a few books so that you do it without even thinking about it instead of making it seem like a big deal.

Action Tactic

To get motivated to read more, consider joining an online book club. Two good ones are Coffeerooms Book*Mark at www.gurlfriends.com/features/books and Online Reading Club at www.net-language.com/readclub.

➤ Join a book club (also known as a reading circle), a group of people who read the same books and then meet to discuss them in someone's home, a café, or some other venue. All right, I know you don't have time to read, so how are you going to get to meetings of a book club or reading circle? Like lots of things people procrastinate about, making reading a group activity is a way to make a commitment to it. If you know you have to have a book read by a certain meeting date, you might be surprised to find free time you didn't know you had.

➤ Read in high-tech style. Be one of the first to start reading electronic books, which are published novels and nonfiction books that you read off a pocket-sized, hand-held device. They weigh in at a mere 22 ounces or so, but they can hold about 10 novels and a dictionary. You can get more information about them at www.rocket-ebook.com.

If you're a purist who enjoys browsing in real live bookstores, not virtual ones, and who likes to turn the pages of a book instead of clicking a button on an electronic doodad, some of these tips probably won't appeal to you. But if they're the only way you can catch up on your reading, don't knock them until you've tried them.

The Least You Need to Know

➤ New Year's resolutions aren't kept because we expect dramatic changes too quickly.

➤ All-or-nothing thinking may be the biggest cause of putting off weight loss or exercise.

➤ Investing a little time and money in preventive health care will save you a lot in the long run.

➤ It's important to make time for hobbies to flex your mental, and maybe even physical, muscles in ways that your job or family commitments don't.

Chapter 17

Death, Taxes, and Other Important Stuff

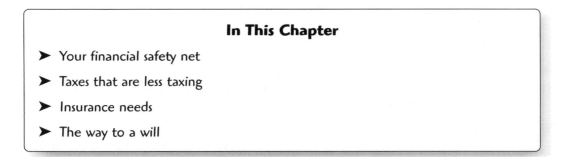

In This Chapter

➤ Your financial safety net

➤ Taxes that are less taxing

➤ Insurance needs

➤ The way to a will

Isn't it amazing how easy it is to put off the things in life that are the most important for your security and well-being? Just about everybody knows how important it is to pay bills on time, plan for a financially secure future, file income taxes, and have an up-to-date will and adequate insurance coverage. But does everyone do it? Hardly.

The fact that so many people procrastinate about such critical matters is proof that fear is not always enough of a motivator to spark action. You know the negative consequences that can result if you don't attend to important stuff, but for some reason, you just can't make yourself deal with it all. This chapter will examine why that's the case and what you can do about it.

Keep in mind that this chapter doesn't take the place of expert advice on such issues as financial planning, tax preparation, writing wills, and selecting insurance policies. Entire books focus on those complex topics. The emphasis in this chapter is on identifying your mental and environmental blocks to taking care of these matters and on strategies for getting past those blocks. Then when you're ready to take action, you can turn to the resources (books, Web sites, and organizations) recommended throughout this chapter and in the appendixes.

Why the Bottom Line Is Often Last in Line

If the greeting card and schmaltzy music industries are right, then love makes the world go around. But ask any regular Joe or Josephine on the street what makes the world tick, and they'll probably tell you it's money. Deep down, we know that money doesn't buy happiness, but it can sure make life a little easier. So why is it that we make our lives harder by procrastinating when it comes to financial matters?

Action Tactic

If traditional personal finance magazines and Web sites (the ones geared toward white males in their mid-40s with $100,000+ a year salaries) aren't for you, take a look at theWhiz.com at www.theWhiz.com. Its unconventional and entertaining—yet substantive and knowledgeable—approach to money matters might get you on the road to doing something about your finances.

Where Did I Put Those Canceled Checks?

Sometimes financial procrastination is simply due to a lack of organization. We have lousy filing systems or none at all, so our paid and unpaid bills, canceled checks, pay stubs, banking and investment statements, and other important documents end up strewn all over the place. We don't know which ones to keep, how long to keep them, or where to put them. That lack of organization makes for one tall obstacle when it's time to file tax returns, prepare a budget, pay bills, or do major financial planning. Instead of chasing down all the papers and figures you need, it's easier to say, "I'll deal with it later."

The obvious solution to that problem is to set up simple and functional filing systems once and for all so that keeping your financial records straight doesn't have to be a big deal. The filing tips suggested in Chapter 10, "A Crash Course in Getting Organized," are a good place to start. For organizational tips more specifically tailored to finances, take a look at the books and Web sites in the "Getting Organized" and the "Finance" sections of Appendixes A and C. In addition, some professional organizers specialize in putting your financial papers in order or do so as part of an overall organizing job. Financial advisors and planners can guide you in determining what to keep and what to get rid of, and personal finance software can help you set up and maintain the records you do need to keep.

Did I Even Need to Save Those Canceled Checks?

Financial procrastination can also result from lack of knowledge. If no one has ever taught you how to keep your finances in order, plan a budget, handle credit responsibly, and invest wisely, you can't be expected to know how to do those things. There's nothing wrong with not knowing how to do something. There is something wrong with not making an effort to learn what you need to know, or when possible, to hire someone to do what you don't know how to do. That's what financial planners, debt counselors, and others who make it their business to keep up to speed on money matters are there for. That's also why financial advice abounds in books and on Web sites, like many of those listed in the appendixes of this book.

Your Love-Hate Relationship with Money

Suze Orman, the author of best-selling books on finding financial freedom and Oprah Winfrey's "finance angel," talks about things like integrity, faith, and courage when she talks about money. Orman warns us not to blame ourselves for get-

You're Not Alone

It isn't enough for you to love money—it's also necessary that money should love you.

—Baron Rothschild

ting into debt or for mismanaging money but to concentrate instead on moving forward by mapping out a plan for improving our situation. She suggests that we put aside our fears and negativity and is known for frequently saying, "Our thoughts create our destiny."

If you're currently in the hate part of a love-hate relationship with money, you might be tempted to discount all that as a bunch of psychobabble. If not enough money is coming your way and too much is leaving your hands, I know it can be difficult to see how things like courage and faith are going to raise your bank balance. Suze Orman's advice makes sense, though. As with any type of procrastination, putting off dealing with your finances often has less to do with a lack of organization or knowledge and more to do with your emotional battle with money. Until you can identify and deal with the irrational, self-defeating thoughts at the root of your money problems, the best nuts-and-bolts financial strategies in the world won't help you.

Paying Bills

You know that life is much easier when you pay your bills and pay them on time. You don't have to avoid answering the phone for fear that it's a bill collector. You keep from having to pay late fees and interest. Your credit rating stays untarnished (or is repaired if it's been less than perfect). Most important, you have peace of mind. Maybe you know all that, but you still can't seem to get those checks in the mail. There are three basic reasons why that happens. See which one rings a bell for you:

1. **No money.** If you don't have the money to pay your bills, you can't pay them. Perhaps you've lost your job, or the breadwinner in your household has. Or maybe you've had some unexpected expenses come up due to a medical emergency or other mishap. To delay paying your bills in those sorts of situations is not really procrastination, given that you might gladly pay if only you had the funds to do so. (There may, however, be procrastination behind the problem. Perhaps you've been putting off preparing a budget, curbing your spending habit, or overusing credit cards. These issues are dealt with in the sections that follow this one.)

219

Solution: Recognize that many people face financial difficulties from time to time through no fault of their own, so there's no need to be embarrassed by your predicament. Rather than ignoring the problem you have paying bills due to lack of money, face up to it and ask your creditors for some leniency. Most will help you work out payment plans that are feasible as you ride out a difficult time.

2. **Lack of organization.** Some people don't pay bills merely because they lose track of what needs to be paid and when to pay it. When their bills come in the mail, they let them get scattered all over home or office and don't keep any logs or schedules of payments due and payments made. They also might not file their payment receipts or bill stubs well, so they can't keep track of what they've already paid.

   Solution: Use the stacking tray sorting system described in Chapter 10 so that you can put all your bills in one place for easy access. Some people prefer to keep their bills in accordion-pleated folders that have pockets in which you can sort bills according to the type of bill or date each month when it needs to be paid. Also, schedule a regular time once or twice a month (or more often, if necessary) during which you sit down and pay bills. That way, you only have to worry about them on those dates and don't have to wonder on the other days what you should have paid already or what is coming due.

3. **Defiance.** Some people put off paying bills despite their fat bank accounts. They have a mental block against writing the checks and getting them in the mail, even though they have plenty of money to back up those checks. It's a way of gaining some small degree of control over their finances and their lives and a way to express their resentment over having to fork over their hard-earned dollars. It's a way of saying to the phone company, the gas company, or whomever, "I'm going to hold onto my money as long as I can to show that you're not so powerful. I'm not going to let you use my money for one single day longer than I have to."

   Solution: Get over it! This act of defiance is bound to backfire on you. Paying bills late or right down to the wire means you end up paying more in late fees and, in cases of repeated offenses, marring your credit rating. Plus, you pay for it in stress.

Budgeting

Budgets have about the same reputation as brussels sprouts. We know they're good for us, but we just can't get too excited about them. If you've been putting off preparing or following a budget, your procrastination may be due to misconceptions about what the task entails. First, you might balk at the idea of putting a budget together because it seems like such a complex project, or you don't know how to do it. It doesn't have to be a major chore. If you've organized all your financial data and bills, and if you use books or software to guide you, then a budget should take no more than part of an evening or a weekday afternoon. You'll probably be pleasantly surprised at how much easier it is than you had expected.

A second reason why people put off preparing a budget—or go through the motions of preparing one but don't use it—is that they think life won't be fun anymore. Living within a budget makes us think of sacrifice and scrimping. It's true that if you're trying to dig yourself out of a financial hole, then you might have to follow a strict budget that doesn't allow for too many splurges. But, in most cases, a budget has room for a few luxuries built into it.

Quicksand!

If you prepare a budget but never look at it again, it's of no use to you. Don't go to all the trouble to make a budget only to bury it in a forgotten folder on your hard drive or in the dark recesses of a file cabinet drawer. Keep it close at hand so that you'll have a constant reminder of what you should be doing with your money.

The idea behind a budget is that it helps you get a handle on where your money is going and how much you can spend on various things in order to remain, or become, financially secure. It also ensures that you're setting aside enough to save or invest to be not just secure, but comfortable in the long run. Having a budget is like having a routine for your regular chores and errands. It should be liberating, not constricting. By putting your expenses and financial plans down on paper, you don't have to worry about whether you're spending too much or saving too little, and about bills that might come out of left field down the road. The budget guides you in making day-to-day financial decisions and helps you anticipate future financial hiccups, but don't take my word for it: Try it for one month and see how it works for you.

Getting out of Debt

Before writing this chapter, I perused many Web sites that focus on personal finance (such as those listed in the Finance section of Appendix C). I wanted to get a sense of just how much debt people around this country are in. I knew that a recent U.S. Census Bureau study found that one out of every five households is touched by financial problems, such as mounting debt and inability to meet expenses. I knew that I'd faced my own struggles with debt and with trying to do something about it. But I wanted to put some real faces—or at least real screen names—to that statistic.

You're Not Alone

Carrying around all the debts I have is like walking around with a 100-pound weight hanging from my neck. I worry about them every day, but I don't do anything about it. I say it's because I don't have the money to pay them off, but I know there must be ways around that. But now the problem has built up so much I feel like I'll never dig myself out of the hole.

—Lee M., editor

It's an Epidemic

What I found wasn't necessarily shocking, because I'd suspected that lots of people were in debt up to their proverbial armpits, but it certainly was discouraging. Pleas for help on message boards, case studies in experts' articles, and people in chat rooms talked of debts in the tens and even hundreds of thousands of dollars. These people are just regular people of all ages. They're not wheelers and dealers who've lost gobs of money playing the market or lost their shirts in risky business ventures. They're ordinary folks who've gotten in debt from student loans or other borrowing, who've lost their jobs and can't keep up with bills, or who've let their spending get out of control.

The Symptoms of Debt Procrastination

You know you're procrastinating getting out of debt if you find yourself using any of these excuses:

"It's too overwhelming to deal with. There's just no hope. I'll never dig myself out of this hole."

Strategy: Realize that there's always hope and that the problem is not going to go away, so you have to tackle it. What you have to do is get the problem out of your head, where it's festering into a major worry, and get it on paper. You might find that it isn't as bad as you thought. But even if the numbers do paint a dismal picture, don't let yourself become overwhelmed. A credit counseling service or financial advisor can help you look at your spending habits and work out a strategy for consolidating your debts (so that you have fewer monthly payments to keep track of) or reducing your debts by negotiating with creditors. Just knowing that you have a plan makes it all seem much less overwhelming.

"I'm afraid to contact any of my creditors because I must be in such deep trouble. I don't want them to take away my house or other property once they get their hands on me."

Strategy: Running away from the problem won't keep the bill collectors away. If you make the effort to contact them and begin chipping away at the debt, most creditors will be willing to work with you rather than immediately pounce on your possessions. In *Surviving Debt: A Guide for Consumers*, a book by The National Consumer Law Center, the authors point out that creditors often have less power than you think to collect a debt. Sure, they have legal means at their disposal, but they would usually rather work out a plan to collect their money than have to take legal action against you.

Matter of Fact

Getting into debt that's way over your head can be an isolating experience. You might be embarrassed, afraid of legal ramifications, and totally clueless about where to turn. Here are two good resources:

Consumer Credit Counseling Services is a nationwide agency offering advice on getting out of debt and restoring or maintaining good credit. Call 800-388-2227 for the number of a local office near you or look it up at www.debthelpnow.org.

Debt Counselors® (www.dca.org or 800-680-3328) offers a wealth of information on credit problems, bankruptcy, and related dilemmas. Its Crisis Relief Team^{SM} includes nationally recognized experts on finance, accounting, and law.

"I'm so embarrassed about my debts. I don't want to ask anyone for help because I don't want anyone to know about them."

Strategy: If you're embarrassed to tell friends or family about your debts, don't be. You don't have to show your laundry list of debts to the world, but seeking advice, emotional support, and possibly even financial assistance from carefully chosen friends or family members can lift a big weight off your shoulders. If you choose the right people, they're not going to ridicule or lecture you; they'll want to help. For more anonymity, you can always turn to a credit counseling service or financial advisor. Remember, they've heard it all, so your situation is not going to shock them. As for the creditors themselves, there's been a movement lately toward training bill collectors to be nicer and more like regular human beings. Although there's a chance that they'll ask you why you haven't been able to pay, they're not likely to grill you or make you feel like a bad person. They just need to know if and when you can make payments. If they do get nasty with you, take their names and report them to their supervisors.

"I don't think my debts are a problem."

Strategy: Being in denial is a big mistake. Maybe your debts aren't a problem now, but they could be if they continue to grow. Or perhaps your financial records and bills are disorganized, so you don't realize how big your debts are. Schedule a time to go through your bills and make a list of debts so that you can see what your true situation is.

Quicksand!

You may think that being in debt is your problem, and yours alone, but remember that it can affect other people down the line. If you need to co-sign a loan or get a joint credit card with a business partner or spouse, your debts and credit rating will come back to haunt not only you, but the other person as well.

"I don't have the money to pay off my debts."

Strategy: You might be surprised to know the extent to which creditors are willing to work something out with you. They might reduce the total amount you owe, reduce the interest being charged, eliminate late fees, spread out monthly payments, or make other arrangements that you can handle. You can try to arrange these deals individually or with the help of a credit counseling service.

"Some of these debts aren't right or are unfair. I shouldn't have to pay them."

Strategy: I remember the day I got a bill for $150 from a long-distance phone carrier for the calling card I'd used in a business I had closed three months earlier. Seems that when I called them to switch my phone service to a new number because I had moved from a regular office to working from home, they didn't cancel the card. I hadn't used the calling card number for three months, but I had been racking up a $50 a month, business-rate, basic service charge without realizing it. I tried to dispute the charge because it seemed incredibly unfair, but I was told that it had been my responsibility to stop the card or to switch the rate to a residential rate. I could've pursued the matter further because I did feel the charge was unjustified, but I made the decision not to. The time and money that would be involved in taking legal action was bound to be more than $150. Even if I didn't take legal recourse, pursuing the complaint more formally was not a way I wanted to spend my time. I hated writing that check, but getting it out of the way gave me peace of mind; pressing the matter would've been a major headache.

You don't necessarily have to make the same decision, especially if you're dealing with larger sums of money or completely unjust charges. Just make sure, though, that the legal costs or general hassle factor are worth the trouble.

No matter which excuses you've been using, getting out of debt requires owning up to the problem, facing it head on by mapping out a strategy, and adjusting your spending habits to make that strategy work.

Planning for a Secure Future

Procrastinators are famous for living in the present. They take the path of least resistance doing what's easiest and most satisfying at any given moment, no matter what the future consequences of that action might be. One of the most dangerous implications of this approach to life is in the area of financial planning, whether that's saving money for retirement, investing money to reach financial goals, or gaining security through insurance coverage.

Saving and Investing

Government statistics show that only 2 out of every 100 people are financially independent when they reach age 65. The rest have to keep working or rely on the government or relatives for financial security. Some careful advance planning, specifically saving and investing, can make those so-called golden years a lot richer. Unfortunately, many people procrastinate when it comes to long-range financial planning.

It's not just retirement planning that gets put off. Saving for kids' college tuition or for future purchases such as a house is something that's usually nagging at the back of procrastinators' minds, but they rarely take action. Here are some of the excuses for delaying:

Action Tactic

If paying college tuition is in your future, get some advice from *Paying for College Without Going Broke* by Kalman Chany. With the helpful strategies and tips it offers, you might get motivated to do something about your financial planning rather than just worry about it.

"I'm too young to have to worry about that now."

"I don't have enough money to save or invest."

"I have plenty of money, so there's no need to worry."

"I don't know where to begin. All the options are confusing."

"I'm afraid of being conned by a financial advisor."

"I'll have to spend too much time monitoring my investments."

"There are too many things I want to spend money on now."

"I have a 401(k) plan through my employer, so I don't need to do anything else."

There are basically two simple truths at work here that you need to be aware of:

1. You're never too young to save and invest, no matter what your future might hold and no matter how little you can put aside each month or each year.

2. Unless finance is your profession, you shouldn't expect yourself to be able to muddle through the dizzying array of savings and investment options. You have to seek expert advice from a qualified professional. The organizations in the Finance section of Appendix B can refer you to the right person, as can some of the financial Web sites listed in Appendix C.

You're Not Alone

Gentlemen prefer bonds.

—Andrew Mellon

Action Tactic

If you've been putting off purchasing life, disability, or health insurance, or changing a current policy, take one simple step to get started. Contact any of these companies, which maintain databases of the top insurers and can help you find the lowest rate and best policy: MasterQuote at 800-337-5433 or www.masterquote.com; QuickQuote at www.quickquote.com; Quotesmith.com at 800-431-1147 or www.quotesmith.com; and TermQuote at 800-444-8376 or www.term-quote.com.

Insurance

People put off getting, maintaining, and updating insurance coverage for many of the same reasons they procrastinate about financial planning. They think they're too young and healthy to need life or disability insurance. They think that damage to homes and property only happens to the natural disaster victims they see on television and won't happen to them. Talk about denial! There's no excuse in the book that can justify assuming nothing is going to happen to you, your family, or your possessions.

If you're willing to acknowledge that, but still find it mind-boggling to try to sort through all the different companies and types of policies offering life, disability, health, auto, and homeowner's insurance, take a look at The Consumer Insurance Guide at www.insure.com. It offers lots of helpful advice for choosing insurance plans or for dealing with ones you already have.

If affording insurance is what's holding you back (as is often the case with health insurance for those not covered through an employer), the Consumer Insurance Guide site, as well as some overall strategizing with a financial advisor, can help you find a way to make it happen.

The Annual Tax Procrastinator's Ball

Each year as April 15 approaches, the U.S. Postal Service expects tens of millions of last-minute income tax filers. Although it would prefer that everybody file long before the midnight deadline, it does extend post office hours around the country and offer conveniences like late mailbox pickups and curbside drop collection points.

Even local businesses get in on the act. According to news releases from the Postal Service (www.usps.gov), festivities in recent years have included:

➤ A Harrisburg, Pennsylvania post office welcomed taxpayers with the world's "Largest IRS Tax Loophole," composed of 1,040 red, white, and blue balloons in the shape of an arch.

➤ The worst procrastinator in Charleston, West Virginia received a trophy from the Charleston Postmaster.

➤ A local radio station broadcasting live from the San Francisco Processing and Distribution Center paid the taxes of one lucky listener.

➤ The Leslie Gore tune, "It's My Party (and I'll Cry if I Want to)," rang out in the lobby of the Springfield, Illinois main post office on tax night courtesy of a local oldies radio station. A disc jockey handed out tax relief packages of Rolaids and aspirin to Springfield customers "Crying" along with Roy Orbison over their 1040s.

Matter of Fact

Taxes may be the last thing on your mind during the lazy, hazy days of summer, but summer is one of the best times to think about them. Doing so gives you a chance to make financial adjustments while there's still time. You can review any new tax-break legislation, and if you're paying estimated taxes, you can look at your year-to-date income to see whether you're paying enough. You'll also still have several months to plan any charitable donations and to make contributions to retirement plans or other investment accounts.

Clearly, the last-minute tax rush can look like more of a party than a bunch of frazzled citizens fulfilling their civic duty. But what if it's a party you'd rather not attend? If you'd like to get over your taxing procrastination, try these tactics:

➤ Break down the project of preparing and filing into steps (such as: obtain forms, assemble records, prepare information, and set an appointment with a tax preparer). Make a list of the steps involved.

➤ Focus on do dates, not the due date. Forget about April 15 for a while and instead schedule dates and times to do each step in the process leading up to April 15.

➤ Keep your financial records well organized so that you won't have to dread rounding up all the information you need.

➤ Don't wait for the motivation or desire to do your taxes, because it may never come. Just accept that you have to do them whether you want to or not.

➤ If possible, have a qualified tax preparer do them for you.

➤ File your taxes online using systems such as www.turbotax.com. The convenience of doing them from your home and the ease of being guided through the process might motivate you to start earlier.

You're Not Alone

We'd been meaning to write wills since our first daughter was born six years ago, but weren't sure who to name as guardians. Plus, we couldn't quite face the thought of dying. Two things finally kick-started us. My brother got married, providing us with perfect guardians. And we felt the need to scratch out last-minute wills before a helicopter ride in Hawaii!

—Becky A., technical writer

➤ Get past your emotional resentment toward the IRS. Nobody likes to pay taxes, and many of us resent some of the things that our tax dollars are used for. But if you think that holding off until 11:59 P.M. on April 15 is sending a message to the government, forget about it. You're only inconveniencing yourself and stressing yourself out. If you want to do something about taxes, write your Congressperson.

➤ Make a fun plan with friends or family, preferably the sort of thing you have to buy tickets for in advance, for the evenings of April 14 and 15, so you'll have an incentive to be finished by then.

The Reality of Mortality

As the saying goes, only two things in life are guaranteed: death and taxes. We know why you put off dealing with taxes; now let's look at why you procrastinate dealing with death. Do you delay putting together or updating a will or doing some serious estate planning for any of these reasons?

➤ You don't think you have enough assets to warrant estate planning.

➤ You're too young to worry about it. It's not an urgent priority.

➤ You don't like to make the sorts of big decisions that will-writing or estate planning would require you to make.

➤ You figure it will all go to the government anyway, so why bother?

➤ You don't want to hurt anyone's feelings by excluding them from your will or giving them less than others.

➤ You don't like to think about dying.

➤ You're superstitious; if you write a will, you'll die soon after.

➤ You can't afford to work with an attorney.

Valid excuses? 'Fraid not. If you die intestate, which means without a will, the state determines what happens with your money and property. In most cases, the laws dictate that your estate goes to your spouse and children, if you have them. That may sound fine, but how do you know they'll divide it up the way you would want? And what if you're single? How does the state know you would want some of your assets to go to your favorite charity or that your book collection should go to your best friend and your big-screen television to your couch-potato cousin? Experts estimate that only 30 percent of the population has a will. The remaining 70 percent dies intestate. You don't want to be one of those.

Wills and Estate Planning

Many people don't understand the difference between estate planning and preparing a will, so they put off doing either. Basically, a will is a part of your overall estate planning. The will is the document that says who gets what, who should be the guardian of any minor children you have, and who you want to serve as executor. (Your executor is the person who handles your estate, whether that estate is a bank account with $100 in it and some personal effects or a multimillion-dollar portfolio of property, cash, and investments.)

Some people only need to write a simple will. But others, with more significant assets, need to do estate planning with the help of attorneys and financial advisors. Estate planning is basically a form of financial planning in which you do things such as set up trusts or invest and bequest your money in ways that will minimize the taxes your heirs will have to pay on the gifts you leave them. According to Stephen Rosenberg in his book *Last-Minute Estate Planning* (a perfect title for procrastinators!), "Estate planning is the process by which, during your life and after your death, you can control your property in the manner you desire, minimizing all fees, taxes, and court interference, preserving for yourself, your family, and those you choose, the estate you have worked so hard to create."

Quicksand!

If you really don't want to be a procrastinator, you can make arrangements and prepayments for your funeral long before you die so that your loved ones won't have to deal with all that. Beware of con artists, though. Scams are all too common. If in doubt, check out the National Funeral Directors Association's *Consumer Tips on Prepaying Your Funeral* at www.nfda.org or call 800-228-6332 for assistance.

You're Not Alone

Ten years ago when I remarried, it crossed my mind that if something happened to me, would my husband know what sentimental items I'd want passed on to my three daughters? We talked about wills then, again three years later when I got pregnant, bought software to make wills two years later, reminded ourselves each year after that, but haven't done it. I think it's procrastination of facing the inevitable—death.

—Cynthia D., professional counselor

The Least You Need to Know

➤ Putting off dealing with finances usually results from lack of organization, lack of knowledge, or emotional problems with money.

➤ Paying bills, budgeting, and getting out of debt are a matter of facing up to your problems and responsibilities and finding the right strategies.

➤ You're never too young or too old to make financial plans for the future.

➤ There's nothing fun about filing your taxes late.

➤ You may not want to think about death, but estate planning and will preparation can let you rest in peace when the time comes.

Chapter 18

Put It in Writing

In This Chapter

➤ The lost—and delayed—art of social correspondence

➤ Complaining while the iron is hot

➤ Strategies for breaking through writer's block

Whether it's that Great American Novel brewing within you or just a note to Aunt Betty thanking her for the lovely ceramic frog, writing is many procrastinators' biggest nightmare. This chapter focuses primarily on writing tasks you might face in your personal life, such as thank-you notes, letters of condolence, complaint letters, and other social or personal business correspondence.

If your writing-related procrastination occurs at work or school, you'll find relevant strategies for getting past writer's block in the "Breaking Through Writer's Block" section of this chapter. You'll find more specific techniques for dealing with the writing projects unique to those settings in Part Four. If your writing, or the writing you'd like to get around to doing, is of a type more personal in nature, such as keeping a diary or journal, writing poetry, or some other self-expressive or creative form, you'll find useful suggestions in Chapter 16, "New Year's Resolutions and Other Self-Improvement Promises."

Dear Jane, Thank You for the 1992 Desk Calendar ...

" 'Tis better to give than to receive." How true that seems when you've received a gift and have to force yourself to sit down and write a thank-you note before yet another day passes. The gift giver's job is done. He or she gets to sit back and bask in the glory of a job well done, while you agonize over what to say in the thank-you note. Or, even worse, you walk around feeling guilty about a note you haven't even tried to write yet.

Action Tactic

Rather than stare at a blank piece of paper wondering, just what is the proverbial right thing to say in a thank-you note, take a look at the tips and sample letters in *Miss Manner's Basic Training: Communication* by etiquette guru Judith Martin. If it's engagement, wedding, or shower gifts that have you stumped, *The Bride's Thank-You Note Handbook* by Marilyn Werner might get that pen moving.

The same goes for thank-yous that need to be sent when you've been a guest in someone's home, attended a special event at a friend's or colleague's invitation, had someone do a nice favor for you, or been the recipient of any other sort of kindness or hospitality. No matter how much you enjoyed the occasion or liked the gift, you may find that acknowledging the gesture is something you just can't get around to doing. And if you hated the gift or had a lousy time at the event, the note is even harder to write.

A thank-you note is not a doctoral dissertation, an epic novel, or a critical business proposal, so why is it so hard to get the darn thing written and in the mail promptly? Here are several of the most common reasons why notes of appreciation get put off:

➤ Unless you're in the midst of a major gift-receiving and fêted time in your life (such as when getting engaged, married, retiring, and the like), writing thank-you notes is not part of your daily routine. They won't get written and mailed unless you make it a priority to set aside time for them.

➤ There's no deadline for them. It's entirely up to you to choose to write a thank-you note and to make yourself do it. Sure, common courtesy dictates that you should write one, but there are usually no deadlines for when to do it, so you can float along indefinitely before getting around to them. (Some occasions, such as wedding gift thank-you notes, have a deadline of one year according to rules of etiquette, but that's so remote it's almost meaningless, and is certainly not imminent enough to spark a sense of urgency in a procrastinator.)

➤ You're worried about sounding trite. If you pride yourself on being a decent writer who can usually come up with at least an occasional clever turn of phrase, then it's easy to be stumped by a thank-you note. You want to say something more interesting and personal than "thank you for the lovely blah, blah, blah" but don't want to go overboard and sound insincere. So, you end up saying nothing, waiting for inspiration to hit.

➤ You didn't like the gift or enjoy the occasion, so you don't know what to say. It's hard to sound like you genuinely enjoyed a dinner party when the meat was tough (and you're a vegetarian anyway) and the company was lousy. The same goes for gifts you can't even identify, much less use or admire.

➤ You don't have the proper stationery or note card to write it on, and it just doesn't seem appropriate to write a thank-you note for monogrammed towels on a post-it note or sheet of notebook paper.

Matter of Fact

Forgive me for sounding smarmy, but whenever I hear a newlywed or new mother say, "Ugh, I have to write my thank-you notes," I'm tempted to say, "Get a grip and stop complaining." Instead of remembering that it's a good thing to have thank-yous to write (because it means they received lots of gifts), some people equate the writing of the notes with cleaning out a closet—yet another onerous chore on the to-do list. Plus, it's not as if all those gifts came as a big surprise. They had to know that writing thank-yous was inevitable, and could've planned for it.

So, how do you get yourself to thank someone for that nice desk calendar while you're still in the same year? Try these strategies for expressing thanks for gifts, favors, or hospitality before it becomes embarrassingly late to do so:

➤ Realize that there is absolutely no excuse for not sending a thank-you note. This is one of the few times when I encourage you to make yourself feel lousy about procrastinating over a task. People who don't send them in a timely manner are being ungrateful and inconsiderate, unless they have a very legitimate excuse. Is that how you want to be? If not, then make it a priority and *Just do it!!*

➤ Use the Stop, Look, and Listen formula in Chapter 12. You might hear yourself saying, "What a great gift. I can't wait to tell so-and-so how much I love it!" followed by the conflicting thought, "I'll write the thank-you note later." When that happens, stop and say to yourself, "Why don't I write the note now? It'll only take a few minutes." The longer you wait, the harder it will be to write, so try to write the note within twenty-four hours of an event or the receipt of a gift.

Action Tactic

The writing of thank-you notes for engagement, wedding, and new baby gifts has traditionally been the responsibility of the wife or mother. How unfair is that?! If you happen to be female and a procrastinator too, why not ask your husband or partner to share the responsibility? As long as he's a decent writer, you can delegate all or part of the task to him.

➤ If you can't write a thank-you immediately, add the task to your to-do list and also make a note on a daily action page of your planner so that you've scheduled a day to do it.

➤ Think of the effort the gift-giver, party host, or whomever it is that you're thanking put into the gesture. You might guilt-trip yourself into getting the note written. This also works when you didn't particularly enjoy the event or like the gift; you can at least express thanks for the thought and effort.

➤ Don't worry about making the note perfect. Sending anything at all, even if it's not the most original note ever written, is better than saying nothing.

➤ Keep an assortment of letter paper, fold-over note cards, and blank greeting cards easily accessible so that you don't get slowed down by having to buy or order stationery or cards or hunt down ones buried in a drawer somewhere. If you aren't sure which kinds to get, refer to an etiquette book for guidelines.

If even these tactics can't get you to put pen to paper, consider sending flowers or fruit with just a note saying "thank you." Acknowledging a gift with a gift isn't appropriate for every situation (such as when you need to write thank-you notes for wedding gifts), but it can come in handy at times.

RSVP—ASAP!!

R.S.V.P. (also sometimes written as "R.s.v.p.") stands for *"Répondez s'il vous plaît,"* which is French for "Respond, please." Unfortunately for the hosts of formal events, it doesn't matter what language procrastinators speak; they don't seem to understand the importance of responding promptly to invitations. I remember the inconvenience caused by procrastinators in the last few days before my wedding as we scrambled to get a final guest list tally. Just about every large, formal affair has a few stragglers who wait until the last minute to reply to an invitation or who never bother to reply but show up anyway. By doing so, they set off a chain of events that inconveniences everyone, from the hosts, to the caterer, to the other guests.

As life has become increasingly informal in recent decades, fewer and fewer invitations require a written reply. Many hosts of parties, corporate events, and other large functions ask that you reply by phone or even e-mail, or they enclose a reply card and self-addressed, stamped envelope with the invitation.

Even invitations to formal weddings now usually come with reply cards and envelopes.

While plenty of procrastinators manage to delay even something as simple as checking off the yes or no box and sticking the reply card in the mail, the bigger problem comes when a written response is called for. If an invitation asks you to reply but doesn't give a phone number to call, then a written response is expected.

Matter of Fact

Etiquette books aren't just for diplomats and social butterflies. Everybody should have one on hand when questions about social correspondence or other manners matters come up. Some of the best, by authors who know their fish fork from a fork in the road, include: *The Amy Vanderbilt Book of Etiquette* by Nancy Duckerman and Nancy Dunnan; *Emily Post's Etiquette* by Peggy Post; *The Complete Idiot's Guide to Etiquette* by Mary Mitchell.

We Want to Attend, but We Don't Know How to Tell You

As with thank-you notes, some people put off sending written replies simply because they don't see any urgency in doing so, don't make it a priority, or don't schedule it into their daily routine. One of the biggest reasons for procrastinating over R.S.V.P.s, however, is that few people outside of diplomatic circles and the Palm Beach party circuit know how to write a proper written reply to a formal invitation. Out of fear of saying the wrong thing, they put off saying anything at all.

There are two simple things you can do to rectify the situation. One is to invest in a good etiquette book which will show you how to write a correct reply. The other is to get used to referring to yourself in the third person (as you'll see in the formal reply that follows)! Etiquette books can walk you through the many slight variations acceptable for formal and informal replies, but the two examples here are standard ones that will at least give you a basic idea of how your responses should sound.

Formal replies to an invitation mirror the wording and layout of the invitation:

Mr. and Mrs. Dewitt Now

accept with pleasure

[or regret that they are unable to accept]

the kind invitation of

Mr. and Mrs. Fancy Pants III

to attend the marriage of their daughter

Tiffany Anne

to Mr. Gold Digger, Jr.

Saturday, the tenth of May

at eight o'clock

If you prefer to send a more casual, personal reply, even to a formal invitation, it's acceptable to do so, especially if you know the hosts or guests of honor well.

We will be delighted to attend

the marriage of Tiffany Anne

on Saturday, the tenth of May

at eight o'clock

Eliza and Dewitt Now

Formal replies are always a safe bet when the invitation itself and the event are formal affairs. But if you know the hosts or guests-of-honor well, or if you happen to be a more informal person, then the more casual option is just fine.

Writing Letters of Condolence

Knowing what to say when you speak directly to the loved one of someone who has died or become critically ill or injured is hard enough; putting the words in writing is even more difficult. Making matters worse is the fact that letters or cards of condolence need to be sent as soon as possible, since the idea behind them is to comfort the people who've just experienced a loss or misfortune.

To make sure that your expressions of sympathy are timely and tactful, follow these do's and don'ts:

➤ DON'T wait for the perfect wording to pop into your head. While you do need to put thought and effort into the letter or card (there's more at stake here than in a thank-you-for-the-lovely-crystal-vase-letter), it's just as important to get the letter on its way quickly.

➤ DON'T assume you know what the other person is feeling. People who are grieving often feel such pain that they can't imagine anyone else understanding what they are going through. If you make comments like, "I know what you're going through," or "I know how you feel," your words come across as more offensive than comforting.

➤ DON'T try to make it all better by saying things like "At least she went quickly and didn't suffer," or "How fortunate that the injuries weren't more severe." If the recipient wants to find a silver lining in the cloud, let him do so himself.

➤ DO play it safe by saying less. When you're trying to be tactful, more is less.

➤ DO say something positive and kind about the deceased person. Relaying a brief anecdote about an experience you had with the person or commenting on his or her character and personality helps keep the memory alive. In the case of someone who is ill or injured, a comment about character will give the recipient hope that he or she can pull through the adversity.

➤ DO take recipients' religious beliefs into account. If they're not religious, don't say things like "We should be happy she's with God now," or "She's in a better place." You may believe that, but the grieving person may find those comments offensive when he'd rather have her on earth than in heaven.

➤ DO offer to help out in any way to get the family through their difficult times.

Quicksand

Just because you send flowers and/or attend a funeral doesn't mean you shouldn't write a note of sympathy in a letter or card. It means a lot to a grieving family to have a written record of condolences, especially when the notes contain comments about the deceased person.

The sample letters below give you an idea of how these DOs and DON'Ts can be put to use.

Sample Letters of Condolence

Unlike formal replies to invitations, which have a fairly standard format, letters of condolence can take an infinite variety of forms. You might add a few warm words to a store-bought sympathy card with a pre-printed greeting, or compose a two-page letter to a close friend who's lost a loved one.

The samples offered here are merely examples of basic, brief condolence letters you might write to people you know reasonably well but aren't extremely close to. (Letters to close friends tend to be a little more casual and personalized.) The first sample demonstrates how to handle the tricky issue of writing about someone you didn't know at all, while the second handles writing about the death of someone you barely knew. (In the case of the death of someone you did know, follow the preceding list of do's and don'ts.)

> **Dear Maria,**
>
> **I was so sorry to hear about the passing of your Uncle Luis.**
>
> **I know you and he were very close, and I always heard such wonderful things about him. Please know that my thoughts are with you and let me know if there's anything I can do to help you now or in the days ahead.**
>
> **Sincerely,**
>
> **Alex**

> *Dear Jake,*
>
> *I was so sorry to hear about the loss of your mother. Though I only met her that one time when she visited you last summer, I was struck by her kindness and energy. I'm sure she will be missed by many who knew and loved her. Please know that my thoughts are with you and let me know if there's anything I can do to help you now or in the days ahead.*
>
> *Sincerely,*
>
> *Barbara*

Consider these samples to be bases from which you can build a more personalized letter reflecting your own style, the relationship you have with the recipient, and any unique characteristics of the deceased.

Postcards from the Edge of Procrastination

Do you often find yourself furiously scribbling notes on postcards and scrambling around for stamps instead of enjoying the last few hours of a vacation? Do all your cards from exotic locales end up having post-marks from the mailbox down the street from your home? It's kind of ironic how many people go on vacation to relax but work themselves into a frenzy over getting postcards written, stamped, and mailed to the folks back home. As with thank-you notes, writing those wish-you-were-here cards becomes more of a chore than a nice, easy gesture.

To solve this problem, you can always choose not to send any cards. Simple as that. Or, if you do want to share news of a trip or tell people you miss them, then carefully select a manageable number of friends and family to write to and don't try to send postcards to everybody you've ever known. If you do end up having a rather lengthy list despite those efforts, consider writing one basic note that you alter slightly for each person. That way, you won't have to reinvent the wheel with each new postcard.

Keeping in Touch

Every time I watch *20/20* and hear Barbara Walters close the show with "… and remember, we're in touch, so you be in touch," I feel guilty. Even though I think she means to be in touch with what's happening in the world at-large, I always find that her comment reminds me of all the friends and business colleagues I've fallen out of touch with.

When was the last time you got a letter in the mail from a friend? Unless you travel in low-tech circles where people still put stamps on envelopes and go to the post office, you probably don't get much more than an occasional "Hello, what's up?" fax or a joke-of-the-day that someone has e-mailed a hundred-or-so close, personal friends. There's nothing wrong with keeping in touch by phone, fax, and e-mail, but there's something about getting a handwritten (or even a typed) personal letter in the mail instead of just bills and catalogs.

If you're a busy person who already has a full plate, I don't recommend increasing your load by adding extensive personal correspondence to your to-do list. But, it never hurts to reconnect with people, both from a warm-and-fuzzy standpoint and for professional networking. So, consider using the following chart to make a plan for

Action Tactic

If you're traveling within your own country, buy postcard stamps before leaving home so you'll have them handy when you get to your destination. Then, buy postcards as soon as you arrive. That way, you'll be two steps closer to getting them done.

You're Not Alone

In the course of any given day, I have about a thousand other ways I need to use my time than writing letters, finding stamps, and getting personal correspondence in the mail. I don't even have time to call friends. I find that e-mailing and faxing is the best way to keep in touch.

—Millie K., corporate attorney

contacting up to ten friends or relatives you've been out of touch with for more than six months. List their names down the left side and put a check under the method of communication you'll use to contact them. It would be great to mail them an actual letter or card, but calling, e-mailing, or faxing is better than nothing. When you've filled in the chart, schedule days or times in your planner when you will contact each person.

Name	Snail Mail	E-mail	Fax	Call

Writing Letters of Complaint

Joe was on his way out of town to be the best man in a friend's wedding the next day, but by the time he arrived, he was more nervous than the caterer, the groom, the soon-to-be-wife, and her mother. First, he was bumped from an overbooked flight because he arrived at the airport too late, due to a clueless cab driver who got lost on the way. Then, he was put on the next flight a couple hours later, but the plane sat on the tarmac for two hours with engine problems. When he finally got to his destination, his luggage was lost somewhere between Maine and California.

He went on to his hotel where his luggage arrived a couple hours later. Even though he had missed the daytime festivities, he could still make it to the rehearsal dinner. He pulled his suit out of his garment bag and found it looking more like crumpled newspaper than something he could wear to a party. The hotel said they could have it pressed in no time, but half an hour later, a sheepish hotel manager appeared at his door with a suit that was burned to a crisp. At that point, the overpriced scotch in the mini-bar was starting to look awfully good.

Later that night at the rehearsal dinner, in a suit borrowed from another groomsman, Joe talked about how he was mad as hell and had been taking names. When

You're Not Alone

Flying home from honeymooning in Hawaii, a loud alarm blasted for the entire six hours. It's hard enough to end an amazing vacation and face reality, but we'd also splurged on first-class tickets, so we wanted a pleasant flight. We planned to file a formal complaint but didn't get around to it until over a year later, at which point it was too late.

—Lisa P., human resources recruiter

he got home, he was going to write a letter to the cab company, the airlines, the hotel, Chambers of Commerce, Attorneys General, and anyone else who would listen. But, did he do it? No. He told his story to all his friends and co-workers when he got home, and he complained about the poor service and treatment for about a week, but he never got around to writing those complaint letters.

Getting Your Outrage Down on Paper

While we're in the midst of a major inconvenience or injustice, complaining to the powers-that-be seems like the biggest priority in our lives. We're all fired up and not gonna take it anymore. We've had it with lousy service, incompetent workers, faulty products, and anything else that slows us down or trips us up. So, why don't we do something about it? The following are four basic roadblocks, along with solutions for getting past them:

1. The fire dies down. In Chapter 12, "The Secret Formula to Overcoming Procrastination," you saw that getting fired up and fed up is an important emotional precursor to taking action. The problem is that when we're no longer experiencing the inconvenience or poor treatment, the fire dies down, so we're less motivated to complain.

   Solution: Close your eyes and visualize yourself back in the situation. Try to revive the feelings of anger and frustration that you felt then. If your complaint is about a faulty product, get it out and try to use it again.

2. We don't know who to complain to. It's hard enough to get letters written to friends and family whose addresses you have at your fingertips. But, when you have to zero in on one name, title, and address within a multinational, multiconglomerate, behemoth of a corporation, there are so many research steps involved before you can get your letter in the mail, most anyone in that situation would procrastinate.

   Solution: Don't get overwhelmed by the thought of tracking down the right person. All it takes is some simple research and a little resourcefulness.

3. You don't think it will do any good to complain so you don't bother to do it.

   Solution: Realize that most companies do take complaints seriously. If your letter is concise, but with all necessary details, and firm but not hostile, it will most likely be read and acted upon. Direct it to the highest person in the organization and accompany it with any necessary documentation (photocopies—not originals!), such as plane tickets, product purchase receipts, photos of a faulty product, and the like.

4. You assume it's too late to complain. If you've procrastinated and let weeks or months pass since the event occurred or since you first bought or used a faulty product, you might assume that your complaint won't be taken seriously.

Solution: Give it a try anyway. If it's been several months or a year or more, you might find that the company will not compensate you in any way, but a matter of weeks or a few months probably won't make a difference.

The rewards that can come from lodging a formal complaint in a timely manner, whether those rewards are actual compensation or just an apology, are usually worth the hassle of making the complaint.

Matter of Fact

The people you need to send complaint letters to do not hide under rocks. You can find hundreds of corporate and government agency contacts in the free *Consumer's Resource Handbook* from the U.S. Consumer Information Center (www.consumer.gov or 719–948–4000). You'll also find them in the appendixes of an excellent book called *Shocked, Appalled, and Dismayed!: How to Write Letters of Complaint That Get Results* by Ellen Phillips.

Breaking Through Writer's Block

If you're tired of staring at a blank screen or sheet of paper or sick of writing at a snail's pace, try the following techniques to get the words flowing:

➤ Analyze your writing style and work with it. If you work in bursts of inspiration with dry spells in between, don't try to force yourself to write at precisely scheduled times of the day. As long as you can control your deadlines enough to allow for the dry spells, you'll do fine.

➤ Play beat the clock to see how much you can get written in a certain period of time. For example, tell yourself you need to write four thank-you notes or two more pages of a report before *"Jeopardy"* comes on or before your office mate gets back from lunch.

➤ Write roughly off the top of your head without editing or worrying about how it sounds. This is especially useful when you're having trouble getting started at all. Once you get something down, you might feel more motivated because your task is then one of editing, not writing.

➤ Use the chip-away technique. Instead of saying, "I have to get this paragraph written," tell yourself to write just one sentence. If that doesn't work, try for one phrase, or even just one word. It's like the one-day-at-a-time idea in 12-step addiction programs. Dwelling on all you have to get done is overwhelming, so the chip-away technique lets you break it down into baby steps.

➤ Do the busywork part of your writing. When I write a book, I have to type certain codes into the manuscript so that the editors know where various headings, bullet points, and other format features should go. When I get stuck writing the text of a chapter, I divert my anxiety away from my writer's block by doing busywork: typing asterisks, brackets, and other symbols in places where I'll be filling in words. It's a simple little trick that gets my fingers moving on the keyboard and propels me back into action.

➤ Keep moving. Similar to the last tip is the idea of not letting yourself get stuck. If you can't think of the right word to use in a particular sentence or don't know what to say to introduce a letter or report, don't dwell on the problem. Move on to another part of the writing and come back to the trouble spot later.

Quicksand!

Whatever you do when faced with writer's block, don't panic! Getting yourself all worked up over the problem will only make matters worse. Use the Stop, Look, and Listen technique from Chapter 12 to pause, take a deep breath, and identify the source of your block.

➤ Talk the task through with someone. If you can't get your thoughts and feelings down on paper, it sometimes helps to have a conversation with a friend or co-worker, explaining to them what it is you want to say. You might find that your thoughts are more well-formed than you thought.

➤ Pretend you're talking to someone about the subject. If you don't want to talk to a real person, or if it's not convenient to do so, try writing as if you were talking to someone. A silly trick I play on myself is to imagine that I'm being inter-viewed on a TV talk show. For example, when I was agonizing over getting the Stop, Look, and Listen formula down in Chapter 12, I imagined I was sitting across from Oprah, Katie, or Diane and explaining my ideas to their viewers. Doing so helped me write about the formula in a way that was much more straightforward and meaningful than if I had written all the jumbled thoughts in my head.

➤ Frequently skim back through what you've already written. Whether it's a short note or a 400-page book you're tackling, when you get stuck, try rereading parts you've already written. It can help get you back on track if you've started to lose sight of what you wanted to say and it can also be encouraging if you find you've written more (or better) than you had thought.

➤ Make sure you're comfortable. The rule about being in a comfortable work envi-ronment is particularly important when you're trying to write. I often find that the only reason I'm blocked is because I'm tired of sitting in my desk chair star-ing at the computer screen. So, I often print out what I've written up to that point, sit in a big comfortable chair or outside, and do some work by hand for a while.

➤ Change your modus operandi. Not only does working by hand enable me to move away from my desk and get comfortable, it also lets me see my work-in-progress in a different vein. If you do your writing on a computer where you can see only a few paragraphs or a page at a time, you might lose sight of where you are in the project. Printing out what you've written can help you have a more big picture view of your work. Plus, it can be encouraging to see what the finished product is going to look like. If you do most of your writing by hand, consider switching to a typewriter or computer. Even if your final product needs to be handwritten, typing a draft might make you more efficient.

➤ Take a break. When you're completely stalled and none of the other techniques is working, drop what you're doing and do something else. Take a walk, make a phone call, surf the 'Net, do anything that will clear your head and relax you. An added benefit of this technique is that, in the process, you might also find inspiration for your writing.

Whether you're trying to write a quick thank-you note or a major report at work, one of the most important things to keep in mind is that being a so-called good writer or bad writer has very little to do with your procrastination. Not having well-honed writing skills can certainly slow you down, but the biggest bouts with writer's block come not so much from how you write, as how you approach the writing task. The psychological and situational obstacles described in this chapter are usually the culprits. Once you recognize what it is that's holding you back, you can start to deal with it, and get those words onto paper.

The Least You Need to Know

➤ Thank-you notes don't have to be perfect; they just need to get written and sent.

➤ Don't be intimidated by formal invitations that require a written R.S.V.P. There's a standard format to follow.

➤ When it comes to condolence letters, short but warm is the best approach (except for those to very close friends).

➤ Make a point of occasionally writing a nice, old-fashioned letter sent through the regular mail to a friend or relative.

➤ When writer's block hits, rely on the grab bag of ten techniques from Chapter 12, as adapted for writing in this chapter.

Part 4

Getting Things Done at Work and School

If your procrastination problems lie more in the realm of professional, rather than personal, life, then this section is for you. These chapters look at why that resumé won't write itself, why that dull paperwork on your job keeps multiplying, and how to get out of career ruts.

If you're a student—whether you're in high school, college, graduate school, or just taking a course or two—you'll find tips for avoiding the last-minute rush to cram for exams, write papers, and get your degree.

Get a Career—or Change the One You Have

A 1999 TV commercial for the career Web site Monster.com premiered during the Super Bowl and caught the nation's attention with its startling question, "What did you want to be when you grew up?" How unfortunate that the answer for many people is not the same as the career they have ended up in. They reach middle age or the retirement years and realize that they've spent most waking hours of their adult lives doing work that is not satisfying or rewarding.

A Career in Procrastination

For many people, jobs are more than a way to earn a living. They're the building blocks of a career, which is the collection of work experiences over a life span that make up a part of one's identity and can be a major source of satisfaction and fulfillment in life. When you put off choosing a new career direction, making a career change, or starting a business you've been thinking about, you limit yourself in many more ways than one. Career-related procrastination can have the following results:

You're Not Alone

Putting off focusing on my career has been my biggest procrastination problem. I've been going through life as if there were all the time in the world to make career decisions. In hindsight, I've realized that the act of not making a choice turns out to be a choice after all—and it's a choice I would not have made if I'd known the consequences.

—April R., artist/paralegal/office administrator

➤ Getting stuck in a job or career field you don't enjoy or value

➤ Never reaching your full potential

➤ Earning less money than you could if you were to make some changes in your job or career

➤ Waiting so long to make a career change that the transition is more difficult and time-consuming than it would have been if you'd done it sooner

➤ Always feeling insecure and uncertain about your job security and career future because you haven't set goals and worked toward them

➤ Not gaining the flexibility and independence that can come from self-employment (if that's something you desire)

Many procrastinators are aware of those consequences, but they still can't seem to get moving in a new career direction.

Why Careers Stagnate

The reasons people put off making career decisions and acting upon them closely parallel those for any type of procrastination. You might find yourself overwhelmed by the many career options to choose from or by the work involved in making a career transition. You may lack knowledge about what's out there in the world of occupations or lack knowledge about yourself in terms of your skills and priorities. If you don't know where to go to find people and information that can help you become more knowledgeable (such as the resources listed in the Careers sections of the appendixes), you'll remain stuck.

Or perhaps your career is stagnating because you haven't gotten fired up enough. Maybe you're reasonably comfortable in your same old job and career field and don't feel an urgent need to make career change a priority, even though, in the back of your mind, you think you'd be happier doing something else. Fear can also be a factor here in that you might be nervous about venturing into the uncharted territory of a new career field or employer, interviewing again after a long absence from the job hunting scene, or returning to school if that's a necessary step in your transition.

Finding Your Direction

In their book, *Do What You Are: Discover the Perfect Career for You Through the Secrets of Personality Type*, Paul Tieger and Barbara Barron-Tieger advise readers to stop defining themselves by their jobs. They recommend that you not force yourself to fit into a job, but that you find a job that fits into you. In other words, do what you are. Their advice is right on target and touches on why so many workers aren't satisfied in their careers and have difficulty finding a new one.

As a career counselor for the better part of two decades, I've heard so many people ask the question, "What's out there?" They want to know what the hot jobs and growing industries are. They want to know what other career fields my clients are going into. They want to know which companies are hiring. Instead of "What's out there?" they should be asking, "What's in here? Who am I and what do I want?" Then they can ask about career and job options that might fit who they are.

Matter of Fact

Some career indecision results from perfectionism, which in this case means feeling that you have to make the perfect choice that will keep you happy the rest of your life. The fact is, very few, if any, career decisions are irreversible, and statistics show that most people have several different careers over a lifetime. Sure, it's nice to be able to choose a career that you're going to stick with for a while, but if you do get into one and find that it's not quite right, you can change it. If you use effective transition strategies, it's never too late to make a career change, and you're never too deeply entrenched in one field or industry to switch to another.

Whether you're a student or recent grad choosing your first career, a parent looking to get back into the work world, or an experienced worker wanting to make a change, knowing how to ask yourself those questions can be difficult, and finding the answers can be even more difficult. If you've been putting off making decisions about your career direction, try the following strategies to motivate yourself:

➤ Realize that there is a method to the madness when choosing a career. You can learn this method by reading books about career planning or by working with a career development professional one-on-one or in seminars. Choosing a career is not a skill you're born with; you have to be educated about how to do it before you can expect to make any good decisions.

➤ Don't get frustrated. Many people attempting to make a career choice on their own begin by thinking about what they enjoy or what they do well. The problem is that most people end up with too many, or too few, options based on those interests and abilities. They often decide at that point that it's too difficult to choose, and then either give up and stay in their same field or just take any

Quicksand!

Don't put off making decisions about a career direction just be-cause you're waiting to find your calling. You might think that the perfect career choice will miraculously come to you some day, but that happens for very few people. You're more likely to choose a career based on a methodical process of elimination than by feeling a calling toward one occupation.

job without making a conscious choice about the career path that job will put them on. In order to work through the frustration of choosing a career, you have to move beyond introspection by turning to outside resources that can teach you that "method to the madness."

➤ Don't take the stab-in-the-dark approach. Many people who need to choose a new career open up the newspaper to the help wanted ads or sign on to a career Web site and peruse the job listings. They start applying for jobs before they've even zeroed in on their overall career goals. Be sure you aren't putting the cart before the horse. Choose a direction first, and then look for jobs within that field or industry.

The books, Web sites, and organizations listed in the appendixes can help you find the tools and experts you'll need to work through the career planning process.

Changing Your Career Field

Identifying a new direction to head in as a result of your desire to make a career change is an important first step in changing careers. But that step won't mean much if you don't use that information to actually make the change. If you find yourself unable to get moving, remember what you learned about the change process in Chapter 6, "Making Sure You'll Really Do It This Time." Whether you're trying to change careers or make any other sort of life transition, change takes time, effort, and support from the right people and resources. It doesn't come easily or quickly. As a result, change is a process that's vulnerable to procrastination every step of the way.

Having watched thousands of would-be career changers strike out on the career transition road with high hopes and enthusiasm, I've observed five main pitfalls that keep many of them from making it through the process to a new career. The following are those pitfalls, along with strategies for avoiding them:

1. **Not having a plan.** Career consultants who guide career changers through the transition process know that you can't get from Point A to Point B without a plan. That plan usually involves steps such as research, networking, self-assessment, preparing tools (such as a transitional resumé), learning to speak the language of the new field, and identifying interim steps (such as moonlighting in the new field or taking courses before you can get a full-time job in it). People who try to

make a career change in a haphazard way without a game plan usually strike out, give up, or say they'll "do it later." To avoid the hit-or-miss approach, you have to devise a strategy, usually with the help of books, support groups, or consultations with a career development professional.

2. **Being overwhelmed.** Trying to change careers can be difficult. Like any project that stretches over a period of time (often several months or a year or more in the case of typical career changes), a career change will involve some setbacks. The key is not to run out of steam when you hit a snag, but to see the snag as a normal, temporary bump in the road to a new work life.

3. **Not thinking about the big picture.** To move from being, say, a computer hardware repair technician to a systems analyst, for example, you have to think creatively, strategically, and analytically. Making a career change requires that you see the connection between what you've done and what you can do in the future. Many people have trouble seeing the path they need to take to get the career they want. They keep saying, "I'd like to be a _____, but ..." Instead of focusing on the barriers and giving in to the "buts," focus on being resourceful, persistent, and creative until you come up with a plan that will work.

4. **Having a negative view of career change.** Some people are miserable in their jobs, feel like fish out of water around the people in their profession or industry, and know that they'd be happier doing something else. But

Action Tactic

Stop thinking about all the things you need to do to change careers and instead identify one simple thing you can do. Maybe that's visiting one Web site listed in Appendix C to read about career transitions. Maybe it's contacting one person to set up a meeting to discuss that person's career field and job. Pick one simple thing and do it in the next 24 hours.

Quicksand!

Don't assume that the only kind of change you can make in your career is a drastic one. Sometimes, staying in your same type of job, but with a new employer or in a different industry, is enough of a change to improve your professional life. Don't make your career quandary more complicated than it needs to be.

no matter how much they would like to make a change, they feel that doing so is somehow wrong. Some people worry that they'll be labeled flaky or a job-hopper.

Others feel guilty about losing the time, money, and effort they've invested in their current career or job. These views are natural, but they are unfortunate and unfounded. Job-hopping is no longer viewed negatively. Changing careers and jobs is more the norm these days than is staying on one track until retirement. As for the guilt factor, who are you helping by being a martyr and staying in a job or career you hate? No one.

5. **Self-defeating beliefs and feelings.** A career change just about always involves venturing into unfamiliar territory. With that realization can come fears (of failure or success), discomfort with the idea of an inevitable identity change, and doubts about one's ability to make the change happen. All the normal but self-defeating emotions and thoughts described in Chapter 4, "It's All in Your Head," can crop up when you're trying to make a career change. The solution is two-fold: (1) Gather enough information about the career transition process and the new field you're headed toward to make that new territory seem less scary; and (2) Seek the support of experts, friends, and family for help along the way.

Striking Out on Your Own: The Advantages of Self-Employment

Business experts, career consultants, and disgruntled employees are singing the praises of self-employment these days the way ambitious sorts touted plastics in the era of *The Graduate*. For several years now, small- to medium-sized start-up companies have been leading the way in the business world, and all indications point to the continuation of that trend. Although being a small-business owner is still not an easy path, with its long work hours and often high degree of risk, it's no longer a lonely path. More and more resources, from magazines, to books, Web sites, advisory groups, and funding sources, are available to help guide entrepreneurs toward success.

Also booming is the option of being a freelancer, consultant, contract worker, or other independent type. Those choices mean that you see yourself more as a free agent who goes from project to project on a short- or long-term basis, rather than someone who runs a company with employees and inventory. Free agents often work from home or at the site of the employer who has hired them temporarily for a project.

Whether you have your own company or function as a free agent, self-employment has many advantages, including autonomy, independence, schedule flexibility, a greater variety of projects, the chance to be creative, and unlimited earning and growth possibilities.

Action Tactic

If you're a budding entrepreneur between the ages of 12 and 16, or know someone who is, contact the Entrepreneur Boot Camp for Teens. This residential summer camp held at the University of Wisconsin helps young people get a head start on building entrepreneurial skills. You can reach the camp by phone at 414-472-2018 or by mail at 1018 Carlson, Whitewater, WI 53910.

What's Stopping You?

So if self-employment is such a great thing, what's holding you back? The following quiz can help you figure that out. Read the 10 statements and circle T for True or F for False to indicate whether each one sounds like something you would think, feel, or say as you contemplate going into business for yourself.

1. I know that I'd like the independence and growth potential that comes with self-employment, but I don't know what sort of business I would be happiest in. **T F**

2. I already have a business idea, but I don't know how, where, or when to begin implementing it. **T F**

3. I'm concerned about dealing with the risk involved in being self-employed. **T F**

4. I can see some advantages of going into business for myself, but I'm just not sure I'm the entrepreneurial type. **T F**

5. I'm worried that I don't have all the skills or experience necessary to handle certain aspects of self-employment (such as marketing, sales, financial management, administrative details, or others). **T F**

6. I don't think I have enough money or access to funds to start and/or maintain self-employment. **T F**

7. I don't know whether I can manage my time well enough to be my own boss. **T F**

8. I'm confused by the choices for a business structure: corporation, sole proprietorship, partnership, franchise owner, freelance worker, consultant, and so on. **T F**

9. I'm not sure whether I truly want to be self-employed or whether I just see it as an option because self-employment and small businesses are such a hot trend these days. **T F**

10. I'm having trouble deciding whether I should work by myself or have partner(s) or employee(s) in my business. **T F**

Scoring: Count the number of times you answered True to the odd-numbered statements and write that amount in the space labeled Odd. Then count the number of times you answered True to the even-numbered statements and write it in the Even space.

Odd: _____

Even: _____

Action Tactic

If the idea of conducting market research to test your business idea seems daunting, try having informal focus groups with friends. Ask them to point out the pros and cons and make suggestions for how to get it going. Have friends over for pizza or take a few business colleagues out to lunch.

What your score means: If the number in the Odd space is higher, then your concerns are related mostly to doubts about your suitability for self-employment. You should do some self-assessment, using exercises in books on career planning or self-employment or by working with a counselor or coach. That self-assessment can help you explore your skills, abilities, temperament, and willingness to take risks and can help you define some priorities and goals for your professional life.

If the number in the Even space is higher, then the problem is lack of information. You need to educate yourself about the realities of self-employment.

Making It Happen

If you find that your mind is racing with business ideas and excitement over the prospect of self-employment, but you're dragging your feet and not getting a business off the ground, try these strategies:

➤ **Research.** Frequent libraries (especially ones with specialized business collections) as well as the business section of bookstores and business-related Web sites. Also, scour magazines and newspapers for ideas, read biographies or memoirs of successful business owners, or use any other source that can help you develop or assess the viability of a business idea. Market research is an essential foundation of any business, product, or service.

➤ **Connect.** Talk to other entrepreneurs, both those in businesses similar to the one you want to start, as well as those in unrelated fields who can speak about self-employment in general. Also connect with experts who can advise you about how to start your business or make it grow.

➤ **Make a plan.** Just as washing one dirty dish may give you the impetus to wash the whole sinkful, writing a business plan can build the momentum necessary to get the business launched. Of course, washing dishes is by no means on an equal plane with starting a business, but tricking yourself into action is the same with both. By starting with the basic step of putting together a business plan, with no expectation that you'll go any further, you make the whole idea of self-employment less overwhelming. You get yourself to move from just considering the idea or worrying about why you haven't started on it to taking concrete action.

➤ **Start small.** If it's feasible for the type of business you want to start, begin gradually. Instead of quitting your day job and plunging headfirst into the uncertainties of self-employment, try to start on a small scale in your off hours to give the business a trial run or a chance to build up slowly before you have to depend on it as your sole source of income and job satisfaction.

➤ **Apprentice.** If you're unfamiliar with the sorts of products or services you'd be dealing with in your business, or you don't have experience working in a certain way, such as in a consulting role, consider learning the ropes from another business before striking out on your own. For example, a public relations (PR) specialist who would like to become an independent consultant but has always worked for companies' in-house PR departments could take a job with an established consulting firm to familiarize herself with the consultant's role.

Matter of Fact

Starting your own business doesn't have to take as much money as you might think. Surveys have shown that many successful small businesses were started with less than $5,000. Some new entrepreneurs begin with pools of small loans from family and friends or by using credit cards (cautiously!). The books, organizations, and Web sites listed in the appendixes can point you toward more formal sources of funding.

Going from the security of a paycheck and the familiarity of being employed by someone to the uncertainties and increased responsibilities of the solo route is bound to stir up some fears and uncertainties. But before you decide it's all too overwhelming and that you'll think about it later, remember the potential rewards that can come from being your own boss. Whether it's the opportunity to make gobs of money, the chance to have ultimate creative license over what you do, or just the prospect of sleeping until noon occasionally that starts your entrepreneurial juices flowing, keep dangling those rewards in front of your nose until you start taking some action toward self-employment.

The Least You Need to Know

➤ Putting off career decisions and transitions limits your potential for growth, satisfaction, and earnings.

➤ Career changes are put off for the same situational and psychological reasons as other types of procrastination.

➤ To choose the right career, you have to start by looking at who you are.

➤ Making a career change, like making any other kind of major change, takes time, effort, and outside support.

➤ To stop putting off going into business for yourself, connect with the right information and people to make it happen.

Chapter 20

Get a Job—and Keep It

In This Chapter

➤ Putting off looking for a new job

➤ Doing your work

➤ Securing your professional future

➤ Going beyond the job description

It's the stuff of songs and movies. It's a source of friction between parents and their grown kids and among couples. It makes students want to stay in school forever and rattles the nerves of middle-agers with mortgages and orthodontists' bills. What is it? It's the prospect of getting a job and keeping it.

All but the independently wealthy, or successful entrepreneurs, rely on a job to put food on the table and a roof over their heads. Most people, of course, hope to do more than that. They hope to bring in enough income to be comfortable, or more than comfortable, not merely enough to eke out an existence. They'd even like to enjoy what they're doing while earning those dollars. As I pointed out in Chapter 19, "Get a Career—or Change the One You Have," jobs are the building blocks of something bigger—the foundation for a career. That career, in turn, reflects, and in some ways shapes, your identity and can give you a sense of fulfillment. That puts a lot of pressure on you not only to get a job, but also to get a good one and keep it. And anywhere there's pressure, you're likely to see procrastination.

Get a Job

You know you want a new job, a better job, or any old job, but you can't seem to do anything about it. One obvious reason for your procrastination may be that you don't enjoy job hunting. There's the prospect of long nights at the computer cranking out cover letters and days spent waiting in line at Kinko's to print up yet another batch of resumés. There are the demoralizing cattle calls at employment agencies, the brush-offs from headhunters, and the rejections after interviews you thought you aced. To add insult to injury, you end up stuck with a big dry-cleaning tab. Job hunting doesn't have to be as miserable as all that; some people find it kind of interesting, even a little fun. But any way you cut it, pounding the pavement (more likely to be the cyberpavement these days with so much online job hunting) is not how most people would choose to spend their time.

The following are four additional reasons why people put off looking for a job:

1. Not having a sense of urgency

2. Not knowing how to go about looking for a job

3. Lack of a clear job target

4. Fear, self-doubt, and other anxieties

Quicksand!

Don't mistake this for a how-to-find-a-job chapter. The focus here is on the mental and situational obstacles that might cause you to put off looking for a job or to delay thinking about ensuring your job security. For the nuts and bolts of how to write resumés, interview, network, or devise a job search strategy, you need to use the career resources recommended in Appendixes A, B, and C.

Let's look at each of those procrastination factors in detail, along with strategies for combating them.

Too Comfortable to Leave, Too Miserable to Stay

When I was in private practice as a career counselor, I often received frantic calls from new or current clients saying that they couldn't stand their jobs anymore and needed to leave immediately and needed to see me immediately to discuss how to find a new one. I often couldn't squeeze them in for an appointment until a couple of days later, but in the meantime, I offered some brief advice by phone to tide them over. The anxious callers would accept it grudgingly, but they claimed they didn't know how they were going to last in their jobs another hour, much less another day or two.

Invariably, when those same people would arrive in my office days later, all sense of urgency was gone.

Maybe the day of the call had turned out to be only an isolated bad day that was easily cured (temporarily, at least) by going home and taking a long, soothing bath or having a stiff drink. Or maybe they looked at their bank balance and realized that unemployment wouldn't help their bottom line, so they were no longer so eager to jump ship. Or perhaps just the passage of time had given them a chance to cool down.

Whatever the reason, many people put off looking for a new job because they don't stay fired up. Just as with letters of complaint that don't get written (as discussed in Chapter 18, "Put It in Writing,"), you might be fed up with your job one day, only to find that a few days later the fire dies down. You forget how miserable, bored, underappreciated, or angry you were. You give in to the comfort factor: the fact that it's often easier to stay in a familiar situation than to venture into uncharted territory, even if the status quo is less than perfect.

Action Tactic

The Five O'Clock Club has been one of the most successful job search clubs in the country for over 20 years, offering group and one-on-one coaching, networking, sharing of job leads among members, and emotional support. To find out whether there's a club branch near you, look it up at www.fiveoclockclub.com or call the New York headquarters at 212-286-9332.

Solution: Every time you hear yourself about to say, "I'll worry about a job later," remember how you felt the last time you were fed up with your job. The idea is to relive that moment until you get fired up again.

Fishing with a Net

Some people put off looking for a job, or give up too soon after starting, because they're going about it the wrong way. They start by putting out a few feelers. Maybe they fax their resumé for a few ads in the paper and don't get a reply, or they post their resumé on a job Web site and don't get any hits. Or they mention to a few friends and professional contacts that they'd like something new, but nobody follows through. After a few days or weeks, or even a few months, of these flash-in-the-pan efforts, they assume that there's just not a better job out there and give up.

Solution: Haphazard, passive approaches to getting a job rarely yield positive results. To motivate yourself from the start and to stay that way, you have to understand that a job search takes time and effort. You have to put thought into developing an effective strategy and make it a priority to implement that strategy every day.

Quicksand!

Don't get hung up trying to write the perfect resumé and never make it past that point to launching the job search. Resumés are difficult to write without a clear job target and an inventory of skills and accomplishments. Self-assessment and research are essential first steps in a successful job search.

No Target to Hit

Behind the haphazard fishing with a net approach to finding a new job is often a problem of not having a job target. Some people put off looking for a job because they don't know what to look for. This is an example of the good kind of procrastination. (Remember that back in Chapter 2, "The Procrastination Epidemic," I said that delaying action is sometimes a smart move?) If you don't know what you want in terms of an ideal type of employer, job duties, salary, and other characteristics, then you don't know where to begin looking because you don't have a clue about what you're looking for.

Sometimes, that lack of a career focus results from the sorts of career-related procrastination described in Chapter 19. It may also result from ambivalence about even wanting a job or a career at all. This ambivalence is especially common among people who have deep connections to, and obligations in, the other life roles beyond Income-Earner and Careerist. (Those and the other eight life roles were described in Chapter 3, "Blame It on the Environment," in case you need a refresher.)

Parents who've been at home raising kids but are ready to do other sorts of work may have doubts about whether that work should be in the form of a full-time or part-time job. People who are starting their own businesses may not be able to decide whether they should work full- or part-time while getting the business off the ground. Other people would like to make a career out of their passions, such as art, acting, or writing, but they don't know how much time to devote to a steady day job while also pursuing their not-yet-lucrative craft.

If you don't know what kind of job you want at all or which structure the job should take (full-time, part-time, telecommuting, or others), you may stall and not embark on a search. If you've been putting off looking for a job because you don't know how or when you want to work, or how you'll manage other demands on your time, the following table can help you sort out the options.

Alternatives to the 9–to–5, Monday Through Friday Rut

Type	Description
Part-time	A position that is usually less than 35 hours a week and is often around 20 hours a week. Work is either a few hours several days per week or a few full days a week. Usually has a set schedule with little fluctuation of days and hours you're scheduled to work. May include benefits in addition to hourly wage, but often does not. Can be permanent or temporary.
Temporary	A full- or part-time position that is intended to last anywhere from one day to a matter of weeks or months. Temporary positions are usually arranged by an agency, which places you at the site of a company needing temporary help and which issues your paycheck. Most temporary positions do not include benefits, but some large employment agencies offer benefits to workers who do temporary work through them on a regular basis.
Job sharing	Two or more people share one full-time job so that each worker has a part-time schedule, but the job duties are covered full-time. As a job sharer, you might work half days for five days or may work full days, which you alternate with your counterpart. Sometimes a job is designed to be shared; other times, a job sharing arrangement is proposed by two employees.
Flextime	A full- or part-time position with days and hours that vary from the traditional 9 to 5 workday. For example, you might work from 7 a.m. to 3 p.m. five days a week or work four 10-hour days a week. The structure of flextime varies widely.
Telecommuting	Working from home or out of an office away from the main one either all or part of the time. Telecommuters stay in touch with the primary office via networked computers, modem, fax, pager, and phone. They may go into the office for regularly scheduled meetings or hardly at all. Some positions are designed with a telecommuting structure; others start out as regular in-office jobs that employees propose to do from home on a full- or part-time basis.

If your job-hunting stalemate is not so much due to confusion over the structure of the job, but the bigger issue of what you want out of life, follow the suggestions offered in Chapter 19 for getting over the hurdle of choosing a career direction. You'll also find ideas in the career resources in this book's appendixes. If you take some time to identify mid- to long-range career goals, you'll know which specific types of jobs and job structures would make good stepping stones to those goals.

Job Hunting Mind Games

Job hunting experts have often compared the process of getting a job to the process of marketing and selling a product. They use phrases like "package yourself" and "sell yourself" when describing how to win over prospective employers. At its core, that advice is on target. Just as the packaging on a box of cereal has to grab a shopper's attention, and television commercials have to entice viewers with the cereal's health benefits or great taste, so too do job seekers have to win over the consumer who is, in this case, an employer.

The downside of that advice, however, is that it adds to the anxiety job hunters are already likely to feel. They might have doubts about their ability to obtain, or succeed in, a new job. They may feel self-conscious about a scattered or lackluster employment history or nervous that a volatile former boss will give them a bad reference. They might feel ill at ease in interviews where it sometimes seems as though charm counts as much as credentials. Whatever is at the root of the feelings, fear, doubt, and anxiety are often on the minds of job seekers, sometimes to such an extent that they lead to job hunting paralysis.

Solution: Realize that rejection in a job search is not a comment on your worth as a person. It simply means that a wide range of factors, many of which were beyond your control, didn't fall into place to make you the right person for the job. Rather than internalizing the rejection and letting it slow you down, accept it and move on to the next iron in the fire.

Action Tactic

If you're in the corporate world and have difficulty finding time to read the thousands of business books published each year, consider subscribing to *Soundview Executive Book Summaries*. These monthly newsletter-style publications distill the essence of the year's best books into eight-page synopses, sort of a grown-up's *Cliff's Notes*. Find them at www.summary.com or call 1-800-521-1227.

Keep Your Job

Once you have a job, your next task is to hang on to it (assuming you like it, need it, and want to keep it). At a minimum, you must handle the basic responsibilities of the position in an effective, efficient, and professional manner while also getting along well with your co-workers and bosses. To ensure your job security more solidly, you have to do more than the job description calls for. In the "Make a Difference" section of this chapter, you'll find out what "doing more" entails and how to get moving on it.

The Bare Necessities

The tasks that most people put off on a day-to-day basis at work are the ones they find boring, tedious, difficult, or unimportant. On the procrastination survey (described in Appendix D), some of the job duties that survey respondents wrote in on the questionnaire included making cold calls; preparing expense reports;

filing; invoicing clients or customers; writing periodic reports; and processing various types of papers. Other tasks that are put off are ones that people don't necessarily dislike doing but simply have trouble finding the time for, such as keeping up with professional reading or dealing with all the mail and other in-basket documents that pour in.

Many of the books in the "Getting Organized" section of Appendix A, "Recommended Books," contain hundreds of tips on how to make better use of your time at work. Professional organizers, too, can be helpful if you're having difficulty setting priorities, staying organized, and keeping one step ahead of the paper avalanche. In the meantime, here are some ways to deal with the specific issue of procrastination on the job:

Quicksand!

Putting off organizing, backing up, and cleaning up your computer can have dire consequences. Be sure to copy files onto disks while projects are ongoing; back up your entire hard drive on a regular basis; and keep your desktop uncluttered so you can access files and applications quickly.

➤ Even if you're kind of fond of your identity as the person with the messiest desk in the office, try to keep your desk and overall workspace as uncluttered and organized as possible.

➤ Schedule dull tasks as if they were just as important as a meeting or other big responsibility. Just as with household chores, working out a routine for when you do paperwork and other dreaded tasks helps you get in the habit of doing them and out of the habit of worrying about them all the time.

➤ Try getting the tasks you usually put off done early in the day, before you get caught up in other projects.

➤ Be sure to use the action launching pad system described in Chapter 10, "A Crash Course in Getting Organized." Sorting your mail and other incoming documents into stacking trays rather than letting them pile up on your desk or in an in-basket makes you more likely to take action on them.

Action Tactic

To reduce the temptation to play computer games, don't keep them on your hard drive. If you have to take the extra step of putting in a game CD, you might be less inclined to waste time playing it.

➤ Be sure to use some sort of mission control system like that described in Chapter 10 to keep a running list of subtasks within large projects and to schedule times to finish them.

➤ Devise systems for getting things done more easily. Suppose that you have to bill clients periodically and that doing so is a hassle because you have to gather lots of random data related to prices, dates, and the like. To make yourself less likely to put off doing it, make it an easier task. Not only should you have a template for bills; you should also have a system for inputting the data little by little while working with the client, rather than having to gather it all at the last minute. Depending on the nature of your work and the types of tasks you procrastinate about, you can develop your own simple systems or use more sophisticated project management software.

➤ Do your best to keep interruptions to a minimum, especially during times when you need to concentrate on a project.

As you use these techniques, don't forget to use the Stop, Look, and Listen formula as well! (That formula was discussed in Chapter 12, "The Secret Formula to Overcoming Procrastination.")

Write Like You Mean Business

If writing is the task you put off at work, whether it's reports, memos, e-mails, proposals, or correspondence, many of the tips in Chapter 18 can get you past your blocks. In addition to trying those strategies, ask yourself these four questions:

1. **Is it a writing style problem?** When writing for business, many people feel that they have to be much more formal than they would be when writing something outside of work. That's why you see lots of business memos that sound something like, "It has come to our attention that, by unanimous consensus, the aforementioned documentation previously distributed was erroneous in its declaration of the holiday time allocation …," instead of saying, "Sorry for the inconvenience, but our offices will close at 4:00 P.M. on the Friday before Labor Day weekend, not at 3:00 P.M. as I had stated in yesterday's e-mail." If you get hung up writing because you're trying to be overly formal, try writing in plain English and see whether the words flow more easily.

Action Tactic

If your writing style leaves a lot to be desired, contact the Association of Professional Communication Consultants at www.apcc-online.org or 918-743-4793 for expert advice and assistance.

2. **Is it an information problem?** Writing on the job often involves gathering lots of information from various files, places, and people. So if you're at a loss for what to say next, don't assume that the problem is a lack of writing ability or a mental block against it. Make sure you have all the information you need.

3. **Is it a problem of organization?** When you collected all the information needed for your report or other written communication, did you organize it well? Is it in clearly marked files or, at the very least, sorted into stacking trays? As you learned in Chapter 3, people often procrastinate on their jobs because their desks and other work areas are cluttered. If you can't find, or easily access, what you need to inform your writing, you'll probably end up putting off the task until later.

4. **Is it a mental block?** As you may know from Chapter 4, "It's All in Your Head," certain tasks are especially likely to raise all sorts of concerns in your mind. Writing is one of those. Your written documents at work reflect your level of professionalism, knowledge, and opinions. They tell the reader whether you have great ideas or are just filling a page with words. They have to pass muster in the eyes of your boss and colleagues. In the case of a proposal, they might be the main way to receive funding or approval for a project or to get new business. Even writing a simple e-mail can be intimidating because it might be read by hundreds or even thousands of people if you work in a large company. The way to get past the mental block is to first identify the anxiety or faulty thinking that's holding you back. Then use the techniques suggested in the "Breaking Through Writer's Block" section of Chapter 18.

Written communication is such an important aspect of so many jobs, and so often a way that colleagues judge your professionalism and knowledge, it's worth it to you to pay special attention to why you procrastinate writing and how you can get past the blocks.

The Human Component of a Job

One of my favorite book titles is *Work Would Be Great If It Weren't for the People* by Ronna Lichtenberg. My sentiments exactly! Of course, I'm someone who can work for 14 hours straight with no human contact other than the guy in my computer who tells me I've got mail, so I'm probably not the norm. But as a career counselor, I've come across many, many people who agree that work would be great if it weren't for the people.

You might be the most outgoing person in the world, who loves the camaraderie of an office and thinks teamwork is the way to go, but I bet there's at least one person in your workplace who bugs you to no end. Some of the things you might be putting off dealing with on the human side of your job include the following:

➤ Coming to terms with a difficult boss

➤ Resolving interpersonal conflicts with co-workers resulting from gender, age, cultural values, work ethic, or personality differences

➤ Dealing with office gossip

➤ Confronting or reporting verbal or sexual harassment

➤ Confronting or reporting an ethical breach you've witnessed

You're Not Alone

Ethics are important to us all because we are accountable for our personal behavior and performance, regardless of our position on the office hierarchy. In some circles, this kind of personal accountability is the mark of a true professional.

—From You Want Me to Do What? When, Where, and How to Draw the Line at Work *by Nan DeMars (Fireside, 1997)*

We often put off these tasks because they can involve tense confrontations that make us dread coming back into work the next day. We may also sweep these issues under the rug because we don't know how to address them. Whole books are written on subjects like managing your boss, navigating office politics, and getting along with co-workers. These skills are learned, so you can't expect to know exactly what to do intuitively. When it comes to serious issues like ethical dilemmas and harassment, it's even more important to seek expert advice. Some career management books cover these topics, but you'll more than likely need to speak to a real, live person. Career coaches, employment or labor attorneys, and employee advocates in human resources departments are good people to turn to. You can also start by seeking advice from a mentor or other trusted business colleague.

Matter of Fact

Whether it's due to a lack of planning or just responsibility overload, lots of businesspeople can't seem to get a break. A national survey of over 5,000 executives by Management Recruiters International found that 82 percent reported doing work while on vacation, and 13 percent have had to cut their vacations short because of work. Survey respondents in the Midwest were the least likely to work during vacation; those in the Northeast were most likely to do so.

Whichever resource you use, the important thing is to do something. The discomfort and awkwardness you might endure when resolving an interpersonal conflict or seeking expert advice about an ethical or legal issue is a small price to pay for peace of mind.

When the Office Is at Home

A revolution has occurred in home-based work in recent years, and the trend is expected to continue. If you work from home as a telecommuter or in your own business, you face special challenges when it comes to battling procrastination. There's no one watching over your shoulder to see if you're doing your work or yet another crossword puzzle.

Most of the techniques discussed in Chapter 12 and in the "Bare Necessities" section of this chapter can get you past bouts of procrastination when working from home. Especially important, though, is the Stop, Look, and Listen formula described in Chapter 12. Because self-discipline is a major issue when working alone amidst all the distractions of your personal life, you have to freeze that impulse to procrastinate before any action techniques can work. In addition, consider these tips:

➤ Turn on your computer first thing in the morning so that you'll feel like the workday has already started (or prepare any other equipment and supplies you use in your work, if not a computer).

➤ If you have the space to do it, locate your office or work area well away from the parts of the house you live in.

➤ If possible, have separate telephone lines for home and work so that you're not distracted by personal calls.

➤ Let family, roommates, and friends know what your work hours are and ask them to pretend that you are off at a job away from home, even if you're just in the next room.

➤ Keep family members informed of your business goals and plans so that they can help support your efforts and won't begrudge having to give you time to get your work done.

➤ Remember that just because something is urgent doesn't mean it's important. Try to set up your workflow and organizational systems in a way that will minimize the need to put out fires and will allow you time to focus on what's important.

➤ Don't work around the clock. You might be tempted to because your office is right under your nose, but if you overdose on work, you'll become less productive. When your workday is done, close the door (or if your workspace is part of a room in which you also live, find some way to close off the area).

You're Not Alone

At first, working from home can seem like Paradise Island ... Like tourists on a holiday, many people working from home start out living it up, indulging in whatever they want to do, but by the end of a few weeks, they realize that if they don't get down to work, they won't have any work.

—from *Working from Home*, 5th Ed., by Paul and Sarah Edwards

No matter which productivity tips end up working for you when you work from home, the most important thing to remember above all else is to work in a way that fits your style of doing things. You are, more than likely, working from home at least in part because you want some freedom from the constraints of a traditional office environment. You may want autonomy over how you dress, the hours of your work-day, whether the radio is on, or other factors. As you struggle with the self-discipline challenges of working at home, keep in mind that you don't have to conform to any one notion of how someone should conduct business at home. As long as you use common sense (such as not having the radio or television blasting when you're on a business phone call), you can work to your own drummer. Doing so will make you more productive in the long run.

Make a Difference

Employers don't hire people just to fill up square footage in the office (or wherever the work takes place). They want employees who don't merely go through the motions of doing a job but who go the extra mile to bring an innovative, visionary, problem-solving approach to improving the organization's bottom line. They want people who can help them not just compete with, but also outsmart and outpace their competitors.

Making the effort to make a difference is not only good for your employer; you bene-fit as well. When you stretch the limits of your abilities and see achievements beyond the basics of what your job requires, you become more marketable. Then, when you set out to land your next job and the one after that, you'll have an impressive track record of accomplishments to discuss on your resumé, in cover letters, in interviews, and when negotiating salary and other terms of a deal.

Unfortunately, most people get so caught up in the day-to-day demands of their jobs and in more pressing matters that they don't make the time to look at what's going on beyond their cubicle walls. If you put off looking at the big picture of your career and your professional community or industry, you may come to regret that procrasti-nation down the road. If you just don't see how you'll find the time to go that extra mile, consider these simple things you can do:

➤ **Be visible.** Become involved in your professional community at large, not just by joining professional and trade associations and reading the newsletter, but by participating in these organizations. Attend meetings and seminars, help coordi-nate events, write for their publications, and even run for office. Schedule a minimum of one activity per month.

➤ **Network.** To stay informed about developments in your profession or industry as a whole, and to connect with people who could help you out in your career down the road, make a point of getting together with people outside of your own company. Schedule breakfast or lunch meetings, keep in touch by phone and e-mail, or connect in any way that's feasible.

➤ **Keep your skills sharp.** Take stock of areas where you could use some improvement. Examples include public speaking, making presentations, working on teams, managing people, project management, oral or written communication, and sales.

You may be tempted to say, "But I don't have time to do those things." I know it might seem like a reach, but making those objectives a priority will save you time in the long run and is therefore worth every minute you'll have to spend on it.

Get Ahead

Do you suspect that you're being underpaid but haven't gotten up the nerve to ask for a raise?

You're Not Alone

On my last job, I focused so much on the needs of my clients and on getting my projects done perfectly, that I forgot I am my number one client. I should always keep in mind that my most important project is advancing in my career.

—Avery B., sales manager

Does your position no longer resemble its original job description because of all the added responsibilities that have been heaped upon you, but your business card still bears the old job title? Are you overlooked for plum assignments no matter how hard you work?

If so, don't just sit there: Do something about it. I know, I know, that's easier said than done. We may know in our own minds that we deserve better. We can present eloquent cases to our spouse, best friend, or dog for why we deserve more. But when it comes to telling somebody who can make it happen, such as a boss, you become a shrinking violet.

Your reticence may be due in part to an internal struggle between the voice in your head that says, "Fight for what you deserve," and the other one that tells you it's bad form to be aggressive or greedy. It might also be due to a lack of negotiating skill or experience. You may have no qualms about fighting for more, because you know that asking for what you've earned is not being greedy. But you hold back because you're worried that you'll make your request in the wrong way.

At this point, a career counselor or coach can come in handy. Working with someone who can teach you career management strategies, including how to negotiate for more money, a better title, or a change in the nature of your job, can help you get moving. Plus, having a career expert confirm that you do deserve more can provide the emotional support and self-confidence you need to get ahead. As an alternative, or complement, to working with a career development professional, take a look at the advice and encouragement offered through the career books and Web sites in Appendixes A and C, respectively.

The Least You Need to Know

➤ Putting off looking for a job is often due to a lack of a clear job target or search strategy or to fears and self-doubt.

➤ Being organized and scheduling routine or periodic tasks are keys to getting work done when you don't enjoy the task.

➤ Employers expect you to add value to their organizations beyond fulfilling the basic requirements of the job description.

➤ Getting raises, promotions, or plum assignments starts with realizing that you do have a right to ask for what you deserve.

Chapter 21

Cramming for Exams and Other Fine Academic Traditions

In This Chapter

➤ Procrastinating in high school, college, and grad school

➤ Putting off returning to school at age 25+

➤ Surviving theses and dissertations

➤ Calling an end to eleventh–hour cramming

If you had been a fly on the ivy-covered wall during my senior year in college, you'd never have believed that I could turn out to be an ex-procrastinator later in life. There I was in the final semester, taking five classes and two independent studies at once, rushing to complete papers, and cramming for exams in order to meet my degree requirements. All this work was due to the fact that I had spent much of my college career dropping courses I didn't like or taking incompletes in ones I had slept through. (How dare they hold classes before noon?!) For three and a half years, I told myself that I would catch up later. I paid for that procrastination by having a stressful, overloaded final semester while most of my classmates were taking it easy, coasting toward their diplomas.

A Procrastination Breeding Ground

Just about every scientific study ever published on procrastination has used college students as its subjects. Lots of studies of human behavior focus on undergrads because they're an easily accessible study group, but procrastination is a particularly

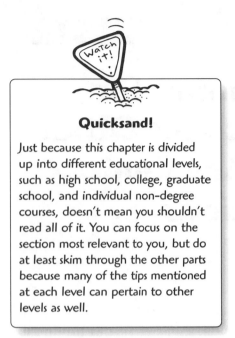

Quicksand!

Just because this chapter is divided up into different educational levels, such as high school, college, graduate school, and individual non-degree courses, doesn't mean you shouldn't read all of it. You can focus on the section most relevant to you, but do at least skim through the other parts because many of the tips mentioned at each level can pertain to other levels as well.

apt topic to investigate on campuses because the world of academia is a procrastination breeding ground.

You have the distractions of extracurricular activities and a social life. You have semester-long projects with faraway deadlines and no one watching over you to make sure you work steadily toward those deadlines. Then you have the pressure of getting good grades, fulfilling requirements, and making sure the tuition is paid. Based on extensive research, social scientists estimate that as many as 70 percent of students on any given campus procrastinate. Most studies have found that writing papers is the biggest area of procrastination, followed by studying for tests and doing homework.

Whether it's in high school, college, graduate school, or even in individual, non-degree courses, the life of a student is brimming with potential distractions and psychological ups and downs. This chapter looks at what some of those procrastination catalysts are and how they can be kept at bay, with a focus on issues unique to each level of education: high school, college, and graduate studies; it deals with issues of older adults returning to school as well. You'll also find strategies for overcoming procrastination related to studying in general at any level, as well as procrastination related to completing a degree.

Procrastination in High School

Bad habits related to doing homework, studying for exams, and writing papers usually start in high school, if not earlier. Sometimes, procrastination starts because your home environment isn't conducive to studying. It might be noisy and chaotic. You may not have a clearly designated study area or anyone encouraging and supporting your academic pursuits. You also might find yourself too loaded down with household chores and family obligations to have time for schoolwork. Other homes have the opposite problem of parents who go overboard in pressuring their kids to excel at school, thus making them rebel or feel overwhelmed and fearful of failure.

Maybe your procrastination comes from inside. You may have a learning disability or attention deficit problem that makes it difficult to prioritize your time, stay focused, and complete your reading or writing. (Such problems are described in more detail in Chapter 4, "It's All in Your Head.") Or maybe you just have lousy study habits.

If you're a high school student who finds yourself cramming for exams at the last minute, starting papers and projects the night before they're due, or always feeling behind, here are some things you can do to be more effective:

➤ Don't give in to all-or-nothing thinking. Instead of leaving all your studying or writing until the last minute and having to spend a whole evening or weekend getting it done, try to break up the project into smaller parts and start earlier. Use the chip-away technique described in Chapter 12, "The Secret Formula to Overcoming Procrastination," to get things done little by little.

➤ Keep your family in the loop. As soon as you find out when big projects or papers are due or when quizzes or exams will be given, let your parents know. That way, they can plan family activities and outings around those dates to avoid conflicts with times you need to be studying.

➤ Don't load up on extracurricular activities just because you think that's the only way to get into a good college. Good grades and recommendations from teachers are just as important for college applications, so don't get your schedule so packed with activities that you can't keep up with academics.

➤ If your home environment is not conducive to studying, study at school or a library whenever possible. Try to schedule two or three specific times per week when you go to that study spot (or even do it every day!). Consider it an appointment that is just as firm and as much a part of your routine as your sports practice, music lessons, or anything else.

➤ If your parents are putting too much pressure on you to excel at school, and you find yourself procrastinating as a way to rebel or because you feel overwhelmed, talk to them about what you're feeling. You may think it's not going to do any good, but you might be surprised to find that opening the lines of communication is all it takes to get them to change. If they still won't listen, talk to a teacher or counselor.

➤ If you're loaded down with household chores, tell your parents that you're willing to do some but that you have to have enough time left to get your schoolwork done, too. Be specific in telling them how much time you need. Add up the number of hours you typically need to spend on homework per day or week and compare that to the amount of time you have to spend on the chores they've assigned you. If you come to them with numbers, rather than just complaints about having to do too many chores, they should respect your mature approach and be willing to adjust their expectations.

Action Tactic

Get ahead on your college-level workload before you even get to college by reading some of the books that you're likely to be assigned there. Arco Publishing's *Reading Lists for College-Bound Students* by Estell, Satchwell, and Wright can help you do that. It contains reading lists from over 100 colleges and has a list of the 100 books most often assigned by all colleges.

➤ If you seem to have more difficulty organizing your time or getting your work done than your friends do, talk to your parents (or a teacher or guidance counselor) about the problem. Ask them if they think you should be tested for learning disabilities or an attention disorder.

➤ If learning difficulties aren't the issue, but you still have trouble getting your work done and organizing your studies, ask your parents about hiring a private tutor for you. Some tutors help with general study skills and organization, not just with learning subject matter. If a private tutor isn't an option, ask your teachers about study skills classes or learning centers at your school or in the community.

If you kick the procrastination habit now, while you're still in high school—or keep yourself from developing the habit in the first place—you'll be much better off down the road as you continue your education.

Procrastination in College

If you're a commuter student, the reasons for your procrastination are probably a lot like those high school students have. You might be working full- or part-time and going to college part-time, so you have the added demands of a job, which can make it hard to keep schoolwork a priority. But what if you're a so-called traditional college student, aged 18 to 24, who lives on campus and takes classes full-time? You have your own set of procrastination challenges.

You're Not Alone

When I was a university student in England, cleaning out the bathroom was a chore I avoided as much as possible. The nearer we got to final exams, however, the cleaner that bathroom got. I'd ask myself, "Shall I study or do more household chores? Hmm, the kitchen and TV room are spotless, I'll go clean the bathroom."

—Tanuja W., corporate treasury manager

Why College Students Procrastinate

The causes of procrastination among college students mirror those of any type of procrastination: environmental factors and psychological ones. The environmental, or situational, causes include the following:

➤ The distractions of a social life

➤ The competing demands of part-time jobs and internships

➤ The lack of structure, as compared to high school (more projects with long-range deadlines and more autonomy to get themselves to class and get work done)

➤ The challenges of living with roommates

➤ A culture of procrastination in which students brag about being far behind in their work and use last-minute studying as a chance to socialize

Matter of Fact

If you tend to be motivated by money and are having trouble completing a college or graduate degree, consider these facts from recent years' findings by the Bureau of Labor Statistics:

Annual earnings of college graduates are nearly twice that of high school graduates. Having a master's degree increases earnings an average of 30 percent. Holding a professional degree (such as law, medicine, engineering, and so forth) means you'll earn an average of 130 percent more than high school graduates.

The internal factors are also much the same as for procrastination in any type of setting. Some students are held back by fear of failure, fear of having their work judged, desire for perfectionism, or being overwhelmed by a workload that is likely to be heavier and more difficult than that encountered in high school. Some students get addicted to the adrenaline rush that comes from doing their work at the last minute. Some have faulty concepts of time, miscalculating how long it will take them to get work done.

What Can Be Done About It

The strategies that work for overcoming procrastination in college are the same ones that help in any other type of situation. If you're a college student struggling with procrastination, be sure to read Chapter 12, if you haven't done so already. Also, keep these points in mind:

➤ Realize that, even though having a high GPA is important, especially for getting highly competitive jobs or getting into some graduate and professional degree programs, you are more than your grades. Employers and graduate admissions officers are often just as interested in your work experience and extracurricular activities as they are in your GPA. So don't let yourself get overwhelmed by the need to make straight As.

➤ Don't get caught up in the culture of procrastination. Think about how silly it is to brag about being far behind or having to cram for an exam at the last minute. There are plenty of other ways to be one of the gang and to interact with your classmates without having to pull all-nighters.

➤ Realize that the adrenaline rush you get from doing work at the last minute may feel good now, but eleventh-hour cramming gets harder to pull off later in life. If you come to rely on the habit now, you'll have a hard time kicking it later.

Action Tactic

If you've been putting off choosing a college major, meet with a counselor in your campus career center to discuss how to narrow your options. While you're in the center, also see whether it has any of the books published by VGM Career Horizons. These books describe career options for over 15 different majors, including *Great Jobs for Psychology Majors* and *Great Jobs for History Majors*.

➤ Although internships, other work experiences, community service, and campus activities are important for a well-rounded college experience, keep your schedule manageable by not taking on too much in any one semester or academic year. College is a time to learn and have fun, not a time to burn out.

If you follow these suggestions, you'll have more time for fun or whatever else it is you want to do besides study. Also, in addition to the pointers I give here, don't forget to use the 10 techniques for overcoming procrastination described in Chapter 12.

Procrastination in Graduate School

If my own experience is at all typical, procrastination is often less of a problem once you reach graduate school, even if you were a big procrastinator in college (until you get to the thesis or dissertation stage, that is!). Most grad students know why they're in school. They usually have reasonably clear career goals or a love of a particular academic subject, which motivates them to work toward an advanced degree. Their classes tend to be small, and faculty advisors tend to be involved in their lives, so they have a built-in support system.

Graduate students also tend to be more mature and responsible and less distracted by social lives and extensive extracurricular activities than their undergrad counterparts. (Those were certainly factors that made me much less of a procrastinator in graduate school than I was in college!)

One Foot in the Ivory Tower, One in Real Life

Before I give too rosy a picture of graduate school, let's remember what procrastination is: It's a habit. No matter how favorable the conditions are for productivity, someone who suffers from the procrastination habit is going to find ways to put off things, even in grad school.

As a graduate student, you are more likely than an undergrad to feel divided between two worlds: the academic world and real life. You may have a burgeoning professional career requiring time, energy, and attention, and possibly a family that demands the same.

What's the solution? The key lies in taking stock of your commitments in the 10 life roles (as described in Chapter 3, "Blame It on the Environment") and making sure that your expectations, and those of your bosses, professors, and family, are realistic.

As you should know by now, you can't be all things to all people and put equal amounts of time and energy into several of those 10 life roles at once. You have to decide which of your competing demands takes priority. Maybe being the star of your master's or doctoral program is currently more important than being a star on the job. As long as you're doing your job adequately and have a reasonable amount of job security, why not let the job take a backseat for a while?

If family obligations are pulling you in too many directions, let those take a backseat as well. That doesn't mean you're declaring that your education or your job is more important than your family. You're simply saying that you have to shift your day-to-day priorities to school and/or work and away from family chores, commitments, and activities for a while. This shift doesn't mean you care any less about your spouse, partner, or kids; it just means that the best thing you can do for them at that point is to get your degree completed successfully and in a timely manner.

Quicksand!

There's more to schoolwork than papers and exams. Keeping on top of academic red tape is important for procrastinators, who might let problems go unresolved until serious consequences develop. Make sure you watch out for deadlines related to financial aid, tuition and fees, course incompletes, and transcript discrepancies.

All But Dissertation, All Because of Procrastination

In *How to Complete and Survive a Doctoral Dissertation*, author David Sternberg cites a personal ad from the November 22, 1979 issue of the *New York Review of Books*: "33-year-old, attractive woman, having just finished her doctorate, is ready to enjoy life again and would like to meet an adventurous man."

Looking for Dr. Goodbar and the good life is what a lot of recent doctorates are ready to do. This ad no doubt speaks for many women and men who felt that, while they were completing their advanced degree, they didn't have much of a life, particularly during the thesis or dissertation stage. Many students proceed through their graduate-level classes just fine, then they get hit with major procrastination when it comes time to start or finish the final project. So many students get stuck at the dissertation stage, in fact, that a couple of decades ago, the term *A.B.D.* (All But Dissertation) was coined to describe them. Unfortunately, many students never make it from A.B.D. to Ph.D., and that's *A.B.P.*: All Because of Procrastination.

A lot of students are unprepared for the massive scope, nebulous deadlines, long duration, and autonomy involved in writing a dissertation. They simply don't have the organizational skills to plan and execute such a major project. Some get hung up at the beginning because they agonize over choosing a topic. Others have no trouble getting started, but they run out of steam along the way as they begin to lose interest, hit writer's block, or become distracted by other responsibilities.

Action Tactic

Many graduate students don't finish theses or dissertations because when they move away from campus after completing coursework, they become isolated and removed from academic life. If you're trying to write your final project from a distance, be sure to stay in the loop by having regular phone meetings with your advisor and staying in touch with your classmates and faculty by e-mail.

Getting from A.B.D. and A.B.P. to Ph.D.

If you find yourself with the dubious distinction of being A.B.D., you probably worry that your career opportunities are limited and you may even feel that your self-esteem has taken a real blow. Being A.B.D. often makes people feel like failures. The answer to getting out of this rut lies in three areas.

First, learn project management skills. Learn how to break the project down into smaller tasks; set mini-deadlines; keep records, files, and other organizational systems; and schedule your daily work routine. Ways to learn these skills include the following:

➤ Take part in any dissertation-writing seminars offered on campus, or form a dissertation support group with peers.

➤ Seek one-on-one advising from a professional organizer, professor, counselor, or advanced graduate student.

➤ Read books on project management, as well as those specifically on managing academic projects, such as those listed in the "Education and Study Skills" section of Appendix A.

Second, get past the psychological roadblocks. Some graduate students put off the dissertation for so long or fall so far behind when they're in the midst of it that their anxiety reaches astronomical proportions. The root of that anxiety may be fear, perfectionism, misconceptions about time, negative self-talk, or any of the other mental maladies described in Chapter 4, "It's All in Your Head" and in Chapter 5, "It's About Time." Rereading those chapters and using the techniques described in Chapter 12 can help you break down the emotional barriers. If a do-it-yourself method is not sufficient, working with a mental health professional or personal coach (as described in Chapter 7, "Rallying Support from the Pros") may be the answer.

Third, rearrange your life to get it done. Whether it's setting up a proper workstation and getting organized, doing some soul-searching about your priorities, changing your daily routine, or putting other responsibilities on the back burner, some degree of sacrifice is necessary in order to start and complete a doctoral dissertation. It's not going to get written unless it becomes a main focus of your life, both in your mind and in your daily planner and calendar.

If you decide, for whatever reason, that you're never going to write your dissertation or thesis, then accept that fact and move on. Don't keep your life on hold forever.

Returning to School Before the Twelfth of Never

Gone are the days when college campuses were populated by nothing but 18- to 24-year-old students. Now, you're likely to see more than a few gray hairs among the jeans and backpacks—in fact, the gray-haired students are likely to be wearing jeans and backpacks themselves. Adults aged 25 and up are going back to school in record numbers—either for the college degrees they never earned when they were younger, for graduate degrees, or just for individual courses.

Returning to school does wonders for your career advancement, income potential, and self-confidence. Plus, you learn interesting stuff. So what's keeping you from doing it? See whether any of these excuses ring a bell:

Quicksand!

If the reason you're delaying the completion of your graduate coursework or dissertation is that you no longer want to go into that field, don't be afraid to admit that you've had a change of heart and move on to new pursuits. Worrying about a degree you haven't completed, and that you have no interest in completing, keeps your life in limbo and your self-esteem deflated.

"I won't fit in with all those younger students."

Reality: It's very unlikely that you'll be the only returning student on campus, particularly if you select a school or program that encourages adult learners. Even if you do feel a little different, which is worse? Feeling a bit out of place or limiting your knowledge, career potential, and self-confidence by not venturing onto campus?

"I don't feel as smart as I used to. My memory is shot."

Reality: Sure, you may have spent a few more brain cells than the perky 19-year-old next to you in class, but that doesn't mean you can't learn. Your maturity, life experience, and genuine desire to learn (three things that that 19-year old may not have) will make up for any cellular breakdown.

"I don't have time to go back to school."

Reality: If you make it a priority, you will have time for it. Many returning students juggle school with job and family responsibilities. If you're concerned about how to keep all the balls in the air, go back to Chapter 3 and reread the description of the 10 life roles. See where you could make some adjustments to allow school to take a more prominent place in your life. You may not have to work toward a full degree or go full-time.

Action Tactic

If disorganization is causing your procrastination at school, check out www.schoolmate.com for nifty planners and organizers designed especially for students.

"I can't afford it."

Reality: You'd be amazed how many sources of financial aid are out there. It just takes advance planning and persistent research to uncover the options and apply for them. Some colleges will let you speak with a financial aid advisor before you're even admitted so you can get a head start on budgeting and applying for loans, grants, scholarships, and fellowships. Also, many of the education Web sites listed in Appendix C provide extensive information on financial aid and links to other resources.

"My grades and standardized test scores were lousy when I was last in school, so I'll never get in anywhere."

Reality: If you've been out of high school or college for several years or more, most admissions officers will be more interested in what you've done recently than in your ancient history. They take your work and life experience into account and usually assume that you're more mature, responsible, and motivated now than you were then. If you're concerned about showing them your full academic potential, take a couple of non-degree courses that are at least somewhat related to what you would want to study now. If you do well in them, you'll have some recent academic accomplishments that can distract admissions departments from your past record.

Matter of Fact

Colleges and universities are making it easier for adults with family and job responsibilities to squeeze education into their busy lives. According to a 1998-99 report from the National University Continuing Education Association (www.nucea.edu), nearly half of all students enrolled in higher education now attend part-time. From 1970 to 1998, part-time enrollments increased by 125 percent (compared with 44 percent for full-time enrollments). In addition to the part-time option, you don't even have to leave home to get a degree. Over one-third of all four-year public universities and nearly 30 percent of all four-year private colleges and universities offer complete degree programs through distance education (taking courses online and by phone and mail).

If you have difficulty accepting any of those realities, don't just take my word for it. Contact the schools you're considering attending and ask whether they can put you in touch with any current students around your age or any who have life circumstances in common with you (such as working full-time or being a parent). Talk to the students about the pros and cons of being a returning student. You might learn that, even though it's a struggle, being back in school gives them a sense of accomplishment and career opportunities that they never could have had without further education.

Do Your Homework!

When I was in the eighth grade, my English teacher, Mr. Morrell, required us to turn in a theme every Monday. The theme was a written report, three to five pages long, with the requisite introductory paragraph, thesis statement, and four or so supporting points. How did I spend every Sunday night of the eighth grade? Writing those damnable themes, of course. Now that I've written six books, I appreciate the fact that he taught us the foundations of coherent writing and instilled the discipline required to meet frequent, regular deadlines. But at the time, all I could think about was the million or so other ways I could have been spending my weekends.

Of course, it wasn't Mr. Morrell's fault that my Sundays were wrecked. It was my own fault. I had all week to get each theme written, but I always put it off until the last minute. I hadn't learned the value of planning ahead. The fact that I was able to write a fairly decent report in a short period of time meant that I could get away with a last-minute approach. That bad habit, and the knowledge that I could come through in the final moments, came back to haunt me in college, where the workload was heavier and the papers much longer.

Whether your procrastination lies in writing papers, preparing projects, studying for exams, or doing routine homework and assigned reading, there are tutors, counselors, teachers, and professional organizers who can help you put an end to eleventh-hour cramming. Knowing how to study is not necessarily an innate talent. The key to breaking the procrastination habit when it comes to academic work is to learn how to study and organize your time. The experts mentioned previously, as well as the study skills books recommended in Appendix A, can help you do that.

You're Not Alone

No one is born knowing how to study. Unfortunately, there isn't nearly as much opportunity to learn how to study as there is to play baseball or the piano. Everyone assumes students will somehow figure out how they are supposed to study. Some are able to develop the skills that make them successful; others need more guidance.

—From The Everything Study Book by Steven Frank

The Least You Need to Know

➤ The procrastination habit often develops during high school.

➤ Procrastination in college often results from the distractions of social life and extracurricular activities.

➤ The close-knit community of students and faculty in graduate school makes it easier to overcome procrastination.

➤ Most excuses adults over age 25 make for not returning to school are based on myths and misconceptions.

➤ Poor study habits can easily be broken by learning effective study skills from counselors, teachers, and books.

➤ The benefits gained by completing a degree far outweigh the inconvenience, cost, and difficulty involved.

Part 5

Living the Life of an Ex-Procrastinator

By this point, I hope you're seeing that there is a way out of your procrastination quagmire. Maybe you plan to implement some of my suggestions for getting your household chores done, and maybe you've already started on a will or taken a close look at your investments for retirement. Or perhaps you've set some professional goals and are already making your way toward them.

Whether you've revamped your entire personal and work life and your household and office, or whether you've just managed to get the dry cleaning pile out the door before it grew legs and walked out on its own, you may be starting to have some concerns about keeping up the new you. In this part of the book, you'll find out why keeping your new act together is not going to be as difficult as you may have thought.

Chapter 22

Your Procrastination Proclamation

In This Chapter

➤ Freeing yourself from the tyranny of procrastination

➤ Taking stock of where you want to spend your time

➤ Identifying your procrastination hot spots

➤ Prioritizing the problems to work on

➤ Making the commitment to change

With his Emancipation Proclamation on January 1, 1863, Abraham Lincoln declared that "... all persons held as slaves ... shall be ... then, thenceforward, and forever free." With your own procrastination proclamation on this date, well over a century removed, you will declare yourself forever free from the slavery of procrastination.

A *proclamation* is an official announcement, a declaration of the way things are going to be. The Procrastination Proclamation you'll put together in this chapter is an announcement to yourself and to others that you will do everything in your power to become an ex-procrastinator.

You're Not Alone

They are able who think they are able.

—Virgil

Quicksand!

If you are about to put down this book to go in search of a pen or pencil and some notepaper, don't even think about it! You might never come back to this important step. Instead, carry the book with you so that you'll be less tempted to say, "I'll do that proclamation thing later."

The Five Steps to Making a Procrastination Proclamation

Think of this proclamation as an action plan. It lays out what you want to accomplish, as well as when and how you plan to accomplish it. You'll go through five easy steps to put together the plan:

1. Define your life roles priorities.
2. Take a procrastination inventory.
3. Choose your procrastination priorities.
4. Make your priority B list.
5. Build in balance.

All you need is a pen or pencil for filling in some blanks and completing a few exercises, along with a pad of paper to jot down any notes you might want to take as you go through each step. With those simple tools, plus a commitment to changing your behavior, you will end up with a completed procrastination proclamation by the time you reach the end of this chapter.

1. Identify Your Life Roles Priorities

In Chapter 3, "Blame It on the Environment," you had the first opportunity to think about the commitments and obligations that occupy your time and energy in 10 areas of your life, which I referred to as your life roles. Now as you get ready to tackle some of your procrastination problems, you need to take stock of which of those 10 life roles are taking up the majority of your time and which ones you'd prefer to place priority on. "My Life Roles Rankings" is an exercise that identifies any discrepancies between where you are currently devoting your time and energy and where you'd rather be putting them.

Exercise: My Life Roles Rankings

Read through the following list of life roles and think about how much of your time and energy are currently going into each role (or will be during the very near future). Rank the roles from 1 to 10, with 1 being the role that is receiving the most time and attention from you and 10 being the role that you are devoting the least time and attention to. Write your rankings in the "Actual Time and Attention" column.

As you rank the roles, don't think about how much you're enjoying them or wanting to spend time in them. Just think about how much time you are spending in them and the mental (or physical) energy you are devoting to them.

Next, go back through the list and think about the roles where you want to spend your time and energy. Do the same sort of ranking, with a 1 next to the role that you would most like to focus on now and in the very near future, and 10 being the role that is of least interest to you. Write these rankings in the "Preferred Ranking" column. In some cases, if you're spending time doing the things you want to do, you might find that roles get the same ranking in each column. But you're likely to find discrepancies between where you're spending your time and where you'd prefer to be.

Life Role	Actual Time and Attention	Preferred Ranking
Family member		
Homemaker		
Income-earner		
Careerist		
Leisurite		
Social being		
Community member		
Learner		
Physical being		
Spiritual being		

Your Procrastination Proclamation: Part One

I, _____, proclaim that I will make a concerted effort to devote more time and attention to the following life roles:

_____   _____   _____

2. Take a Procrastination Inventory

If you read the chapters in Part 3, "Tips and Tricks for Getting Things Done" and in Part 4, "Getting Things Done at Work and School," you have a sense of all the possible tasks, chores, projects, and goals a person could procrastinate about. You probably read about procrastination problems that you were already all too aware you have, as well as some you hadn't even realized you have. Now it's time to take a complete inventory of everything you procrastinate about: the big, important things, as well as the trivial but annoying ones.

The Procrastination Hot Spots Checklist

Read through the following lists and check off any task that you procrastinate about, either often or very often. You may have procrastinated on all or most of the items on this list at some point in your life, but in this exercise, just check off the ones that you have been putting off recently. The tasks are grouped into categories so that you know the context in which the activity occurs.

If a task isn't applicable to you, then skip it. (For example, if you aren't currently in school, then don't check off any of the school-related tasks, even if you used to procrastinate when you were a student.) Only check off what applies to your life now or in the very recent past.

Work

- ❏ Reading and dealing with mail
- ❏ Doing routine paperwork
- ❏ Writing reports
- ❏ Writing correspondence
- ❏ Writing memos or other business documents
- ❏ Starting projects far in advance of a deadline
- ❏ Completing projects after starting them
- ❏ Implementing new ideas or procedures
- ❏ Returning phone calls
- ❏ Making phone calls
- ❏ Paying bills
- ❏ Billing clients or customers
- ❏ Keeping up with professional reading
- ❏ Organizing my office
- ❏ Improving my on-the-job productivity or performance
- ❏ Dealing with office politics or workplace relationships
- ❏ Getting involved, or more active in, professional associations
- ❏ Professional networking (not just association involvement)
- ❏ Looking for a new job
- ❏ Setting career goals
- ❏ Making a career change
- ❏ Starting a business

Other work-related tasks or projects, such as:

- ❏ _____
- ❏ _____

School

- ❑ Writing papers and reports
- ❑ Studying for tests
- ❑ Doing homework
- ❑ Choosing a thesis or dissertation topic
- ❑ Doing research for a project
- ❑ Finding an internship (or summer or part-time job)
- ❑ Choosing a major
- ❑ Choosing courses
- ❑ Meeting with professors or teaching assistants
- ❑ Requesting letters of recommendation
- ❑ Dealing with academic red tape (such as financial aid)
- ❑ Making the decision to return to school for a degree
- ❑ Applying for a degree program
- ❑ Signing up for individual courses for professional development
- ❑ Completing a degree
- ❑ Enrolling my child/children in school

Other education-related tasks or projects, such as:

- ❑ _____
- ❑ _____

Personal/Social Life

- ❑ Dealing with relationship problems
- ❑ Improving my social relations skills
- ❑ Making an effort to make new friends or date more
- ❑ Returning phone calls
- ❑ Making phone calls
- ❑ Getting together with old friends
- ❑ Getting together with people I've just recently met
- ❑ Writing letters to friends or family
- ❑ Writing and sending thank-you notes
- ❑ Replying to invitations
- ❑ Sending birthday cards (or cards for other occasions)
- ❑ Sending birthday gifts (or gifts for other occasions)
- ❑ Shopping for major holidays such as Christmas or Valentine's Day
- ❑ Leaving home on time to get to appointments
- ❑ Getting organized (in general)

continues

Personal/Social Life   (continued)

- ❏ Keeping up with things I want to read
- ❏ Taking up new hobbies or renewing old ones

Other tasks or projects, such as:

- ❏ _____
- ❏ _____

Home

- ❏ Routine household cleaning
- ❏ Routine tidying up around the house
- ❏ Clearing out closets, drawers, and other cluttered spaces
- ❏ Clearing out and organizing the attic
- ❏ Clearing out and organizing the garage
- ❏ Doing laundry
- ❏ Taking clothes to the dry cleaners or picking them up
- ❏ Taking out the trash or recyclables
- ❏ Reading and dealing with mail
- ❏ Mailing letters and other correspondence
- ❏ Replying to e-mails
- ❏ Buying groceries
- ❏ Making home repairs or arranging for others to do them
- ❏ Furnishing or decorating
- ❏ Washing the car
- ❏ Maintaining the car
- ❏ Watering indoor plants
- ❏ Yard work/gardening
- ❏ Returning rented videos
- ❏ Returning library books
- ❏ Returning borrowed items from friends

Child care tasks, such as:

- ❏ _____
- ❏ _____

Other household tasks or projects, such as:

- ❏ _____
- ❏ _____

Self

- ❑ Making doctor's/dental appointments
- ❑ Stopping smoking

Breaking other bad habits, such as:

- ❑ _____
- ❑ _____
- ❑ Losing weight
- ❑ Gaining weight
- ❑ Taking vitamins
- ❑ Exercising
- ❑ Learning something new
- ❑ Focusing on my spirituality or religion
- ❑ Getting involved in community service
- ❑ Dealing with my mental health issues

Making major life decisions, such as:

- ❑ _____
- ❑ _____

Other self-improvement tasks or projects, such as:

- ❑ _____
- ❑ _____

The Big Stuff

- ❑ Preparing or updating a will or other estate planning
- ❑ Organizing and maintaining financial records
- ❑ Investing/saving for the future
- ❑ Preparing a budget
- ❑ Preparing and filing income taxes
- ❑ Changing the batteries in the smoke alarm(s)
- ❑ Childproofing
- ❑ Taking fire safety precautions
- ❑ Burglar-proofing
- ❑ Getting or changing insurance coverage

Other important tasks or projects, such as:

- ❑ _____
- ❑ _____

Action Tactic

Before filling out the following form for Part Two of the Procrastination Proclamation, photocopy it or type up your own version on a computer to use as a template for any procrastination priorities you want to work on in the future.

3. Choose Your Procrastination Priorities

The Procrastination Hot Spots Checklist gave you a bird's-eye view of all the things you procrastinate about. At this point, you need to zero in on the one or two major issues that you most need to work on. These neglected tasks, projects, or goals are having the biggest negative impact on your life now or might in the near future. In Step 4, you'll choose several smaller, easier-to-tackle issues. For now, concentrate on major ones such as finding a job, dealing with a relationship problem, losing weight, and the like.

By choosing only one or two issues to work on, you keep yourself from getting overwhelmed by too many problems to solve at once. These two issues become your procrastination priorities. Take some time to consider all your choices and make a careful decision, because the idea here is that you are making a commitment to do something about these two problems. Feel free to choose only one major issue to work on if you don't have two or if you're concerned that two is too much to handle right now.

Your Procrastination Proclamation: Part Two

I, _____, proclaim that:

My top priority is to stop procrastinating about _____

_____.

It is important to me that I start this (or finish it if already started) because

_____

_____.

I believe that I have been procrastinating on this because of

_____

_____.

The steps or subtasks I need to complete in order to accomplish this task or reach this goal, and the dates I plan to do them, are as follows:

Step or Sub-Task	Date Scheduled in My Planner

When I stop procrastinating over this and get it done, my life will improve in the following ways: _____
_____.

4. Make Your Priority B List

As you know by now, trying to change too many aspects of your behavior at once is a bad idea. Trying to quit smoking, lose weight, start a business, and renovate your kitchen simultaneously, for example, is not only masochism, it's also a sure way to accomplish none of those tasks. That's why I recommended that you choose no more than two major procrastination priorities to work on first.

When it comes to simple, fairly mundane tasks, however, you can probably handle at least a few of those while working on the bigger issues. Clearing the trash out of the car when you get home every evening or taking clothes out of the dryer before they get wrinkled are fairly minor-league issues.

Action Tactic

If for some reason you cannot take the time now to schedule all of the steps or subtasks required for overcoming your procrastination priority, at least schedule a block of time when you will plan the project and fill in those dates.

What I want you to do now is to look back over all the items you checked off in the Procrastination Hot Spots Checklist and choose anywhere from 5 to 10 minor-league items that you would like to work on in the near future. List those here:

1. _____
2. _____
3. _____
4. _____
5. _____
6. _____
7. _____
8. _____
9. _____
10. _____

From this list, choose no more than two items that you want to start working on immediately. These two go in Part Three of the Procrastination Proclamation.

Your Procrastination Proclamation: Part Three

I, _____, proclaim that, starting today, I will stop procrastinating about _____ and _____.
Of the 10 strategies for getting things done described in Chapter 10, the ones that are most likely to help me get over these two problems are:

_____, _____, _____, and _____.

Quicksand!

When selecting your top priorities and your B list priorities to work on, make sure that the tasks you choose or goals you set are truly important to you and are not things you think you should be doing.

5. Build in Balance

Enough talk about doing laundry, gutting the kitchen, and breaking bad habits you're attached to. Now it's time to make sure that you'll do some things simply because you want to, not because you have to, somebody's making you, or they're good for you. Daydream about what you would be doing if your time weren't filled with all the responsibilities and obligations you currently have. Using whatever comes to mind, compile a wish-to-do list.

Wish-To-Do Lists

To give you an example of the kinds of things a wish-to-do list might include, here are two sample lists. One is from Molly, an overworked management consultant and mother of a toddler and preschooler, and the other is from James, a computer specialist and father of a toddler.

Here's Molly's list:

1. Turn the backyard into a massive cutting garden and fill the house with fresh flowers.
2. Go to the pool more than twice a summer.
3. Paint *en plein air.*
4. Pedicures, manicures, and facials!
5. Plan and host festive dinner parties: outdoor things with twinkling lights and candles and wine.
6. Become a savvy stock picker (and profit from it).
7. Learn how to cook.
8. Needlepoint things for my daughters.
9. Buy a rustic retreat and furnish it with "finds" from the local auctions and junk shops.
10. Jog or walk daily.

Here's James' list:

1. Sleep!
2. Write letters.
3. Catch up on reading.
4. See movies.
5. Spend relaxing time with family.
6. Take drives to nowhere in particular.
7. Browse the Internet.
8. Read several newspapers a day.
9. Help friends get up-to-speed on their home computers.
10. Swim.

What would your list include? You'll make that list in Part Four of the Procrastination Proclamation.

Your Procrastination Proclamation: Part Four

I, _____, proclaim that, starting today, I will try to find the time to do some of the things on my wish-to-do list, at least occasionally:

1. _____
2. _____
3. _____
4. _____
5. _____
6. _____
7. _____
8. _____
9. _____
10. _____

The Procrastinator's Oath of Effectiveness

Your Procrastination Proclamation, the statement of what you want to accomplish and when and how you plan to do it, is a little like promises made during a political campaign. After a candidate is elected to office, he or she either forgets those promises or makes good on them (and we all know which they're more likely to do). That's where you stand now. You can either make good on your promises to yourself and others, or you can go on living life as a procrastinator, forgetting about the action plan you've laid out here.

If you are truly committed to banishing procrastination from your life, then you're ready to take The Procrastinator's Oath of Effectiveness. By signing your name to this oath, you agree to abide by the rules of behavioral change and the bylaws and constitution of the Kingdom of Recovering Procrastinators. So if you're ready to bestow this honor upon yourself, then grab two people who can bear witness to this historic occasion, place your left hand on this book, raise your right hand, and repeat after me:

Action Tactic

Write your wish-to-do list on an index card that you carry in your wallet, purse, or briefcase. Also copy it onto a second index card or a larger piece of paper that you post near your desk, on the inside of your bathroom medicine cabinet door, on your refrigerator, or any place where you'll see it daily.

I, _____, do solemnly swear that

➤ I understand that procrastination is no joke, that it diminishes the quality of my life and the lives of people around me.

➤ I pledge that, whenever I feel myself about to procrastinate, I will use the Stop, Look, and Listen formula (see Chapter 12), no matter how tempting it may be to act on impulse.

➤ I declare that, before I make negative statements such as, "I just can't make myself do this," I will try as many of the 10 strategies for getting things done (also in Chapter 12) as necessary until I take some positive action.

➤ I will not let fear, perfectionism, or other self-defeating thoughts and feelings control my life.

➤ I will not be overly judgmental of my behavior or put unnecessary pressure on myself. I will recognize that I'm only human and will not always be perfectly efficient—nor should I want to be.

➤ I will keep my priorities and goals in sight at all times.

➤ I will make it a priority to have fun, relax, take care of myself, and connect with my family and friends as often as possible.

I will faithfully execute my Procrastination Proclamation and will, to the best of my ability, preserve, protect, and defend the Procrastinator's Oath of Effectiveness.

_____   _____

Signed   Date

Witnessed by:

1. _____

2. _____

Congratulations! Have the band strike up a rousing chorus of *Hail to the Chief*. You are now inducted into the hallowed halls of recovering procrastinators. Armed with your Procrastination Proclamation, you're ready to get out there and get doing.

The Least You Need to Know

➤ Your Procrastination Proclamation is an announcement to yourself and the world that you are fed up with being a procrastinator and plan to take concrete steps toward becoming an ex-procrastinator.

➤ Before taking action toward your goals, you have to see which of your life roles are taking up the most of your time and energy and compare the results with where you would like to devote your time and energy in the future.

➤ The key to developing an action plan that you will carry out is to keep it simple and not try to tackle too much at once.

➤ Thinking about how your life will be better if you can stop procrastinating on certain matters is a powerful incentive for making good on the goals you set in your action plan.

➤ By taking the Procrastinator's Oath of Effectiveness, you make a commitment to yourself and others to carry out your Procrastination Proclamation.

Chapter 23

Dealing with the Procrastinators Around You

In This Chapter

➤ What to do if you don't procrastinate but others do

➤ How to deal with slackers in the workplace

➤ How to keep family and roommates from turning home into chaos

➤ When to confront procrastinating friends and when to let them be

➤ How to correct kids without stifling them

In their book, *Winning with Difficult People*, Arthur Bell and Dayle Smith have a clever name for people who make life difficult for others. They call them S.O.P.s, Sources of Pain. As you begin the life of a recovering procrastinator, you're likely to come across more than a few S.O.P.s. They might be old partners-in-crime from your procrastinating days who try to suck you back into a life of delaying and denying. Or they may be new friends or business colleagues whose procrastinating behavior frustrates and concerns you now that you've seen the light. Then again, maybe it wasn't you who had the procrastination problem in the first place; maybe you're reading this book to figure out what to do about the procrastinators who drive you bonkers. If so, this chapter will be particularly relevant to you.

Convert Them? Or Turn the Other Cheek?

So what do you do with these sinners (at least, that's how you see them)? Is it your place to show them the error of their ways, or should you look the other way and forget about it? The answer lies in how much harm, or at least inconvenience, the other procrastinators are causing you and themselves.

If their procrastination is having a negative impact on your life, either at work, home, or elsewhere, then you have a right to do something about it. But if you aren't particularly affected by their delaying tactics and last-minute rushes, the matter is not so clear-cut. If it's someone you care about, and you see that procrastination is keeping that person from reaching his or her full potential, then you probably ought to say something about it. But if it's someone you don't know well and don't have frequent contact with, your concern might be misinterpreted as meddling.

If you are a recovering procrastinator and do decide to intervene in a procrastinator's life, tread carefully. Remember what it was like to be one yourself. You may have been ashamed of your habit or afraid someone would find out how far behind the eight ball you were. Or you might've been proud of the habit in an odd sort of way and in denial about its effects on your and others' quality of life, brushing it off as a charming idiosyncrasy.

You're Not Alone

I'm surrounded by procrastinators. At work, it's colleagues who don't do their share. At home, it's a husband who's a dear but just doesn't get things done. I try to make plans with friends who can't commit to a simple lunch date until the last minute. I don't know whether to nag or just let it go. It drives me crazy!

—Adrienne L., office manager

You may not see a procrastination habit as a personal hot button akin to a drug, alcohol, or gambling habit, but a habit is a habit. Anytime you confront people about their behavior, you're likely to meet resistance and resentment. This is especially true if you forget your roots in procrastination and come across like an overzealous missionary who's been born again in some sort of religion of efficiency.

Do's and Don'ts for Dealing with Procrastinators

Whether the slackers around you are in your home or office or are just friends or colleagues you deal with on occasion, there are some basic do's and don'ts to follow regardless of the setting.

Confronting the Procrastinator

When you've decided to approach a procrastinator about his or her problem, tread carefully. Flying off the handle or getting into a major debate without some advance planning is a mistake. Take some time to consider how, when, and where you'll approach the other person, and follow these do's and don'ts:

Don't expect the other person to be a mind reader.

Do communicate with the person before expecting any behavioral changes to take place.

Don't confront the other person with anger.

Do approach the person in a calm, nonconfrontational manner to make the person more receptive to what you have to say.

Don't label the other person. Avoid even using the term *procrastinator*. Name-calling won't get you anywhere.

Do focus on discussing the behavior rather than the character of the person.

Don't focus too much on the details of exactly how the person procrastinates when discussing the annoying behavior.

Quicksand!

Watch out for rationalizing other people's procrastination or denying that they have a problem in order to protect them. Making excuses or covering for them does them no good in the long run. Taking over the chores or doing the work that they don't get around to does you no good.

Do talk instead about the negative impact the procrastinating behavior has on you, on the procrastinator, and/or on other people. In other words, focus on the end result of the behavior more than on the details of the behavior itself.

Don't humiliate the other person by chastising him or her in front of others.

Do find an appropriate time to speak privately.

Don't assume guilt before innocence.

Do take the time to listen to the other person's reasons for not doing something. You might find that there is a perfectly logical explanation for the procrastination. (Then again, the reasons might be lame, but it's worth a shot!)

Don't assume you know what will solve the problem.

Do ask the other person for input into what might work to help him or her get moving.

Trying to Solve the Problem

When you have the lines of communication open and have pointed out to the other person that he has a problem behavior that is affecting himself or others negatively, the time inevitably comes when you have to discuss what's going to be done about it. Consider the following do's and don'ts when you get to that stage:

Don't make it a me-against-you situation in which you seem completely at odds with the other person and wanting to control him or her.

Do talk about common goals, shared objectives, and how you can work together to reach mutually beneficial results.

Don't simply demand that the other person take action.

Do involve the person in the problem-solving process.

Don't delegate a task that the other person isn't capable of doing.

Do choose the right family member, co-worker, committee member, or friend for the task you're delegating, based on their talents, experience, temperament, and schedule.

Don't give vague instructions to someone for how to do something and fail to give that person all the necessary resources and tools.

Do be explicit when telling someone how to do something, especially if it seems that person has been procrastinating because he or she didn't know how to do the task or didn't have the tools to do it with.

Matter of Fact

When dealing with someone whose ethnic background, national origin, or native language is different from yours, you must take those cultural differences into account. Each culture has its own unique perspective on time and the value it places on efficiency. Even language affects how and when we get things done. For example, in Arabic, the word *bukra* means both tomorrow and future. So if a native Arabic speaker says, "Tomorrow, when I do X," but X doesn't happen the next day, it might be because he meant, "In the future, when I do X"!

Don't give overly detailed instructions if the person has been procrastinating as a way to rebel against your control.

Do let the person have more control over how, when, and where the task should be done. Empowering a rebellious type is more effective than becoming even more controlling.

Don't send the person off to fend for himself or herself until the due date or final deadline.

Do follow the "do dates, not due dates" strategy by establishing mini-deadlines and checkpoints.

Don't use ultimatums except as a last resort. (An example of an ultimatum is: "If you don't have your stuff cleared off the kitchen table by Monday, I'm throwing it all out!")

Do try everything in your power to work with the other person before taking drastic measures. If nothing works, then you can throw out all the stuff.

The Recovery Process

After you've had an initial discussion with a procrastinator who's been bugging you, you will no doubt be keeping a careful watch for changes in that person's behavior. This time can be frustrating because the results may not come as quickly as you'd like, and things may not get done in the way you want them to be handled. You might also be unsure of how much you should follow up and keep discussing the problem. These do's and don'ts may make the time a little less confusing for you:

Don't expect miracles overnight.

Do remember what the change process is all about (as discussed in Chapter 6, "Making Sure You'll Really Do It This Time"). It takes time.

Don't nag.

Do try to maintain the same attitude you had in the initial discussion, one of wanting to work with the person, not simply criticizing or nagging.

Don't deny the other person his or her share of the glory or treat the person like a child.

Do praise the recovering procrastinator when you see some real changes in his or her behavior, but don't go overboard.

Don't be inflexible or rigid if things don't go exactly as you had hoped.

Do recognize that everyone has different styles of doing things and try to appreciate that the other person's goals and objectives might be different from yours, but just as valid. Even if you can bring about only small changes, that's a significant accomplishment.

Procrastinators in the Workplace

Getting your own work done is hard enough, but what about those people who turn the workplace into Procrastination Central? They make your job even harder. You may end up having last-minute assignments dumped on your desk or have to take on an extra heavy workload to make up for coworkers or subordinates who don't do their share. Whether the procrastinators are at your job or in a business you run or they are people you deal with while doing volunteer work or serving on committees in your professional community, there are special techniques to use to maintain not only your sanity, but also your job security.

Action Tactic

For more ideas on making changes at work when you're not in a position of authority, read *Getting Things Done When You Are Not in Charge* by Geoffrey Bellman.

When You're Not the Boss

Lydia is a secretary whose boss always gives her assignments at the last minute with very little instruction, and then flips out when she's even the least bit late turning them in. Janet is the manager of a computer help desk in a major corporation. Whenever she tells her manager she wants to discuss a new procedure that would improve the help desk technicians' productivity and internal customer service, he says he'll get to it later. By the time he gets around to listening to her and approving the implementation of the new idea, she's had to bear the brunt of complaints and crises that have arisen from the old procedures.

Having a procrastinator as a boss is a little like having a dysfunctional parent. You have to take on more responsibility than your position warrants and possibly more than your skills and experience make feasible. When everything comes crashing down, you're the one who gets penalized, when in fact the boss's procrastination is really to blame.

If you're experiencing this situation, rest assured that there are steps you can take to rectify the situation:

➤ Make sure you're not the problem. Before assuming that your manager's procrastination is fully to blame for your own difficulty in getting your work done, think about any role you might be playing in the situation. You can't expect to sit back and be told what to do every step of the way. You have to take responsibility for finding out what needs to be done and when and how to do it.

➤ Realize that you can have some control over the situation even if you're not officially in a position of power. You provide a service that your managers depend on, so making your working conditions conducive to getting things done is in their best interests.

➤ When discussing the problem with your boss, keep the focus professional, not personal. Rather than making statements that start with phrases like, "You are …," "You should be more …," or "You do …," talk instead about how you want to change systems and procedures. In other words, don't make personal attacks (even ones that you think are pretty gentle); do discuss how policies and procedures could be different. Even if the boss is the procrastinator behind those faulty procedures, you don't need to humiliate or alienate him or her by calling attention to that fact.

➤ Focus on how the boss's procrastination affects your job performance, not how it makes you feel. Give specific examples of how you could do your job better if your boss planned ahead, were more organized, or whatever.

Quicksand!

If you want to take over projects, be careful how you make the request. Never let on that you're afraid the boss will leave the project to the last minute or mess it up. Instead, make it sound like you want the opportunity to have more responsibility or to learn something new.

➤ Focus on your desire to be a team player. Make it clear that you want to support the boss's objectives, not undermine them.

➤ Ask for more check-ins and meetings. These will help you keep tabs on your boss and will alert you to danger that lies ahead. (If your boss is on a real power trip, make it sound like you need the meetings to check in about your own work rather than to check up on him or her.)

➤ Take over projects whenever possible, rather than getting into a teamwork situation with your boss. If you are fully in charge of planning and executing a project, then you're not at the mercy of your boss's work habits.

When You're in Charge, but Not in Control

If you're in a management or supervisory role, then you have the opposite problem. Your position provides the authority to do something about the procrastinators on your staff, but exerting that authority in the wrong way can backfire. Being in control but not controlling in the negative sense is a tricky tightrope act. Many of the general do's and don'ts offered in the earlier "Trying to Solve the Problem" section of this chapter apply to this particular dilemma, but the following are some additional tips to consider when dealing with a subordinate's procrastination problem:

➤ At first, address the problem face-to-face rather than in writing, so as not to come across as threatening.

Action Tactic

These tips on dealing with procrastinators you manage aren't just for the corporate world. You can use the same strategies with household workers or anyone else you might supervise.

➤ Initially, focus on discussing specific examples of problem performance (such as tasks that aren't getting done or projects that don't flow according to schedule) rather than the big, general procrastination problem.

➤ Follow up an initial face-to-face discussion with a written summary of the specific performance problems that were discussed to establish a written record of the reprimand in order to protect yourself in the event that the employee ends up having to be fired.

➤ Make sure you're delegating the right assignments to the right people. As a manager, it's your job to recognize and develop the talent on your staff. If you keep asking the wrong people to do the wrong tasks, you're not making the most of that talent pool.

➤ Delegate without hesitation. Don't be afraid to wield some authority when assigning a task or putting someone in charge of a project. You have to make it clear that you're turning it over to the other person. Otherwise, your staff may have it in the back of their minds that you'll take over if they don't get it done.

➤ When you turn assignments over to your staff, give them the tools, resources, and support they need. Don't leave them hanging high and dry.

➤ Don't shift gears while someone is trying to finish something that you said was a top priority. Priorities do change, and employees have to be flexible, but before pulling them off projects midstream, make sure that it is absolutely necessary to do so, and tell them why. Don't upset their workflow and sense of concentration just because you want them to indulge your whims.

➤ Establish checkpoints around "do dates" rather than waiting until the due date to see how employees have done the work.

➤ If your employees don't show improvement on a specific performance or productivity problem, then you should have the discussion about procrastination as a general problem.

When Your Coworkers Are Slackers

Working with people who don't hold up their end of the workplace bargain is a major hassle. You end up taking on extra work because they don't do their share, and they might even end up getting credit for doing the whole job. You risk your integrity when you have to cover for them. You fall behind in your own work because they slow down the teamwork process or disrupt the overall workflow.

Matter of Fact

If you're a boss, sometimes it's best to let someone else teach your employees how to be responsible and efficient. Referring your employees to an executive coach or a productivity or time management seminar not only ensures that they'll get more expert advice than you might be able to offer, it also helps you avoid complicating the manager-subordinate relationship unnecessarily. If you don't know how to find a one-on-one coach or a seminar, ask your human resources department for a recommendation, or use the resources listed in the "Careers" and "Coaches" sections of Appendixes B and C in this book.

The general do's and don'ts for confronting any type of procrastinator, as described earlier in this chapter, apply to dealing with co-workers. In addition, consider the following twists on those tips, as well as ones unique to the workplace:

You're Not Alone

The ideal committee is one with me as chairman and two other members in bed with flu.

—Lord Milverton

➤ Don't go straight to the boss. Try to work the problem out with the person directly before making a major case out of it.

➤ Don't badmouth the procrastinator to other co-workers. Either deal with the procrastinator directly or keep your mouth shut.

➤ If and when you do confront the co-worker, remember you have to work together after the discussion is over. Don't lash out and say things you'll regret later.

➤ Keep a written record of examples of co-workers' procrastination, as well as a log of work you have to do to cover for them or take up the slack.

No matter what you do, try to strike a balance between supporting your co-worker in solving the problem and making sure you aren't being taken advantage of.

When You Live with a Procrastinator

You've asked your wife to take out the trash when she leaves for work, but she seems to be wearing blinders each morning as she steps over the piles of trash bags to get out the door. Your roommate agreed to vacuum the shared living room once a month (gee, that often?), but several major religious and federal holidays have passed since you last saw the true color and texture of your carpet. Your 10-year old son is supposed to clean up his room every night before bedtime, but somehow you always find yourself tiptoeing through the toys long after he's snoozing. If you can't live with them, but can't live without them, follow the do's and don'ts suggested earlier in this chapter. Also, consider a few additional tips that work for the particular type of person you're dealing with.

Matter of Fact

The key to getting people to do their share of a workload may lie in the reward you offer—at least that's what a psychology theory from the 1920s, called *expectancy theory*, tells us. It explains that people in groups will work hard if they believe that their efforts will be rewarded and if that reward is something they value. For example, a study by University of Florida psychology professor James Shepperd (reported in the *Personality and Social Psychology Bulletin*, August 1998) found that college students were willing to work diligently at creating as many uses as possible for a knife because they would be rewarded with a certificate for free pizza.

Spouses and Partners

To keep from spending many nights sleeping on the sofa after confronting your wife, husband, or life partner about a procrastination problem, keep these pointers in mind:

➤ Emphasize the "we're-in-this-together" aspect so that the other person doesn't feel ganged up on.

➤ Don't let other baggage from the marriage or relationship muddy the issue. Focus only on specific, current (or recent) behavioral examples.

➤ Don't be overly vigilant about checking for progress after your partner agrees to try to kick the procrastination habit. Because you live together, you're in a position to check up far more often than is healthy for either of you.

➤ Remember that relationships have to be based on some degree of compromise. Try to correct problem behaviors that are dragging you both down, but accept that you have differences and may never approach efficiency the same way.

Roommates

If your roommate is a slob straight out of a sit-com, try these strategies before giving him or her the boot:

> ➤ Establish clear ground rules about household chores and other shared responsibilities from the beginning. If you've already lived together a while, it's never too late to do so.

> ➤ Don't badmouth your roommate to other roommates or the roommate's friends.

> ➤ Think about your expectations for the way the household is maintained and be sure you're being realistic. Your idea of a livable environment may not be everybody else's vision.

Quicksand!

If other relatives besides a spouse or children live with you, don't be afraid to stand your ground if they procrastinate. A mother-in-law, sibling, or anyone else who comes into your household should expect to respect the rules of that home.

> ➤ Don't let your anger or frustration bottle up inside you. Deal with the problem soon after it happens.

> ➤ Clarify your expectations for how and when household tasks should be done. Just saying, "I wish you'd vacuum more," isn't always specific enough.

> ➤ Don't be an enabler. If you go around cleaning up roommates' messes, they might not even see the mess they've made. Let them live in their own squalor for a while (if you can stand it) and maybe they'll clean up their act. Then again, their tolerance for squalor might outlive yours, in which case you may have to resort to cleaning it up yourself just to be able to live there.

> ➤ Remember that roommates are more expendable and easily replaceable than spouses, romantic partners, and friends. If you can't live with them, get rid of them. If it's not your place, move out.

Children

Dealing with your kids' procrastination is tricky. When they say, "I really will do it when I come home from school, Mom," and "Daddy, I just forgot to do it," you can see the procrastination habit sprouting in them and want to nip it in the bud. You want to teach them a sense of responsibility and help instill good habits early on. You also want some sanity in your home life.

Matter of Fact

A handy product for keeping a household running smoothly is the Mission Control Family Organizer. This magnetic, write-on/wipe-off board comes with 60 movable chore and event magnets. You stick it on the refrigerator so that all family members, roommates, babysitters, and cleaning people can keep track of what's happening when and who's supposed to do which chores. It was developed by a husband and wife who forgot to pick up their son at preschool one day because they each thought the other was doing it. I have one on my own fridge and highly recommend it. Look for it at www.familyproducts.com. If you prefer to call, it's in East Montpelier, Vermont at 802-223-7189.

The tricky part comes in when you look at why children procrastinate. Sometimes it is downright rebellion or disorganization; you can do something about these causes. Other times, though, it's part of a toddler's or child's developmental process. Children exert power over their world to stake out their independence. What we see as disobeying us may simply be a way for them to have some control over what they do with their time:

➤ You shouldn't let kids get away with anything they want, but neither should you be overly rigid in what you expect them to do. To find the happy medium, use many of the same do's and don'ts that work with adult procrastinators.

➤ Let kids have a say in how and when a task might be done, but don't completely give up your authority to enforce the rules.

➤ Provide an environment that encourages kids to get things done. Make sure your household is well-organized and that they have the tools they need. For example, you can't expect them to look forward to putting away their toys if the place they have to put them in is too crowded and difficult to get to.

➤ When appropriate, don't bail them out. For example, if your high-schooler always waits until the last minute to prepare a project for class, warn him that you're not going to stay up until midnight working on it with him the next time. Then, when the next time comes, stick to your promises and leave him to do it on his own.

➤ Perhaps the most important point is to set a good example. Kids soak up what they observe like sponges. If you're a procrastinator, you can't expect your children to be productive.

Friends

The tricky thing about dealing with friends who procrastinate is that, on the surface, there seems to be less justification for you to try to do anything about their problem. At work, your justification is that other people's procrastination jeopardizes your job security and makes you shoulder an unfair portion of the workload. When dealing with procrastinators you live with, you have a right to expect them to change because you have a right to live in a peaceful, well-functioning home and in harmony with loved ones (as opposed to chaos and living hell).

With friends, however, the expectations are different. Sure, you're supposed to be considerate and supportive of each other, but you do lead separate lives. There's no built-in authority as in a boss-subordinate relationship. Also, there's no implicit contract that allows you to meddle in each others' lives like you can in a marriage or roommate situation.

You're Not Alone

Contrary to popular belief, some procrastinators do feel bad about letting friends down. Take this comment from a friend of the author:

Michelle, you realize I've been asked to contribute a quote, story, or wry comment to your last two books, and I always miss the deadline. I guess I even procrastinate with people who really matter to me!

—Eric M., slacker and sometime accountant

The reality, however, is that friends who procrastinate can drive you just as crazy. Here's how they might do that:

➤ You can never get them to make plans in advance, so you have to keep your life on hold in order to get together with them.

➤ When plans are set, if you leave them with the responsibility for anything, from buying tickets to an event to making the baked goods you'll both take to a party, they may leave you in the lurch by not doing it or doing it at the last minute.

➤ They inconvenience you when they put off getting to appointments. They show up late or miss an appointment altogether, which is not only a nuisance, it also shows disrespect for you and your time.

➤ They don't get around to returning things they've borrowed from you.

➤ They bug you by complaining about all the work they're behind on.

➤ You have to endure countless stories about their hopes and dreams, but you never hear how they're going to start making those dreams a reality.

If these problems sound familiar, it may be time to have a talk with your friend. Once again, the general do's and don'ts for confronting any type of procrastinator, as described earlier in this chapter, apply to dealing with friends. Pay special attention to letting your friend know how his or her procrastination makes you feel. You can talk

311

about how you feel disrespected and inconvenienced, as well as how you feel concern for the friend because he or she is not reaching his full potential or is having to deal with too much stress. If your procrastinating friends care about you, they should receive your criticism as constructive, not vindictive, and should want to rectify the situation.

The Least You Need to Know

➤ You do have a right to confront people about their procrastination habit if the habit affects your quality of life or job security.

➤ You also owe it to other people—friends, co-workers, or family—to help them work out their problem if you see that it is keeping them from reaching their goals for living a stress-free life.

➤ When dealing with procrastinators in the workplace, work with them as a team player, not as an adversary.

➤ When trying to live with procrastinators, let them know how their problem makes you feel and focus on specific examples of procrastination rather than labeling them a bad person.

Sigh...

Chapter 24

Keeping It Going

In This Chapter

➤ Staying fired up long after you close this book

➤ Keeping clutter out and organization in

➤ Starring in the balancing act

➤ Sorting out priorities and values

Unless you've skipped ahead to this chapter (hey, there's no law against it), then you've come a long way. You've learned why you procrastinate and why it's so important to stop doing so. You've seen what it takes to become an ex-procrastinator: understanding the change process, finding support from other people, getting organized, and making good decisions. You've also found out that any urge to procrastinate can be overcome by doing three simple things: Stop, Look, and Listen. Once you've taken control of your impulse to procrastinate, you'll then be using the 10 techniques described in Chapter 12, "The Secret Formula to Overcoming Procrastination," to start taking action in the specific ways suggested in Parts 3 and 4.

I hope that, at this point, you've already started to break the procrastination habit and are seeing some changes in your approach to life, even if they're only minor ones for now. If not, then I hope, at least, that you've been motivated to do something about your problems, particularly the ones you focused on in the Procrastination Proclamation, and that you feel better equipped to get working on them than when you started this book. In other words, I hope you have not only a fire in your belly but also a strategy in mind.

Four Simple Things to Remember

The goal of this final chapter is to remind you of the most important points offered throughout the book. It's a summary of four main themes that help you overcome procrastination:

1. Change will occur only if you give yourself a reality check about your procrastination habit, get fired up to break it, and stay that way.

2. Keeping clutter from re-accumulating is more important than you might think; it's a key to keeping your organized act together and being productive.

3. Productivity is enhanced by having a balanced life, one in which you get things done but have fun and relax as well.

4. To know what to do on a day-to-day basis, that is, what your priorities are, you have to know what your overall life values are. You also have to understand the difference between values and priorities.

You're Not Alone

We only become what we are by the radical and deep-seeded refusal of that which others have made us.

—Jean-Paul Sartre

In reminding you of those four points, this chapter goes from something of the ridiculous to the sublime. You'll go from reading about seemingly trivial matters like how to keep too many wire clothes hangers or empty take-out food containers from re-cluttering your life to how to sort out complex issues of values and priorities when faced with your own mortality and that of your loved ones.

Here We Go Again? No, Not This Time

So the first step to keeping it going is to get fired up and stay that way as you take the steps in your Procrastination Proclamation. But what if that fire starts to go out and that strategy becomes fuzzy? I know you don't want your determination to go the way of past efforts to lose weight, get fit, stop biting your nails, get your house in shape, start a business, or whatever it is that you've begun with gusto in the past, only to lose steam before reaching your goals.

This time you're not going to give up. Whether it's something as easy as getting the trash out the door or as complex as resolving a relationship problem (I realize some of you might see those two tasks as being one and the same!), you're going to make it happen this time. You'll do it by following five simple rules:

1. **Be realistic about change.** Don't expect miracles overnight. Reread Chapter 6, "Making Sure You'll Really Do It This Time," if you've forgotten what change is all about.

2. **Take it one day at a time.** Don't let yourself be overwhelmed by the process you're embarking on. Focus on taking one baby step each day.

3. **Shed your old identity.** Just because everyone around you has come to know you as a procrastinator, and you've internalized their view, don't get stuck with that label. I'm not asking you to change the core you and become someone you're not, but I do want you to stop thinking of yourself as someone who can't get things done. You're becoming someone who does have your act together. Adopting the identity of an ex-procrastinator is one of the quickest ways to become one.

4. **Use the techniques.** Just reading this book doesn't mean that you will automatically start using the Stop, Look, and Listen formula or any of the other strategies for taking action. It takes sheer determination to get yourself to pause long enough to become aware that you are on the brink of procrastinating and to do something about it. Unfortunately, determination is not something I can give you through words on paper.

5. **Admit when you need help.** If you are having difficulty taking control of your behavior and using the action strategies, or if you need some help understanding the strategies better, then you have to be willing to get some help. Whether you turn to a support team of family and friends or an expert such as those described in Chapter 7, "Rallying Support from the Pros," connecting with real, live human beings is essential for making the strategies work.

These five rules, together with a genuine desire to stop procrastinating, get things done, and reach your goals, will make it happen.

Keeping Your Act Together

Another thing you're going to do is make an effort to keep your act together. You have to keep clutter at bay, stay organized, and not let your schedule and life roles get overloaded again. Believe me, if you're not vigilant about those things, they'll all go back to the way they were.

Prevent Clutter from Piling Back Up

You've cleared out all the unnecessary junk from every closet, corner, and cabinet (or plan to do so soon) and are feeling like a new person. Beware!

Action Tactic

Keep a small spiral notebook close by at all times to jot down notes, phone numbers, something you hear mentioned on the radio, and any other information. It doesn't matter that all the bits of data are unrelated. Having them in your handy-dandy notebook means you don't have to search through scraps of paper, cocktail napkins, Post-it notes, and other assorted places to find something.

Some things in your home or office will multiply like cells dividing in a petri dish. In Chapter 8, "Lightening Your Load," I suggested that every time you bring something new across the threshold, you throw away, give away, or sell a comparable item that you already possess. Out of all the tips offered in this book, that's one of the most important ones to remember. Be particularly watchful of the following items, which can easily reclutter your spaces in the blink of an eye:

➤ Pens that don't write

➤ Coupons

➤ Dead or terminally ill plants

➤ Plastic grocery sacks

➤ Plastic containers and cutlery from take-out food

➤ Empty glass jars and bottles

➤ Wire clothes hangers

➤ Little packets of salt, ketchup, Chinese mustard, and other condiments

➤ Cardboard boxes and gift boxes

➤ Catalogs

➤ Broken items

Quicksand!

Don't forget that you have to look at your to-do lists on a regular basis, schedule times to do the things on them, and follow your schedule. Setting up these organizational systems is only the first step. If you ignore them, they won't work.

That list contains the sorts of things that we hang onto out of habit. Most of us know that, unless we're planning to open a dry cleaners, we don't need 400 wire hangers. If the coupons are for items we'd never buy even if they were free, we know there's no reason to stick them under a refrigerator magnet, but we do it anyway—just in case. Remember, you have to start thinking like someone who gets things done, which means you have to stop and think before you let clutter reaccumulate and slow you down.

Put Things in Their Places

I began this book with the sad tale of a man who might have won 12 million dollars if only he could have found the winning lottery ticket. He had procrastinated setting up a simple organizational system for keeping his lottery tickets in one place. But would that have been enough? No. Designating a file folder, box, or drawer as the place for tickets would not have kept him organized. He would have had to actually put the tickets in that spot to stay organized.

Many people set up beautiful filing systems or closets with neat stacks of sweaters and tidy rows of shoes, but find that order soon turns to chaos. That's because they don't maintain their organizational systems by putting things back where they belong.

They revert to their old ways of tossing stuff anywhere and everywhere.

Remember how important getting organized is as a foundation for overcoming procrastination? If not, revisit Chapter 9, "Getting Your Act Together," and Chapter 10, "A Crash Course in Getting Organized." When you let chaos creep back into your life, you're not just becoming disorganized, you're also allowing obstacles to get in the way of action.

Avoid Overload

If you've already begun to take on fewer obligations or plan to as soon as you get past a current crunch period, then your next task is to keep your plate from getting too full again. Learn from your past mistakes and remember how miserable, tired, and cranky you were when your schedule was overloaded.

Matter of Fact

Even though you can never foresee unexpected demands on your time that might arise, there is one simple thing you can do to prevent overload: Leave room for the unexpected. For example, always take on one less commitment or project than you're inclined to, even if your life has room for it. Always schedule one less daily appointment, even if you have time for it. That way, when an unexpected demand on your time arises, you won't go into overload. If the unexpected doesn't happen, then you end up with a lighter schedule, which is always a nice surprise.

Make Balance a Priority

I know it's easier said than done, but even if you make just a little effort toward keeping some balance in your life, you might be surprised at the positive changes that result. The best way to do this is to keep in mind that balance is not achieved by a mechanical process. It's not a matter of scheduling times into your daily planner to take a walk in the park, meditate or pray, go to the zoo with a child, do something artistic, or just sit and do nothing. It's more of a mindset. It's understanding what the best ways are for you to nourish your mind, body, and soul.

In a poll conducted by the Monster.com Web site, 37,558 people answered the question: "If money were no object, what would you do with your time?" The survey results provide a sort of sneak peek into what nourishes the mind, body, and soul of a big slice of the general public:

Percent of Respondents	How They Want to Spend Their Time
43%	Traveling
29%	With family and friends
13%	Pursuing artistic endeavors
9%	Doing volunteer work
4%	Making more money for the sport of it

How would you have answered that poll? Did any of the activities on that list sound like things you wrote on your wish-to-do list from Chapter 22? The interesting thing about the poll's results is that they reflect the three main keys to having a balanced life:

➤ **Have fun.** Do things you enjoy while still meeting your responsibilities.

➤ **Be grateful.** Make a conscious effort to think about, and be thankful for, what's good in your life. Even the busiest person, who claims not to have time to lead a more balanced life because of work, school, or family demands, can take a minute to do this. If you really do have only a minute to spare in your day, use that minute to—and forgive how corny this sounds—cherish the moment. If you have more than a minute, you can be grateful for what you have by giving something back through volunteer work, as you saw in the poll results.

➤ **Connect.** Connect with the things you do and the people around you instead of just going through the motions.

Action Tactic

When you feel yourself taking on too much, too fast and getting out of balance, pop the cassette tape *Slow Down...and Get More Done* (Listen & Live Audio, 1996) into your Walkman or stereo. It's by Marshall Cook and is based on a wonderful book of the same name.

By the way, there's nothing inherently wrong with scheduling balance into your calendar, if that's the only way to ensure that you'll start making the time to have fun, be grateful, and connect. But true balance is a frame of mind, not an appointment.

Value Your Priorities and Prioritize Your Values

Ultimately, being a more effective, efficient, and accomplished person becomes an issue of working in harmony with your values and keeping your priorities straight. "Gee, umm, that sounds good ... I guess ... but what does it mean?" you might ask. Allow me to illustrate the point by sharing one last personal anecdote with you.

Another Sort of Wake-Up Call

For nearly four decades, one question has been woven into the fabric of American popular culture more than perhaps any other: Where were you when Kennedy was shot? Unfortunately, a new question has been added: Where were you when you heard that JFK Jr.'s plane was missing and then that he and his wife and sister-in-law had died?

I know where I was. It was a steamy July weekend, and I was at home about to get back to writing this chapter, just days from my final deadline for the book. In addition to the numbness and profound sadness I felt over the surreal tragedy—feelings experienced across the United States and around the world—I began to have the sort of thoughts that many people have when faced with a reminder of how fragile our lives are.

Being Hit over the Head with Your Values

My first thought was that I need to treasure my husband, daughter, and other loved ones like never before because they might not be here tomorrow. My next thought was that I need to live each day to the fullest, accomplishing my goals while I still can because I might not be here tomorrow.

Family and work are the two things I care about, that is, value, above just about everything else, so those thoughts were nothing new. But when mortality slaps you in the face, especially when it's the death of three people who are close to your own age, the importance of those values is magnified to the *n*th degree.

When "What Did You Do Today?" Takes on New Meaning

Then, back down on earth, I looked at my to-do list for the weekend:

➤ Wrap up two near-finished chapters of the book

➤ Write a draft of an article for *The New York Times*

➤ Call hotels to make reservations for a vacation

➤ Buy a birthday gift for a friend

➤ Go to the gym

➤ Get milk

You're Not Alone

It seems that the older I get, the more my priorities change, and some tasks end up on hold longer. My house was once one of my main concerns. Now, I don't redecorate as often. I value more spending time with people I love and care for.

—Judy T., homemaker, grandmother, and co-owner/manager of a 375-acre Texas cattle ranch

Before I woke up to the shocking news of our national tragedy, I had planned to spend the entire weekend at the computer, cranking out chapters and an article as fast as I could. My husband had planned to spend most of the weekend driving our daughter around town to visit some of our friends. The idea was that he would keep her "out of my hair" (a phrase I should erase from my vocabulary) so that I could get some work done, given that my deadlines for two writing projects were approaching so quickly.

Okay, so that plan fit with my work value: Reach your goals while you can because you might not live to see tomorrow (and because you enjoy the work). But what about the other value of treasuring loved ones? It looked like I was facing a conflict of values. What good would it do to have a book finished and an article published in a big-deal paper if my husband and daughter went out that day and well ... I don't even want to think about it. On the other hand, I can't abandon my responsibilities and quit doing work that I find fulfilling and just sit around and hug them all the time. What's the solution?

Sorting Out the Values and Priorities Confusion

The answer lies in realizing that values and priorities are not the same thing. I thought I was facing a values conflict that weekend, but I wasn't. I was facing a question of how to prioritize my time.

That weekend, working had to be a priority. Sure, I could've said to hell with it and spent both days playing with my family. But there's a time and a place for that sort of semi-reckless abandon. This weekend was not one of those. I needed to have a draft of the newspaper article in the editor's box first thing Monday morning. My world would not crumble, nor would his, if I didn't have it there on time, but some negative consequences would undoubtedly result. It was the same with the book. I could've chosen to procrastinate and catch up on the final chapters later that week, but there was no time to catch up with just a matter of days left before the deadline.

By choosing to work, I wasn't saying that my work was more important than my family. I was recognizing that work had to be a priority that weekend. I was acknowledging that not meeting my professional obligations would end up having serious negative consequences—not just for myself and my career, but for the people on the other end of my work who were counting on me. Even my family would end up suffering if I had to rush to catch up on extra work a few days down the road.

Getting It Done

So there you have it. I wouldn't let myself feel guilty, because that wouldn't do anyone any good either. Instead, I finished my writing, despite having one eye and ear focused on the disturbing, round-the-clock television news (just as my parents had been glued to the television watching the news of JFK's death when I was a toddler). I also managed to squeeze in a quick workout and to pick up a birthday gift at the bookstore next to the gym. I delegated the milk purchase to my husband, and the vacation planning was grudgingly put off until a few days later.

I also did two things that hadn't been on my to-do list. I made a point of telling my husband how much I appreciated his help in getting my book written. And I gave my daughter a hug like she'd never felt before and thanked my lucky stars for her. It took only about one minute total to do both of those things, but I did more in that one minute than I would have done in an entire Sunday afternoon in the park with them.

It's Up to You

In Chapter 5, "It's About Time," I asked, "Who controls your time?" The only correct answer was "you." Despite all the obstacles that might be thrown your way from people, places, and things, and despite all the mind games you might inadvertently play on yourself, you are in control of your behavior. You can choose to waste time (which is allowed, even encouraged, now and then), or you can choose to make good use of it. You choose what you want to value and which actions you want to, or need to, make a priority on any given day.

Quicksand!

Values and priorities are not the same thing. Values are what matters to you, the guiding principles of your life. Priorities are the actions you deem important at any given time. Don't try to behave every day as if every value you hold is a priority, or you'll face constant ethical dilemmas. For example, you may value family over work but sometimes have to make work a priority.

You can use this book as a reference tool, keeping it handy so that you can refer back to the strategies offered throughout it when you need them. Or you can give in to the "yes, buts" and say, "Aww, these techniques aren't going to work for me," and let the book gather dust on the shelf. It's entirely up to you.

As you struggle to make those choices, think about this old Saudi Arabian proverb: "If a camel once gets his nose in the tent, his body will soon follow." I want you to keep that image in mind as you try to overcome procrastination. You might feel a little clumsy as you stretch and strain to get things done, just like that gangly dromedary. But if you take just one step toward your goals—merely poke your nose in the tent—and vow to stay determined, then success will follow.

The Least You Need to Know

➤ All the strategies in this book are useless if you don't summon up the determination to use them.

➤ Staying organized is an easy way to keep your procrastination-busting efforts working.

➤ A balanced life comes from having fun, being grateful, and staying connected to others.

➤ Values and priorities are not one and the same.

Recommended Books

If you want more detailed advice on any of the topics covered in *The Complete Idiot's Guide to Overcoming Procrastination*, you'll find it in the books listed here. All of these titles are available in bookstores, both the real kind you walk into and the online kind you sign onto.

Careers: **Choosing or Changing**

Best Jobs for the 21st Century by J. Michael Farr and LaVerne Ludden. JIST Works, 1999. ISBN: 1563704862.

Career Smarts: Jobs with a Future by Martin Yate. Ballantine Books, 1997. ISBN: 0345395956.

Career Change: Everything You Need to Know to Meet New Challenges and Take Control of Your Career by David P. Helfand. VGM Career Horizons, 1999. ISBN: 0844242691.

The Complete Idiot's Guide to Changing Careers by William Charland and David E. Henderson. Alpha Books, 1998. ISBN: 0028619773.

Dare to Change Your Job and Your Life by Carole Kanchier. JIST Works, 1995. ISBN: 156370224X.

Do What You Are: Discover the Perfect Career for You Through the Secrets of Personality Type by Paul D. Tieger and Barbara Barron-Tieger. Little Brown & Co, 1995. ISBN: 0316845221.

I Could Do Anything If I Only Knew What It Was: How to Discover What You Really Want and How to Get It by Barbara Sher. Bantam Doubleday Dell, 1995. ISBN: 0440505003.

It's Never Too Late: 150 Men and Women Who Changed Their Careers by Robert K. Otterbourg. Barrons Educational Series, 1993. ISBN: 0812014642.

The Pathfinder: How to Choose or Change Your Career for a Lifetime of Satisfaction and Success by Nicholas Lore. Fireside, 1998. ISBN: 0684823993.

Targeting the Job You Want by Kate Wendleton. Five O'Clock Books, 1997. ISBN: 0944054110.

Zen and the Art of Making a Living by Laurence Boldt. Penguin, 1999. ISBN: 0140195998.

Careers: Job Hunting

CAREERXROADS: The Directory to the 500 Best Job, Resumé and Career Management Sites on the World Wide Web by Gerry Crispin and Mark Mehler. MMC Group, (annual). ISBN: 0965223930.

Change Your Job, Change Your Life: High-Impact Strategies for Finding Great Jobs in the 21st Century by Ronald L. Krannich and Caryl Rae Krannich. Impact Publications, 1997. ISBN: 1570230668.

The Complete Idiot's Guide to Getting the Job You Want by Marc Dorio. Alpha Books, 1998. ISBN: 0028627237.

Cover Letters (*Job Notes* series) by Michelle Tullier. The Princeton Review/Random House, 1997. ISBN: 067977873X.

Cyberspace Resumé Kit: How to Make and Launch a Snazzy Online Resumé by Mary Nemnich and Fred Jandt. JIST Works, 1999. ISBN: 1563704846.

Gallery of Best Resumés: A Collection of Quality Resumés by Professional Resumé Writers by David Noble. JIST Works, 1994. ISBN: 1563701448.

Gallery of Best Resumés for Two-Year Degree Graduates by David Noble. JIST Works, 1996. ISBN: 1563702398.

Getting from Fired to Hired: Bounce Back from Losing Your Job and Get Your Career Back on Track! Martin Elkort. Arco, 1997. ISBN: 0028617371.

Guide to Internet Job Searching: 1998-99 by Margaret Riley. VGM Career Horizons. ISBN: 0844281999.

Job Smart: What You Need to Know to Get the Job You Want by Michelle Tullier, Timothy Haft, Margaret Heenehan, and Marci Taub. The Princeton Review/Random House, 1997. ISBN: 067977355X.

Jobs '99 by Kathryn Petras. Fireside/Simon & Schuster, 1998. ISBN: 0684818264.

Knock 'Em Dead: The Ultimate Job Seeker's Handbook by Martin Yate. Adams Media, 1999. ISBN: 1580620701.

Networking for Everyone: Connecting with People for Career and Job Success by Michelle Tullier. JIST Works, 1998. ISBN: 1563704404.

Professional's Job Finder 1997-2000 by Daniel Lauber. Planning/Communications, 1997. ISBN: 1884587046.

Resumés That Knock 'Em Dead by Martin Yate. Adams Media, 1997. ISBN: 1558508171.

Trashproof Resumés by Timothy Haft. The Princeton Review/Random House, 1995. ISBN: 0679759115.

Unofficial Guide to Acing the Interview by Michelle Tullier. Macmillan, 1999. ISBN: 0028629248.

Using the Internet and the World Wide Web in Your Job Search by Fred Jandt and Mary Nemnich. JIST Works, 1997. ISBN: 1563702924.

Careers: Managing and Advancing In

Dancing with the Dinosaur: Learning to Live in the Corporate Jungle by William Lareau. Winchester Press, 1997. ISBN: 0832905054.

Get More Money on Your Next Job by Lee Miller. McGraw-Hill, 1997. ISBN: 0070431469.

Getting Things Done When You Are Not in Charge by Geoffrey Bellman. Fireside, 1992. ISBN: 0671864122.

Job Savvy: How to Be a Success at Work by LaVerne Ludden. JIST Works, 1998. ISBN: 1563703041.

Jobshift: How to Prosper in a Workplace Without Jobs by William Bridges. Perseus Press, 1995. ISBN: 0201489333.

Six Months Off: How to Plan, Negotiate, and Take the Break You Need Without Burning Bridges or Going Broke by Hope Dlugozima, James Scott, and David Sharp. Henry Holt, 1996. ISBN: 0805037454.

Toxic Work: How to Overcome Stress, Overload, and Burnout and Revitalize Your Career by Barbara Reinhold. Plume, 1997. ISBN: 0452272750.

Unofficial Guide to Earning What You Deserve by Jason Rich. Macmillan, 1999. ISBN: 0028627164.

Work Less, Make More: Stop Working So Hard and Create the Life You Really Want! by Jennifer L. White. John Wiley & Sons, 1999. ISBN: 0471354856.

Work Smart: 250 Smart Moves Your Boss Already Knows by Marci Taub and Michelle Tullier. The Princeton Review/Random House, 1998. ISBN: 0679783881.

Change and Transitions

Getting Unstuck: Breaking Through Your Barriers to Change by Sidney B. Simon. Warner Books, 1989. ISBN: 0446390240.

Managing Transitions: Making the Most of Change by William Bridges. Perseus Press, 1991. ISBN: 0201550733.

We Are All Self-Employed: The New Social Contract for Working in a Changed World by Cliff Hakim. Berret-Koehler, 1995. ISBN: 1881052796.

Decision-Making

The Confident Decision Maker: How to Make the Right Business and Personal Decisions Every Time by Roger Dawson. Quill, 1995. ISBN: 0688142281.

The Creative Problem Solver's Toolbox: A Complete Course in the Art of Creating Solutions to Problems of Any Kind by Richard Fobes. Solutions Through Innovation Publ., 1993. ISBN: 0963222104.

Decision Traps: Ten Barriers to Brilliant Decision-Making and How to Overcome Them by J. Edward Russo and Paul Schoemaker. Fireside/Simon & Schuster, 1990. ISBN: 0671726099.

Smart Choices: A Practical Guide to Making Better Decisions by John S. Hammond, Ralph L. Keeney, and Howard Raiffa. Harvard Business School Press, 1998. ISBN: 0875848575.

Education and Study Skills

The Adult Learner: Strategies for Success (A *Fifty-Minute Series* Book) by Robert Steinbach and Kay Keppler. Crisp, 1993. ISBN: 1560521759.

The Adult Student's Guide to Survival & Success by Al Seibert and Bernadine Gilpin. Practical Psychology Press, 1997. ISBN: 0944227120.

The Art of Academic Finesse: How Ordinary Students Achieve Extraordinary Grades by Eric Evans. Hohm Press, 1998. ISBN: 1889057096.

Back to School: A College Guide for Adults by LaVerne Ludden. JIST Works, 1996. ISBN: 157112070X.

The College Learner: Reading, Studying, and Attaining Academic Success by Jalongo, Tweist, and Gerlach. Prentice Hall, 1998. ISBN: 0137555709.

50 Ways to Bring Out the Smarts in Your Kid by Marge Kennedy. Peterson's Guides, 1996. ISBN: 1560795905.

How to Study by Ronald Fry. Career Press, 1996. ISBN: 1564142299.

Financial Planning

The Complete Idiot's Guide to Doing Your Income Taxes by Gail A. Perry and Paul Craig Roberts. Alpha Books, 1999. ISBN: 0028620003.

The Complete Idiot's Guide to Investing Like a Pro by Edward T. Koch. Alpha Books, 1999. ISBN: 0028620445.

The Complete Idiot's Guide to Managing Your Money by Christy Heady. Alpha Books, 1999. ISBN: 0028627229.

The Courage to Be Rich: Creating a Life of Material and Spiritual Abundance by Suze Orman. Riverhead Books, 1999. ISBN: 1573221252.

Getting Rich in America: 8 Simple Rules for Building a Fortune and a Satisfying Life by Dwight R. Lee and Richard B. McKenzie. HarperBusiness, 1999. ISBN: 0066619823.

The 9 Steps to Financial Freedom by Suze Orman. Crown, 1997. ISBN: 0517707918.

10 Minute Guide to Household Budgeting by Tracey Longo. Macmillan, 1997. ISBN: 0028614429.

Getting Organized

Clutterology: Getting Rid of Clutter and Getting Organized by Nancy Miller. CPM Systems, 1999. ISBN: 0962994405.

The Complete Idiot's Guide to Organizing Your Life by Georgene Lockwood. Alpha Books, 1997. ISBN: 0028610903.

The Organized Executive: A Program for Productivity: New Ways to Manage Time, Paper, People, and the Electronic Office by Stephanie Winston. Warner Books, 1994. ISBN: 0446395285.

Organizing for the Creative Person by Dorothy Lehmkuhl and Dolores Lamping. Crown, 1994. ISBN: 0517881640.

Organizing from the Inside Out by Julie Morgenstern. Holt, 1998. ISBN: 0805056491.

Stephanie Winston's Best Organizing Tips: Quick, Simple Ways to Get Organized and Get on with Your Life by Stephanie Winston. Fireside, 1996. ISBN: 0684818248.

30 Days to a Simpler Life by Connie Cox and Chris Evatt. Plume, 1998. ISBN: 0452280133.

Health/Fitness/Diet/Nutrition

The American Dietetic Association's Complete Food & Nutrition Guide by Roberta Larson Duyff. John Wiley & Sons, 1998. ISBN: 0471346594.

8 Weeks to Optimum Health by Andrew Weil. Fawcett Books, 1998. ISBN: 0449000265.

Healing the Hungry Self: The Diet-Free Solution to Lifelong Weight Management by Deirdra Price. Plume, 1998. ISBN: 0452279402.

The New Fit or Fat by Covert Bailey. Houghton Mifflin, 1991 (revised). ISBN: 0395585643.

The Optimum Nutrition Bible by Patrick Holford. Crossing Press, 1999. ISBN: 1580910157.

Smart Exercise: Burning Fat, Getting Fit by Covert Bailey. Houghton Mifflin, 1996. ISBN: 0395661145.

Stretching by Jane Anderson and Bob Anderson. Random House, 1980. ISBN: 0936070013.

Stretching at Your Computer or Desk by Bob Anderson. Shelter, 1997. ISBN: 0679770844.

Unofficial Guide to Dieting Safely by Janis Jibrin. Macmillan, 1998. ISBN: 0028625218.

Inspiration and Motivation

Find Your Calling, Love Your Life: Paths to Your Truest Self in Life and Work by Martha Finney and Deborah Dasch. Simon & Schuster, 1998. ISBN: 0684831694.

Getting Out from Under: Redefining Your Priorities in an Overwhelming World by Stephanie Winston. Perseus Press, 1999. ISBN: 0738200980.

Life Strategies: Doing What Works, Doing What Matters by Phillip C. McGraw. Hyperion, 1999. ISBN: 0786865482.

Simple Steps to Impossible Dreams: The Fifteen Power Secrets of the World's Most Successful People by Steven K. Scott. Simon & Schuster, 1998. ISBN: 0684848686.

Too Tired to Keep Running, Too Scared to Stop: Change Your Beliefs, Change Your Life by Joyce Patenaude. Element, 1998. ISBN: 1862043493.

Wishcraft: How to Get What You Really Want by Barbara Sher and Annie Gottlieb. Ballantine Books, 1986. ISBN: 0345340892.

Interpersonal Relationships and Social Skills

Beyond Shyness: How to Conquer Social Anxieties by Jonathan Berent and Amy Lemley. Fireside/Simon & Schuster, 1994. ISBN: 0671885251.

The Complete Idiot's Guide to Dating by Judith Kuriansky. Alpha Books, 1999. ISBN: 0028627393.

The Complete Idiot's Guide to a Healthy Relationship by Judith Kuriansky. Alpha Books, 1998. ISBN: 0028610873.

The Complete Idiot's Guide to Managing People by Arthur Pell. Alpha Books, 1999. ISBN: 0028610369.

Difficult People: How to Deal with Impossible Clients, Bosses, and Employees by Roberta Cava. Firefly Books, 1997. ISBN: 1552091252.

That's Not What I Meant! How Conversational Style Makes or Breaks Your Relations with Others by Deborah Tannen. Ballantine Books, 1992. ISBN: 0688048129

Unofficial Guide to Divorce by Sharon Naylor. Macmillan, 1998. ISBN: 0028624558.

What Do I Say Next? Talking Your Way to Business and Social Success by Susan Roane. Warner Books, 1999. ISBN: 0446674265

Winning with Difficult People by Arthur Bell and Dayle Smith. Barrons, 1997. ISBN: 0812098943.

Working with Difficult People by Muriel Solomon. Prentice Hall, 1990. ISBN: 0139573909.

Mental Health

Answers to Distraction by Edward Hallowell. Bantam Books, 1996. ISBN: 055337821X.

Anxiety & Phobia Workbook by Edmund Bourne. Fine Communications, 1997. ISBN: 1567310745.

The Complete Idiot's Guide to Beating the Blues by Ellen McGrath. Alpha Books, 1998. ISBN: 0028623916

Depression: How It Happens, How It's Healed by John Medina. New Harbinger, 1998. ISBN: 1572241004.

Driven to Distraction: Recognizing and Coping with Attention Deficit Disorder from Childhood through Adulthood by Edward Hallowell and John Ratey. Simon & Schuster, 1995. ISBN: 0684801280.

I Don't Want to Talk About It: Overcoming the Secret Legacy of Male Depression by Terrence Real. Fireside, 1998. ISBN: 0684835398.

Just Checking: Scenes from the Life of an Obsessive-Compulsive by Emily Colas. Washington Square Press, 1999. ISBN: 0671024388.

Obsessive-Compulsive Disorder: The Facts by Padmal de Silva and Stanley Rachman. Oxford University Press, 1998. ISBN: 0192628607.

Questions Most Asked about Anxiety and Phobias: A Lively, Down-to-Earth Guide for Overcoming Panic by Jane Miller. Pretext Press, 1998. ISBN: 096548730X.

The Sky Is Falling: Understanding and Coping with Phobias, Panic, and Obsessive-Compulsive Disorders by Raeann Dumont and Aaron Beck. W.W. Norton & Company, 1997. ISBN: 0393316033.

You Mean I'm Not Lazy, Stupid, or Crazy?!: A Self-Help Book for Adults with Attention Deficit Disorder by Kate Kelly. Fireside, 1996. ISBN: 0684815311.

Personality and Behavior

The Complete Idiot's Guide to Breaking Bad Habits by Levert, McClain, and Ferber. Alpha Books, 1998. ISBN: 0028621107.

Get Out of Your Own Way: Overcoming Self-Defeating Behavior by Mark Goulston and Philip Goldberg. Perigee, 1996. ISBN: 0399519904.

Gifts Differing by Isabel Briggs Myers and Peter Myers. Consulting Psychologists Press, 1995. ISBN: 089106074X

Imperfect Control: Our Lifelong Struggles with Power and Surrender by Judith Viorst. Simon & Schuster, 1998. ISBN: 0684801396.

Never Good Enough: Freeing Yourself from the Chains of Perfectionism by Monica R., Ph.D. Simon & Schuster, 1999. ISBN: 0684849631.

Too Perfect: When Being in Control Gets Out of Control by Allan E. Mallinger and Jeannette Dewyze. Fawcett Books, 1993. ISBN: 0449908003.

Self-Employment

Be Your Own Business by Marcia Fox. JIST Works, 1998. ISBN: 1571120823.

The Complete Idiot's Guide to Making Money in Freelancing by Christy Heady and Janet Bernstel. Alpha Books, 1998. ISBN: 0028621190.

The Complete Idiot's Guide to Starting Your Own Business by Ed Paulson and Marcia Layton. Alpha Books, 1998. ISBN: 002861979X.

Going Indie: Self-Employment, Freelance, and Temping Opportunities by Kathi Elster and Katherine Crowley. Kaplan, 1997. ISBN: 0684837560.

The Small Business Money Guide: How to Get It, Use It, Keep It by Terri Lonier and Lisa Aldisert. John Wiley & Sons, 1998. ISBN: 0471247995.

What No One Ever Tells You About Starting Your Own Business: Real Life Start-Up Advice from 101 Successful Entrepreneurs by Jan Norman. Upstart, 1999. ISBN: 1574101129.

Working from Home: Everything You Need to Know About Living and Working Under the Same Roof by Paul Edwards and Sarah Edwards. Putnam, 1999. ISBN: 087477764X.

Working Solo: The Real Guide to Freedom & Financial Success with Your Own Business by Terri Lonier. John Wiley & Sons, 1998. ISBN: 0471247138.

Working Solo Sourcebook: Essential Resources for Independent Entrepreneurs by Terri Lonier. John Wiley & Sons, 1998. ISBN: 0471247146.

Time: Making the Most of It

The Business Traveler's Survival Guide: How to Get Work Done While on the Road by June Langhoff. Aegis Pub Group, 1997. ISBN: 1890154032.

The Complete Idiot's Guide to Managing Your Time by Jeff Davidson. Alpha Books, 1998. ISBN: 0028610393.

First Things First by Stephen R. Covey. Fireside, 1996. ISBN: 0684802031.

The 7 Habits of Highly Effective People: Powerful Lessons in Personal Change by Stephen R. Covey. Fireside, 1990. ISBN: 0671708635.

The Time Bind: When Work Becomes Home and Home Becomes Work by Arlie Russell Hochschild. Henry Holt & Company, 1997. ISBN: 0805044701.

Time for Life: The Surprising Ways Americans Use Their Time by John P. Robinson, Geoffrey Godbey, and Robert Putnam. Pennsylvania State University Press, 1997. ISBN: 0271016523.

Time Management for the Creative Person by Lee T. Silber. Three Rivers Press, 1998. ISBN: 0609800906.

Wills and Estates

The Complete Idiot's Guide to Wills and Estates by Stephen Maple. Alpha Books, 1997. ISBN: 0028617479.

Estate Planning: Step-By-Step (Barron's *Legal-Ease* Series) by Martin Shenkman. Barrons Educational Series, 1997. ISBN: 0812098064.

The Complete Will Kit by Bruce Gentry and Jens Appel. John Wiley & Sons, 1996. ISBN: 0471141372.

Writing

Miss Manners' Basic Training: Communication by Judith Martin. Crown, 1997. ISBN: 0517706733.

The Complete Idiot's Almanac of Business Letters and Memos by Tom Gorman. Alpha Books, 1997. ISBN: 002861741X.

The Plain English Approach to Business Writing by Edward Bailey. Oxford University Press, 1997. ISBN: 0195115651

Words at Work: Business Writing in Half the Time with Twice the Power by Susan Benjamin. Addison-Wesley, 1997. ISBN: 0201154846

Vest Pocket Guide to Business Writing by Deborah Dumaine. Prentice Hall, 1997. ISBN: 013440355X

Useful Organizations and Associations

Connecting with people who can provide information, resources, or support is an important step in overcoming procrastination. If you're not sure where to get that help, check out the organizations listed in this appendix. Some can provide referrals to professionals in your area. Some offer support groups or seminars. Others focus on educating or informing you about a particular issue.

Careers

If you need to find a career development professional to help you choose, change, or manage your career or find a job, the following organizations are good places to start. They can refer you to career counselors, coaches, or consultants in private practice or other settings and may offer group career counseling and seminars.

Career Planning and Adult Development Network

408-559-4946 or info@careertrainer.com

www.careertrainer.com

Five O'Clock Club

212-286-9332

www.fiveoclockclub.com

International Association of Career Management Professionals

650-359-6911

www.iacmp.org

National Association for Female Executives (NAFE)

1-800-634-NAFE

www.nafe.com

National Board for Certified Counselors

336-547-0607

www.nbcc.org

National Career Development Association

1-888-326-1750

www.ncda.org

Coaching

The following organizations can refer you to a coach for assistance in setting and reaching personal or professional goals.

Coach University Coach Referral Service

1-800-48COACH

www.coachu.com

The Coaches Training Institute Coaching Referral Service

1-800-691-6008

www.thecoaches.com

International Coach Federation

1-888-BEMYCOACH

www.coachfederation.org

Education

For assistance in selecting and applying to schools, colleges, and special educational programs, members of the following organization can be a valuable resource. Most independent educational consultants work with children, adolescents, and young adults, but some provide guidance for older adults wishing to return to school. Some also offer, or can refer you to, testing for academic aptitude or learning disabilities as well. (For more education-related resources, see the education Web sites listed in Appendix C.)

Independent Educational Consultants Association

703-591-4850

www.educationalconsulting.org

Finance

If you need information on getting out of debt or getting ahead financially, or referrals to financial planning experts, these organizations can come to your rescue:

Debt Counselors of America

1-800-680-3328

www.dca.org

Institute for Certified Financial Planners

1-800-282-7526

www.icfp.org

International Association for Financial Planning

1-800-945-IAFP

www.iafp.org

National Association of Personal Financial Advisors

1-888-FEE-ONLY

National Foundation for Consumer Credit

1-800-388-2227

www.nfcc.org

Health/Fitness/Diet/Nutrition

When you're fed up with your feeding frenzy or need to get in shape, or if you need help with an eating disorder, these organizations might get you on the right track:

Aerobics and Fitness Association of America

1-800-225-2322

www.afaa.com

American Council on Exercise

619-535-8227

www.acefitness.org

American Dietetic Association

1-800-366-1655

www.eatright.org

American Holistic Health Association

1-714-779-6152

www.ahha.org

IDEA: The Association for Fitness Professionals

1-800-999-4332

www.ideafit.com

The National Eating Disorders Organization (NEDO)

1-918-481-4044

www.laureate.com

Overeaters Anonymous

1-505-891-2664

www.overeaters.anonymous.org

Society of Certified Nutritionists

www.certifiednutritionist.com

Learning Disabilities and ADD

These organizations educate the public about learning disabilities and Attention Deficit Disorder (ADD). Some provide referrals to qualified professionals who can diagnose and treat such problems. In addition to these groups, see the appendix of the book *Driven to Distraction: Recognizing and Coping with ADD from Childhood through Adulthood* by Edward Hallowell, M.D., and John Ratey, M.D., for a list of ADD support groups nationwide.

Children and Adults with Attention Deficit Disorder

1-800-233-4050

www.chadd.org

International Dyslexia Society

1-800-ABCD123

www.interdys.org

National Attention Deficit Disorder Association

1-800-487-2282

www.add.org

National Center for Learning Disabilities

1-212-545-7510

www.ncld.org

Mental Health

When your battle with procrastination seems like more than you can handle on your own, these organizations can provide referrals to mental health professionals, as well as general information:

American Association for Marriage and Family Therapy

202-452-0109

www.aamft.org

American Association of Pastoral Counselors

703-385-6967

www.aapc.org

American Counseling Association

1-800-347-6647

www.counseling.org

American Mental Health Counselors Association

1-800-326-2642

www.amhca.org

American Psychiatric Association

202-682-6000

www.psych.org

American Psychological Association

1-800-374-2721

www.apa.org

Anxiety Disorders Association of America

301-231-9350

www.adaa.org

National Association of Cognitive-Behavioral Therapists

1-800-853-1135

www.nacbt.org

National Association of Social Workers

202-408-8600

www.naswdc.org

National Mental Health Association

1-800-969-NMHA

www.nmha.org

Obsessive-Compulsive Foundation

203-878-5669

www.ocfoundation.org

Organizers

To whip your closets, office, or any other space at home or work into shape, the places to turn to for expert assistance are the following organizations:

National Association of Professional Organizers

512-206-0151

www.napo.net

National Concierge Association

312-782-6710

www.conciergeassoc.org

Self-Employment/Business Development

If you've been putting off pursuing a business idea or making improvements in a business you're already in, these organizations have information, resources, and advisors that can motivate you to get cracking:

American Association of Home-Based Businesses

301-466-8070

www.aahbb.org

American Institute for Small Business

1-800-328-2906

http://members.aol.com/aisb

American Society of Women Entrepreneurs

1-888-669-2793

www.aswe.org

American Women's Economic Development Institute

212-692-9100

International Franchise Association

202-628-8000

www.franchise.org

National Association of Women Business Owners

301-608-2590

www.nawbo.org

National Association for the Self-Employed

202-466-2100

www.nase.org

National Minority Business Council

212-573-2385

www.nmbc.org

SCORE – Service Corps of Retired Executives

1-800-827-5722 (Small Business Administration)

www.score.org

Small Business Administration

1-800-827-5722

www.sba.gov

U.S. Chamber of Commerce Small Business Institute

1-800-429-7724

www.usccsbi.com

Young Entrepreneurs Network

310-822-0261

www.yenetwork.com

Appendix C

Online Resources

The Web sites listed here provide the information and support you need to make things happen in your career, education, business, finances, health, or home front.

Careers

AdviceZone: www.advicezone.com

America's Job Bank: www.ajb.dni.us

CareerMosaic: www.careermosaic.com

HeadHunter.Net: www.headhunter.net

HotJobs: www.hotjobs.com

Job Trak: www.jobtrak.com

Monster.com: www.monster.com

O*NET – The Occupational Information Network: www.doleta.gov/programs/onet

Riley Guide: www.dbm.com/jobguide

Telecommuting jobs: www.tjobs.com

Telecommuting, Teleworking, and Alternative Officing: www.gilgordon.com

Coaches

Coach University Coach Referral Service: www.coachu.com

The Coaches Training Institute Coaching Referral Service: www.thecoaches.com

International Coach Federation: www.coachfederation.org

Education

    College Board Online: www.collegeboard.org

    College Planning Network: www.collegeplan.org

    Education Index: www.educationindex.com

    ERIC Clearinghouse on Higher Education: www.eriche.org

    Kaplan Educational Centers: www1.kaplan.com

    Petersons Education and Career Center: www.petersons.com

    The Princeton Review Online: www.review.com

    Study Web: www.studyweb.com

Finance

    CNNfn The Financial Network: cnnfn.com

    Debt Counselors of America: www.dca.org

    E*TRADE: www.etrade.com

    EduStock: tqd.advanced.org/3088

    iVillage Money Life: www.ivillagemoneylife.com

    Money.com Financial Strategy Center: www.pathfinder.com/money/aol/index.html

    Nolo.com Self-Help Legal Center/Wills and Estate Planning: www.nolo.com

    Personal Finance 101: www.ralphphillips.com/personalfinance/

    Quicken.com: www.quicken.com

    Quote.com: www.quote.com

    Yahoo! Finance: finance.yahoo.com

Health/Fitness/Diet/Nutrition

    AdviceZone: www.advicezone.com

    Healthfinder: www.healthfinder.gov

    Health World Online: www.healthy.net

    National Library of Medicine's MEDLINEplus: www.nlm.nih/gov/medlineplus

    OnHealth: www.onhealth.com

Household Organizations

Hints from Heloise: www.Heloise.com

Householdtips.com: www.householdtips.com

Tipz Time: www.tipztime.com

Learning Disabilities and ADD

National Institute of Mental Health's online pamphlet on ADHD: www.nimh.nih.gov/publicat/adhd.htm

Mental Health

Go Ask Alice: www.cc.columbia.edu/cu/healthwise/alice.html

HandiLinks to Mental Health Counselors: www.ahandyguide.com

Internet Mental Health: www.mentalhealth.com

Mental Health Net – Self-Help Resources: www.cmhc.com

National Clearinghouse for Alcohol and Drug Information: www.health.org

Psych Central: www.grohol.com

Psych Web: www.psych-web.com

Web of Addictions: www.well.com/user/woa

Planners

The following are sites where you can purchase or obtain information about appointment books, calendars, and organizers:

BOSS Custom Day Planner Products: www.bossplanners.com

Day Runner Online Store: www.dayrunner.com

Day-Timer Store: www.daytimer.com

Filofax: www.TheDailyPlanner.com

Franklin Covey: www.franklinquest.com

Self-Employment/Business Development

American Success Institute: www.success.org

Business Resource Center: www.morebusiness.com

Eweb: Education for Entrepreneurship: www.slu/edu/eweb

Small Business Development Center Research Network: www.smallbiz.suny.edu

Start Up biz.com: www.StartUpbiz.com

Working from Home: www.paulandsarah.com

Working Solo: www.workingsolo.com

The Procrastination Survey

I conducted a survey over a four-month period in 1999 to find out what people procrastinate about most. A brief look at the results was included in Chapter 1, "The Procrastinator's Wake-Up Call." More results, as well as some background information on the survey itself, are provided in this appendix.

Survey Method

The survey began with a questionnaire that I distributed by e-mail to 73 people: professional colleagues, friends, and family in my own e-mail address book. Of those 73 people, 59 returned the completed survey, giving a response rate of 81 percent. Several people in that group forwarded the questionnaire on to people in their own e-mail address books, and I also sent out approximately 30 more questionnaires to add to the initial group of 73.

The questionnaire continued to circulate in cyberspace, as respondents forwarded it on to their friends and family, who then forwarded it on to their friends and family, and so forth. I ultimately received a total of 309 responses to the survey. It's not possible to calculate a final response rate (the percentage of people who answered out of those who received it) because I do not know how many people received the questionnaire. Note: 64 of the 309 respondents completed a printout of the questionnaire, which they mailed or faxed back to me (or, in a few cases, hand-delivered) instead of receiving and returning it by e-mail.

Who the Participants Are

Demographic data is available for only 278 of the 309 respondents, because an early version of the questionnaire did not ask for such personal information as age, race, and so on. So all statistics reported here are for the pool of 278, not 309.

The respondents ranged in age from early 20s to 70s, with the breakdown as follows:

Age	# of Respondents	Percentage of Total
Younger than 20	0	0%
20–29	33	12%
30–39	66	24%
40–49	63	23%
50–59	48	17%
60–69	18	6%
70+	6	2%

Male	Female
30%	70%

Race	Percentage
Caucasian/White	70%
African-American/Black	5%
Other*	4%

Household Situation	Percentage
Live with spouse or other family, partner, or roommate	51%
Live alone	39%
Have children in household between age 7 weeks and 34 years at the time of the survey, with age 10 being the average	24%

Work Status	Percentage
Work full-time (not as a homemaker/parent)	70%
Work part-time (not as a homemaker/parent)	9%
Full-time student	3%
Part-time student	4%
Full-time homemaker and/or parent	3%
Part-time homemaker and/or parent	4%
Retired	1%
Semi-retired	4%

The Other category includes Hispanic, Asian-American, Arab-American, Native American, Indian, Pacific Islander, and Tibetan. The remaining 21 percent not accounted for are participants who chose not to identify their race.

The Questionnaire and Instructions

In this section is a copy of the questionnaire that was used in this survey as well as the instructions that survey participants were given for how to complete it.

Procrastination Survey

Please read through the list below and type an asterisk next to any task/activity that you tend to procrastinate—things you either delay doing or start but don't finish. You've probably put off many of these tasks at some point in your life, but just put an asterisk next to the ones that you procrastinate about currently, or have in the recent past.

Then go back and choose the three biggest problems—the ones that belong in your "Personal Procrastination Hall of Fame." You can think of these as the three things that you have most often put off throughout your life or that you are most concerned about. Type two additional asterisks next to each of those three items for a total of three asterisks. Also, feel free to write in any comments that come to mind as you complete the survey.

➤ Routine household cleaning
➤ Routine tidying up around the house
➤ Cleaning out closets, drawers, and other cluttered spaces
➤ Doing laundry
➤ Taking clothes to the dry cleaners or picking them up
➤ Taking out the trash or recyclables
➤ Reading and dealing with your mail (at home or work)
➤ Mailing letters and other correspondence (the actual stamping and mailing, not the writing)
➤ Replying to e-mails
➤ Buying groceries
➤ Making home repairs or arranging for others to do them
➤ Washing your car
➤ Maintaining your car (having the oil changed, checking the tires, etc.)
➤ Returning rented videos
➤ Returning library books
➤ Returning borrowed items from friends
➤ Returning phone calls (work-related)
➤ Returning phone calls (personal ones)
➤ Doing routine paperwork (at work)
➤ Paying bills

- Keeping up with things you want to read (personal)
- Keeping up with your professional reading
- Looking for a new job
- Making a career change
- Starting a business you've been thinking about
- Taking up new hobbies or renewing old ones
- Getting together with old friends
- Writing letters (personal correspondence)
- Writing and sending thank-you notes
- Replying to invitations (RSVPing)
- Sending birthday cards or gifts
- Shopping for major holidays such as Christmas or Valentine's Day
- Making medical/dental appointments
- Stopping smoking
- Breaking other bad habits (please specify)
- Losing weight
- Exercising
- Making major life decisions (please specify)
- Returning to school for a degree or individual courses
- Writing papers and reports (at work)
- Writing papers and reports (for school)
- Studying for tests
- Doing homework
- Completing a degree
- Preparing a will or other estate planning
- Keeping or organizing financial records
- Investing/saving for the future
- Preparing a budget
- Preparing and filing income taxes
- Changing the batteries in your smoke alarm(s)
- Leaving home or work to get to appointments
- Getting organized (in general)
- Reaching long-term goals (personal or professional)
- Other:

Survey Results

The following list of questionnaire items is reordered to show you how each task ranked—in other words, how often it was cited as a problem. The task ranked as #1 is the task that was noted by the largest number of survey participants as being a problem for them. The task ranked as #47 was the one least likely to be a problem. Tasks with the same rank indicate items that were tied.

The number in parentheses after each item shows the percentage of respondents out of the total 309 who cited that task as a problem. (Decimal points of percentages were rounded to nearest whole number, so items with the same percentages did not tie, unless those items have the same ranking.)

1. Cleaning out closets, drawers, and other cluttered spaces (62 percent)
2. Exercising (57 percent)
3. Making home repairs or arranging for others to do them (40 percent)
4. Keeping up with things you want to read (for pleasure, not for work) (40 percent)
5. Writing letters (personal correspondence, not work-related) (40 percent)
6. Routine household cleaning (39 percent)
7. Keeping up with professional reading (38 percent)
8. Keeping or organizing financial records (37 percent)
9. Washing your car (35 percent)
10. Preparing a will or other estate planning (34 percent)
11. Writing and sending thank-you notes (34 percent)
12. Making medical/dental appointments (33 percent)
13. Losing weight (33 percent)
14. Getting together with old friends (32 percent)
15. Doing routine paperwork at work (30 percent)
16. Reading and dealing with mail at home or work (30 percent)
16. Investing/saving for the future (30 percent)
17. Routine tidying up around the house (29 percent)
18. Sending birthday cards or gifts (29 percent)
19. Getting organized (in general) (27 percent)
20. Paying bills (27 percent)
21. Shopping for major holidays (26 percent)
22. Taking up new hobbies or renewing old ones (25 percent)
23. Taking clothes to the dry cleaners or picking them up (25 percent)
23. Preparing and filing income taxes (25 percent)

23. Preparing a budget (25 percent)

24. Changing the batteries in smoke alarm(s) (23 percent)

25. Returning phone calls (personal ones) (23 percent)

26. Writing papers and reports (at work) (22 percent)

27. Maintaining your car (21 percent)

28. Mailing letters and other correspondence (20 percent)

29. Replying to invitations (RSVPing) (18 percent)

30. Making a career change (17 percent)

31. Looking for a new job (17 percent)

32. Leaving home or work to get to appointments (17 percent)

33. Taking out the trash or recyclables (15 percent)

34. Doing laundry (15 percent)

34. Starting a business you've been thinking about (15 percent)

35. Writing papers and reports (for school) (14 percent)

36. Buying groceries (14 percent)

37. Studying for tests (12 percent)

38. Reaching long-term goals (12 percent)

39. Returning borrowed items from friends (11 percent)

40. Returning phone calls (work-related) (11 percent)

40. Returning to school for a degree or individual courses (11 percent)

41. Doing homework (11 percent)

42. Replying to e-mails (10 percent)

43. Returning library books (9 percent)

44. Returning rented videos (9 percent)

44. Stopping smoking (9 percent)

45. Making major life decisions (8 percent)

46. Completing a degree (6 percent)

47. Breaking other bad habits (4 percent)

Tasks not listed on the original questionnaire, which survey respondents wrote into the Other category, included the following:

➤ Booking a babysitter

➤ Buying a home

➤ Cooking dinner

➤ Depositing checks in the bank

➤ Evening childcare routines during "meltdown" time of the day

- ➤ Getting haircuts or coloring
- ➤ Getting reimbursements
- ➤ Grading papers
- ➤ Having children
- ➤ Learning to drive
- ➤ Making restaurant reservations
- ➤ Mending and ironing
- ➤ Organizing photos and assembling albums
- ➤ Planning vacations
- ➤ Putting gas in the car
- ➤ Returning items to stores
- ➤ Selling a home
- ➤ Unpacking boxes after a move
- ➤ Writing sympathy notes
- ➤ Yard work

In the "Breaking Bad Habits" category, respondents listed

- ➤ Collecting junk
- ➤ Drinking too much beer
- ➤ Drinking in general
- ➤ Eating sugar/sweets/fats/junk food
- ➤ Nail biting
- ➤ Other unhealthy eating habits

Index

A

abuse, safety issues, 188
ADD (Attention Deficit Disorder), 51
addictions, procrastination as, 19
administrative files, filing systems, 125-126
adrenaline rushes, causes of procrastination, 49
alarms, smoke alarms, 186
all-or-nothing thinking, 171
ambition, lack of, 22
anxiety disorders, 52
appointments
    being on time, 110
    medical/dental appointments, excuses/responses, 210-211
assessing procrastination, 287, 291
    areas to improve, priorities, 292-294
    home, 290
    personal health, 291
    personal/social life, 289-290
    school, 289
    work, 288
assistance
    career development professionals
        career coaches/ consultants, 84
        career counselors, 84
        Career Planning and Adult Development Network, 82
        types, 82-83
    education consultants, 85
    mental health professionals, 79
        psychotherapists, 80-82
        Shrink to Fit: Answers to Your Questions About Therapy, 80

personal coaches, 84-85
professional help, assessing need, 77-79
professional organizers, 85-86
questions to ask when seeking, 86-87
Association of Image Consultants International Web site, 206
Attention Deficit Disorder (ADD), 51

B

balancing work/fun
    organization, 111
    maintaining change, 317-318
    managing time, 60-61
benefits of procrastination, 20
Beyond Love and Work: Why Adults Need to Play, 192
bills, reasons for not paying, 219-220
birthdays cards/gifts, 195-196
books
    Beyond Love and Work: Why Adults Need to Play, 192
    changing behaviors, 72
    children, having, 182
    Complete Idiot's Guide to Managing Your Time, The, 58
    Complete Idiot's Guide to Organizing Your Life, The, 170
    Do What You Are: Discover the Perfect Career for You Through the Secrets of Personality Type, 248
    etiquette, 235
    Getting Things Done When You Are Not in Charge, 304
    Last-Minute Estate Planning, 229

Organizing for the Creative Person, 127
Reading Lists for College-Bound Students, 273
reading more, 215-216
Seven Habits of Highly Effective People, The, 61
Shrink to Fit: Answers to Your Questions About Therapy, 80
Simplify Your Christmas: 100 Ways to Reduce the Stress and Recapture the Joy of the Holidays, 197
Slow Down...and Get More Done, 318
Stress Management Sourcebook, The, 10
Surviving Debt: A Guide for Consumers, 222
boring tasks, causes of procrastination, 50
bosses, as procrastinators, 304-305
broken promises
    exercising, self-defeating thoughts, 205-207
    hobbies, taking up, 211-212
    journals/diaries, keeping, 214-215
    learning new skills, 214
    New Year's resolution, flaws, 204-205
    reading more, 215
    see also proclamations
budget preparation, 221
burglaries, safety issues, 187-188
businesses, starting, *see* self-employment

C

calendars, monthly calenders, 128
cards, birthdays, 195

career development
professionals
    career coaches/
        consultants, 84
    career counselors, 84
    Career Planning and
        Adult Development
        Network, 82
    types, 82-83
Career Planning and Adult
    Development Network, 82
career-related procrastination
    changing careers
        pitfalls/strategies for
            avoiding, 250-252
        self-employment,
            252-254
    dangers of procrastinating,
        7-9
    *Do What You Are: Discover
    the Perfect Career for You
    Through the Secrets of
    Personality Type,* 248
    direction, lacking, 248-249
    effects of, 247-248
    guidelines for dealing
        with, 249-250
    home-based offices,
        266-268
    job searches
        reasons for procrastina-
            tion, 258-262
        resumés, 259
    keeping jobs
        essentials, 262-263
        extra efforts, 268-269
        interpersonal problems,
            265-266
        Soundview Executive
            Book Summaries, 262
        writing problems,
            264-265
    reasons for
        procrastinating, 248
categories of
    procrastination, 14-15
causes of procrastination, 44
    adrenaline rush, 49
    boring tasks, 50
    frustrating tasks, 49
    overwhelming tasks, 49
    perfectionism, 48
    physical problems, 52

psychological disorders,
    50-51
    anxiety disorders, 52
    Attention Deficit
        Disorder (ADD), 51
    depression, 52
    Obsessive-Compulsive
        Disorder (OCD),
        51-52
    rebellion, 50
    unrealistic view of
        time, 50
change,
    books, 72
    difficulty of change, 73
    failure, reasons, 70-71
    likelihood of change
        (quiz), 75
    maintaining, 314-315
        balancing work/fun,
            317-318
        clutter, avoiding,
            315-316
        organization, 316-317
        overcommitment,
            avoiding, 317
        values/priorities,
            318-320
        success, 314
    reasons, 73
childproofing, safety issues,
    188-189
children
    books, 182
    childproofing, safety
        issues, 188-189
    cost considerations, 183
    procrastinators, 309-310
    timing, 183-184
    www.babycenter.com, 183
chip-away technique
    completing tasks, 157
    household chores, 167
chores, *see* home-related
    procrastination
cleaning services, 169
cleaning up
    household chores
        all-or-nothing
            thinking, 171
        complaints about
            opposite sex, 171
        easing the burden, 169

gender-related
    statistics, 170
guidelines for dealing
    with, 169-170
professional services, 169
scheduling tasks, 169-170
clothing, 32
clutter
    assessing (quiz), 90-93
    avoiding
        collectibles, 34
        computer hard drives,
            34-35
        maintaining change,
            315-316
        papers, 33
    clearing out, 171-172
    decluttering, 101-102
    excuses for purchases/
        solutions, 94
        guilt, 94, 96
        historical reasons, 97
        hopes/dreams, 98-99
        identity, 99-100
        practical purposes, 97-98
        sentimental reasons,
            96-97
        value, 95
    household chores, 171-172
    rationalizing, 93-94
    trash cans, 108
coaches, personal coaches,
    84-85
collectibles, 34
college students, 271
    graduate students, 276-277
        dissertations, 277-279
    guidelines, 275-276
    majors, choosing, 276
    reasons for procrastination,
        274-275
    returning to school
        excuses, 279-281
        National University
            Continuing Education
            Association, 280
    saving for college, 225
comfort, 31
    career-related
        procrastination, 258-259
    clothing, 32
    completing tasks, 154
    room temperature, 31-32

commitments
  backing out, 113-114
  overcommitment
    avoiding, 35
    life roles, 36-38
complaints
  letters of complaint,
    240-241
    excuses/solutions,
      241-242
completing tasks
  strategies, 151-152
    chip-away
      technique, 157
    comfort, 154
    isolation, avoiding,
      154-155
    motivating yourself, 152
    organization, 152
    positive self-talk,
      155-156
    prioritizing, 153
    rewards/treats, 158-159
    scheduling, 153, 157
computer hard drives
  clutter, avoiding, 34-35
  environmental factors, 34
computers, distractions, 38-39
condolence letters
  considerations, 236-237
  samples, 238
consultants
  career coaches/
    consultants, 84
  education consultants, 85
Consumer Information
  Center, 242
correspondence
  condolence letters
    considerations, 236-237
    samples, 238
  etiquette books, 235
  keeping in touch, 239-241
  postcards, 238-239
  R.S.V.P.s, 234-235
    samples, 236
  thank-you notes
    guidelines for writing,
      233-234
    reasons for
      procrastination, 232
co-workers, as procrastinators,
  306-307

crowding schedules, 109
crunch periods, time
  management, 58
cubicles, environmental
  factors, 31-32
cultural differences, others'
  procrastination, 302
current projects, filing
  systems, 125

D

daily action pages,
  organization, 128-129
dangers of procrastinating,
  3-5
  career-related, 7-9
  financial, 5-7
  health-related, 9-11
  home-related
    consequences, 11
  relationship-related
    consequences, 11
  safety-related, 12
dating
  ending relationships,
    199-200
  guidelines, 198-199
  hindrances, 198
day planners, types, 127-128
deadlines vs. due dates,
  156-157
dealing with procrastinators
  attempting to resolve,
    301-303
  confronting, 300
  cultural differences, 302
  family, 307-308
    children, 309-310
    spouses, 308-309
  follow-up action, 303
  friends, 311
  rationalizing, 301
  roommates, 309
  workplace
    bosses, 304-305
    co-workers, 306-307
    *Getting Things Done
      When You Are Not in
      Charge*, 304
    subordinates, 305-306

debts, paying off, 221
  excuses/responses, 222-224
  *Surviving Debt: A Guide for
    Consumers*, 222
  widespread epidemic, 222
decision-making
  delaying, 134
  difficulties, 134-135
    internal struggles,
      136-137
    lack of choices, time, or
      money, 135-136
    too many choices/too
      much information, 135
  major decisions, 137-138
  poor choices, 134
  process
    addressing
      roadblocks, 144
    analyzing
      information, 143
    gathering
      information, 142
    gut feelings, 142-143
    importance of
      decision-making, 141
    priorities, 142
    readiness, 141
  stress, 144
  styles, 138
    assessing, 140-141
    facts vs. feelings, 140
    future-oriented vs.
      present-oriented,
      139-140
    gathering
      information, 140
decluttering
  categorizing items, 101-102
  considerations, 102
dental/medical appointments,
  excuses/responses, 210-211
depression, 52
diaries, keeping, 214-215
dieting
  broken promises, 205
  guidelines for dieting,
    207-209
difficult tasks vs. simple
  tasks, 61
discipline, lack of, vs.
  procrastination, 21

dissertations, 277
    completing, 278-279
distractions, 38
    computers, 38-39
    environmental factors, 38-39
    television, 38-39
do dates vs. due dates, 156-157
Do What You Are: Discover the Perfect Career for You Through the Secrets of Personality Type, 248
domestic violence, safety issues, 188
dreams/hopes, excuses for clutter, 98-99
dry cleaning, 173-174
due dates vs. do dates, 156-157

E

e-mail, 194
education consultants, 85
effectiveness, Oath of Effectiveness, 296
environmental factors
    categories, 29
    clutter
        collectibles, 34
        computer hard drives, 34
        papers, 33
    comfort, 31
        clothing, 32
        lighting, 32
        room temperature, 31-32
    common examples, 28
    distractions, 38-39
    overcommitment, 36-38
    peer pressure, 30
estate planning vs. wills, 229
etiquette books, 235
evaluating reasons for procrastination
    considerations, 148-149
    listening to thoughts/feelings, 149
    removing distractions, 149

exercising
    broken promises, 205
        self-defeating thoughts, 205-207
    guidelines, 207-209
    Web sites, 208
expected events, 109-110

F

failure
    difficulty of change, 73
    fear of, 45
    reasons, 70-73
family
    as procrastinators
        children, 309-310
        friends, 311
        guidelines, 307-308
        roommates, 309
        spouses, 308-309
    children
        books, 182
        childproofing, 188-189
        cost considerations, 183
        timing, 183-184
    habits, 168
    marriage
        considerations, 181-182
        reasons for procrastination, 180-181
        statistics, 179-180
    www.familyproducts.com, 310
fears
    causes of procrastination, 44-45
    failure, 45
    judgement, 45-46
    role of, 12-14
    success, 46-47
feelings/thoughts
    all-or-nothing thinking, 171
    effects of, 42
    fear of success, 46-47
    frustrating tasks, 49
    gut feelings, 142-143
    listening to, 149
    not thinking enough, 43-44
    overwhelming tasks, 49

perfectionism, 48
self-defeating thoughts, 205-207
thinking too much, 42
time constraints, 56
filing systems, 122
    administrative files, 125-127
    cabinets, 123-124
    current projects, 125
    folders, 123
    key people/places files, 126
    pending projects, 124-125
    topic files, 126
finances
    advice, 218-219
    bills, paying, 219-220
    budgets, preparing, 221
    dangers of procrastinating, 5-7
    debts, paying off, 221
        excuses/responses, 222-224
        Surviving Debt: A Guide for Consumers, 222
        widespread epidemic, 222
    insurance coverage, 226
    investments, 225
    love-hate relationship with money, 219
    organization, lack of, 218
        not paying bills, 220
    savings, 225
fire safety, 185
    guidelines, 186-187
    smoke alarms, 186
    Web sites, 186
FireHouse.com, 186
Five O'Clock Club (job searches), 259
friends (procrastinators), 311
frustrating tasks, 49

G

Get Organized Week, 107
getting things done
    strategies, 151-152
        chip-away technique, 157

comfort, 154
Getting Things Done When You Are Not in Charge, 304
isolation, avoiding, 154-155
motivating yourself, 152
organization, 152
positive self-talk, 155-156
prioritizing, 153
rewards/treats, 158-159
scheduling, 153, 157
Getting Things Done When You Are Not in Charge, 304
gifts, buying, 195-196
going out, 192
Beyond Love and Work: Why Adults Need to Play, 192
ending relationships, 199-200
finding time, 192-193
following through, lack of, 193-194
guidelines, 198-199
hindrances, 198
graduate students, 276-277
dissertations, 277-279
grocery lists, 185
guilt, 94, 96

H

habits, others', 168
health and fitness
dangers of, 9-11
effects of procrastination, 10-11
exercising
broken promises, 205-207
guidelines, 207-209
Web sites, 208
medical/dental appointments, 210-211
weight loss, 205
high-school students, 272-274
Reading Lists for College-Bound Students, 273
historical reasons, excuses for clutter, 97

hobbies
broken promises, 211-212
taking up, 211-213
www.forhobbies.com, 212
holidays
gifts, buying, 195-196
preparing for, 196-197
Simplify Your Christmas: 100 Ways to Reduce the Stress and Recapture the Joy of the Holidays, 197
home-based offices, 266-268
advantages, 252
disadvantages, 255
quiz, 253-254
strategies, 254-255
home-related procrastination, 24,163-164, 172
chip-away technique, 167
chore categories, 166
cleaning up
all-or-nothing thinking, 171
Cleaning Encyclopedia, The, 170
complaints about opposite sex, 171
easing the burden, 169
guidelines, 169-170
professional services, 169
scheduling tasks, 169-170
clutter, clearing out, 171-172
dangers of, 11
dry cleaning, 173-174
gender-related statistics, 170
guidelines, 167-168, 175-176
imaginary gadgets, 165
laundry, 172-173
reasons for procrastination, 164-165
strategies, 165
tidying up, 167
trash (taking out), excuses/responses, 174-175
Web sites, Tipz Time, 165
yard work, 176-177
see also safety issues
hopes/dreams, excuses for clutter, 98-99

I

identity (source of) excuses for clutter, 99-100
IECA (Independent Education Consultant Association), 85
improvements/repairs, 175-176
income taxes, 226-227
guidelines, 227-228
indecision, *see* decision-making
Independent Education Consultant Association (IECA), 85
insurance coverage, reasons for procrastinating, 226
Internet
auctions, 95
socializing online, 194
interpersonal problems, job-related procrastination, 265-266
investments, 225
isolation, avoiding, 154-155

J

job searches
Five O'Clock Club, 259
reasons for procrastination, 258
comfort, 258-259
job structure, 260-261
lack of career focus, 260
lack of success, 259
rejection, 261-262
resumés, 259
jobs, *see* job searches; keeping jobs
journals, keeping, 214-215
judgement, fear of, 45-46

K

keeping jobs
essentials, 262-263
extra efforts, 268-269
interpersonal problems, 265-266

Soundview Executive Book
    Summaries, 262
    writing problems, 264-265
key people/places files, filing
    systems, 126-127

L

*Last-Minute Estate
    Planning*, 229
laundry, household chores,
    172-173
laziness vs.
    procrastination, 21
learning new skills, 214
letters of complaint, 240-241
    excuses/solutions, 241-242
    see also correspondence
life roles
    identifying, 286
    overcommitment, 36-38
    prioritizing, 287
lighting, environmental
    factors, 32
lists
    to-do lists, 108
        organization, 129-130
    wish-to-do lists, 294-296
long-term goals vs. short-term
    goals, 61
losing weight, broken
    promises, 205

M

major decisions, 137
managing time, 55
    balancing work/fun, 60-61
    *Complete Idiot's Guide to
        Managing Your Time,
        The*, 58
    crunch periods, 58
    inability to control time,
        55-56
    multitasking, 60
    pressed for time, 56
    priorities, 61-63
    reminders, 60
    renders, 59
    right time, 63
    short-term vs. long-term
        goals, 61

simple vs. difficult
    tasks, 61
survey, 57
time-saving tips, 63-64
marriage
    considerations, 181-182
    reasons for procrastination,
        180-181
    statistics, 179-180
medical/dental appointments,
    excuses/responses, 210-211
men
    having children
        books, 182
        cost considerations, 183
        timing, 183-184
    household chores
        complaints about
            women, 171
        statistics, 170
    marriage
        considerations, 181-182
        reasons for
            procrastination,
            180-181
        statistics, 179-180
    see also family
mental health
    professionals, 79
    psychotherapists
        roles/duties, 80
        *Shrink to Fit: Answers to
            Your Questions About
            Therapy*, 80
        types/credentials, 80-82
minor decisions, 138
Mission Control Family
    Organizer, 310
money, *see* finances
monthly calendars, 128
motivation, 152
multitasking, 60
Myers-Briggs Type
    Indicator, 139

N

National Association of
    Professional Organizers
    (NAPO), 85,107
National Domestic Violence
    Hotline, 188

National University
    Continuing Education
    Association Web site, 280
New Year's resolutions
    flaws, 204-205
    rationalized
        procrastination, 205
notes
    R.S.V.P.s, 234-235
    samples, 236
    thank-you notes
        guidelines for writing,
            233-234
        reasons for
            procrastination, 232

O

Oath of Effectiveness, 296
Obsessive-Compulsive
    Disorder (OCD), 51-52
organization
    commitments
        backing out, 113-114
        balancing, 111
    *Complete Idiot's Guide to
        Organizing Your Life,
        The*, 170
    completing tasks, 152
    Container Store, 111
    crowding schedules, 109
    daily action pages, 128-129
    filing systems, 122
        administrative files,
            125-126
        cabinets, 123-124
        current projects, 125
        folders, 123
        key people/places files,
            126-127
        pending projects,
            124-125
        topic files, 126
    guidelines, 106
    lack of
        bill payments, 220
        finances, 218
        inconveniences to
            others, 110
    maintaining change,
        316-317
    methods, 118-120
    monthly calendars, 128

National Association of Professional Organizers (NAPO), 107
organizers (day planners), types, 127-128
Organizing for the Creative Person, 127
papers, categorizing, 107, 120-121
places for things, 106
procrastination-organization link, 114
professional organizers, 85-86
proper place for items
  finding, 118-119
  keeping them there, 120
saying "no"
  difficulties/strategies to overcome difficulties, 111-112
  guidelines, 113
scheduling tasks
  advantages/disadvantages, 108
  guidelines, 130-131
stacking trays, 121-122
Stop-the-World-I-Wanna-Get-Off day, 152
to-do lists, 108, 129-130
trash cans, number of, 108
unexpected events, 109-110
see also clutter
organizers (daily planners)
Mission Control Family Organizer, 310
types, 127-128
others (procrastinators), 300-301
  attempting to resolve, 301-303
  cultural differences, 302
  family, 307-308
    children, 309-310
    spouses, 308-309
  follow-up action, 303
  friends, 311
  rationalizing, 301
  roommates, 309
  workplace
    bosses, 304-305
    co-workers, 306-307

Getting Things Done When You Are Not in Charge, 304
  subordinates, 305-306
overcommitment
  avoiding, maintaining change, 317
  environmental factors, life roles, 36-38
  social life, 194
overwhelming tasks, causes of procrastination, 49

P-Q

paper
  clutter, avoiding, 33
  environmental factors, 33
  filing systems, 122
    administrative files, 125-126
    cabinets, 123-124
    current projects, 125
    folders, 123
    key people/places files, 126-127
    pending projects, 124-125
    topic files, 126
  organization, 107
  stacking trays, 121-122
past efforts, failure
  difficulty of change, 73
  reasons, 70-73
paying bills, not paying, 219
  defiance, 220
  lack of money, 219-220
  lack of organization, 220
peer pressure, 30
pending projects, filing systems, 124-125
perfectionism, causes of procrastination, 48
personal coaches, 84-85
physical problems, causes of procrastination, 52
positive self-talk, 155-156
postcards (writing), 238-239
practical purposes, excuses for clutter, 97-98

prioritizing
  areas to improve, 292-294
  categories, 62-63
  completing tasks, 153
  life roles, 287
  maintaining change, 318-320
  time management, 61
    categories, 62-63
  vs. values, 320-321
proclamations
  assessing procrastination, 287, 291
    areas to improve, 292-294
    home, 290
    personal health, 291
    personal/social life, 289-290
    school, 289
    work, 288
  balance
    samples, 295
    wish-to-do lists, 294, 296
  effectiveness, Oath of Effectiveness, 296
  essentials, 286
  life roles, 286-287
  sample, 297
procrastination, 19
  as an addiction, 19
  character flaw vs. behavior problem, 20
  vs. lack of ambition, 22
  vs. lack of discipline, 21
  vs. laziness, 21
  word origins, 18
professional help, 77
  assessing need (quiz), 78-79
  career development professionals
    career coaches/consultants, 84
    career counselors, 84
    Career Planning and Adult Development Network, 82
    types, 82-83
  choosing, questions to ask, 86-87
  education consultants, 85

mental health
  professionals, 79
    psychotherapists, 80-82
    *Shrink to Fit: Answers to
      Your Questions About
      Therapy*, 80
  personal coaches, 84-85
  professional organizers,
    85-86
psychological disorders,
  causes of procrastination,
  50-52
psychotherapists
  roles/duties, 80
  *Shrink to Fit: Answers to
    Your Questions About
    Therapy*, 80
  types/credentials, 80-82

R

R.S.V.P.s, 234-235
  guidelines, 235
  samples, 236
repairs/improvements,
  175-176
rationalized procrastination
  New Year's resolutions, 205
rationalizing
  others'
    procrastination, 301
*Reading Lists for College-Bound
  Students*, 273
reading more
  broken promises, 215
  guidelines, 215-216
  online book clubs, 215
rebellion, causes of
  procrastination, 50
relationship-related
  procrastination
  dangers of, 11
  see also dating; family
resolutions, New Year's
  flaws, 204-205
  rationalized
    procrastination, 205
responsibilities
  distractions, 38
  overcommitment, 35
  life roles, 36-38

rewards/treats, completing
  tasks, 158-159
right timing, 63
roles, life roles
  identifying, 286
  prioritizing, 287
room temperature,
  environmental factors, 31
roommates
  habits, 168
  procrastinators, 309
routines
  advantages/disadvantages,
    108
  freedom in, 153
  household tasks, 169-170
  see also scheduling tasks

S

safety issues, 185
  burglaries, 187-188
  childproofing, 188-189
  dangers of
    procrastination, 12
  domestic violence, 188
  fire safety, 185
    guidelines, 186-187
    smoke alarms, 186
    Web sites, 186
savings, 225
saying "no"
  difficulties/strategies to
    overcoming, 111-112
  guidelines, 113
scheduling strategies for
  completing tasks, 153, 157
scheduling tasks
  advantages/
    disadvantages, 108
  crowding schedules, 109
  guidelines, 130-131
  household chores, 169-170
school-related
  procrastination, 271-272
  college students
    guidelines, 275-276
    majors, choosing, 276
    reasons for
      procrastination,
      274-275

graduate students, 276-277
  dissertations, 277-279
high-school students,
  272-274
  *Reading Lists for College-
    Bound Students*, 273
returning to school
  excuses, 279-281
  National University
    Continuing Education
    Association, 280
self-employment
  advantages, 252
  disadvantages, 255
  home-based offices,
    266-268
  quiz, 253-254
  strategies, 254-255
self-esteem
  Association of Image
    Consultants
    International, 206
  weight, 206
self-talk, positive, 155-156
Seminar Finder Web site, 214
sentimental reasons, excuses
  for clutter, 96-97
*Seven Habits of Highly Effective
  People, The*, 61
shopping
  gifts, 195-196
  grocery lists, 185
short-term goals vs. long-term
  goals, 61
*Shrink to Fit: Answers to Your
  Questions About Therapy*, 80
simple tasks vs. difficult
  tasks, 61
*Simplify Your Christmas: 100
  Ways to Reduce the Stress and
  Recapture the Joy of the
  Holidays*, 197
skills, learning new skills, 214
*Slow Down…and Get More
  Done*, 318
social life, changes, 191-192
  *Beyond Love and Work: Why
    Adults Need to Play*, 192
  dating
    ending relationships,
      199-200
    guidelines, 198-199
    hindrances, 198

getting out, 192
    finding time
    following through,
        lack of, 193-194
    guidelines, 192-193
    overcommitment, 194
    socializing online, 194
Soundview Executive Book
    Summaries, 262
spouses as procrastinators,
    308-309
stacking trays, 121-122
stages of changes, 73-74
Stop, Look, and Listen
    formula
    evaluating reasons for
        procrastination, 148-149
    listening to feelings/
        thoughts, 149
    putting into action,
        150-151
    stopping avoiding tasks,
        147-148
Stop-the-World-I-Wanna-Get-
    Off day, 152
stopping avoidance of tasks,
    147-148
stress, 10, 144
Stress Management Sourcebook,
    The, 10
students
    college students
        guidelines, 275-276
        majors, choosing, 276
        reasons for
            procrastination,
            274-275
    graduate students, 276-277
        dissertations, 277-279
    high-school students,
        273-274
        Reading Lists for College-
            Bound Students, 273
    organizers (daily
        planners), 280
    returning to school
        excuses, 279-281
        National University
            Continuing Education
            Association, 280
    study habits, 281

subordinates as
    procrastinators, 305-306
success
    difficulty of change, 73
    essentials, 314
    fear of, 46-47
    lack of, reasons, 70-73
    likelihood of change
        (quiz), 75
    maintaining change,
        314-315
        balancing work/fun,
            317-318
        clutter, avoiding,
            315-316
        organization, 316-317
        overcommitment,
            avoiding, 317
        values/priorities,
            318-320
    stages of change, 73-74
support of others
    changing behavior, 75-76
    finding support, 87
    see also professional help
Surviving Debt: A Guide for
    Consumers, 222

T–U–V

taxes, 226-227
    guidelines for doing,
        227-228
technology, effects of, 22-23
televisions, distractions, 38-39
thank-you notes
    guidelines for writing,
        233-234
    reasons for
        procrastination, 232
therapists, psychotherapists
    roles/duties, 80
    Shrink to Fit: Answers to
        Your Questions About
        Therapy, 80
    types/credentials, 80-82
thoughts/feelings
    all-or-nothing
        thinking, 171
    effects of, 42

fear of success, 46-47
frustrating tasks, 49
gut feelings, 142-143
    listening to, 149
not thinking enough,
    43-44
overwhelming tasks, 49
perfectionism, 48
self-defeating thoughts,
    205-207
thinking too much, 42
tidying up, 167-168
time, unrealistic views of, 50
time management, 55
    balancing work/fun, 60-61
    Complete Idiot's Guide to
        Managing Your Time, 58
    crunch periods, 58
    inability to control time,
        55-56
    multitasking, 60
    pressed for time, 56
    priorities, 61
        categories, 62-63
    reminders, 59-60
    right time, 63
    short-term vs. long-term
        goals, 61
    simple vs. difficult
        tasks, 61
    survey, 57
    time-saving tips, 63-64
Tipz Time Web site, 165
to-do lists, 108
    organization, 129-130
topic files, filing systems, 126
trash (taking out),
    excuses/responses, 174-175
trash cans, number of, 108
treats/rewards, completing
    tasks, 158-159

value, excuses for clutter, 95
values
    maintaining change,
        318-320
    vs. priorities, 320-321
violence (domestic violence),
    safety issues, 188

W-X-Y-Z

Web sites, 188
   American Red Cross, 186
   Coffeerooms
      Book*Mark, 215
   Consumer Information
      Center, 242
   Container Store, 111
   exercising, 208
   fire safety, 186
   Five O'Clock Club, 259
   gift shopping, 196
   Improvements
      catalogue, 175
   Independent Education
      Consultant Association
      (IECA), 85
   National Association of
      Professional
      Organizers, 85
   National University
      Continuing Education
      Association, 280
   Online Reading Club, 215
   Seminar Finder, 214
   Soundview Executive Book
      Summaries, 262
   Tipz Time, 165
   www.forhobbies.com, 212
   www.babycenter.com, 183
   www.familyproducts.com,
      310
   www.rocket-ebook.com, 216
   www.schoolmate.com, 280
weight loss
   dieting
      broken promises, 205
      guidelines for dieting,
         207-209
   exercising
      guidelines for exercising,
         207-209
      self-defeating thoughts,
         205-207
      Web sites, 208
women
   having children
      books, 182
      cost considerations, 183
      timing, 183-184

household chores
   complaints about
      men, 171
   statistics, 170
marriage
   considerations, 181-182
   reasons for
      procrastination,
      180-181
   statistics, 179-180
   see also family
workplace
   bosses, 304-305
   co-workers, 306-307
   crunch periods, time
      management, 58
   cubicles, environmental
      factors, 31-32
   *Getting Things Done When
      You Are Not in Charge*, 304
   subordinates, 305-306